BELIEFS IN GOVERNMENT

Volumes of a Research Programme of the European Science Foundation

Series Editors: Max Kaase, Kenneth Newton, and Elinor Scarbrough

THE SCOPE OF GOVERNMENT

This set of five volumes is an exhaustive study of beliefs in government in post-war Europe. Based upon an extensive collection of survey evidence, the results challenge widely argued theories of mass opinion, and much scholarly writing about citizen attitudes towards government and politics.

The **European Science Foundation** is an association of its fifty-six member research councils, academies, and institutions devoted to basic scientific research in twenty countries. The ESF assists its Member Organizations in two main ways: by bringing scientists together in its Scientific Programmes, Networks, and European Research Conferences to work on topics of common concern, and through the joint study of issues of strategic importance in European science policy.

The scientific work sponsored by ESF includes basic research in the natural and technical sciences, the medical and biosciences, the humanities, and the social sciences.

The ESF maintains close relations with other scientific institutions within and outside Europe. By its activities, ESF adds value by co-operation and co-ordination across national frontiers, offers expert scientific advice on strategic issues, and provides the European forum for fundamental science.

This volume arises from the work of the ESF Scientific Programme on Beliefs in Government (BiG).

Further information on ESF activities can be obtained from:

European Science Foundation
1, quai Lezay-Marnésia
F-67080 Strasbourg Cedex
France

Tel. (+33) 88 76 71 00
Fax (+33) 88 37 05 32

BELIEFS IN GOVERNMENT VOLUME THREE

THE SCOPE OF GOVERNMENT

Edited by

OLE BORRE

and

ELINOR SCARBROUGH

OXFORD UNIVERSITY PRESS

1995

Oxford University Press, Walton Street, Oxford OX2 6DP
Oxford New York
Athens Auckland Bangkok Bombay
Calcutta Cape Town Dar es Salaam Delhi
Florence Hong Kong Istanbul Karachi
Kuala Lumpur Madras Madrid Melbourne
Mexico City Nairobi Paris Singapore
Taipei Tokyo Toronto
and associated companies in
Berlin Ibadan

Oxford is a trade mark of Oxford University Press

Published in the United States
by Oxford University Press Inc., New York

British Library Cataloguing in Publication Data
Data available

Library of Congress Cataloging in Publication Data
The scope of government/edited by Ole Borre and Elinor Scarbrough.
—(Beliefs in government; v. 3)
Includes bibliographical references.
1. Government spending policy—Europe—Public opinion. 2. Welfare state—Public opinion.
3. Taxation—Europe—Public opinion. 4. Public opinion—Europe. I. Borre, Ole, 1932–
II. Scarbrough, Elinor. III. Series.
HJ7755.S38 1995 336.3'9'094—dc20 95–10793
ISBN 0–19–827954–X

1 3 5 7 9 10 8 6 4 2

Typeset by J&L Composition Ltd, Filey, North Yorkshire
Printed in Great Britain
on acid-free paper by
Biddles Ltd, Guildford and King's Lynn

FOREWORD

This is one of five volumes in a series produced by the Beliefs in Government research programme of the European Science Foundation. The volumes, all published by Oxford University Press in 1995, are as follows:

i *Citizens and the State*, edited by Hans-Dieter Klingemann and Dieter Fuchs
ii *Public Opinion and Internationalized Governance*, edited by Oskar Niedermayer and Richard Sinnott
iii *The Scope of Government*, edited by Ole Borre and Elinor Scarbrough
iv *The Impact of Values*, edited by Jan van Deth and Elinor Scarbrough
v *Beliefs in Government*, authored by Max Kaase and Kenneth Newton

The first chapter of *Beliefs in Government* presents a brief history of the research project, its general concerns, approach and methods, and an outline of the relationship of each volume to the project as a whole.

All five books share a debt of gratitude which we would like to acknowledge on their behalf. The European Science Foundation (ESF) supported and funded the research programme throughout its five long and arduous years. Eleven of the research councils and academies which are members of the ESF have made a financial contribution to the overall costs of the project—Belgium, Denmark, Finland, France, the Federal Republic of Germany, Ireland, Italy, the Netherlands, Norway, Sweden, and the United Kingdom. We would like to thank the ESF and these member organizations five times over—once for each book.

All five volumes were copy-edited by Heather Bliss, whose eagle eye and endless patience are unrivalled in the Western World. At Oxford University Press we were lucky indeed to have two understanding editors in Tim Barton and Dominic Byatt.

In particular, John Smith, the Secretary of the ESF's Standing Committee for the Social Sciences, and his staff put in huge efforts and gave us encouragement at every stage of the project. Having gone through the process with other ESF research programmes a few times before, they knew when we started what an immense task lay in wait for us all, but were not daunted. We cannot lay claim to any such bravery, and have only our innocence as an excuse.

Max Kaase
Kenneth Newton
Elinor Scarbrough

December 1994

PREFACE

This volume, the third of the five volumes in the Beliefs in Government series, is the work of a group of twelve scholars from eight European countries. Apart from thanking our colleagues in the research group, the editors wish to thank several people and institutions for their assistance in various aspects of this project.

We are grateful to the European Science Foundation for initiating the project and supporting it throughout. Our research group first met in the autumn of 1989 and over the next five years it met in eight different places across Europe, from Umeå to Lisbon. From the perspective of administration, such habits must be a challenge. Dr John Smith in particular deserves to be warmly thanked for the smooth administration of our project.

Retrieving and distributing the data files upon which our study builds is a considerable problem in a comparative project such as ours. We are indebted to the Zentralarchiv in Cologne, especially to Ekkehard Mochmann, as well as to the ESRC Archive at Essex University and the Scandinavian and Dutch data archives, for providing us with the data and codebooks needed for the analyses in this volume.

Our work benefited from the criticism of our colleagues in the three other research groups and from other scholars. Particularly valuable were the comments, sometimes severe, offered by Professor William Lafferty and Professor Albert Weale at the Strasbourg Conference held in the summer of 1993. Thanks to their critique, several chapters were reworked and improved during the last phase of the project.

This volume is in every way a collaborative product, in which the contributions of the authors go far beyond their own chapters. At every stage, all members of the group were involved in the design, and redesign, of the volume. But the final product also owes much to Helen Sibley and Sharon Duthie, who wrestled to bring order to unruly disks, manifold tables, and the idiosyncrasies of several different languages.

Ole Borre
Elinor Scarbrough

December 1994

CONTENTS

LIST OF FIGURES

LIST OF TABLES

ABBREVIATIONS

AGIP	Azienda General Italiana dei Petrolii
BBC	British Broadcasting Corporation
CIS	Centro de Investigaciones Sociologicas
EC	European Commission
ENEL	Ente Nazionale per l'Energia Elettrica
ICO	Instituto de Crédito Oficial
INI	Instituto Nacional de Industria
IRI	Instituto per la Riconstrucione Industriale
ISSP	International Social Science Programme
SIPRI	Stockholm International Peace Research Institute
TF1	Télévision France 1

Standard country abbreviations used in the tables and figures are:

AU	Austria
BE	Belgium
DK	Denmark
FI	Finland
FR	France
GB	Britain
GE	Germany
GR	Greece
IC	Iceland
IR	Ireland
IT	Italy
LU	Luxembourg
NL	The Netherlands
NO	Norway
PO	Portugal
SP	Spain
SV	Sweden
SW	Switzerland

LIST OF CONTRIBUTORS

ACHILLE ARDIGÓ, Professor of Sociology, and Chair of Postgraduate School of Health Sociology, University of Bologna.

OLE BORRE, Professor of Political Sociology, Department of Political Science, University of Aarhus.

MARIA M. CONFALONIERI, Associate Professor of Public Administration, Faculty of Political Sciences, University of Bologna.

PETER GOLDING, Professor of Sociology, Department of Social Sciences, University of Loughborough.

MICHAEL GOLDSMITH, Professor of Government and Politics, and Pro-Vice-Chancellor, University of Salford.

BEATE HUSEBY, Research Fellow, Department of Sociology and Political Science, University of Trondheim.

OLOF JOHANSSON, Senior Lecturer, Department of Political Science, University of Umeå.

KENNETH NEWTON, Professor of Government, Executive Director of European Consortium for Political Research, Department of Government, University of Essex.

PER ARNT PETTERSEN, Professor of Political Science, Department of Sociology and Political Science, University of Trondheim.

EDELTRAUD ROLLER, Senior Research Fellow, Science Center Berlin.

LEO B. VAN SNIPPENBURG, Associate Professor, Department of Communication, University of Nijmegen.

JOSE MANUEL VIEGAS, Lecturer, Department of Sociology, University of Lisbon.

1

The Scope of Government

OLE BORRE AND MICHAEL GOLDSMITH

What governments do or should do has been one of the most hotly debated topics across Western Europe over recent years. In some countries, such as those of southern Europe, the continuing development of welfare provision remains a major objective, while in others, such as Britain, there has been a reformulation of the services provided by the state. In major parts of Eastern Europe, the form of the state itself has been transformed, while in others, such as the former Yugoslavia, the state has effectively collapsed. Thus debate about the old question as to what should be the proper role of the state in society continues to be relevant.

Historically, states have always undertaken some functions. First, they have had a major concern with defence, to protect and promote the territory which the state encompasses. Much of the development of modern Europe has been shaped by the endeavour of states to impose their power over one another. In the post-war period, defence expenditure has been a major element in the budgets of many West European governments, at least until the ending of the Cold War. A second traditional concern for states, linked to external security, has been law enforcement. Upholding law and order is a prerequisite of much of what modern states do: economic activity depends on a legal basis of property and contract, people have to be prepared to pay taxes (Olson 1965: 98–100), and ways and means have to be established for resolving disputes between individuals, companies, and states.

Moreover, as economies have grown, so states have grown. A growing economy requires infrastructural developments, such as roads, railways, and other communication networks. The process of economic development also brought with it new technology which, in turn, led to an increasingly differentiated society and political heterogeneity. And as states and economies developed, pressure grew for those in power to accept responsibility for the well-being of their populations, in the form of social security provision, education and training, housing, or cultural activities. Finally, states exhibit a need for ideological and symbolic legitimation. During the period of absolutism, the splendour of Versailles and other courts consumed considerable state revenues. Today, it often takes the form of cultural support for museums or opera houses, or sponsorship of national football teams, all of which are intended to promote the identification of the citizens with their society.

What is clear is the impact which the great technological discoveries, the large standing armies, and the administrative systems developed in the fifteenth and sixteenth centuries had on the growth of the centralized state. We do not distinguish between 'state' and 'government' in this context but note that, from that period on, the scope and functions of government have continued to grow. Among the factors accounting for the historical growth of the state, however, the opinions of the populace have counted for little, at least until recent times. It was not until the Civil War in seventeenth-century England and, from the mid-eighteenth century, the Enlightenment in Europe that a public sphere emerged in which policy could be proposed and debated. Thereafter, most European countries saw the emergence of an industrial, commercial, and intellectual middle class capable of persuading government to adopt policies favouring its ideas and interests. The progressive extension of the franchise meant that, by the end of the nineteenth century, political parties representing the working class became commonplace. In the twentieth century, governments throughout most of Western Europe have come to adopt the kinds of programmes and policies advocated by reformers of the left and the right in the 1920s and 1930s, giving rise to the modern state with which most people in Western Europe today are familiar.

Democratic Crisis

These developments have led democratic theorists of various persuasions to suggest a key role for the public in relation to the policy process and the behaviour of government. For classical liberal theorists such as de Tocqueville and Mill, public opinion was important in moulding society, in protecting the individual against the state, and in passing judgement on the activities of government. By contrast, writers of the left have portrayed voters as manipulated by the interests of capital. According to Marx, the state acts in the interests of capital; governments lack the autonomy to develop policies and activities which work against the interests of capital. More recently, neo-Marxists such as Miliband (1969) and Poulantzas (1978), as well as critical sociologists such as Habermas (1975) and Offe (1984), reformulated Marx's arguments to permit the state a certain autonomy in handling the problems posed by the capitalist system. For many writers in this vein, the conflict between the 'true' nature of the state and the ideology of the state as the caretaker of society would cause a crisis of legitimacy, if not the collapse of the capitalist system itself. Other writers in this tradition, such as O'Connor (1973), saw the ever-increasing pressures on government to expand its activities—in order to mitigate the worst excesses of capitalism—bringing about a fiscal crisis of the state, which implied the collapse of capitalism. In this context, the expansion of the state is seen as a consequence of the imperatives of capitalism rather than as a reflection of the preferences of voters.

These predictions of a 'crisis of democracy' coincided with rather different analyses by neo-liberal critics of welfare state systems writing at about the same time. Writers such as King (1975), Rose and Peters (1978), and Birch (1984) all suggested that governments, unable to keep pace with the demands being placed upon them by the rising expectations of the public, were 'overloaded'. These critics, to put it simply, saw today's luxuries becoming tomorrow's necessities: people had become used to rising standards of health, welfare, and education, and expected such improvements to continue, with government solving all their problems. As King put it: 'Once upon a time, man looked to God to order the world. Then he looked to the market. Now he looks to government' (1975: 166).

Other writers, such as Niskanen (1973), placed the blame for 'overload' on ever-growing bureaucracies which were concerned to maximize their budgets and extend their activities. Moreover, to secure reelection, politicians seek support from different electoral publics by expanding the services they offer, with little regard for either parliamentary control or the growth in public expenditure. These tendencies lead to incremental increases in public expenditures and to information overload for the public. According to these theories, by the late 1970s and early 1980s, West European publics were increasingly concerned about the extent of government intervention in society and the tax levels associated with such activities.

These kinds of analyses imply something about people's beliefs concerning the scope of government. In the traditional perspective of representative democracy, mass beliefs about the scope of government are critical because, ultimately, public opinion controls the state; thus society, through the vehicle of the state, has conscious control over its destiny. From the critical perspective, however, the beliefs of the mass public have little part to play; either they represent a false consciousness, or else they demand more than the state can deliver. As the scope of government everywhere in Western Europe has expanded vastly during the post-war period, understanding popular beliefs about the role of government is crucial to understanding the politics of contemporary West European societies. And examining the way in which these beliefs have changed over time, between nations, and amongst different social and political groups, is an important exercise in comparative politics. This task is the objective of this volume.

Beliefs about the Scope of Government

What do we mean by the scope of government? In this volume, it refers to both the *range* of government activity and the *degree* to which governments engage in activities which have an impact on people's daily lives. By 'range', we mean the whole gamut of government activities, such as spending on services, taxing people, regulating their behaviour, providing for defence, improving the environment—and sometimes doing nothing about a problem. For example, in one country the state may be responsible for providing electricity, whereas in another provision is in the hands of the private sector. Thus the range of government activity is different in these two countries: in the one, electricity supply is within the scope of government, in the other, it is outside. By 'degree', we mean the intensity with which government pursues a particular activity. The growth of health care is a good example: most governments have been concerned with some form of health care to deal with illness, but more recently some governments have adopted health promotion programmes which involve, for example, regulating water purity and food additives. This constitutes an increase in the degree of government activity.

Why should beliefs about the scope of government be a concern for political scientists? One reason is that, however measured, the scope of most governments and the impact of government on everyday life are far greater today than ever before. Thus the extent to which people support such a wide range of activities by their governments is important in terms of their support for the political system as a whole. The general process of economic growth during the post-1945 period has permitted governments almost everywhere to extend the range of goods and services provided for their citizens. According to Wilensky, 'economic growth and its demographic and bureaucratic outcomes are the root cause of the general emergence of the welfare state' (1975: xiii). We might therefore expect widespread support for the extension of the welfare state to be demonstrated over this period, especially as the growing economic cake permitted governments to increase the share of the cake going towards welfare services without, necessarily, imposing heavier tax burdens on their citizens. In other words, as people have become accustomed to the success of governments in solving economic and social problems, we would expect to find an expansionist view of the scope of government—reinforced by the desire of bureaucrats to expand their activities.

Changing circumstances can also lead to demands that government do more. Here we might note the 'new politics' agenda (Baker, Dalton, and Hildebrandt 1981), associated with issues relating to the environment, gender, and to the position of ethnic minorities. For example, when there is public concern about, say, global warming or acid rain, this usually leads to new demands for the regulation of behaviour, especially changes in industrial practice. Such changes may well have other, perhaps unacceptable, consequences, such as job losses or industrial decline. Similar demands for changes in practices can arise from the issues of equal rights for women and ethnic minorities. In all these cases, some new action is probably expected from government—which involves a change in the scope of government.

Continually rising levels of government activity could be supported so long as national economies continued to grow. Growth meant that government tax incomes continued to rise without the imposition of higher taxation. More and better public services could be provided without fear of a public backlash. From the early 1970s onwards, however, especially following the 1973 oil crisis, economic growth in many West European countries either slowed down or started to decline. Furthermore, extensive changes in the locus of manufacturing forced the restructuring of much of Western Europe's industrial activity, further aggravating the economic problems facing governments. Extending, or even maintaining, levels of welfare state activities in such circumstances only remains possible if governments are prepared to contemplate higher tax burdens. With the likelihood that tax increases incur electoral punishment, such increases seem untenable. Wilensky, writing before the financial collapse of New York and the Californian tax revolt, had already predicted middle-class resistance to high taxation and to 'health and welfare spending that favors the poor' (1975: 54–8). Moreover, given the heated debate in many West European countries over recent years concerning the level of public expenditure, the size of government, and its involvement in people's daily lives, we might expect beliefs about the scope of government to be moving in a contractionist direction, reversing the former expansionist trend.

However, there is at least one alternative to the welfare backlash argument, reflecting a different kind of process. People might change their beliefs about the scope of government because they accept arguments about individual responsibility. Self-help comes to replace government help, with a consequent reduction in the scope of government. There can be a shift of function from the state to the individual. For example, to 'roll back the state' by making individuals less dependent on government action was one of the objectives pursued by the Conservative governments of the 1980s in Britain. Mrs Thatcher and her governments hoped thereby to reduce government expenditures in areas such as welfare and health care. Similar concerns were shared by Chancellor Kohl in Germany and by Prime Minister Schlüter in Denmark in the early 1980s.

Mass Beliefs and Government Action

That people's beliefs may change raises important questions about how people's beliefs about the scope of government are formed and what are their consequences. Traditional liberal democratic theory sees mass opinion influencing political élites or government, a position we review frequently throughout this book. But it is also possible that mass beliefs follow the lead given by governing élites; rather than public opinion influencing government policy, the policies adopted by government may shape people's beliefs. In other words, identification with parties of the left or the right may influence people's beliefs about what government should or should not do. If so, is a sense of party identity more important than social variables? And if parties are a major influence, then we might expect people's beliefs about government to change rather quickly—simply because parties constantly search out new issue positions in order to compete more effectively against their opponents. Furthermore, if parties are constantly redefining the issue packages on which they campaign—in effect, redefining what they consider to be the proper scope of government—do peoples' beliefs have any effect in constraining this process? Certainly, the attempts by government in some countries, such as Britain, to cut back the welfare state in the 1980s did not seem to be much constrained by the high levels of public support for the welfare state reported at the time (Taylor-Gooby 1985; Edgell and Duke 1984).

This example does not necessarily challenge the assumptions of liberal democratic theory. Perhaps governments are able to pursue such policies because other policy concerns are higher on people's agendas. Or perhaps people make trade-offs between the range of government activities and their intensity, accepting less activity in one area in return for maintaining the general scope of government. More likely, however, is the effect of lags between a change in the scope of government and people's evaluations. Changes in government policy, in service provision, or in the means by which such services are provided, all take time to work through. People may even be unaware that there have been any changes until they are exposed to some direct consequence. There are likely to be yet further lags before negative evaluations of a policy change come to influence their beliefs about the scope of government.

Alternatively, beliefs may change because the environment in which they develop changes. From the 1970s onwards, West European governments operated in a more difficult economic environment. These straightened circumstances had political consequences throughout Europe. They led to new ideas about what government should or should not do, to policies of deregulation and privatization, and to an increasing emphasis on the market rather than the state to provide for people's well-being. But do such policy changes, lagged over time, produce changes in the kinds of beliefs which people hold about the scope of government? In other words, are there crucial points in time when, on account of shocks or a radical change of direction in élite thinking, beliefs change quite markedly?

Moreover, beliefs about the scope of government may change because the demographic and social structure of a society changes over time. During the last twenty to thirty years, across much of Western Europe, women have entered the labour force, the birth rate has declined, older people make up a growing proportion of national populations, and the large family has almost disappeared, at least among urban populations. Such demographic changes affect what people expect from government. Likewise, the last thirty years have seen the advent of mass education, and the educated are likely to differ from less-well-educated generations in their ideas about the nature of the good life and how it might be achieved.

It is also likely that there are national differences in beliefs about the scope of government. In this context, Wilensky distinguishes between welfare state leaders and welfare state laggards, making the important point that different countries have introduced different levels of welfare provision. Wilensky notes (1975: xiii):

> At an advanced stage of affluence and in countries matched for per capita income . . . we find differences in the organization and level of welfare and in the politics of welfare. For instance, the student of public spending quickly notes large differences in the proportion of resources these countries spend on social security.

It is reasonable to hypothesize that these differences reflect real differences in the beliefs which different nationalities have about the scope of government. Identifying such differences is an important objective for us.

This discussion raises several questions about how people in Western Europe understand the scope of government. It would be rewarding if we could provide answers to all of them. However, as we shall see on more than one occasion, we lack the kind of data which would permit us to answer these questions as extensively or precisely as we would wish. But we can address questions about the direction of such beliefs across a range of West European countries over time, highlighting differences within and between countries. We can also examine, empirically, some of the general arguments about the impact of government activity.

In particular, we can address the question of 'ungovernability' raised by the neo-liberal critique of the welfare state already touched on. These theories suggested that changes in people's beliefs about the scope of government will lead to a loss of support for the political regime. Because people have rising expectations about what government can achieve, and because these expectations cannot be met due to limitations on resources, dissatisfaction with government policies both increases and becomes more widespread. As people's dissatisfaction becomes more widespread, it will be generalized, leading to a decline in political support for the system as a whole. Such loss of support might also follow from a change in beliefs which leads people to favour a contraction in the scope of government. The argument in this case suggests that people want government to do less because they are increasingly dissatisfied with its performance. Again, in the long run, this dissatisfaction will be generalized, leading to declining support for the system as a whole.

At the centre of these rather different propositions is the level of dissatisfaction about government performance over time—with the expectation that changes in the level of dissatisfaction will lead to a decline in the legitimacy of the political system. Under such conditions, Easton (1965) suggests, the future of both the regime and the political system, as well as the society it sustains, is threatened.

At a very general level, then, we expect both the activities of government—the scope of government broadly defined—to change over time, and people's beliefs about the scope of government to change over time. The task is to pin down some of the reasons why people's beliefs change and the direction of such changes. We have suggested that beliefs can become more expansionist, either because new demands come on to the political agenda or because expectations about what government can achieve are rising amongst people in general or amongst politicians and bureaucrats. But people can also develop a narrower view about the scope of government, their beliefs becoming more contractionist, either because of reactions against the cost of government activities—the 'welfare backlash'—or because people come to believe that government is inefficient or too heavily involved in their daily lives.

The importance of such changes in beliefs, especially when set against people's evaluations of the way government performs, we have argued, may have consequences for the overall evaluation of the political system. In brief, negative evaluations and increasing dissatisfaction may lead to a decline in political legitimacy and declining political support more generally. We return to these issues in the latter chapters of this volume. Here we go on to consider more specifically some matters of definition, the dimensions we explore, the nature of the available data, and the general plan of this volume.

Defining the Scope of Government

The first problem centres on what we mean by the scope of government, which we defined as the range and degree of government regulation. Such regulation can vary in several ways. In comparing two countries with regard to medical care, for example, we may say that the scope of government is larger in one of them if the care programme covers (i) more people, (ii) more diseases and treatments, or (iii) the programme incurs a larger share of public expenditure. The first two amount to more extended coverage (range), the last to more intensive coverage (degree). Expansion of the government programme in any of these ways, however, represents a larger scope of government, since it implies that the government intervenes in a greater number of acts or events. But statements about the scope of government may apply to only one of these developments. For example, in some countries the economic problems of the 1980s led to reductions in levels of social security payments, hitting the living standards of the unemployed. But owing to increasing levels of unemployment, making more people eligible for these payments, expenditure on social security has often increased. From one perspective, this constitutes a reduction in the scope of government; from another perspective, an increase. Unfortunately, when it comes to public debate about the scope of government, it is not always clear which kind of change is involved.

This example reveals another problem: many government policies have consequences which may be difficult to determine exactly. For instance, one consequence of improved health care is that people generally live longer and thus are likely to require both more health care and social support. Similarly, an emphasis on roads in transport policy may have implications for environmental protection policy. Moreover, the degree of government involvement in a policy area may grow without any change in government policy, as when expenditure on unemployment benefits increases because unemployment is rising, reduced benefit levels notwithstanding. Such structural characteristics and interdependencies underlie many government activities, leading to constant change both within and across policy areas. It is important to bear this in mind, especially as much of our subsequent discussion of specific policy areas precludes such considerations.

Setting aside these complexities, the general trend in the scope of government is clear: over the last thirty years West European governments have greatly expanded their activities. One indicator of this growth is the size of public expenditure in various policy areas. While this is not the sole measure of what governments do, the relevant data are readily accessible, and we use them extensively throughout this volume. As we shall see in Chapter 2, by and large the scope of government has increased in different countries both because spending on certain policy areas has increased relative to national income and because new areas have been added. As a result, a much larger share of national income is channelled through government activities, and governments in most countries have increasingly engaged in activities which were previously performed by private firms and households—if they were performed at all. According to OECD statistics, expenditure on 'general government', including local government, has grown as a percentage share of national income in all countries, although not at the same rate. For example, in Sweden it grew dramatically from 26.2 per cent in 1950 to 63.8 per cent in 1990, whereas in Britain it grew more moderately from 33.5 per cent in 1950 to 39.5 per cent in 1990.

However, a change in government functions is not always adequately reflected in public expenditure. In medical care, for example, public expenditure data do not tell us anything about different types of coverage, the number of patients and personnel, the number of contacts, the length of the treatments, and so forth. Moreover, and perhaps most importantly, many government functions have little do to with money at all. Public expenditure data tell us little about the impact of abortion laws on people's behaviour, for example. The same is true in other fields. A government that imposes price regulation, or laws preventing industrial firms from polluting the environment, generally does not reimburse firms for the losses thereby inflicted. Thus, public expenditures are at best a rough indicator of the functions or the scope of government, and then only on selective points.

Much the same limitations apply to other tangible measures, such as the number of people employed in various branches of government. The number of soldiers, policemen, teachers, or nurses paid from the public purse may give some rough indication of national differences in the scope of government in a particular policy area. But, as our example of medical care indicates, physicians and patients as well as government employees depend on government for their standard of living and welfare. Moreover, in the case of administrative bureaucracies, one cannot assume that personnel numbers are proportionate to the effects they have in regulating people's behaviour.

Another problem concerns the nature of government itself. Modern governments are expected to be dynamic, constantly introducing new legislation to deal with the exigencies of modern industrial societies. Nowhere has this been more true than in relation to the welfare state. Governments also introduce new interpretations of their activities, set new performance targets for government agencies, introduce new regulations in some policy areas whilst deregulating others. Thus, given that the scope of government is constantly changing, getting a handle on what people believe is, and should be, the proper scope of government is always going to be difficult.

Beliefs about the Scope of Government

Understanding something of the complexity of government and the way we simplify measures of government activity is important when it comes to understanding what we mean when we talk of people's beliefs about the scope of government. However, the focus of our study is not the scope of government as such but, rather, beliefs about the scope of government. We are concerned with the beliefs held by the public about what the government should do, can do, will do, or is actually doing. We define such beliefs as the sum total of ideas circulating in the public domain about actual or possible government activities.

One of the most important type of beliefs in our study concerns positive and negative evaluations of government policies. We will often speak rather loosely of the attitude of a group towards a certain policy, using it interchangeably with support for that policy. Moreover, within each policy area one can distinguish a number of policies, or specific types of activity. Sometimes support for policies may be ordered into policy positions constituting successively stronger forms of intervention, giving rise to a political conflict in which it is possible to identify a liberal—or non-interventionist—position, an interventionist position, and less-well-defined 'centre' positions. One of these positions can usually be identified, roughly, with the current policy of the government, whereas the other positions are removed at successively larger distances from the actual policy. Our interest here is whether, for example, the distance between voters' attitudes and government policy makes a difference to their view of the political system.

Attitudes, however, are not the only indicators of beliefs about the scope of government. Attitudes may be underpinned by a series of cognitive beliefs, which may or may not be accurate or realistic. For example, support for strong law and order policies may stem from the belief that severe punishments reduce crime rates. In other instances, it is less clear what informs an attitude. Someone opposed to a policy may think that the policy is inefficient, too costly, that it has harmful side effects, or that it will serve the interests of a disliked group. Beliefs of this kind are important; information which verifies or falsifies them may have the effect of changing the beliefs. In our study, however, such cognitive beliefs play a comparatively small role because, unfortunately, they have rarely been investigated systematically.

Both attitudes and cognitive beliefs have a critical role in the interaction between state and society. Support for policy positions may become expressed as *demands* (Easton 1965; Almond and Powell 1978). In Easton's terms, demands are messages coming into the political system from various parts of society. In focusing more sharply on particular government activities, however, demands reflecting policy positions differ from some of the other messages flowing from society to government. Election outcomes, for example, are unfocused, since they aggregate the public's perception of policies and policy agents—candidates, parties, and government officials—into a simple signal, the vote. Demonstrations and petitions usually focus on specific policies, but they are not representative of the public, which may include a 'silent majority'. Interest groups, opinion polls, newspapers, official reports—all have a part in conveying messages to the government about the popularity or otherwise of policies.

In our approach, attitudes relating to policy positions constitute the input side of Easton's model whereas cognitive beliefs about what the government is currently doing, or what, in practice, it can do, relate to the output side. But neat as this distinction may be, people often do not distinguish between the input side and the output side, or at least they jump easily from one side to the other. A demand for government action in a particular area may be supported by the belief that government is doing very little, and could do much more. Thus changes in normative beliefs may follow from changes in the underlying cognitive beliefs. For instance, a report showing that government is trying to create more jobs may dampen the demand for more government action in that field.

Our study, then, is an attempt to construct the input parameters of the political system as affected by the output parameters, and vice versa. In other words, we aim to close the circle between these two sides of politics as stipulated by Easton. We expect to find that sometimes the connection is so close in people's minds that it looks like a short circuit. For example, to say that the government is doing very little in a policy area almost amounts to demanding that it does more. In other cases, we expect the connection to be broken, as shown by the 'something for nothing' syndrome discussed in Chapter 5.

Survey Items

Ideally, our analysis would be based on a range of comparative surveys covering all West European countries at regular intervals since 1945. In the event, the only comparative surveys which deal with the scope of government, even then in a rather limited way, are the International Social Survey Programme (ISSP) surveys of 1985 and 1990. The Eurobarometer series and the two Political Action surveys, conducted in 1973–6 and 1979–81, include a limited number of relevant questions. Thus, if we want directly to compare beliefs about the scope of government in West European countries, we have to work with quite restricted data sources. Indeed, perhaps more than the other concerns of the Beliefs in Government project, our topic reveals the lack of systematically comparative survey data.

National data, too, are limited. Given the history of social science, this is hardly surprising; even in the homeland of social surveys, the United States, election surveys are a post-war phenomenon. Several West European countries have rich data sets but their usefulness, for our purposes, is limited by differences in question wordings, sporadic attention to the scope of government as a research topic, and the quite different timings of surveys featuring relevant questions. Moreover, the national data sources are largely confined to the countries of north-west Europe: Germany, Britain, the Netherlands, and the Scandinavian countries. Even then, these data seldom extend back much beyond the early 1970s.

For the most part, then, the studies in this volume use data from the ISSP surveys and the Eurobarometer series, augmented by data points from national surveys where these are available. However, even the comparative data sources do not always cover the same countries or questions over time. These are the typical problems of secondary analysis. So in searching for items which have face validity in measuring beliefs about the scope of government, we distinguish between certain types of survey items.

Responsibility items. One line of questioning in surveys asks respondents whether or not it should be the government's responsibility to take care of various specific social and economic problems. Responses may vary from 'Yes, definitely' to 'No, definitely not'. With these items, responses are taken as indicators of beliefs about the range rather the degree of government intervention.

Position items. Simple position items giving the respondent a choice between two, three, or four policy alternatives are fairly common in both national and comparative surveys. For example, in the 1985 and 1990 ISSP surveys, respondents were asked whether they preferred electricity works to be (i) owned by the state, (ii) controlled but not owned by the state, or (iii) neither controlled nor owned by the state. The distribution of respondents over these three policy positions is easily computed. If we then assume equal distances between these positions on the same axis, we can compute a single statistic showing the average position for any group of respondents, such as voters of a particular party, people in different countries, or the entire sample. The position of respondents may also be compared with the policy of governments or parties which take stands on the issue, and with the actual ownership of electricity works. Moreover, various measures of policy distances can be computed by subtracting one position from another.

Policy change items. These are survey items asking respondents whether the government should do, or spend, 'more or less' in a policy field such as medical care, housing, control of private firms, or censorship of the media. Items of this kind often differentiate between five positions: (i) much more, (ii) more, (iii) same as now, (iv) less, and (v) much less. Responses to this type of question are indicators of policy distances but not policy positions. By assuming equal distances between these five positions on the same axis, we can compute the average distance between the policy favoured by any group of respondents and what they believe to be government policy.

Likert items. The very common 'agree or disagree' items are used extensively in our analysis. Nevertheless, we have to be aware of their shortcomings: while 'agree' responses indicate support for the policy position in question, it is not always clear what 'disagree' responses signify as alternative policy lines are not specified. Likert items work best when several items constitute a scale. Unfortunately, we often have to carry out analyses for which this is not the case.

Agenda items. Some survey questions invite respondents to speak out about important problems, but the responses give no clues about who should be held responsible for solving them. The respondent may, for example, be concerned about inflation or the high crime rate, but this is not the same as saying that the government should do something to curb inflation or crime. Respondents might, with further probing, reveal that they think businessmen should cut prices or parents should be stricter with children, or they might say nothing can be done. Hence we cannot interpret such items as measures of beliefs about the scope of government.

With other survey questions, however, it is obvious that only the government can do something to remedy the problem, even though the item does not refer explicitly to the government. When, for example, a respondent complains that taxes are too high, or that the rich do not pay enough, we may regard it as a policy position, however rudimentary. Thus questions about important problems which suggest a political agenda, or the issue priorities of the public, are mainly useful for our purpose when they can be related with other items on beliefs about the scope of government. In Chapter 3, agenda items are treated as antecedent to policy attitudes.

Performance items. A common type of survey question invites respondents to evaluate the performance of their government in various policy fields as good, adequate, or poor. Such questions may appear to resemble the 'more or less', or policy change, items. However, they tell us very little about the preferred policy of those responding that the government is doing a poor job. These respondents may want the government either to increase or reduce its efforts on the policy in question. Or they may think the scope of government is about right, only the government is not efficient in pursuing the policy. For example, they may believe that social security goes to the wrong people—the 'undeserving poor'—or that it is too easy for rich people to evade taxes. Hence, performance items are not used in our analyses.

Trade-off items. Surveys often ask respondents to choose between two policy lines which researchers assume to be incompatible. For example, choosing between fighting unemployment or fighting inflation, or between protecting the environment and securing economic growth. These items resemble agenda items in that the response suggests which of two policy goals is the most important to the respondent. We have to be aware, however, that the choice is 'forced' on the respondent who may not perceive the two goals as incompatible. Such items make more sense when the choice is between, for example, cutting taxes and improving public services than when it is between fighting pollution and securing economic growth. Therefore we use these items with caution.

Perception items. Finally, some surveys seek to measure perceptions concerning what the government is actually doing in various fields—that is, perceptions about the current scope of government. Likewise, people have cognitive expectations about what the state will do or can do in a particular instance, or in the future; for example, whether or not taxes will continue to rise. However, there are few examples of these kinds of data in the available surveys; in particular, there seem to be no time series or comparative data allowing cross-national analysis. Even if these data existed, they might well disappoint us, for on the subject of 'what government is actually doing', people's perceptions are likely to be grossly inaccurate. When respondents are asked to estimate public expenditure on some programme or in some policy area, their estimates often vary by a factor of ten or more. Apparently the public consider information about government activity to be a technical matter, but ignorance does not prevent them having opinions on policy matters.

Types of Relationship Explored

The limitations of the available data mean that the studies in this volume are more about demands—in the Eastonian sense—in the fields of economic and social policy, and their development in the 1970s and 1980s, rather than changing beliefs about government between 1945 and 1990. On many questions, we can make inferences only from observations at a single time-point. In large part, the data problems we have to confront stem from the lack of a long-standing research tradition focusing on people's attitudes and beliefs about the scope of government in general and public policies in particular (Almond and Powell 1980). Consequently, often we have had to resort to surrogate measures, using them to infer something about the way in which people's beliefs about the scope of government have either changed or are changing.

Nevertheless, we address some interesting and important questions in this volume concerning both differences between countries and differences within countries. Differences between countries may be due to different political traditions or cultures, to government initiatives, or to recent conspicuous events. But differences in attitudes—or policy demands—may also vary, in the aggregate, according to levels of economic development. In general, we anticipate some weakening of demands for government intervention as societies become wealthier. For example, Inglehart notes the tendency of people in economically advanced societies to oppose any further expansion of welfare or reduction of income inequalities, as well as opposing government management of the economy and the nationalization of industry (Inglehart 1990: 256). Such variations between countries also suggest that demands for government action are not insatiable. Elementary public choice theory may hold true here: people above a certain income level tend to respond negatively to the expansion of welfare because the cost of these public goods, in terms of taxation, outweighs any personal benefit. In many less-developed countries, on the other hand, income distribution is highly unequal and upper-income people are in a minority, which makes for strong pressure for expanding welfare and reducing income differences. In mature economies, however, upper-income people are on the way to becoming a majority. Even so, that strong opposition to further expansion can be mustered in advanced welfare societies does not mean that their populations want to give up significant parts of their welfare systems. Indeed, as we shall demonstrate later in the volume, this seems to be the lesson learnt by many governments of the 1980s.

Economic factors, however, must be supplemented with other factors in explaining beliefs about the scope of government. For example, comparing British and American public demands on government, Davis (1986) found that in seven policy fields British people were much more likely than Americans to assign responsibility to the state. Part of the difference might be ascribed to differences in average income, but what we find in these data is the contrast between the American ethic of free enterprise and self-reliance and the European tradition of relying on a strong state. Thus, we anticipate finding national differences which can only be ascribed to different historical traditions. Where the data permit, we have tried to identify these differences.

As to differences within countries, we assume that beliefs about the scope of government reflect the needs and interests of different groups in society. Thus we anticipate that the demand for welfare expenditure is strongest among groups whose income depends, or may come to depend, on those expenditures. Similarly, during periods of high inflation, we expect the demand for government control of prices to come especially from people with relatively constant incomes, such as pensioners, unskilled workers, and government employees. Demands for crime prevention are likely to be strongest among those who are most likely to become the victims, such as women and old people; and so forth. Differences in beliefs probably also reflect the values and norms which prevail in different generations. Hence, we expect older generations to emphasize the traditional law and order functions of government, whereas middle generations—who grew up during the 1960s—probably emphasize welfare state functions. In addition, among younger generations, we expect to find greater interest in new policy fields such as foreign aid, sexual equality, and technological research.

To some extent, these kinds of tendencies work in the same direction, since values and tangible interests often go together. In other cases, they supplement each other. For instance, no one group in particular seems to have a greater interest than other groups in expenditure on defence or foreign aid. In such cases, different policy demands are associated with different values and life-styles.

Responses to several survey items often indicate a line of conflict in the population. How many such lines of conflict can be identified? Obviously we do not suggest that a new line of conflict is opened up every time an item is inserted in a questionnaire, so we have to distinguish and label those conflict lines which recur in the survey data. To a large extent the differences between the ideas of the conservative, liberal, social democratic, and communist parties might be defined in terms of beliefs about the scope of government. Historically, such beliefs have been among the important factors shaping the party systems in Western Europe. This is especially true with regard to beliefs about the regulation and nationalization of business, the provision of public services, the scope of income transfers, and the strength of internal and external security. Even parties which are formed ostensibly around non-material goals and ideas, such as the Christian parties and the green parties, tend to have a characteristic profile of beliefs about the scope of government. Christian parties, for instance, traditionally resisted government influence in schools but advocate surveillance of public morality; green parties emphasize the role of government in fighting pollution and protecting the environment.

Thus partisan orientations are associated with government intervention in some areas but not in others. So we assume that beliefs about the scope of government will, to some extent, turn out to be structured according to leading ideological conflicts, particularly on issues associated with the left–right axis. Left-wing voters are assumed to favour government intervention chiefly in the economic sphere, including job security and welfare, whereas right-wing voters are assumed to favour intervention to ensure internal and external security. In addition to this classical conflict line, we endeavour to identify an emergent new conflict line associated with non-material values as opposed to tangible interests. Several studies have indicated that 'new politics' constitutes a distinctive dimension (Baker, Dalton, and Hildebrandt 1981; Inglehart 1990) in contemporary political conflicts. Our data allow us to track the growth and influence, or otherwise, of this dimension from the 1970s through the 1980s.

Plan of the Book

The subsequent chapters of this volume deal with different types of beliefs about the scope of government. The chapters in Part I start with general questions about the scope of government, or with attitudes in different policy fields. First, in Chapter 2, Michael Goldsmith provides an overview of developments in the scope of government in West European countries between 1960 and 1990. Using aggregate-level time series, the analysis points to both cross-national similarities and differences in general trends. This broad picture provides a general backdrop to our study.

In Chapter 3, Edeltraud Roller addresses the question of how personal agendas for government action are formed. Here, the distinction between the range and the degree of government intervention is elaborated. She also investigates whether the choice of agenda items conforms to theories of value change and new politics. Beate Huseby, in Chapter 4, continues this line of enquiry by examining whether people's ideas about government responsibility are matched by their attitudes towards the general growth of government. An important question in this chapter is whether expansionist attitudes on several issues are matched by an expansionist attitude towards government in general.

In Part II, we turn to examine attitudes in policy fields which are major pillars of the welfare state. The older functions, discussed at the beginning of this chapter, constitute the general background against which the more recent functions discussed in these chapters developed. In Chapter 5 and Chapter 6, Maria Confalonieri and Ken Newton examine attitudes towards personal taxation. Taxes vary over time and between nations in their level, their progressiveness, and their visibility. These parameters are not always spelled out when people are asked about their attitudes. Nevertheless, the authors are able to test several hypotheses within a cross-national framework.

Beliefs about welfare policies are examined in Chapter 7 and Chapter 8. Welfare services and income transfers are designed to provide material security and to promote a greater degree of economic equality. This distinction is important because adverse attitudes to welfare policies may be confined to the equality aspects. In Chapter 7, Edeltraud Roller first discusses the distinction between the security and equality goals of welfare policies and then focuses on questions about equality. In Chapter 8, Per Arnt Pettersen examines attitudes towards security goals, concentrating on old-age pensions, health care, and unemployment benefits. And then, in Chapter 9, Ole Borre and José Manuel Viegas deal with beliefs about economic policy, especially management of the economy and the nationalization of industry. An important question in that chapter is whether attitudes in this policy field form a general interventionist versus liberal dimension. Whether there is the same social and partisan basis for economic intervention in all West European countries is also explored.

Developments in newer policy fields are examined in Part III. In Chapter 10, Peter Golding and Leo van Snippenburg deal with communications policy, examining attitudes towards media content and media access. Questions about media content engage ethical principles, whereas media access raises questions about democratic attitudes. A central concern is whether such attitudes are autonomous and consistent, or whether they are rather unpredictable, driven by events and technological innovation. In Chapter 11, Olof Johansson examines attitudes towards environmental policy, discussing, among other things, their relationship to the classic left–right values of industrial society and to newer postmaterialist values. National differences in the priority given to environmental policy are particularly important here, since some measure of international consensus seems to be a prerequisite for an effective policy of environmental protection.

Finally, in Part IV, we have three chapters presenting general assessments of the role of beliefs in the wider context of policy formation and attachment to the political system. Whereas earlier chapters are largely concerned with establishing the structure and sources of beliefs about the scope of government, in Chapter 12 Ole Borre assesses the consequences of policy distance for political support. A particular concern in that chapter is what happens when a large number of people disagree with a policy being pursued by their government. In Chapter 13, the findings from our several studies are summarized and some of their implications outlined. Chapter 14, by Achille Ardigó, is a provocative postscript to our volume. Developments in health policy during the 1980s serve as an illustration that public opinion, as measured by surveys, is not always a reliable guide to actual policy. Thus the chapter voices a note of caution about some of the assumptions underlying the project reported in this volume.

PART I

General Issues

2

The Growth of Government

MICHAEL GOLDSMITH

The purpose of this chapter is to outline the general growth of government activity, as illustrated by the growth in government revenues and expenditure, over the period 1950 to 1990. But first it is important to set this topic in context, with a brief discussion of why governments grow—or their activities change—over time.

Within the context of this volume, two reasons can be advanced for changes in the scope of government. In systemic terms (Easton 1965*a*), the scope of government changes because there has been a change either in the level of demand or in support for the political system and its range of outputs. To put the point rather differently, the scope of government changes because there has been a change in the needs which demand government action; or there has been a change in the things people want governments to do; or there has been a change in the level of public support for various kinds of government activity.

Changes in the level of needs can come from a variety of sources. Changing demography has been a major factor, with ageing populations a common feature of many West European countries since 1945. Changes in employment levels, especially rising unemployment, bring pressures on tax and benefit levels. Thus, for example, falling unemployment generally means higher tax revenues for governments and may permit reductions in taxation whilst also reducing expenditure on unemployment support. Similarly, changes in the world economy, especially in the locus of manufacturing activity, can bring about a need for governments to restructure different economic sectors—as the decline in the West European coal and steel industry has demonstrated in recent years.

Changes in wants are harder to quantify, and it is harder to see how they affect the scope of government, although they obviously have an impact on the beliefs people hold about what governments should or should not do. At the simplest level, governments may be expected to maintain and improve the general well-being of the populations they serve, however well-being is defined (Wolman and Goldsmith 1992). Thus people may want both lower taxation and more extensive or improved welfare services (Taylor-Gooby 1983*a*; Edgell and Duke 1984, 1991). They may want reductions in defence expenditure—especially since 1989—but at the same time expect government to provide for national security. The post-war period has seen a significant increase in the salience of issues relating to the environment and to gender, giving rise to new kinds of wants which people expect governments to meet. Moreover, some wants may be difficult to uncover from survey or attitudinal data, simply because the values they represent are taken for granted in most West European countries, yet they depend on government action to see that they are met. Freedom of speech or association, for example, were not so readily guaranteed by the state in countries like Spain, Portugal, or Greece until the mid-1970s or later.

Even allowing that needs and wants can be expressed politically, there is inevitably a delay before political action is taken to meet them. Needs and wants have to be perceived, articulated, and processed by the political authorities—the government—of the day. A need for more public housing, or better quality housing, for example, not only has to be identified but also has to be accepted as a problem about which governments should do something. Despite recognizing needs and demands, the government may well decide to leave the matter to the market. Common sense suggests that lags between the recognition of demands and government action are likely to be quite long—years or even decades in some cases. Thus changes in public beliefs about the scope of government may not actually be translated into government action for several years.

In the meantime, several different political processes are typically under way: public debate of the problem, policy debate among experts, pressure on government from interest groups, contestation about appropriate policy between the political parties. For those matters brought forward by parties, an election may settle which sets of changes in government action are adopted. For issues decided within government, new policy statements and legislation, together with some commitment to expenditure, or to regulate/deregulate, will be needed. In all, the process of translating needs or wants into demands, and then into government action, tends to be lengthy and tortuous.

This general description of the policy process, however, conceals a central problem for the studies in this volume: the direction of the causal flow in the relationship between people's beliefs about government and what governments actually do. The simplest model would propose that as people's beliefs change so governments change their policy and behaviour. We could demonstrate this relationship empirically by looking for an increase in, say, public support for expenditure on health care, and then looking for (appropriately lagged) increases in government expenditure on health care. If the outcome is positive, we might suggest that there is a direct relationship between change in people's beliefs about government and government action.

But such a model is too simplistic and mechanical. First, it ignores intervening variables, such as parties and pressure groups, which moderate and aggregate people's demands. Moreover, the government may moderate these demands still further. Secondly, such a model presents beliefs as influences on government behaviour, rather than asking whether or not government, or élite behaviour, influences beliefs. Much government behaviour is essentially of a legitimating kind, seeking support for its actions, moulding public opinion or beliefs about what government should do. The national debates which followed the signing of the Maastricht Treaty are an example—although also demonstrating, as in the case of the subsequent Danish referendum, that governments may not always be successful in persuading electors to accept their proposals. Parties act in a similar fashion, seeking to persuade electors that their view of the proper scope of government action, rather than that of other parties, is to be preferred (Castles 1982; Budge and Hofferbert 1990; Hofferbert and Klingemann 1990; Karran 1985).

This discussion simply draws attention to what we already know from the limited literature on beliefs about government. However, the kind of data on which we have been able to draw does not allow us to unscramble the relationship between beliefs in government and what governments actually do. Even so, we need to be aware of the problem when we make assertions about the impact of mass opinion on government policies. In the context of this chapter, however, the problem is much simpler: to identify the way in which governments have changed their scope over the period since 1945. That the activities of government change over time is readily apparent. That governments grow, and have grown since 1945, is universally recognized. What governments do today is very different from what they did in 1972, and even more so than in 1952. Accounting for these changes has occupied much of the research agenda in recent years. Most studies have been concerned with the introduction of the wide range of services which together comprise what is called the welfare state. Writers such as Flora, Heidenheimer, and Alber have seen the growth of state activities partly as a process of modernization and partly as a process of development (Flora 1986*a*, 1986*b*; Flora and Heideheimer 1981), with their roots in reactions to the 'evils of capitalism' in the nineteenth century and the movement towards mass democracy. The two processes combined to give rise to the first elementary labour laws and social insurance schemes, and subsequently to much more extensive provision. The developmental process also involved considerable extension to the idea of individual rights (cf. Marshall 1950), which was linked to the growth in mass support for parties of the left or left-of-centre in the post-war period throughout much of Western Europe. A variant on this developmental model is more firmly rooted in economics and is associated with Wagner's 'law', asserting that government expenditure, in relation to the size of the economy, inevitably rise as a nation advances (Wagner 1890).

It is difficult to see in these accounts what part was played in the development of the welfare state by people's beliefs about the scope of government. Clearly writers like Flora and Heideheimer allow little room for such influences, seeing the development of the modern welfare state as much more the result of the interaction between markets, associations, and bureaucracies (Flora and Heideheimer 1981: 42). Certainly the British case provides little support for the notion that mass beliefs about the scope of government influenced the early development of the welfare state. For example, nineteenth-century reforms concerning hours of work and child labour owed more to the efforts of individual social reformers than to any serious consideration of mass beliefs, although historians have argued that fear of the 'revolting residuum' was a powerful motivator of elites in proposing social reforms (Stedman-Jones 1984). Equally, however, historians have demonstrated the extent to which local elites opposed centrally introduced poor law and public health reforms in the middle and late nineteenth century (Garrard 1983; Fraser 1979). Furthermore, the franchise was limited in Britain at the time. Thus, for example, although there were extensions to the male franchise in 1832, 1867, and 1884, women did not obtain the vote until 1928, and full universal suffrage did not come to Britain until after the Second World War in 1948.

The simple point being made here is that, for most countries of Western Europe, much of the scope of government was set by the time mass electorates arrived. Indeed, it was set long before the kind of data on mass beliefs and attitudes which allow us to see what people believe about the scope of government. Thus, what we consider in this chapter is the way in which that scope, or the range of government activity, has changed over the post-war period. Here we are talking of essentially marginal adaptations, except perhaps when a radical shift occurs in values more generally. Such value change probably occurs once in a generation or so, notwithstanding the extent to which the pace of policy transfer and adaptation has quickened over recent years. Thus, for example, the shifts in values involved in post-Francoist Spain or in Thatcherite Britain during the 1980s may be considered more general and widespread than those associated with the emergence of post-industrial society (Inglehart 1977, 1990). These shifts are likely to have more impact than marginal changes in people's beliefs about the need for expanding or reducing particular state activities.

This discussion suggests that we need to identify three sets of changes in people's beliefs about the scope of government. First, we have to identify the more common, gradual, and marginal changes in beliefs which have an impact on the growth of the welfare state generally. In so far as the welfare state was a central feature of the 'post-war consensus' (Bowles and Gintis 1982; Pierson 1991), we can assume that the balance of mass opinion about the scope of government for much of the period since 1945, throughout Western Europe, supported the expansion of welfare state provision. Thus we would expect to find a steady increase in state expenditures on such services throughout much of the post-war period, allowing for the impact of differing economic growth rates.

Secondly, the emergence of new values—reflected in postmaterialist theory (Inglehart 1977, 1990)—leads us to expect changes in some aspects of state activities and expenditure. The dissemination of 'green' values is likely to lead to more expenditure on environmental matters and the extension of government regulation. Although some gender issues, such as women's participation in the labour market, have met with a measurable response from several governments through, for example, extended and improved child-care facilities, issues like gender discrimination prove more difficult to regulate. Whilst data on such matters is less readily available, on the face of it we might argue that many West European governments, over the last decade or so, have adopted the kind of policies associated with the move to a postmaterialist culture.

Thirdly, we would expect significant changes in the level of state activity and expenditure following the impact of other kinds of shift in values or beliefs, even allowing that such shifts might be élite led. For example, we would anticipate that the transitions in Spain, Portugal, and Greece would have led to considerable increases in public expenditure on developing welfare state systems, notwithstanding the capacity of the newly emergent democratic states to finance such services. We might also expect such countries to adopt very liberal legislative measures in relation to individual freedoms or the regulation of market forces, whatever the political complexion of governments. In Britain, under the influence of the 'new right' (Bosanquet 1983; King 1987), we would expect not only larger reductions in the level of state expenditures than we find in other countries facing similar degrees of fiscal stress, but also an increase in state activity concerned with the deregulation and privatization of industry and business. The whole issue of market and individual values, as compared to the collectivist values assumed by previous welfare-orientated regimes, has been the dominant focus of political debate in Britain throughout the 1980s, and remains an influence into the 1990s. But arguably the growth of public support for the neo-liberal values associated with 'Thatcherism' initially followed changes in policy, rather than preceding them, only gathering full force after some experience of the sea change in ideological focus has been felt.[1]

Nevertheless, if Britain is perhaps an extreme case, the size and scope of government has been a major problem in a number of countries from the early 1970s onwards, receiving attention not only from academics (Clark and Ferguson 1983; Rose and Peters 1978) but from those in political office as well. Along with Britain, countries like the United States and Denmark had governments in the 1980s committed to cutting back government activity, attempting to reduce public expenditure, and to changing the balance between the public and private sectors. More recently, similar policy thrusts have become more common in other countries such as Sweden, Finland, Norway, and the Netherlands, whilst Germany has had to grapple—in addition—with the consequences of re-unification.

Other West European countries, such as Spain and Portugal, coming to industrialization and democracy later, have been concerned with extending the role of the state. By contrast to the more developed countries of north-west Europe, these less-developed countries have faced pressures to introduce the kind of welfare state associated with the Nordic countries or the level of welfare provision found in Britain, the Netherlands, and Germany. Their capacity to provide such services is limited by their relative poverty and the contending needs for infrastructural development and industrial investment.

We now go on to examine trends in general macro-level indicators which provide a measure of the pressures on government expenditures and the responses of governments in key policy fields. In the next section, we consider some of the demographic changes which have taken place in Western Europe as an indication of how the demand for government activity has changed in the post-war period. We then examine the capacity of governments to finance policy responses to those changing demands, reviewing both the actual increase in the Gross Domestic Product (GDP) per capita and the rate of GDP per capita growth. Higher per capita incomes and faster rates of GDP growth are likely to make it easier for government to finance a large range of activities. Finally, we review the relative growth—and decline in some instances—in government activity across Western Europe over the last thirty years or so.

Changing Demographics

The increase in population in West European countries from 1950 to 1990 is outlined in Table 2.1. On average the population of Western Europe increased by about a quarter over the period. Although there is considerable variation in the magnitude of growth, every one of these countries, without exception, has experienced steady increases in the size of their population. The largest increases, over 30 per cent in each case, have been in the Netherlands, Switzerland, Spain, France, and Greece. At the other extreme, Austria, Britain, Belgium, Ireland, Portugal, and Denmark have seen their populations grow by less than 20 per cent. In simple, rather crude terms, we would expect countries with faster growing populations to experience more pressure for government activity than those with slower population growth.

Two groups in the population, the young (under 14) and the elderly

TABLE 2.1. *Population growth in Western Europe, 1950–90*

	1950	1970	1990	% change 1950–90
Denmark	4.3	5.0	5.1	18.6
Finland	4.0	4.6	5.0	25.0
Norway	3.3	3.9	4.2	27.3
Sweden	7.0	8.0	8.6	22.9
Austria	6.9	7.4	7.7	11.6
Belgium	8.6	10.0	10.0	16.3
Britain	50.6	55.4	57.4	13.4
France	41.7	50.8	56.7	36.0
Germany	50.0	60.7	63.3	26.6
Ireland	3.0	2.9	3.5	16.7
Luxembourg	0.3	0.3	0.4	33.3
Netherlands	10.1	13.0	15.0	48.5
Switzerland	4.7	6.3	6.8	44.7
Greece	7.6	8.8	10.1	32.9
Italy	47.1	53.7	57.6	22.3
Portugal	8.4	9.0	9.8	16.7
Spain	28.0	33.8	39.0	39.3
Total	285.6	333.6	360.2	26.1

Notes: Entries are in millions. The total percentage change 1950–90 is calculated here, as in subsequent tables, on the basis of the totals shown, not as an average of the percentage change by country shown in the final column.

Sources: *United Nations Demographic Yearbook* (1964, 1988, 1992).

(over 65), are particularly likely to need state welfare services. Both groups place relatively heavy demands on health services, whilst the young are particularly demanding on education budgets and the elderly on transfer payments such as pensions. Table 2.2 gives some details of the changing size of these two age groups between 1950 and 1990. As we can see, the trends in the size of these two groups run in opposite directions.

All West European countries experienced a decline in the proportion of young people in their population—amounting, in all, to a drop of some 25 per cent. The decline is modest but clearly discernible in Ireland, France, Belgium, and Britain, but is a notable 30 per cent and more in Denmark, Finland, Germany, the Netherlands, Italy, Greece, and Portugal. In stark contrast, with the exception of Ireland, the proportion of the population over sixty-five increased quite dramatically in every West European country between 1950 and 1990. In

TABLE 2.2. *Age structure of West European populations, 1950–85*

	14 years and younger				65 years and older			
	1950	1970	1990	% change 1950–90	1950	1970	1990	% change 1950–90
Denmark	26.3	23.3	17.1	−35.0	9.1	12.3	15.6	71.4
Finland	30.0	24.6	19.3	−35.7	6.6	9.1	13.4	103.0
Norway	24.4	24.5	18.9	−22.5	9.7	12.9	16.3	68.0
Sweden	23.4	20.9	17.9	−23.5	10.3	13.7	17.8	72.8
Austria	22.9	24.4	17.4	−24.0	10.6	14.1	15.1	42.5
Belgium	20.6	23.6	18.1	−12.1	10.6	13.4	14.9	40.6
Britain	22.6	24.1	19.0	−15.9	10.9	13.2	15.7	44.0
France	22.6	24.8	20.1	−11.1	11.2	12.9	19.0	69.6
Germany	23.3	23.2	15.2	−34.8	9.4	13.2	15.3	62.8
Ireland	28.9	31.3	27.3	−5.5	10.7	11.2	11.4	6.5
Luxembourg	19.8	22.1	17.7	−10.6	9.5	12.6	13.5	42.1
Netherlands	29.3	27.3	18.2	−37.9	7.1	10.2	12.8	80.3
Switzerland	23.4	20.9	16.5	−29.5	9.6	11.4	15.0	56.3
Greece	28.4	24.6	19.4	−31.7	6.6	11.1	13.8	109.0
Italy	26.1	22.9	15.0	−42.5	8.2	10.5	15.3	86.6
Portugal	29.4	28.8	19.3	−34.4	7.3	9.3	19.1	161.6
Spain	26.2	28.0	19.7	−24.8	7.3	9.5	13.4	83.6
Average	24.9	24.6	18.5	−25.7	9.3	12.0	15.3	64.5

Note: Entries are percentages of total population.

Sources: See Table 2.1.

Finland, Greece, and Portugal, the proportion more than doubled; in Spain and the Netherlands, the proportion came close to doubling. Only Ireland shows a negligible increase; in every other case the increase is never less than 40 per cent. We might see this 'greying' of the West European population as a reflection of greater life expectancy following improvements in health care, one of the fastest growing elements in the expenditure of most governments. This probably applies even in the countries of southern Europe, despite the late development of the welfare state in those countries.

The Economic Environment

Several commentators have portrayed the growth of government as a reflection of growing economic prosperity. The data in Table 2.3 allow us to see how the economic base of West European countries has changed since 1950, reflecting the general rise in per capita incomes which all countries have experienced during the period.

The increase in the average GDP per capita is over 200 per cent. The lowest increases (Switzerland and Britain) represent more than a doubling of GDP per capita, whilst the highest increases represent a quadrupling of national wealth. Such dramatic increases are largely concentrated in the countries of southern Europe, closely followed by Norway, Germany, and Austria. However, despite the general picture of economic growth across Western Europe, the gap between the richest and poorest countries widened over the period. Indeed, as Table 2.3 makes clear, there has been little overall change in the rank order: those countries with the highest per capita GDP in 1950 are, by and large, the same as in 1990. On the other hand, by the end of the period, Norway, Finland, and Germany had joined Switzerland, Sweden, Denmark, Luxembourg at the top of the ranking. Similarly, countries with the lowest per capita GDP in 1950 remain in the bottom ranks in 1990: Portugal, Greece, Spain, Ireland, and Italy. With the exception of Ireland, however, this latter group of countries had the fastest rate of increase in per capita GDP. Indeed, some of the richest countries—such as Switzerland and Sweden—had the slowest rate of increase in GDP per capita over the period. The largest drop in the rank ordering is experienced by Britain, which fell from fifth to twelfth place and had the second slowest rate of increase in per capita GDP. The strongest climber was West Germany, moving up from ninth to sixth place.

What is interesting about Table 2.3 is that it helps us to understand why some countries may be better able to cope with rising demands to extend the range of state activities, whereas others suffer from demand 'overload'. This problem is discussed more fully in Chapters 3 and 4. Thus we would not be surprised to find that countries with constantly high and rapidly growing per capita GDP, such as Norway, Finland, Germany are better placed to meet changing demands or are more willing to widen the scope of state activities and services. Similarly, we would expect poorer countries such as Portugal and Greece to have lower levels of state expenditures, or lower increases in levels of expenditure. In Britain and the Netherlands, on the other hand—with

TABLE 2.3. *GDP per capita, 1950–90*

	1950	1970	1990	% change 1950–90
Denmark	4,395	8,283	12,183	177.2
Finland	3,207	7,182	12,838	300.3
Norway	3,372	8,008	14,812	339.3
Sweden	4,975	9,418	13,023	161.8
Austria	2,279	5,718	9,832	331.4
Belgium	2,929	5,784	9,367	219.8
Britain	3,677	6,146	9,287	152.6
France	2,904	6,948	10,706	268.7
Germany	2,639	7,401	11,387	331.5
Ireland	2,025	3,541	6,654	228.6
Luxembourg	4,336	6,957	11,216	158.7
Netherlands	3,187	6,899	9,607	201.4
Switzerland	6,620	12,207	15,649	136.4
Greece	729	2,246	3,579	390.9
Italy	1,891	5,098	8,545	351.9
Portugal	536	1,486	2,636	391.8
Spain	1,108	3,254	5,298	378.2
Average	2,989	6,269	9,801	227.9

Note: Entries are in US$1985 prices/exchange rates.

Sources: OECD (1968, 1983, 1992).

relatively modest GDP per capita and slower growth rates—we would anticipate fiscal stress or demand overload leading to changing expectations about the scope of government.

If West European countries have experienced remarkable increases in GDP per capita, how is this reflected in changes in government activity? Or, more precisely, which government activities have grown since 1945? One important area of activity, and still somewhat neglected among researchers, is the changing nature of government legislation and statutory provision (Rose 1983*b*; Page 1982). Introducing new services requires legislation, so does changing a service or dropping it. Similarly laws are necessary to regulate behaviour, whether they relate to institutions such as the stock market, environmental pollution, or speeding car drivers. However, we concentrate on changes in two aspects of government central to the studies in this volume: government income and government expenditure.

Government Income

Government income is necessary to finance services, and rising income is necessary to meet growing levels of public expenditure. Similarly, falling income constrains the capacity of governments to maintain overall levels of expenditure, exerting pressure to review welfare provision or to revise the balance of expenditure between different areas of government activity. We deal first with the growth in government income over the period 1950 to 1990 and, then, in the next section, with the growth of government expenditure. Our principal data source is the *Political Data Handbook* (Lane, McKay, and Newton 1992), with some adaptions for our purposes.

Data on government incomes in Western Europe over the post-war period, expressed as a proportion of national GDP, are presented in Table 2.4. Income here refers to the current receipts of government,

TABLE 2.4. *Government receipts as a percentage of GDP, 1950–90*

	1950	1965	1975	1985	1990	% change 1950–90
Denmark	21.7	31.4	46.2	57.0	55.9	157.6
Finland	30.3	33.5	38.8	40.5	40.8	34.7
Norway	29.6	37.7	49.6	56.1	56.3	90.2
Sweden	26.2	42.0	50.7	59.4	63.8	143.5
Austria	27.9	36.1	42.9	47.7	46.6	67.0
Belgium	24.2	30.7	40.4	46.5	49.5	104.5
Britain	33.5	32.8	40.8	43.7	39.5	17.9
France	32.6	37.7	40.3	48.5	46.4	42.3
Germany	31.6	36.2	42.7	45.4	43.2	36.7
Ireland	23.4	28.0	35.2	44.3	40.3	72.2
Luxembourg	31.7	35.2	49.0	53.0	n/a	—
Netherlands	33.0	36.8	53.2	54.4	51.9	57.3
Switzerland	25.5	25.4	32.1	34.4	34.1	33.7
Greece	15.5	23.4	27.4	34.9	34.2	120.6
Italy	21.0	31.6	31.2	37.5	42.3	101.4
Portugal	20.0	20.4	24.8	n.a.	37.6	88.0
Spain	n.a.	19.3	24.4	33.2	37.9	—
Average	26.7	31.7	39.4	46.0	45.0	68.5

Notes: Receipts consist mainly of direct taxes and social security contributions paid by employers and employees. General government consists of all departments, offices, organizations, and other bodies that are agents or instruments of the central, state, or local public authorities.

Sources: See Table 2.3.

largely comprising direct and indirect taxes, plus state insurance contributions. The figures reveal that, broadly, government incomes rose on average from 26.7 per cent of GDP in 1950 to 45 per cent in 1990. In 1950, government incomes were highest—about one third of GDP—in Britain and the Netherlands, closely followed by France and Germany. By 1990, the Scandinavian governments, led by Sweden, were far ahead, receiving well over half the total GDP as income.

The figures in Table 2.4 show other interesting features. First, government income has not grown evenly throughout Western Europe over the post-war period. In Britain, for example, government income grew, overall, by less than 20 per cent, and in some other countries (Finland, Germany, and Switzerland) it grew by something around a third. Government income more than doubled, however, in Denmark, Sweden, Belgium, Greece, and Italy. Secondly, within the general pattern of steadily increasing government revenues evident until the mid-1980s, the pace of increase varied. Growth appears generally to have been most rapid between 1965 and 1975, at a time when many countries were not only expanding their welfare systems, but also saw their economies growing at a rate which could support increased government expenditure. Between 1975 and 1985, however, although government incomes continued to grow, the rate of growth slowed in most countries. Thirdly, by 1990, the general pattern of ever-growing government revenues was broken. Compared to 1985, government income (as a percentage of GDP) declined in several countries, most notably in Britain and Ireland, and, in effect, was stationary in Finland and Norway. Only four countries—Sweden, Belgium, Italy, and Spain—show continued expansion of government revenues into the 1990s; and even in these countries, expansion was considerably less than in earlier periods.

Clearly, one of the keys to understanding government income—and, thus, expenditure—is the rate of economic growth in particular countries, and indeed in the world economy as a whole. Government income grows when economies grow—and, as we shall see, so do government expenditures (Wolman and Goldsmith 1987). Gould points out that growth in public expenditure was faster in the 1960s than in the 1970s, supporting the idea that economic growth is the more important determinant of both government income and expenditure. As he notes, after examining budgeting, 'governments have generally been guided to a very great extent in their short-term expenditure plans by the projected increase in tax revenues deriving from the estimated increase in GDP' (Gould 1983: 39).

Government Expenditure

In examining government expenditure, we deal first with changes in the overall level of expenditure and then review some of the more important specific sectoral expenditures, such as health, education, and defence. By adopting this approach we can see both how the general pattern of government activity has changed over time and the way in which specific sectors have developed. Note that services can be financed out of direct and indirect taxation, from state insurance contributions, or from specific charges.

In Table 2.5 we present figures for general government expenditure

TABLE 2.5. *Government expenditure as a percentage of GDP, 1950–90*

	1950	1960	1970	1980	1990	% change 1950–80	% change 1950–90
Denmark	10.2	12.7	19.8	26.7	25.2	161.8	147.1
Finland	11.6	12.6	14.7	18.6	21.1	60.3	81.9
Norway	11.1	14.0	16.9	18.9	21.0	70.3	89.2
Sweden	14.0	17.1	21.6	28.9	27.1	106.4	93.6
Austria	11.2	12.9	14.7	17.8	17.9	58.9	59.8
Belgium	12.6	12.6	13.7	18.5	14.3	46.8	13.5
Britain	16.4	16.8	17.7	21.5	19.9	31.1	21.3
France	12.8	12.9	13.4	15.2	18.0	18.8	40.6
Germany	14.3	13.6	15.8	20.2	18.4	41.3	28.7
Ireland	11.8	12.2	14.7	21.5	15.6	82.2	32.2
Luxembourg	12.1	10.1	9.9	16.5	16.3	36.4	34.7
Netherlands	12.5	13.5	16.3	18.0	14.8	44.0	18.4
Switzerland	11.4	10.2	10.5	12.7	13.3	11.4	16.7
Greece	11.6	11.4	12.6	16.3	21.1	40.5	81.9
Italy	11.6	12.1	13.8	16.4	17.3	41.4	49.1
Portugal	11.2	10.9	14.2	14.7	16.7	31.3	49.1
Spain	n.a.	8.8	8.5	11.6	15.2	—	—
Average	12.3	13.0	14.6	19.4	18.4	57.7	49.6

Note: Expenditure is for goods and services for public administration, defence, and education, excluding all transfer payments.

Sources: See Table 2.3.

as a proportion of GDP. For our purposes, general government expenditure consists of expenditure on public administration, defence, health, and education, but excludes all transfer payments. Thus the figures underestimate the total amount of government expenditure as a share of GDP. Nonetheless, these figures provide an overview of the way in which government expenditure has changed between 1950 and 1990.

Again the general picture is of considerable expansion. On average, across Western Europe, government expenditure grew by 50 per cent over the period, rising from 12.3 per cent of GDP in 1950 to 18.4 per cent in 1990. But this average figure conceals the wide variation between, for example, Denmark, where government spending more than doubled, and Belgium, where it grew, overall, by only rather more than 10 per cent. On this measure, however, the rank order of the countries changed over the period: Britain, Germany, and Sweden had the highest spending governments in 1950 but by 1990 the Nordic countries, along with Greece, had the highest spending governments—with Sweden and Denmark far ahead of the field. As with government revenues, increasing government expenditure was generally more evident during the 1960s and 1970s but with downturns in several countries during the 1980s. In most instances, the decline in government expenditure was fairly modest, but quite dramatic in the case of the Netherlands, Ireland, and Belgium. By 1990, apart from the southern countries, government expenditure continued to grow only in France, Finland, and Norway. Moreover, although the governments of richer countries tended to spend more, this is not invariably the case: despite having the highest per capita incomes, Switzerland had both the lowest spending government in 1990 and almost the lowest increase in government expenditure over the period since 1950. Again, whereas governments in Spain, Portugal, and Ireland are among the lowest spenders, low spending is not confined to the poorer countries—witness the 1990 spending levels in Belgium, the Netherlands, and Switzerland.

What makes government expenditure grow? Reviews of the factors contributing to the growth of public expenditure have often drawn attention to the impact of demographic change (especially ageing populations), urbanization, the relative price effect, and the high income elasticity for public goods (especially social welfare goods), as well as displacement effects relating to social upheaval (Tarschys 1975; Peacock and Wiseman 1979; Gould and Roweth 1980). In addition, a number of political and budgeting influences come into play, such as electoral competition, the partisan nature of government, budgetary incrementalism, and bureaucratic budget maximization strategies.

Modelling the effects of these different factors is complex, and the models are difficult to test. Gould, for example, notes that 'there is clearly a rather complex, multidimensional process at work' (Gould 1983: 38). However, his analysis suggests that there is generally 'only a poor or even reverse association between differences in public expenditure growth relative to GDP . . . and a number of variables which might be expected to exhibit a strong relationship' (Gould 1983: 64). For the period 1960–79, he found that total public expenditure grew faster than GDP in all countries, a finding generally supported by the figures we present. On the other hand, according to Gould, this finding is not significantly related in any predictable way to differences either in the level of economic development or in the partisan composition of governments (Gould 1983: 40, 51). Subsequent work by Saunders largely confirms Gould's findings, in particular concluding that there is 'no evidence that the decline in economic growth after 1973 bears any systematic relation to the growth of public expenditure' (1985: 14). On the other hand, Saunders notes that those countries which had the largest public sectors before 1973 were also characterized by lower rates of economic growth (1985: 19).

If we consider the rate of growth of government expenditure, the fastest rate of growth was generally in the 1970s. Although some countries—notably Luxembourg and West Germany—actually reduced expenditure between 1950 and 1960, the steady growth of expenditure was a consistent feature of government activity across Western Europe into the 1980s. As we noted earlier, only half a dozen countries avoided cutbacks in public expenditure. The British figures reveal both the effects of the 1976 crisis—when the government resorted to negotiating a sizeable loan from the IMF[2]—and the early years of the Thatcher governments, with expenditure falling from 1975 onwards. On the whole, cuts in expenditure reached other countries later, with the result that the rate of decline in expenditure was actually more marked in the short term than was the case in Britain—as in the case of Belgium and the Netherlands.

These data thus confirm the picture outlined by Gould and Saunders. Quite clearly government has grown throughout Western Europe in terms of 'getting and spending' (Pliatsky 1982). The data also show that both government income and expenditure tend to be higher in the social democratic Scandinavian states with their extensive welfare systems, and lower—although expanding more rapidly over recent years—in the newly democratized countries of southern Europe. In addition, the data in Tables 2.4 and 2.5 reveal that the growth in both government income and expenditure has been uneven over the period.

What Has Grown?

The data allow us to compare changes in two different sources of government income: taxes and social security contributions. In principal, the latter are contributions to a social security fund on which individuals can draw, be it for sickness or unemployment benefits, or old age pensions. Several countries distinguish between taxes and social security contributions, whilst others finance the social security system from general tax revenues. In practice, however, many governments treat social security contributions as simply another contribution to general government revenues. Hence, we have to be cautious in interpreting the data on levels of taxation and social security contributions.

In Table 2.6, we present the picture for the growth of tax income. As a percentage of GDP, average government income from taxation rose by 40 per cent between 1950 and 1990. As with expenditure, government taxation income rose faster from 1970 onwards, which is what we would expect from the general expansion of welfare states. By 1990, taxes were highest in the Scandinavian countries, led by Denmark and Sweden, remained lowest in Switzerland and Spain, and have generally been most stable in West Germany and the Netherlands. The table also shows that the rate of growth in government tax incomes tended to slow after 1980; in some instances, especially Norway, there was even a drop on the 1980 levels. Indeed, in Britain during the 1980s, taxation as a percentage of GDP actually fell by 3.7 per cent compared to the 1950 base—reflecting the place of lower taxation as a major plank in the programme of the Conservative governments.

However, the data do not permit us to distinguish between direct and indirect taxation, and they cover taxes raised by public authorities at all levels of government. They include not only income tax, but also local taxes and such indirect taxes as VAT, petrol, and other kinds of sales based taxes. Thus these data do not allow us to trace the tendency, during the late 1970s and the 1980s, by several West European

TABLE 2.6. *Taxes as a percentage of GDP, 1950–90*

	1950	1960	1970	1980	1990	% change 1950–80	% change 1950–90
Denmark	15.5	23.8	38.2	44.4	46.6	186.5	200.6
Finland	25.2	24.9	27.0	29.5	32.6	17.1	29.4
Norway	26.1	26.6	31.5	38.6	34.8	47.9	33.3
Sweden	21.9	27.0	33.2	35.3	40.9	61.2	86.8
Austria	22.4	24.4	27.4	29.2	29.3	30.4	30.8
Belgium	17.9	19.2	23.9	29.9	29.3	67.0	63.7
Britain	29.7	23.8	31.5	30.3	28.6	2.0	−3.7
France	20.8	22.2	22.4	23.3	23.0	12.0	10.6
Germany	22.4	24.2	24.0	25.7	23.7	14.7	5.8
Ireland	20.3	21.2	28.4	30.4	30.5	49.8	50.2
Luxembourg	24.1	21.4	21.7	30.8	n/a	27.8	—
Netherlands	26.1	12.3	25.2	27.9	28.1	6.9	7.7
Switzerland	16.1	15.9	18.2	20.7	20.8	28.6	29.2
Greece	12.3	14.1	18.0	19.0	23.0	54.5	87.0
Italy	14.2	18.4	16.7	21.2	25.0	49.3	76.1
Portugal	14.4	13.5	18.0	20.8	24.4	44.4	69.4
Spain	n.a.	13.1	11.5	13.3	21.9	—	—
Average	20.6	20.9	24.5	27.7	28.9	34.5	40.3

Note: Includes direct and indirect taxes, and social security contributions paid by employers,and employees.

Sources: See Table 2.3.

governments to shift the tax burden from direct or 'visible' taxes, especially income tax, to indirect, 'invisible' taxes.

Some countries impose high tax burdens, which the public may or may not be willing to carry. For example, we noted that Sweden leads the field in terms of government income, yet already in 1985 Hadenius reported that 83 per cent of Swedes felt that tax levels were too high—although 56 per cent adopted a positive attitude towards the balance between the taxes they paid and the benefits they received from state expenditures (Hadenius 1985). He concludes, however, that the 'somewhat controversial policy of substantially reducing the progressive nature of income tax would seem to be strongly supported at the grassroots level' (Hadenius 1985: 362). Similar ambivalence towards taxation levels and welfare benefits are reported by a number of British studies in the 1980s (Edgell and Duke 1982, 1984, 1991; Hibbs and Madsen 1981; Taylor-Gooby 1983a; Lewis 1980; Lewis and Jackson

1985). As far as parties are concerned, parties of the left can be expected to favour progressive taxes, whilst those on the right may well seek to secure a reduction in the level of taxation. However, the influence of parties is likely to be limited to certain types of tax or to setting tax rates rather than overall tax levels (Karran 1985).

Social security contributions constitute a sizeable share of these taxes, but as shown in Table 2.7, we find very considerable differences between countries. For example, in 1990, social security contributions amounted to only 1.5 per cent of GDP in Denmark but 19.3 per cent of GDP in the France. Differences of this magnitude reflect national differences in revenue regimes which we noted earlier. Even so, taking these data at face value, the general pattern we found on earlier indicators is repeated here. On average, social security contributions rose steeply from 4 per cent of GDP in 1950 to 11 per cent in 1980. Thereafter, however, there was either a levelling off of further increases

TABLE 2.7. *Social security contributions as a percentage of GDP, 1950–90*

	1950	1960	1970	1980	1990	% change 1950–90
Denmark	1.3	1.5	1.9	0.9	1.5	15.4
Finland	2.6	2.6	4.4	4.8	4.8	84.6
Norway	1.9	5.5	9.7	12.1	12.2	542.1
Sweden	0.7	3.8	7.6	14.3	15.3	2,085.7
Austria	5.4	6.1	8.8	12.5	12.3	127.8
Belgium	5.1	6.4	10.3	12.5	15.5	203.9
Britain	3.4	3.6	5.2	6.2	6.3	85.3
France	9.3	11.2	12.9	18.4	19.3	107.5
Germany	7.7	9.7	11.6	15.5	15.8	105.2
Ireland	1.0	1.1	4.3	7.6	7.2	620.0
Luxembourg	6.9	9.0	9.5	14.0	n/a	—
Netherlands	4.3	8.1	14.6	18.2	17.0	295.3
Switzerland	4.2	4.7	5.6	9.1	9.8	133.3
Greece	2.5	4.5	6.6	9.0	9.7	288.0
Italy	4.9	8.7	10.7	12.6	12.9	163.3
Portugal	3.6	2.7	4.6	8.9	10.4	188.9
Spain	n/a	3.5	6.6	12.0	12.2	—
Average	4.1	5.5	7.9	11.1	11.4	178.0

Note: Includes all compulsory contributions as payments to institutions of general government providing for social security benefits.

Sources: See Table 2.3.

or, in some cases, a downturn—notably in the Netherlands. The increases over the forty-year period were highest—by a very long way—in Sweden followed by Ireland and then, at a considerable distance, by Portugal and Spain.[3] Setting aside Denmark, where the revenue emphasis is on taxation rather than social security contributions, the lowest increases were in Italy and Britain. Note, however, that no country shows a fall from 1960s levels in the proportion of GDP taken up by social security contributions, and that, with the exception of Denmark, increases in contributions have been larger than increases in taxation.

To get a fuller picture of what grows, we need to look at a breakdown of government spending in different policy areas. In Table 2.8 we show developments in social security transfers as a percentage of GDP. As we can see from the average figure, the general pattern is again one of considerable increase over the post-war period, but with a marked gap

TABLE 2.8. *Social security transfers as a percentage of GDP, 1950–90*

	1950	1955	1965	1975	1985	1990	% change 1950–90
Denmark	5.8	6.7	8.3	13.9	16.5	18.5	219.0
Finland	4.5	5.0	7.0	9.6	11.6	11.0	144.4
Norway	4.8	6.4	9.7	13.6	14.8	19.5	306.3
Sweden	6.3	7.4	10.0	15.1	19.3	20.8	230.2
Austria	7.8	9.4	12.3	16.9	20.1	19.9	155.1
Belgium	9.7	9.0	12.4	18.8	22.0	22.2	128.9
Britain	5.4	5.4	7.4	10.9	14.6	12.8	137.0
France	11.2	13.1	16.1	20.6	26.6	21.5	92.0
Germany	12.3	11.4	13.0	18.4	16.6	15.9	29.3
Ireland	4.7	5.6	6.9	14.9	18.2	15.8	236.2
Luxembourg	7.7	10.4	13.6	19.9	23.2	—	—
Netherlands	6.7	7.2	14.0	25.6	28.5	26.1	289.6
Switzerland	4.9	5.3	7.3	10.1	13.7	13.6	177.6
Greece	5.7	4.9	7.5	7.4	15.0	14.8	159.6
Italy	6.3	9.4	13.4	16.0	16.9	18.4	192.1
Portugal	2.5	2.6	3.4	8.5	10.9	12.3	392.0
Spain	n.a.	n.a.	5.7	9.3	16.0	15.9	—
Average	6.6	7.5	9.9	14.7	17.9	17.4	163.6

Note: Transfers consists of social security benefits, social assistance grants, unfunded employee pension and welfare benefits, and transfers to private non-profit institutions serving households.

Sources: See Table 2.3.

between the highest (Portugal and Norway) and the lowest (Germany and France) increases. In some measure, however, these differences reflect differences in social security regimes. In 1990, social security transfers were highest in the Netherlands, Belgium, and France, lowest in Portugal, Finland, and Britain. But again, we find a repetition of the earlier pattern: with the exception of West Germany, social security transfers increased steadily during the 1960s and 1970s but by 1990 further increases of comparable magnitude are found in only four countries (Denmark, Norway, Italy, and Portugal).

Another important aspect of government is division into central and local administration. The data in Table 2.9 give a limited picture of spending at the subnational, or local level. As a share of GDP, expenditure rose on average by 20 per cent between 1975 and 1990.

TABLE 2.9. *Regional and local government consumption as a percentage of GDP, 1975–90*

	1975	1980	1985	1990	% change 1975–90
Denmark	n.a.	18.2	17.2	17.3	—
Finland	10.6	11.7	13.4	14.1	33.0
Norway	11.0	11.3	11.4	12.6	14.5
Sweden	15.5	19.8	19.9	19.4	25.2
Austria	7.1	7.5	7.6	7.5	5.6
Belgium	3.0	3.7	3.6	4.0	33.3
Britain	9.1	8.2	8.0	7.8	−14.3
France	2.8	3.3	3.8	4.4	57.1
Germany	9.9	10.1	9.7	9.2	−7.1
Ireland	9.2	10.5	9.4	7.5	−18.5
Luxembourg	4.0	4.6	4.6	—	—
Netherlands	9.0	9.2	8.0	7.0	−22.2
Switzerland	4.1	4.0	4.0	4.1	0.0
Greece	2.0	3.8	4.1	4.9	145.0
Italy	6.2	6.7	8.6	7.5	21.0
Portugal	n.a.	1.1	1.4	n.a.	—
Spain	n.a.	2.2	4.2	5.7	—
Average	7.4	8.0	8.2	8.9	20.2

Note: Consists of goods and services for public administration, defence, health, and education, excluding all transfer payments. Regional and local government includes all types of sub-central governments.

Source: OECD (1987*b*).

However, the pattern here is much more mixed than we have seen so far. Over the course of these fifteen years, spending at the local level more than doubled in Greece and increased by over 50 per cent in France, but fell by 22 per cent in the Netherlands and some 18 per cent in Ireland. Again, whilst local expenditure remained fairly constant in Switzerland, it fell consistently from 1975 through to 1990 in Britain. Clearly, then, no general trend of either expansion or contraction is evident from these data. Note, moreover, that local level expenditure is consistently higher in the Nordic countries (averaging almost 16 per cent in 1990) compared, in particular, with the federal states (Austria and Germany) and countries which introduced regional tiers of government during the 1970s and 1980s (France, Italy, and Spain).

In an earlier study, Gould (1983) identified expenditure by regional and local governments as the second fastest growing component of public expenditure, growing faster than central government expenditure as a whole between 1960 and 1980. Unfortunately our data do not extend further back than 1975. However, two explanations can be offered for the general growth of local expenditure up to 1980. First, the period 1950–70 was when the governments of north-west Europe extended their welfare state services, generally delegating the delivery of such services to lower tiers. Thus, the relatively high expenditure levels found in the Nordic countries reflect both the extent of the decentralization of service delivery, and are linked to their relatively high levels of welfare expenditure. Secondly, the period since 1970 has generally seen a decentralization of functions from central government to lower tiers, particularly with the regionalization programmes in Spain, Italy, and France, and federalization in Belgium. Hence, in those countries, we would expect spending at the lower tier of government to have grown as a share of public expenditure. The fall in local expenditure levels in, for example, the Netherlands, reflects the general squeeze on public expenditure witnessed during the 1980s.

Compared with these areas of either rapid or modest growth of government, external security has been an area of decline. Defence expenditure attracts attention in many countries, particularly as parties of the left tend to see it as a ready target for spending cuts. What is striking about defence budgets, however, is their variability across West European countries. In Britain, for example, defence expenditure has featured frequently and prominently in policy reviews, most recently with the prospect of a so-called 'peace dividend' following the collapse of the Soviet Union. But this largely reflects the relatively high proportion of GDP given over to defence—which, in Britain, in 1990, was second only to Greece. In countries with a tradition of neutrality, as in Sweden and Switzerland, we might expect levels of military expenditure to be relatively low. In the event, in 1975, both countries still committed 10 per cent of the public budget to military expenditure. We would expect countries faced with internal violence, as in the case of Britain in Northern Ireland, or fearful of its neighbours, as in the case of Greece, to have relatively high levels of military expenditure. And this is what we find—but France too is among the relatively high spenders on defence.

Despite different national debates about levels of military expenditure, Table 2.10 reveals that, on average, defence expenditure fell across Western Europe by more than a quarter in terms of their share of GDP between 1950 and 1990. Over the period as a whole, defence expenditure was squeezed in every country except Denmark, Norway, and Austria, and was held constant only in Finland and Ireland. The

TABLE 2.10. *Military expenditures as a percentage of GDP, 1950–90*

	1950	1960	1970	1980	1990	% change 1950–90
Denmark	1.7	2.7	2.4	2.4	2.0	17.6
Finland	1.8	1.7	1.4	1.9	1.8	0.0
Norway	2.4	2.9	3.5	2.9	3.2	33.3
Sweden	3.5	4.0	3.6	2.9	2.4	−31.4
Austria	0.7	1.2	1.1	1.2	1.0	42.9
Belgium	n.a.	3.6	2.9	3.3	2.4	—
Britain	6.6	6.5	4.8	4.9	3.9	−40.9
France	5.5	6.5	4.2	4.0	3.6	−34.5
Germany	4.4	4.0	3.3	3.3	2.8	−36.4
Ireland	1.3	1.6	1.3	1.9	1.3	0.0
Luxembourg	1.3	1.0	0.8	1.0	1.1	−15.4
Netherlands	4.8	4.1	3.5	3.1	2.7	−43.8
Switzerland	2.6	2.5	2.2	1.9	1.6	−38.5
Greece	6.0	4.9	4.8	5.7	5.9	−1.7
Italy	4.3	3.3	2.7	2.1	2.1	−51.2
Portugal	3.8	4.2	7.1	3.5	3.1	−18.4
Spain	n.a.	2.2	1.6	3.1	1.8	—
Average	3.4	3.4	3.0	2.9	2.5	−26.5

Sources: *SIPRI World Armaments and Disarmament 1980* (table 1A.4); *1988* (table 6A.3); *1990* (table 7A.3).

largest cuts were imposed in Italy, the Netherlands, and Britain—countries with some of the highest military expenditures during the 1950s. The particularly large percentage increase in Austria only brought military expenditure more into line with average spending levels.

Explanations for the general decline are perhaps not hard to find: wars in Europe have been a rare phenomenon since 1945—the conflicts in Eastern Europe and former Yugoslavia notwithstanding. Yet, as has often been argued (Peacock and Wiseman 1967; Tilly 1975; Hintze 1975), war has been an important element in the development of public expenditure and the growth of the modern state. This finding is confirmed by Rasler and Thompson (1985), who also endorse Peacock and Wiseman's 'displacement theory' that government expenditures increase during periods of national crisis, and, despite some decline in the post-crisis period, they will remain at high levels. West European countries have generally not faced that kind of national crisis since 1950, thus permitting reductions in levels of defence expenditure. The freeing of defence monies leaves governments with income to use in other directions, unless they choose to pass on the benefits in the form of tax reductions. On the whole, most West European countries have not taken up the latter option.

What Has Grown Most?

If defence expenditure has fallen over the years, and increases in expenditure on administration have been relatively modest, yet both taxes and government spending have continued to rise, then governments must have been spending their resources on other activities. The obvious candidates are welfare services such as education and health, with the expectation that social expenditures broadly defined will generally have risen since 1950. Unfortunately our data here are limited to the twenty-year period 1960–80.

Looking at social expenditures generally, shown in Table 2.11, we can see that they increased in all the countries for which we have data. Although there are quite large national differences, the average level of expenditure almost doubled in just twenty years. The largest increases were in Switzerland, Norway, Ireland, and the Netherlands; the smallest in Germany and Austria. The biggest spenders in 1980 were Belgium and the Netherlands, with Denmark and Sweden not far behind—all

TABLE 2.11. *Total social expenditure as a percentage of GDP, 1960–80*

	1960	1965	1970	1975	1980	% change 1960–80
Denmark	n/a	n/a	26.2	32.4	33.3	—
Finland	15.4	17.7	19.9	23.3	25.4	64.9
Norway	11.7	15.8	22.5	26.2	27.2	132.5
Sweden	15.4	18.6	23.0	26.8	32.5	111.0
Austria	17.9	19.7	21.6	24.5	27.1	51.4
Belgium	17.6	21.4	25.3	34.5	38.2	117.0
Britain	13.8	16.2	18.5	22.4	22.0	59.4
France	n.a.	n.a.	n.a.	24.2	28.3	—
Germany	20.5	22.4	23.5	32.6	30.8	50.2
Ireland	11.7	13.9	17.1	23.1	25.7	119.7
Netherlands	16.2	23.0	29.1	37.1	35.6	119.8
Switzerland	8.0	10.3	12.6	19.1	20.0	150.0
Greece	8.5	10.1	10.9	10.6	13.4	57.6
Italy	16.8	20.1	21.4	26.0	26.9	60.1
Average	14.5	17.4	20.9	25.9	27.6	90.3

Notes: Includes expenditure on education, health, pensions, unemployment compensation, and other social expenditure such as sickness, maternity, or temporary disablement benefits. Data for Luxembourg, Portugal, and Spain are not available.

Source: OECD (1985*a*: annex C).

spending some one-third or more of GDP on social provision of one kind or another. Greece had by far the slimmest social expenditure budget in 1980, spending barely 14 per cent of GDP on social provision. Levels of national wealth seem an unlikely explanation for these differences: Switzerland, the second lowest spender in both 1975 and 1980, had the highest per capita GDP, and social expenditure in Ireland was close to the West European average despite having one of the lowest GDP per capita. We should also note that in three countries—Germany, the Netherlands, and Britain—overall social expenditure fell between 1975 and 1980. In the case of the Netherlands and Britain, these falls reflect the fiscal stress we anticipated earlier (see Table 2.3), whereas the reduction in Germany may owe more to worries about inflation and investment levels. Moreover, in several other countries, earlier step increases were modified to modest levels. Only in Sweden were earlier sizeable increases continued into 1980.

A number of observers (Alber 1982; Cameron 1978; Castles 1978; Stephens 1979) have emphasized the role of parties of the left in promoting social expenditure; broadly speaking, the stronger the left, the more likely social expenditure is to grow. But, as Uusitalo (1984) points out, it is still a matter of debate as to exactly which political variables are the most significant. For example, Wilensky (1981) highlights the importance of Catholic dominance as an explanation for social expenditure, whereas Castles (1978) emphasizes societal consensus as the precondition for the political consensus required to build and sustain advanced welfare states. Implicit in these arguments is a form of class mobilization explanation for the growth of the welfare state in general and social expenditure in particular. An alternative explanation places far more weight on the logic of industrialism. For example, both Wilensky (1975) and Flora (1986*a*, 1986*b*) emphasize the effects of economic development, particularly its impact on the age structure of a society, as more powerful determinants of welfare programmes than either parties or ideology.

After testing these hypotheses, however, O'Connor and Brym (1987) conclude that different theories explain different aspects of the welfare state. They found that unitary countries with a corporatist style of government—Belgium, Denmark, the Netherlands, and Norway[4]—are likely to have well-developed welfare state systems. But they also found that old age dependency, or the proportion of the population over 65, is the second most important factor explaining differences in the development of welfare state systems. They conclude that researchers should be cautious before 'generalizing about a global concept of welfare effort' (O'Connor and Brym 1987: 57, 64).

Obviously social security expenditure, especially unemployment benefits and old age pensions, are the two key elements in welfare state provision. But increasingly, spending on health and education feature prominently in debates about the responsibilities of governments. Public debate about social security expenditure tends to focus on benefit levels, with only the occasional radical on the right suggesting that social security is not the business of government. Debate about health and education expenditure, however, goes further, challenging not just spending levels but the role of government in providing services in the public sector which can equally, if not better, be provided in the private sector. This latter debate reflects the success of 'new right' thinking in placing the privatization of welfare services on the political agenda.

We review health expenditures in Table 2.12. As a West European average, health expenditure almost doubled (as a percentage of GDP) over the period 1960–90. The largest increases were in Norway,

TABLE 2.12. *Total health expenditure as a percentage of GDP, 1960–90*

	1960	1970	1975	1980	1990	% change 1960–90
Denmark	3.6	6.1	6.5	6.8	6.7	86.1
Finland	4.2	5.6	5.8	6.3	7.8	85.7
Norway	3.3	5.0	6.7	6.8	8.0	142.4
Sweden	4.7	7.2	8.0	9.5	8.6	83.0
Austria	4.4	5.3	6.4	7.0	8.4	90.9
Belgium	3.4	4.1	5.5	6.3	7.9	132.4
Britain	3.9	4.5	5.5	5.8	6.0	53.8
France	4.3	6.1	7.6	8.5	8.8	104.7
Germany	4.8	5.6	8.1	8.1	8.8	83.3
Ireland	4.0	5.6	7.7	8.7	7.6	90.0
Luxembourg	n.a.	4.9	5.9	6.6	7.0	—
Netherlands	3.9	6.0	7.7	8.3	8.4	115.4
Switzerland	3.3	5.2	7.1	7.2	7.9	139.4
Greece	2.9	3.9	4.0	4.2	4.9	69.0
Italy	3.9	5.5	6.7	6.8	8.1	107.7
Portugal	n.a.	n.a.	6.4	6.1	6.1	—
Spain	n.a.	4.1	5.1	5.9	6.4	—
Average	3.9	5.3	6.5	7.0	7.5	92.3

Note: Includes current general government expenditure on health care and household final consumption on medical care and health expenses.

Sources: OECD (1985*b*: table 2; 1993: i.18).

Switzerland, and Belgium; the smallest in Britain and Greece. And here again we encounter something of the same pattern as we saw earlier: the increase in health expenditure proceeded uninterrupted from 1960 to 1980 (except in Portugal), but either turned down or levelled off between 1980 and 1990. Although not large, downturns are evident in Ireland and Sweden, whilst Denmark, the Netherlands, Britain, and Portugal saw a halting of further increases. However, in the other countries, health expenditures continued to grow during the 1980s; in Finland, Norway, Austria, Belgium, and Italy, health expenditure rose by more than 1 per cent of GDP between 1980 and 1990.

Finally, we look at the figures for education expenditure in Table 2.13. Again, our data are restricted to the twenty-year period 1960–80. Overall, in contrast to the health sector, increases in spending on education have been fairly modest—rising, on average, by less than two-thirds over the period. Again, there are some wide differences

TABLE 2.13. *Education expenditure as a percentage of GDP, 1960–80*

	1960	1970	1980	% change 1960–80
Denmark	n.a.	7.1	7.7	—
Finland	6.6	6.3	6.2	−6.1
Norway	3.9	6.4	6.3	61.5
Sweden	4.6	6.2	6.5	41.3
Austria	2.0	2.7	3.8	90.0
Belgium	4.5	6.0	8.0	77.8
Britain	3.6	5.3	5.6	55.6
France	n.a.	n.a.	5.7	—
Germany	2.4	4.0	5.1	112.5
Ireland	3.0	5.2	6.5	116.7
Netherlands	4.5	6.7	7.2	60.0
Switzerland	3.1	4.1	5.5	77.4
Greece	1.6	1.9	2.4	50.0
Italy	3.7	4.5	5.6	51.4
Average	3.6	5.1	5.9	63.9

Notes: Includes expenditure on pre-primary, primary, secondary, tertiary, education affairs and services, and subsidiary services to education. Data for Luxembourg, Portugal, and Spain are not available.
Source: See Table 2.11.

between the countries, especially between the doubling of expenditure in Ireland and West Germany and the 6 per cent fall in Finland. For the most part, the largest increases occurred during the 1960s with continued but more modest increases during the 1970s.

In all, then, we can see that West European countries are now spending a larger proportion of GDP on both health and education than they were forty years ago. On the other hand, the data also show that the 1980s saw a slowing down of increases in social expenditure. Certainly, the 1980s did not witness the rapid growth in welfare expenditures which characterized the 1960s.

Scope of Government

Overall, the data show general increases in government revenues and expenditure over the post-war period. In so far as government activity entails collecting and spending on a large scale, these increases testify to the ubiquitous growth of government in Western Europe over the last forty years. Some of this growth reflects a general widening of the scope of government, with the state becoming involved in a larger number of policy fields; some of the growth reflects higher levels of government involvement in well-established policy fields. This widening and deepening of government activity is evident, in particular, in those policy fields which, together, constitute the welfare state—whether of pre-war or post-war origin.

As to specific policy areas, only in the case of defence do we find a general trend towards declining expenditure. Even so, a few countries defy the general trend, and expenditure reductions, as a proportion of GDP, have been largely shavings at the margin. Moreover, this 'demilitarization' of public budgets has not been accompanied by reductions in either taxation levels or public expenditure. Rather, over the post-war period as a whole, expenditure has risen generally in the policy fields most closely associated with the welfare state. This is particularly true for social security payments and education expenditures. Health expenditure also increased over the period as a whole, but, in some countries, earlier increases were followed by reductions, or some levelling off of expenditure during the 1980s. Finally, and almost as a corollary of expansion, most West European countries devolved the delivery of welfare services to subnational tiers of government.

Although these developments are generally common across Western Europe, there are differences between countries. In particular, the countries of northern Europe, especially the Scandinavian countries, tend to be larger revenue raisers and spenders than the countries of southern Europe. In some part, this reflects the greater wealth per capita in the advanced industrial societies; it also reflects late democratization in Greece, Spain, and Portugal. More recently, however, these southern countries have been closing the gap, both as revenue raisers and spenders.

This broad overview of the growth of government in Western Europe during the post-war period provides the general backdrop to the studies in subsequent chapters. What is needed now is to see whether or not there is overall public support for both the general increase in levels of government spending and for increasing expenditure on particular services, as evidenced in the survey data available for the period. The scope of government in Western Europe has widened and deepened, although with some contraction more recently, but have the expectations of the public developed in parallel?

NOTES

1. The influence of demographic change is also important. Apart from the effect of changes in the demographic profile of national populations, which are broadly common across Western Europe, there are also more localized effects. For example, there are now generations in Northern Ireland which have never known peace in their region; in 1994, there is a generation of British voters who have not known any form of government other than by the Conservative Party.
2. In the event, the loan was not called upon.
3. Comparable figures (1985) for Australia (0.6 per cent), Canada (4.4 per cent), the United States (7.2 per cent), and Japan (8.3 per cent) are all well below the West European average, perhaps a reflection of generally lower welfare benefit systems in those countries.
4. This group would have included Britain before 1979.

3

Political Agendas and Beliefs about the Scope of Government

EDELTRAUD ROLLER

One of the best-known hypotheses concerning beliefs about the scope of government predicts a spiral of rising expectations. Although supported by a number of rather different arguments (Bell 1976; Brittan 1975; Crozier, Huntington, and Watanuki 1975; Douglas 1976; Janowitz 1976; King 1975; Luhmann 1990), the most common form of the hypothesis suggests increasing expectations among citizens about the range of activities for which the government is held responsible (King 1975). However, the arguments often refer not only to expectations about the range of government activity, but also suggest that expectations about government are increasing with respect to the degree of government activity within each policy area for which the government is responsible (Bell 1976; Luhmann 1990).

The hypothesis of a spiral of rising expectations has been stated in various theoretical contexts, but there is considerable agreement on the underlying logic of the process. It is assumed that the expansion of the scope of government, especially the implementation of economic and social policies, has given people experience of the problem-solving capacity of governments, which has been generalized to create a widespread belief among citizens about the universal responsibilities of governments. In consequence, as a matter of course, people expect their governments to solve problems whenever they occur: the perception of a new problem is followed by the expectation that the government should do something about it. This, in turn, leads to an expansion of their expectations about government in general. It is irrelevant to the argument whether the perceived problem has been identified by citizens themselves or identified by politicians and then presented to citizens.[1]

The hypothesis of a spiral of rising expectations is connected to a more general 'model' of the development of beliefs about the scope of government. The determinants of these beliefs are developments in the scope of government at the macro level and the perception of problems at the micro level. The widened scope of government at the macro level created a general belief in the universal responsibilities of government and, given this general belief, perceptions of problems at the micro level result in further, more specific, beliefs about the scope of government.

The general, macro-level, expansion of government in Western Europe during the last three decades was analysed in the previous chapter, using data on government expenditure. This chapter concentrates on analysing perceptions of problems at the micro level. We analyse two questions which follow from the general 'model'. The first is whether individual-level perceptions of problems have undergone such a change that we can expect beliefs about the scope of government to have changed too. The second question is whether there really is such a close relationship between perceptions of problems and beliefs about the scope of government, as hypotheses about rising expectations suggest.

At first glance, the relationship between the perception of problems and beliefs about the scope of government seems to be very specific, in the sense that the analysis is connected to the model of rising expectations alone. But looking at the general model of the political process suggested by systems theory (Almond and Powell 1978; Easton 1979), it becomes clear that the model of rising expectations is a special case of the general model. Systems theory conceptualizes the political system as an input–output process with demands and support as the two relevant types of input. Demands are defined 'as an expression of opinion that an authoritative allocation with regard to a particular subject matter should or should not be made by those responsible for doing so' (Easton 1979: 38). The main characteristic of demands in the model is that they are directed towards political objects (Easton 1979: 39). This aspect of direction also characterizes beliefs about the scope of government: these beliefs refer to expectations about the goals of policies, with goals defined as the various desirable conditions for which the government is responsible. Further, these demands can be differentiated along the dimensions of *range* and *degree* (Roller 1992:

39–47). Following the flow model of the political process, demands are 'determined' by—or 'arise' from—wants, which are located sequentially before demands (Easton 1979: 38–47, 71–2). Contrary to demands, however, wants are not necessarily directed towards political objects. Hence, although wants are located in the environment of the political system, they may not be politicized. Wants include preferences, interests, as well as perceptions of problems (Easton 1979: 41–7).

Applying this general model, the analysis in this chapter focuses on the relationship between wants and demands at the specific level of the perception of problems and beliefs about the scope of government. This is a central phase in the political process on the input side of the political system. The conversion of wants into demands—the politicization process—is the crucial point at which it is determined whether or not something is relevant for the political process.

We start our analysis with the first question, dealing with developments in the perception of problems among West European publics. Research on changes in the political agenda (Baker, Dalton, and Hildebrandt 1981) and related theories of value change in Western democracies (Inglehart 1977, 1990) are important here, providing frameworks from which we develop some hypotheses. In subsequent sections we analyse the relationship between perceptions of problems and beliefs about the scope of government. Before starting on this first question, however, we have to specify more precisely what we mean by the perception of problems.

Perception of Problems: Analytic Dimensions

What people perceive to be problems, and how they come to these perceptions, has been analysed in various ways, especially in research on voting behaviour, agenda-setting, and political values. Consequently, many analytic dimensions and different indicators have been suggested. However, we shall discuss only those dimensions and indicators which are relevant to our research questions. The discussion follows the two basic dimensions by which attitudes can be classified: the object of evaluation and the criterion of evaluation. Since most research on the perception of problems has been in relation to the notion of issues, our discussion also focuses on issues.

When we consider problems as the object of evaluation, we are confronted with the fact that there is an infinite number of things which can be perceived as problems. Therefore, we restrict ourselves to certain types of problems, identified in terms of our dependent variable: beliefs about the scope of government. As these are beliefs about the goals of policies (Roller 1992: 39–47), we can restrict the problems to the goals of policies. In other words, according to the terminology of issue research, we confine ourselves to goal-defined issues—or problems which 'are defined more in terms of goals or values that government may achieve' in contrast to policy-defined issues which 'are defined in terms of alternative courses of government action' (Butler and Stokes 1974: 277).

In restricting problems to the goals of policies, we need to know what goals belong to which policy areas. We can suggest an analytic classification of policy goals (see Roller 1992: 89), based on different taxonomies (cf. Almond and Powell 1978; Pennock 1966) specified by macro-theoretical studies of specific policies (cf. Flora and Heidenheimer 1981) and extended by the new policy goals discussed in the context of 'new values' (Inglehart 1977; Baker, Dalton, and Hildebrandt 1981). We assume that this classification, shown in Table 3.1, includes all relevant policy goals. As we are interested in a comprehensive picture of changes in what are perceived as problems, and in analysing the relationship between perceptions and beliefs about the scope of government covering all these goals, we need indicators which, according to the object of evaluation, refer to a wide range of goals.

The central criterion for evaluating problems is *importance*. This is the criterion that survey respondents are invited to use to identify problems which are significant for them; and what they perceive as the most important problems is likely to have an impact on other

TABLE 3.1. *Classification of policy goals*

Policy goals
External security
Internal security
Liberty as freedom from regulation and protection of privacy
Wealth
Socio-economic security (goal of the welfare state)
Socio-economic equality (goal of the welfare state)
Free development of personality
Protection of the environment

Source: Roller (1992: 89).

attitudes or patterns of behaviour. We need to note two points about the importance criterion. First, the distinction between intrapersonal and perceived importance which has been suggested by agenda-setting research (Funkhouser 1973: 69). Intrapersonal importance refers to the individuals' assessment of their own problems irrespective of the priorities of their environment, whereas perceived importance refers to individuals' perceptions of the priorities of other people or groups. Questions about perceived importance are of minor interest in our study, because the Beliefs in Government project, above all, is interested in the personal feelings of citizens and the consequences of those feelings. Hence, our indicators have to measure the intrapersonal importance of problems.

The second point is the distinction between absolute and relative priority which has been developed in value research (Rokeach 1973). Absolute priority refers to the importance of something irrespective of the importance of other things; relative priority means assessing the importance of something in relation to the importance of other things. In measurement theory, this distinction is essentially about ranking versus rating. Relative priority is of particular interest when many problems are given high absolute priority. Relative priority is also especially relevant in the case of political decisions which entail a choice between alternatives; for example, between economic expansion and protecting the environment. Therefore, we have to look for measures which use either rating or ranking methods.

The indicators we need, then, are measures of the intrapersonal importance of problems, using either rating or ranking methods, and covering a wide range of policy goals. We also had to decide between using 'open' or 'closed' questions. RePass (1971: 391) suggested that open-ended questions measure those issues which are really important to citizens, but it is often difficult to compare the categories of open-ended questions and the problem of missing data is usually severe. Therefore, we chose to use responses to 'closed', or fixed-response questions.

The Data

There are some longitudinal comparative data on important problems which fulfil our requirements. Rating measures of important problems on a broad range of policy goals are included in several Eurobarometer studies,[2] but a disadvantage of these studies is that the problems included in the surveys vary over time. The main difficulty, however, is that these studies cover only the period after 1976. The first Political Action study is the only other comparative study—before 1976—which includes intrapersonal ratings of important problems, but these data are available for only one additional time point. Moreover, not only are the items in the Political Action and the Eurobarometer studies not directly comparable but the interval between the first Political Action study (1973–6) and the first Eurobarometer study (1976) is only three years at most. Hence, we do not include the Political Action data in the longitudinal analysis. On the other hand, ranking measures of important problems are included in the Political Action study and, again, in several Eurobarometer studies.[3] Unfortunately, the questions in all these surveys either refer to a different set of problems or differ in the ranking method used. Therefore, these data are not practicable for longitudinal analyses.[4]

For the period before the mid-1970s, only national surveys are available. Indicators measuring the importance of problems are included in almost all national election studies. The longest series are the election studies conducted in West Germany, the Netherlands, Britain, Denmark, Norway, and Sweden. But, with the single exception of West Germany, almost all these studies use open-ended questions which, in some cases, do not measure the relevant dimension of the intrapersonal importance of problems. It is not only that the wording of the questions and the categories are not comparable between countries, but, in addition, the wording of the questions and the response categories sometimes differ within the country series. Faced with this situation, our empirical analysis relies on the two comparative studies—Eurobarometer and Political Action—which include those indicators measuring the relevant analytic dimensions. These indicators use closed questions and a rating method to measure the intrapersonal importance of problems, and they cover a wide range of policy goals.

Empirical Dimensions of Important Problems

Rather than specific statements about specific problems, we are interested in more general statements about problems which can be identified according to our classification of policy goals in Table 3.1. The essential precondition for this kind of analysis is that respondents themselves perceive as belonging together those problems which, analytically, we have related to the same policy goal. For example, according to our classification, housing and job security belong to the policy goal which we define as socio-economic security. What we need to know is whether respondents perceive this kind of link. In other words, we need to explore the empirical dimensions of important problems to see if they match our analytic classification.

In analysing the dimensional structure of important problems, we have to take into account research on the 'old' and 'new' agenda of politics (Baker, Dalton, and Hildebrandt 1981: 136–59), which is closely connected to discussions about the political consequences of value change in Western democracies (Inglehart 1977, 1990). The notion of a political agenda refers to 'what people believe are the most important issues facing society' (Baker, Dalton, and Hildebrandt 1981: 136–7). Research in this field is based on indicators measuring the intrapersonal importance of problems, and hypotheses about certain clusters of problems have been formulated and tested. The findings suggest that there are two different kinds of political agenda: an old politics agenda dominating the political process in Western democracies until the late 1960s, and a new politics agenda emerging at the end of the 1960s as a consequence of value change.

According to Baker, Dalton, and Hildebrandt, the new politics agenda includes policy goals such as environmental protection, renunciation of nuclear energy, women's equality, human rights, helping the Third World, and peaceful international coexistence. By contrast, the old politics agenda centres around concerns about economic and non-economic security. Economic security includes such matters as economic growth, fighting rising prices, job security, and other social security concerns. Non-economic security includes strong defence together with firm law and order policies. However, Flanagan (1987: 1305) suggests that, for theoretical and empirical reasons, linking together economic and non-economic security concerns is not justified. Instead, he suggests that these are two separate dimensions, which he identified as materialism and authoritarianism.[5] Hence, according to 'new politics' arguments, we can expect a two-dimensional structure to the problems which people consider important; according to Flanagan, we can expect a three-dimensional structure.

To uncover the empirical structure of perceptions of important problems, we performed a factor analysis of a set of problems. We anticipated finding factors according to, first, our classification of policy goals and, secondly, the distinction between old and new politics.

Relating the different agendas to our classification of policy goals, we expected the new politics agenda to include the policy goals of freedom, socio-economic equality, and environmental protection. External security, however, can be differentiated along a conflictual–co-operative dimension which is strongly related to the old and new politics dimension (Baker, Dalton, and Hildebrandt 1981: 105–35). Thus, we expected co-operative foreign policy issues, such as foreign aid and peaceful international coexistence, to belong to the new politics agenda. By contrast, the old politics agenda should include those policy goals of external security which have a conflictual character—such as strong defence—as well as the goals of internal security, wealth, and socio-economic security. However, if Flanagan is right, this old politics agenda falls apart into two policy areas; that is, there will be a further distinction between external security, which is restricted to conflictual aspects, and internal security on the one hand, and wealth and socio-economic security on the other.

Before moving on to the empirical analysis, we should add three remarks about the notion of an old and new politics agenda. First, the attributes 'old' and 'new' are time-bound. Something which seems new at first becomes old when we get accustomed to it. So, to avoid confusion, the terms 'old' and 'new' are used here to refer to the end of the 1960s, which is when Baker, Dalton, and Hildebrandt identify the distinction between the two agendas. Secondly, the term 'new politics agenda' suggests that completely new goals emerge. Looking at the elements of the new politics—environmental protection, human rights, helping the Third World, women's equality—it becomes obvious that these goals did not just appear, suddenly, in the late 1960s. Rather, they are 'firmly rooted in the modern political philosophies of the last two centuries' and have a 'contemporaneous' character (Offe 1985: 849–50). Hence, we have to guard against over-emphasizing the 'newness' of the new politics agenda.

Our third remark follows from the previous point. We have subsumed policies aiming at socio-economic equality under the label 'new politics agenda'. However, looking at different specific policies such as women's equality or the reduction of income differences between the rich and the poor, it becomes clear that the general category 'policies aiming at socio-economic equality' includes policies that belong to the new politics agenda (women) as well as to the old politics agenda (income differences). Whereas the old equality policies concentrate on income differences and the concerns of workers as a social group, the new equality policies entail an expansion of the principle of equality to other areas, such as rights for example, and other social groups, such as women and homosexuals. Therefore, at first glance, it seems logical to divide policies aiming at socio-economic equality into old and new policies—as with policies aiming at external security. However, the political programmes of the actors in new politics reveal that they often take up old themes and refashion them. Thus, for example, the green parties in Western Europe have picked up the old themes of socio-economic equality and integrated them into their position (Goodin 1992: 197). In this sense, they have reactivated the old equality policies. Moreover, comparative studies have demonstrated that these two dimensions also go together among the mass public (Farah, Barnes, and Heunks 1979: 416). Hence, there are good reasons to assume that all policies aiming at socio-economic equality belong to one agenda.

If our reasoning is correct, the question is whether policies for socio-economic equality should be subsumed under the heading of the old or the new politics agenda. We opted to assign them to the new politics agenda because such an enlarged understanding of socio-economic equality is new in character. At a more general level, however, this conception of the new politics agenda is more ambiguous than the agenda suggested by the adherents of value change theory, because it comprises two parts. It includes new policies, such as environmental pollution, human rights, and women's equality, which emerged at the end of the 1960s. But it also includes, at the same time, reactivated policies which originally belonged to the old politics agenda—such as the old socio-economic equality policies discussed above.[6] Whether this broader conception of a new politics agenda holds true at the level of the mass public is examined in the analysis which follows.

We analysed the dimensional structure of important problems using data from Eurobarometer, No. 6 (1976) in which respondents were asked about the importance to them personally of twelve problems. This study was chosen because it includes the broadest range of problems,[7] covering six of the eight policy goals identified in Table 3.1.[8] The only policy goals not included in our analysis are 'personal development' and 'internal security'. The factor analysis was based on a pooled sample from nine West European countries, weighted according to the size of the country. The data were pooled because we are interested in the empirical structure of important problems among citizens in Western Europe as a whole rather than among the publics of the individual countries.

The factor analysis, reported in Table 3.2,[9] generated three factors. The first is defined by freedom and socio-economic equality and, to a lesser degree, by environmental protection. These are the dimensions which we assigned, a priori, to a broader notion of the new politics agenda. The second and third factors consist of the problems of the old agenda. The second is defined by external security restricted to the conflictual aspect (defence), whilst the third includes wealth and socio-economic security. But two of the items measuring socio-economic security—'modernize education' and 'protection of the public against fraudulent selling and misleading advertising'—show rather lower loadings on this third factor (−0.34 and −0.35). At the same time, they have reasonable loadings on the first factor (0.27 and 0.30), defined by the new politics agenda. This result can be explained by the multifunctional character of these goals. From the perspective of the new politics agenda and its underlying value structure, education, for example, refers to interest in self-improvement and intellectual enrichment. From the perspective of the old politics agenda, education is seen as a means to economic success (Baker, Dalton, and Hildebrandt 1981: 142). A comparable interpretation is also possible for the second item. Therefore, this lack of clear structure need not detain us.

But the factor analysis reveals another, less readily explained, 'anomaly': the item 'environmental protection' which—according to all theories—emerged in the late 1960s, shows reasonable loadings on the first factor defined as the new politics agenda (0.34) and on the third factor defined by the economic concerns of the old agenda (−0.35). If one accepts that the first factor is interpreted as a new politics factor, environmental protection—contrary to the claims of Baker, Dalton, and Hildebrandt—is not an exclusive element in the new agenda. Instead, it holds some intermediate position between the new politics agenda and the economic concerns of the old agenda.

None the less, in all, the items that belong, analytically, to a distinct policy goal consistently have their highest loadings on the same factor. Therefore, we can combine the single problems measuring one goal into a summary index. Additionally, the important problems divide into an old and a new politics agenda, with the old politics agenda being further subdivided into concern for economic security and concern for non-economic security (confined to conflictual aspects). This finding seems to refute the claims made by adherents of materialist–postmaterialist value change and to confirm Flanagan's (1987: 1305) interpretation which suggested exactly this kind of dimensionality. The fact that the

TABLE 3.2. *Empirical dimensions of important problems*

Policy goals	Items	F1	F2	F3
External security (conflictual)	Strengthen our military defence against possible enemies	−0.19	0.85	−0.02
	Defend our interests against the superpowers (United States, Soviet Union, etc.)	0.22	0.69	−0.10
Freedom	More self-government for the regions	0.68	0.22	0.25
Wealth	Fighting rising prices	−0.15	0.10	−0.74
Socio-economic security	Providing for sufficient housing	0.14	−0.00	−0.53
	Fighting unemployment	−0.07	−0.05	−0.75
	Modernize education to meet today's needs	0.27	0.19	−0.34
	Protection of the public against fraudulent selling and misleading advertising	0.30	0.15	−0.35
Socio-economic equality	Try and reduce the number both of very rich people and very poor people	0.65	−0.25	−0.15
	Reducing differences between regions of the country by helping the less developed regions	0.56	−0.00	−0.18
	Controlling activities of the multinational or international firms	0.75	−0.02	−0.03
Environmental protection	Protecting nature and fighting pollution	0.34	−0.08	−0.35
Explained variance (in %)		26.5	11.0	9.6
N = 6,219				

Notes: Entries are factor loadings from principal component analysis with oblique rotation and listwise deletion. Correlation between factors is: F1 × F2 = 0.13; F1 × F3 = −0.34; F2 × F3 = −0.10. Data are based on responses to the question: 'Here is a list of problems the people of [country] are more or less interested in. Could you please tell me for each problem whether you personally consider it a very important problem, important, of little importance, or not at all important?' Respondents are 18 years and older from nine West European countries: Denmark, Belgium, Britain, Germany, Ireland, Luxembourg, the Netherlands, France, and Italy. Weighted data.

Source: Eurobarometer, No. 6.

new politics agenda is mainly defined by freedom and socio-economic equality and, to a lesser extent, by environmental protection, also seems to be a limitation of the original concept developed by the proponents of materialist–postmaterialist value change. That environmental protection as well as two other items (education and protection of the public against fraudulent selling and misleading advertising) show significant effects on the factor which is defined as the economic part of the old politics agenda can be interpreted as a further indication of the ambiguous character of the new politics agenda. This close relationship between the new politics agenda and the economic part of the old politics agenda is also represented by the correlation between factor 1 and factor 3: it is significantly higher (−0.34) than the correlations between the other factors (0.13, −0.10). In other words, it is only the non-economic security part of the old politics agenda which effectively stands alone.

Development of Important Problems, 1976–91

Hypotheses about the development of important problems can be deduced from theories of value change in Western democracies (Inglehart 1977, 1990) and the development of a new politics agenda (Baker, Dalton, and Hildebrandt 1981). One of the basic hypotheses is that the politics agenda has been changing fundamentally since the end of the 1960s. The old politics agenda dominated the political process until the late 1960s, but a new politics agenda had emerged by the end of that decade (Baker, Dalton, and Hildebrandt 1981: 136).

Two models of this development can be suggested. The first proposes that the old politics agenda was replaced by a new agenda. The second model suggests that the politics agenda was expanded, generally, in such a way that a new politics agenda has been added to the old one. The first model is called the proximity model, the second the dominance model (Baker, Dalton, and Hildebrandt 1981: 343). The proximity model seems more in line with the value change hypothesis, although—as the authors of the theory admit—it does not really exclude the dominance model (Baker, Dalton, and Hildebrandt 1981: 343). The overlapping of the two models follows from the assumption that a new politics agenda would appear. Accordingly, we can expect the policy goals of external security (restricted to co-operative aspects), freedom, socio-economic equality, and environmental protection to have grown in importance. The models differ, however, with respect to the development of the old politics agenda which includes the policy goals of external security (restricted to conflictual aspects), internal security, wealth, and socio-economic security. Whereas the proximity model suggests that the rise of a new agenda will be accompanied by a decline in the old agenda, the dominance model claims that the old politics agenda continues to exist.

The comparative data at our disposal do not cover the 1960s, the period when the new politics agenda is thought to have emerged. They cover only the 1970s, 1980s, and the early 1990s. So we cannot test the hypothesis about the emergence of a new politics agenda in the 1960s. However, we can examine its consolidation. According to the dominance model, we can expect that the old and new agendas coexisted during the period from the 1970s through to the 1990s. According to the proximity model, we expect the old politics agenda to fade and the new politics agenda to grow in importance during the period.

We examine the development of the various agendas by analysing items about problems which were posed on at least three occasions in the Eurobarometer surveys conducted in 1976, 1978, 1983, 1987, 1989, and 1991. The eight problems which fulfil this condition refer to five of the eight policy goals classified in Table 3.1: external security (both the co-operative and the conflictual aspects), wealth, socio-economic security, socio-economic equality, and environmental protection. Survey respondents were asked to say whether, for each problem, they consider it to be very important, important, of little importance, or not at all important. In Table 3.3 we report the proportion who thought these problems were 'very important' and 'important'.

The data for 1976 and 1978 indicate that during the 1970s, in all the countries covered, all the problems were regarded as important. With only occasional exceptions, more than 50 per cent of respondents, on average, thought these eight problems either important or very important. Moreover, as the distributions in the table indicate the extent of agreement within a country about the importance of a problem, we can group the policy goals according to three 'levels' of importance. At the highest level are problems related to the policy goals of wealth, socio-economic security, and environmental protection. Over 90 per cent of respondents identified problems in these policy areas as important. Problems belonging to the policy goals of external security (excluding defence) and socio-economic equality, considered important by between 70 and 80 per cent of respondents, are at the next highest

TABLE 3.3. *Rating of important problems, 1976–91*

Policy goals	Items		DK	BE	GB	GE	IR	LU	NL	FR	IT	GR	SP	PO	Average
External security															
Conflictual	Strengthen our military	1976	58	42	76	59	74	35	65	57	48	—	—	—	57
	defence against possible	1978	57	42	81	66	72	27	50	49	46	—	—	—	54
	enemies	1983	54	58	83	60	60	28	53	66	49	89	—	—	57
		1987	48	48	75	52	56	46	42	66	49	88	72	71	54
	Defend our interests	1976	83	84	82	81	78	79	83	91	86	—	—	—	83
	against the superpowers	1978	83	85	83	80	76	81	81	87	84	—	—	—	82
	(United States, Soviet	1983	84	80	89	85	69	67	76	89	88	94	—	—	81
	Union, etc.)	1987	80	68	80	81	60	75	63	86	85	90	86	83	75
Co-operative	Helping underdeveloped	1978	75	60	52	50	70	72	78	70	80	—	—	—	67
	countries in Africa, Latin	1983	75	66	62	73	64	77	73	72	71	69	—	—	70
	America, Asia, etc.	1987	78	67	72	86	63	89	79	71	82	73	82	82	76
	1983, poor countries	1989	67	64	75	79	85	73	76	68	84	82	86	88	75
		1991	80	75	87	84	93	85	82	77	89	87	96	92	84
Wealth	Ensuring energy supplies	1983	97	92	98	94	96	97	91	94	94	94	—	—	95
	are maintained	1987	97	88	93	92	84	97	89	89	94	91	86	85	91
		1991	97	97	99	98	99	98	97	97	98	98	98	97	98
Socio-economic security	Fighting unemployment	1976	99	98	97	98	100	97	98	99	99	—	—	—	98
		1978	100	97	97	92	99	90	99	99	99	—	—	—	97
		1983	98	97	99	98	99	96	98	98	99	98	—	—	98
		1987	98	94	96	97	98	98	98	99	99	98	97	99	97
		1989	98	96	96	97	100	92	97	99	99	98	100	99	97
		1991	97	98	99	98	99	97	97	99	99	99	100	100	98

Socio-economic equality	Try and reduce the number both of the very rich people and the very poor people	1976	84	83	53	68	81	82	83	91	96	—	—	—	80
		1978	82	88	50	63	83	76	90	91	88	—	—	—	79
		1983	72	89	70	79	88	82	82	84	87	91	—	—	81
		1987	73	79	69	81	78	86	77	84	83	93	87	93	79
	Reducing the differences between regions (of the country 1976, 1978) by helping the less developed regions	1976	88	81	79	65	88	86	83	90	90	—	—	—	83
		1978	83	77	76	64	86	73	84	90	93	—	—	—	81
		1983	70	80	83	80	83	76	70	85	81	91	—	—	79
		1987	69	69	83	81	71	80	63	80	86	95	92	94	76
		1989	76	77	90	87	91	68	66	89	88	90	96	99	81
		1991	81	84	92	92	96	81	80	89	92	98	98	97	87
Environmental protection	Protecting nature and fighting pollution	1976	98	97	92	95	91	99	98	98	97	—	—	—	96
		1978	98	95	92	90	91	85	98	96	97	—	—	—	94
		1983	98	90	92	97	88	98	93	93	97	98	—	—	94
		1987	99	89	94	98	85	98	96	97	99	94	93	97	95
		1989	100	99	98	99	99	97	99	98	100	97	99	100	99
		1991	100	99	99	100	99	99	100	99	99	100	100	100	99

Notes: Entries are percentages of respondents who consider this problem as a very important or important problem. The 'Average' figure excludes Greece, Spain, and Portugal. See notes to Table 3.2 for question wording. The sample size varies between approximately 300 (Luxembourg) and 1,000 (all other countries).

Sources: Eurobarometer, Nos. 6, 10, 20, 28, 31*a*, and 35.

level. At the third level, identified by about 55 per cent of respondents, is concern with defence which belongs to the conflictual aspect of external security. This picture holds for all nine countries investigated.

According to these data, then, there was no major difference in the importance accorded to the policy goals of the old and the new politics agendas in the middle of the 1970s. All these policy goals, without exception, were important to a majority of citizens. However, three policy goals—wealth, socio-economic security, and environmental protection—showed unusually high importance, whilst concern about the conflictual aspect of external security (defence) showed lower importance.

The picture remains much the same for the 1980s (1983, 1987, 1989) and the early 1990s (1991), with one exception: external security. The two policy items which relate to the conflictual aspect of external security (military defence, defend interests against the superpowers), and thus belong to the old politics agenda, become less important over the period as a whole. This development had already started in the 1970s and continued steadily during the 1980s. In the case of 'defend our interests against the superpowers', the decline in importance is almost linear. For the item 'military defence', this process is briefly interrupted in 1983, when a slight increase is evident. However, the extent of the change between 1976 and 1987 is small, ranging, on average, between a fall of 3 percentage points in the case of 'military defence' and a fall of 8 percentage points for 'defend our interests against the superpowers'. Conversely, the item 'helping the Third World'—which refers to the co-operative dimension of external security, and thus belongs to the new politics agenda—gained momentum. Between 1978 and 1991 the increase amounts to 17 percentage points. Similarly, the importance of 'reducing the differences between regions', which from 1983 onwards also measures the co-operative aspects of external security[10], increased after 1983.

Research on beliefs about national security has shown that citizens respond to the policy environment in a systematic way (Eichenberg and Stoll 1990: 4). According to this line of argument, declining support for the conflictual aspect of external security and increasing support for the co-operative aspect seem to be a reaction to the international climate of *détente* starting in the 1970s. But there are three countries which show some deviation from this pattern, namely Belgium, Luxembourg, and France, where increasing importance is attached to military defence between 1978 and 1987. Nation-specific events and policies would seem to be at work in these instances.

If we grant, then, that a new politics agenda appeared in the 1960s, we can see a wider politics agenda for the 1970s and 1980s. In so far as a new politics agenda exists alongside the old politics agenda, the dominance model seems to be confirmed. So far as the non-economic security part of the old politics agenda seems to wane, the proximity model is confirmed. But this decline does not take place in all West European countries: with the exception of support for 'military defence' in Denmark, Belgium, Luxembourg, the Netherlands, and Italy, more than 50 per cent of respondents still considered the conflictual aspects of external security to be important in 1987.

So far the analysis is at the aggregate level. But it is difficult to see from these data whether it is the dominance model or the proximity model which is really confirmed because these models require information about the composition of the agendas of individual citizens. Hence, we need to analyse the development of political agendas since the 1970s at the individual level. According to the dominance model, the proportion of respondents who show simultaneous support for all three agendas—the old agenda with economic and non-economic security concerns as well as the new politics agenda—should increase. Alternatively, according to the proximity model, the proportion of citizens who support the new politics agenda but give no support to the old politics agenda should increase.

To measure individual agendas, the ratings for the three agendas are combined in such a way that we can identify which citizens show simultaneously high ratings (measured by the responses 'very important' and 'important') for all three agendas, for only two agendas, or for only one agenda or none. The double and single agendas were further differentiated according to the specific combination of agendas. Thus the typology shown in Table 3.4 covers eight types of individual agendas—but for the purposes of presentation the several 'single agendas' and 'no agenda' are collapsed into one. The old politics agenda referring to non-economic security is measured by the items 'military defence' and 'defend interests against the superpowers'; the old politics agenda centred on economic concerns is measured by the item 'fighting unemployment'; and the new politics agenda is measured by 'reducing the number of very rich and very poor people', 'reducing differences between regions', and 'fighting pollution'. To weigh all three agendas equally, a mean index was constructed for the two agendas for which

TABLE 3.4. *Development of individual agendas, 1976–87*

	Old (security, economic) + new agendas	Old agenda (security, economic)	Old (security) + new agendas	Old (economic) + new agendas	Single agenda or no agenda
Denmark					
1976	59	2	1	37	1
1978	57	2	—	39	2
1983	56	5	1	34	4
1987	53	3	1	39	4
Belgium					
1976	47	1	—	47	5
1978	47	4	1	43	5
1983	56	2	1	35	6
1987	45	2	1	40	12
Britain					
1976	56	14	1	22	7
1978	59	16	1	17	7
1983	73	8	1	16	2
1987	61	8	1	24	6
Germany					
1976	54	6	—	31	9
1978	49	10	4	26	11
1983	56	6	1	33	4
1987	52	2	1	41	4
Ireland					
1976	68	2	—	26	4
1978	61	5	—	28	6
1983	55	2	1	36	6
1987	45	4	—	40	11
Luxembourg					
1976	36	3	1	56	4
1978	28	4	1	51	16
1983	29	—	—	65	6
1987	46	—	—	48	6
Netherlands					
1976	63	3	1	30	3
1978	52	2	—	44	2
1983	49	4	—	41	6
1987	38	3	—	51	8

TABLE 3.4. *Cont.*

	Old (security, economic) + new agendas	Old agenda (security, economic)	Old (security) + new agendas	Old (economic) + new agendas	Single agenda or no agenda
France					
1976	64	1	1	33	1
1978	59	1	—	38	2
1983	68	3	1	25	3
1987	66	4	—	26	4
Italy					
1976	57	1	—	40	2
1978	49	1	—	47	3
1983	52	2	1	41	4
1987	54	1	1	40	4
Greece					
1983	88	1	1	9	1
1987	86	1	1	11	1
Spain					
1987	71	—	—	24	5
Portugal					
1987	69	1	—	27	2
Average					
1976	56	4	1	36	4
1978	51	5	1	37	6
1983	55	4	1	36	5
1987	51	3	—	39	7

Notes: Entries are percentage of respondents who consider this agenda as very important or important. The average figure excludes Greece, Spain, and Portugal. Old agenda (security) = mean of 'military defence' and 'defend interests against superpowers'; old agenda (economic) = 'fighting unemployment'; new agenda = mean of 'reducing the number of very rich and very poor people', 'reducing differences between regions', and 'fighting pollution'. See notes to Table 3.2 for question wording and sample size.

Sources: Eurobarometer, Nos. 6, 10, 20, and 28.

more than one item is available and the values of the means were rounded according to the four response categories (very important, important, of little importance, not at all important) of the original variables.[11]

Looking at the frequencies in the table, the most interesting finding is that only two of the eight possible types of individual agendas show reasonable levels of support. The triple agenda, which includes both old and new agendas, is widely supported. So is the double agenda, which consists of the economic aspect of the old agenda and the new agenda. All other combinations show very low frequencies. The old agenda enjoys significant support only in Britain, averaging 15 per cent by the late 1970s (1976 and 1978). However, as we can see in Table 3.3, British adherence to the old agenda alone declines from 1976 to 1987. Thus, in all of the countries, the new politics agenda coexisted with the old agenda at the individual level. It is only in Britain that such an accommodation had not been realized before the beginning of the 1980s. This finding is also interesting from the perspective of 'issue publics', questioning Converse's (1964) hypothesis suggesting that mass publics concentrate their attention on only a few but diverse topics and, therefore, their concerns are fragmented into a multitude of narrow and only partially overlapping issue publics.

What about change over the period? In 1976, the triple agenda outweighs the double agenda everywhere with the exception of Luxembourg: some 47–68 per cent of respondents in the other countries held this kind of triple agenda. From 1976 to 1987 the proportion of respondents with a triple agenda declines in favour of the double agenda. Thus, by 1987, Luxembourg is joined by the Netherlands where those with a double agenda outweigh those with a triple agenda. As we saw earlier, however, the decline of the triple agenda is not a linear development. Indeed, as an overall average, there was a minor increase in support for this mixture of old and new agendas in 1983. Moreover, some countries deviate from the general trend: in Britain, Luxembourg, and France, support for the triple agenda increases between 1976 and 1987, and there was no overall change in Belgium over the period.

According to this analysis, then, by the late 1980s the old and new politics agendas coexisted at the individual level as well as at the aggregate level. As the two most frequent agendas at the individual level, the coexistence between the new politics agenda and the economic part of the old agenda is almost complete, suggesting that the two agendas were almost fully integrated. But, as the distribution of the triple agenda shows, integration between the new politics agenda and the non-economic security part of the old agenda is only partial. Thus, according to the distribution of individual agendas and their development, the dominance model is working with respect to the economic part of the old politics agenda, whilst the proximity model seems to be at work with respect to the non-economic security part of the old politics agenda.

The longitudinal analyses of what mass publics see as important problems indicate that change has taken place in the micro-level determinants of beliefs about the scope of government. In the 1970s and 1980s there existed an extended politics agenda, including both old and new agendas. But, with the exceptions of Belgium, Luxembourg, and France, the non-economic security part of the old politics agenda has been in decline. If the hypothesized positive relationship between the perception of problems and beliefs about the scope of government exists, this development is relevant for the development of beliefs about the scope of government. However, before exploring this question, we look at group-specific differences in identifying important problems.

Important Problems and Political Cleavages

The analyses of the longitudinal development of important problems identified some changes, although these changes are fairly moderate in character. It is possible that there are specific groups among whom more change is manifest during this period. Therefore, we have to analyse the development of important problems among certain groups. We can do this by employing hypotheses about the determinants of the old and new politics agendas associated with the notion of political cleavage.

It is assumed that the old politics agenda is related to what Inglehart (1984) calls the 'old class cleavage' whereas the new politics agenda is related to what he calls the 'new value cleavage'. Following the dominance model and the proximity model, we expect two kinds of relationship between political agendas and political cleavages. According to the proximity model, we would expect variations between the old and the new political cleavages with respect to both agendas. On the one hand, the groups in conflict over the old class cleavage—labour and capital—generate support for the old politics agenda and opposition or indifference to the new politics agenda. On the other hand, the 'new values' group in conflict with these old groups generates support for the new politics agenda and detachment from the old agenda. According to the dominance model, we would expect no differences with respect to the old politics agenda but we would expect differences with respect to the new politics agenda. The group identified by 'new values' will support the new politics agenda whereas the groups in conflict over the old class cleavage would not.

To measure the old and new political cleavages according to Inglehart's conception, we turn to an instrument which combines left–right self-placement with the materialism–postmaterialism index developed by Inglehart (Klingemann 1982; Fuchs 1989). According to Dalton (1986), it was assumed that the emergence of new political cleavages presupposes some general political orientation (Fuchs 1989: 150). Left–right self-placement measures just such a general political orientation, while the materialism–postmaterialism index measures the emerging new values (cf. Inglehart 1977: 27–9). Both variables were dichotomized and combined so that four types of political orientation could be identified: materialist left, postmaterialist left, materialist right, and postmaterialist right. Each agenda was measured by using the means index used earlier for the typology of individual agendas. To keep our account parsimonious, the longitudinal analyses are confined to only two measurement points, 1976 and 1987.

We need only summarize the results from our analysis of the relationship between people's perceptions of important problems and their political orientation. For both 1976 and 1987, we found no differences in support for the economic concerns of the old agenda or support for the new agenda among people in the four political orientation groups (data not shown). However, in view of the widespread support for these agendas, we should not be surprised by this. But the picture is quite different when it comes to the non-economic security part of the old politics agenda. These results are shown in Table 3.5. In 1976, except in Italy and Luxembourg, the old agenda receives less support among the postmaterialist left than among the other groups. However, the difference between the groups is only really noteworthy in Denmark, Britain, Germany, and the Netherlands. In 1987, this kind of difference is also evident in Luxembourg, France, and Portugal.

In all, in most of these West European countries, the postmaterialist left is a deviant group. However, their 'deviant' behaviour is confined to just one feature: support for the non-economic security part of the old politics agenda is systematically lower among this group than the other three groups. This lends some confirmation to the proximity model, although only partial confirmation since there is no variation concerning the new politics agenda. The data also reveal that the concerns of the postmaterialist left shifted between 1976 and 1987. As we can see from the 'change' columns in Table 3.5, with the exception of Belgium, the

TABLE 3.5. *Old politics agenda (security) and political orientation: change, 1976–87*

	Materialist left	Postmaterialist left	Materialist right	Postmaterialist right
Denmark				
1976	58	42	75	68
1987	50	37	70	70
Change	−8	−5	−5	2
Belgium				
1976	45	43	49	55
1987	46	45	47	48
Change	1	2	−2	−7
Britain				
1976	73	62	72	77
1987	68	58	81	75
Change	−5	−4	9	−2
Germany				
1976	63	39	66	61
1987	54	36	73	56
Change	−9	−3	7	−5
Ireland				
1976	70	63	74	67
1987	48	49	53	48
Change	−22	−14	−21	−19
Luxembourg				
1976	29	45	29	62
1987	48	36	49	47
Change	19	−9	20	−15
Netherlands				
1976	68	48	75	76
1987	34	25	56	43
Change	−34	−23	−19	−33
France				
1976	61	56	80	73
1987	74	52	79	81
Change	13	−4	−1	8
Italy				
1976	49	53	66	61
1987	54	46	66	62
Change	5	−7	—	1

TABLE 3.5. *Cont.*

	Materialist left	Postmaterialist left	Materialist right	Postmaterialist right
Greece				
1987	89	88	91	82
Spain				
1987	77	80	69	59
Portugal				
1987	73	65	100	100
Average				
1976	57	50	65	67
1987	53	43	64	59
Change	−4	−7	−1	−8

Notes: Entries are percentages of respondents who consider this agenda as very important or important. Security is the mean of 'military defence' and 'defend interest against superpowers'. The average figure excludes Greece, Spain, and Portugal. See notes to Table 3.2 for question wording and sample size.

Sources: Eurobarometer, Nos. 6 and 28.

postmaterialist left became even less interested in non-economic security. Yet, in most countries, support for the non-economic security part of the old politics agenda also declined amongst the other three groups—the materialist left, materialist right, and the postmaterialist right. Hence, the concerns of the postmaterialist left do not seem to have changed any more profoundly than the concerns of people in the other three groups. Thus, the general fading of support for the non-economic security part of the old politics agenda seems to reflect period effects—probably, as we suggested earlier, in response to the politics of *détente*.

Important Problems and Beliefs about the Scope of Government

Our analyses of perceptions of problems reveal that some changes have occurred in the political agendas of citizens in Western Europe over the last twenty years or so. Various theories assume that there is a positive relationship between the perception of problems and beliefs about the scope of government. If this is so, then changes in the political agenda would have consequences for development in beliefs about the scope of government. Thus, we come to our second question: is there a positive relationship between perceptions of problems and beliefs about the scope of government? However, since the theoretical arguments are formulated in very general terms, we have to specify what relationship we expect. This is especially the case with the type of beliefs about the scope of government we have been examining.

It has been argued theoretically and demonstrated empirically that beliefs about the scope of government can be differentiated along the two dimensions, range and degree (Roller 1992: 39–47). Range refers to the number of policy goals or areas for which the government is responsible. Indicators measuring this dimension ask whether the government, in principle, should take over responsibility for realizing a specific goal. Degree refers to the intensity of government activity within a policy goal or area. Indicators measuring this dimension ask about preferred degrees of government activity within a policy goal or area. Strictly, the theoretical arguments claim that there is a relationship between important problems and the range of beliefs about the scope of government. This follows from the assumption that there is a general, widespread belief in the universal responsibility of government. We assume that this relationship can be extended to take in beliefs about the degree of government activity. It seems plausible that a greater sense of urgency about problems is followed by a corresponding desire for more government activity to achieve these goals. Consequently, we expect a positive relationship between the perception of problems and beliefs about the scope of government—both in range and degree.

Is a change in perceptions of important problems followed by a change in beliefs about the scope of government? Ideally, the question requires a dynamic analysis of important problems and beliefs about the scope of government based on, at least, two separate time series. Such data would allow us to examine whether an increase in the number and importance of problems is followed by a more expansive view of the scope of government, and whether or not a decline in the number or importance of problems involves a dampening of beliefs about the scope of government. Unfortunately, such data are not available, but there are some comparative studies which include both measures of important problems and beliefs about the scope of government. If the expected relationship between important problems and beliefs about the scope of government exists, we would expect it to exist also at a cross-sectional level.

The relationship between perceptions of important problems and beliefs about the scope of government which refer to the range dimension can be analysed with data from the first Political Action study. Respondents were asked to rate the importance of problems, and assess the responsibility of government, on twelve issues that belong to five of the policy goals identified in Table 3.1. According to both criteria of evaluation—importance and responsibility—respondents could answer by using a four-point scale which runs from very important to absolutely unimportant, and from essentially the responsibility of the government to the government having no responsibility at all. In the analysis, these data are summarized by constructing a mean index for the five policy goals. Our findings are reported in Table 3.6.

Clearly there is a very close relationship between important problems and beliefs about the scope of government. Using Pearson's *r* as a coefficient of association, all coefficients are significant at the 1 per cent level. On average, Pearson's *r* is about 0.51, but there are some

TABLE 3.6. *Relationship between important problems and beliefs about the scope of government: 1*

Policy goals	FI	AU	GE	NL	SW	GB	IT	Average
Internal security[a]	0.36**	0.40**	0.55**	0.49**	0.59**	0.48**	0.37**	0.46
Wealth[b]	0.41**	0.45**	0.58**	0.58**	—	—	0.46**	0.50
Socio-economic security[c]	0.33**	0.51**	0.55**	0.44**	0.59**	0.48**	0.38**	0.47
Socio-economic equality[d]	0.67**	0.61**	0.70**	0.68**	0.66**	0.70**	0.60**	0.66
Environmental protection[e]	0.41**	0.43**	0.55**	0.53**	0.48**	0.54**	0.42**	0.48
Average	0.44	0.48	0.59	0.54	0.58	0.55	0.45	0.51

**$p < 0.05$

Notes: Entries are Pearson's *r*. Question items are: [(a)]'Guaranteeing neighbourhoods safe from crime'; [(b)]mean of 'Guaranteeing the supply of energy' and 'Fighting rising prices'; [(c)]mean of 'Looking after old people', 'Providing good medical care', 'Providing adequate housing', 'Seeing to it that everyone who wants a job can have one', and 'Providing good education'; [(d)]mean of 'Trying to even out differences in wealth between people', 'Guaranteeing equal rights for men and women', and 'Providing equal rights for minorities'; [(e)]'Fighting pollution'. Data for important problems are based on the question: 'Now we would like to know how you feel about some of the particular issues and problems that people often talk about these days. Tell me how important is this issue in your own view. Is it (1) very important, (2) important, (3) not very important, or (4) absolutely unimportant?' Data for scope of government are based on the question: 'Tell me how much responsibility you think government has for dealing with the problem. Is it something that you feel (1) essential for government to do, (2) something that government has unimportant responsibility to do, (3) some responsibility to do or (4) no responsibility at all?'

Source: Political Action (1973–6).

variations between the countries. The lowest coefficient is found in Finland (0.44), the highest in Germany (0.59). There are also some variations between the policy goals. The lowest value is found for internal security (0.46) and the highest for the policy goal of socio-economic equality (0.66). Based on these data, we can conclude that a relationship between the perception of important problems and beliefs about the scope of government does exist and is substantial: increasing importance results in preferences for more government responsibility.

These results seem to confirm the hypothesis that the importance people give to problems is a relevant determinant of their beliefs about the scope of government, at least concerning the range of government activity. However, it could be argued that this relationship is artificial, because importance and responsibility items were asked one after the other within one battery of questions in the Political Action study. If respondents attached high importance to a problem, they might assign, out of consistency, high responsibility to government 'for dealing with the problem'. We need to avoid this potential problem by using data from a study which has questions on important problems and beliefs about the scope of government located in different parts of the questionnaire.

Eurobarometer, No. 19 (Spring 1983), provides such data. In contrast to the Political Action survey, it includes questions which measure beliefs about the degree of the scope of government, and measures the importance of problems with a ranking rather than a rating method. Respondents were confronted with seven problems and were then asked to identify the three most important ones. However, our analysis is based on three problems relating to three different policy goals because these are the only problems for which corresponding data on beliefs about the scope of government are available. Our findings are presented in Table 3.7.

The relationships between important problems and beliefs about the scope of government are again positive. That is, the preference for intensive government activity increases with the importance of problems. However, the coefficients are considerably weaker than in Table 3.6. Even so, except in three instances—relating to the conflictual aspects of external security—all these relationships are significant at the 5 per cent level at least. On average, Pearson's r is about 0.19, compared with 0.51 in the earlier analysis. There are also variations between policy goals and between countries. On policy goals, the lowest average coefficient is for external security restricted to

TABLE 3.7. *Relationship between important problems and beliefs about the scope of government: 2*

Policy goals	DK	BE	GB	GE	IR	LU	NL	FR	IT	GR	Average
External security (conflictual)[a]	0.16**	0.10**	0.15**	0.14**	0.09*	0.10	0.24**	0.19**	0.13**	0.04	0.13
External security (co-operative)[b]	0.25**	0.25**	0.34**	0.23**	0.14**	0.39**	0.38**	0.39**	0.27**	0.13**	0.28
Environmental protection[c]	0.14**	0.08*	0.20**	0.30**	0.08*	0.15*	0.23**	0.22**	0.18**	0.09**	0.17
Average	0.18	0.14	0.23	0.22	0.10	0.21	0.28	0.27	0.19	0.09	0.19

$^{*}p < 0.05$ $^{**}p < 0.01$.

Notes: Entries are Pearson's *r*. The problem and belief question items are: [(a)]'Protect [country's] security against external threats both present and future' and 'Western Europe should make a stronger effort to provide adequate military defence'; [(b)]'Help the countries of the Third World' and 'Economic aid to the Third World countries should be increased'; [(c)]'Protect the environment and fight pollution' and 'Stronger measures should be taken to protect the environment against pollution'. Data for important problems are based on the question: 'There are a number of present day problems. Which 3 [out of 7] would you consider the most important?' 0 = not mentioned, 1 = mentioned. Data for scope of government are based on the question: 'We'd like to hear your views in some important political issues. Could you tell me whether you agree or disagree with each of the following proposals? How strongly do you feel?' 4 = agree strongly, 3 = agree, 2 = disagree, 1 = disagree strongly.

Source: Eurobarometer, No. 19.

conflictual aspects (0.13), the highest for external security restricted to co-operative aspects (0.28). In terms of countries, the lowest average coefficient is found in Greece (0.09), the highest in the Netherlands (0.28).

The results of this analysis show that the relationship between important problems and beliefs about the scope of government persists even under survey conditions which are less conducive to producing consistent attitudes. The relationship is not strong, but it is strong enough to confirm that the suggested relationship between important problems and beliefs about the scope of government does, indeed, exist.

These analyses support the claim that there is a relationship between people's perceptions of important problems and their beliefs about the scope of government. That is, the high perceived importance of problems goes along with a desire for government to assume responsibility (range) and for high level of government activity (degree). Thus, the hypothesis derived from the different theories seems to be confirmed. Moreover, as the relationships are linear, it means that perceptions of problems and beliefs about the scope of government travel in tandem: when high importance is attached to a problem, people expect the government to address the problem and attempt to solve it; when a problem is not considered important, people tend not to expect government to take action. This point is particularly relevant with respect to those theories which anticipate a spiral of rising expectations, suggesting that beliefs about the scope of government never become more restrictive, or that expectations of government are irreversible (cf. Eichenberger 1977: 107). According to these theories, the low importance of a problem will not necessarily go along with low expectations about the scope of government. Our analyses, however, show a linear relationship between perceptions of important problems and beliefs about the scope of government. Therefore, we conclude that beliefs about the scope of government are probably not irreversible. But we have to keep in mind that an adequate examination of the irreversibility thesis requires dynamic analysis of the kind not available to us.[12]

Conclusion

We argued on the basis of different theories that perceptions of problems are a relevant determinant of beliefs about the scope of government at the individual level. We have examined two questions resulting from this hypothesis. First, whether perceptions of problems have changed in Western Europe such that we might expect changes in people's beliefs about the scope of government. Secondly, whether the hypothesized relationship between the perception of problems and beliefs about the scope of government actually exists.

On the first question—the development of people's perception of problems—theories of value change have been used as a reference point. These theories assume a change in important problems which is captured in the notion of political agendas. According to these theories, a change took place in the 1960s when a new politics agenda emerged as a consequence of value change. Unfortunately, the available data do not allow us to examine this change directly, so we could only address a consequence of the change, asking whether the new politics agenda was consolidated in Western Europe in the mid-1970s and 1980s, and whether the old politics agenda still exists. The empirical analysis reveals an expanded politics agenda in the 1970s and 1980s, which includes both the old and new political agendas. On the other hand, for most of the countries investigated, our analysis reveals a trend towards slowly declining support for the non-economic security part of the old political agenda. The postmaterialist left gives the least support to this agenda. However, the decline in the non-economic security part of the old agenda is not restricted to the postmaterialist left. Therefore, it seems that this decline is largely a response to the changing policy environment of *détente*.

From the perspective of value change theory, it is interesting to note here that the new political agenda had already gained strong support amongst all West European citizens (for which we have data) by the mid-1970s. Hence, it is difficult to imagine that the new political agenda has grown slowly with the gradual spreading of postmaterialism, as the adherents of value change theory suggest. Moreover, it is surprising that there is so little change with respect to the old agenda. Confronted with the relatively high stability in the rating of important problems, it seems more plausible to suggest that the assumed shift from materialist to postmaterialist values had, at best, only minor consequences for the absolute priority of policy goals. Indeed, the consequences are perhaps restricted to the relative priority of policy goals—as measured by Inglehart's materialism–postmaterialism index.

The analysis of the second question—the relationship between important problems and beliefs about the scope of government—reveals the expected positive relationship. That is to say, the high perceived importance of problems goes along with strong beliefs about the scope of government and vice versa. Such results have interesting consequences for the study of beliefs about the scope of government. In a static perspective, the political agenda gives strong hints concerning beliefs about the scope of government. In a dynamic perspective, the results suggest that each expansion of the political agenda will automatically result in a more expansive view of the scope of government. Conversely, a narrowing of the political agenda is followed by a more restrictive view of the scope of government. This could mean that beliefs about the scope of government can be turned back, contrary to the often implied assumption of irreversibility. Finally, given the positive relationship between perceptions of problems and beliefs about the scope of government, as well as the results from our longitudinal analyses of perceptions of problems, we can suggest that people in Western Europe generally have a wide range of beliefs about the scope of government. Only on external security by conflictual means—that is, on defence—is it likely that people expect their governments to do less.

NOTES

1. This perspective is most clearly suggested by Brittan (1975) and Luhmann (1990).
2. These are Eurobarometer, Nos. 5 (Spring 1976), 6 (Autumn 1976), 10 (Autumn 1978), 20 (Autumn 1983), 28 (Autumn 1987), 31*a* (Summer 1989), and 35 (Spring 1991). Ratings of important problems are also included in Eurobarometer, No. 36 (Autumn 1991), but these data were unavailable at the time of writing.
3. These are Eurobarometer, Nos. 5 (Spring 1976), 10 (Autumn 1978), 19 (Spring 1983), 25 (Spring 1986), 31 (Spring 1989), and 31*a* (Summer 1989).
4. Almost all Eurobarometer studies include the materialism–postmaterialism instrument designed by Inglehart (1977: 27–9) based on the ranking of four important goals. These data are not included in our analyses of goals because they cover only a small range of policy goals. Three of the studies mentioned (Political Action; Eurobarometer, Nos. 5 and 10) also include the extended materialism–postmaterialism instrument which is based on thirteen different goals. However, these data cover only a short period. Moreover, the four-item and the thirteen-item instruments are not strictly comparable.
5. Note that Baker, Dalton, and Hildebrandt (1981: 141) explicitly expanded their concept of old politics from economic to non-economic security concerns.
6. In principle, such a reactivation of old politics is also possible for other policy goals, such as the goal of freedom.
7. Moreover, Eurobarometer, No. 6 forms the starting point of our longitudinal analysis. Obviously, we cannot exclude the possibility that the dimensional

structure of the political agenda changed further during the 1980s. It can be suggested, for example, that the old and new politics agendas go together as a result of the increasing number of people who hold old and new values at the same time (Klages 1984). Factor analyses based on the other Eurobarometer studies reveal no fundamentally different results.

8. The item 'more self-government for the regions' measures the preference for decentralization. The goal of autonomy is a more strict interpretation of the item.
9. Advocates of materialist–postmaterialist value change based their dimensional analyses on the second factor of a principal component analysis without rotation. They argue that their method is appropriate because they conceive materialism and postmaterialism as opposite ends of a single dimension (Baker, Dalton, and Hildebrandt 1981: 342 n.17; Inglehart 1990: 130–44). In contrast to value research, we are interested in the dimensions of problem priorities and a simple factor structure, so rotation seems more appropriate (Nie *et al.* 1975: 482). Since we are interested in a 'realistic' description, we use principal components analysis with oblique rotation (cf. Nie *et al.* 1975: 483).
10. The question wording of the item 'reducing the differences between regions . . . ' changed slightly between 1978 and 1983. Before 1983 the regions were specified as the regions of the country, but this has been omitted since 1983. The latter formulation not only includes exchange between different areas within a country but also exchange between different countries. Therefore, the item can be subsumed under both the policy goal of socio-economic equality and the policy goal of external security (co-operative aspects).
11. For the economic part of the old politics agenda, especially, we would have wished to have more items measuring this agenda. In particular, the policy goal of wealth, one of the main constituents of this old politics agenda, is missing. We had to rely on 'fighting unemployment', since it was the only item measured four times between 1976 and 1989. To check whether this sample of items is a valid indicator for these agendas, we created an index for these individual agendas based on all items presented in every survey and examined the correspondence between the extended and 'restricted' indices. The correspondence is relatively high, so we use the 'restricted' index in the analyses.
12. There are some longitudinal studies which reject the irreversibility thesis. Reversibility seems to take place not with respect to the range of expectations but only with respect to the degree of expectations (Roller 1992: 108–28).

4

Attitudes towards the Size of Government

BEATE M. HUSEBY

This chapter examines attitudes towards the size of government in Western Europe. Our central concern, in line with the major theme in this volume, is whether attitudes towards government can be described as expansionist or contractionist. By expansionist, we mean that people take the view that government should expand its activities and services; by contractionist, that government should reduce its activities and services. Of course, many people may feel that government should expand its activities in some policy areas but reduce them in others. However, in this chapter, we focus on attitudes towards the overall size of government and certain policy areas, rather than support for specific policies.

The question of what government should do has more than one dimension. According to Rose (1984: 17), governments do three things; mobilize resources, combine resources into programmes, and deliver outputs. Although we study attitudes towards government, which is different from studying government itself, Rose's approach is useful for us as well, for it is attitudes towards programmes and the outputs of programmes—goods and services intended to benefit citizens—which are central in this chapter.

It was shown in Chapter 3 that attitudes towards the goals of government can be described in two dimensions: *range* and *degree*. Range defines the extent of the areas in which government intervenes; degree taps the intensity with which government intervenes in any area. These two dimensions are important when studying attitudes about the size of government, too, although they are probably best studied relative to specific government activities or policy programmes.

However, the tendency to support specific policies may not be consistent with people's more general attitudes about the overall size of government. Additionally, attitudes about the power of government may reflect attitudes towards the authority of government, which adds a further dimension to attitudes about the size of government.

We examine attitudes towards government, then, by analysing responses to questions about (i) the range of government responsibility, (ii) whether government should increase or reduce spending in specific areas, and (iii), in general, how much power government should have. That is, we examine attitudes about the size of government in terms of the dimensions *range* and *degree*, and according to a scale from specific to more general attitudes. We also examine the social and partisan origins of these attitudes.

Ideally, we would have comparable data from all West European countries for the post-war period. This is not the case. The welfare states of Scandinavia have commonly been considered the most comprehensive in the world, so questions about attitudes towards public expenditure are most often found in national surveys in those countries. However, differences in the formulation of survey questions mean that these data cannot be used for direct comparison. Fortunately, two comparative surveys about attitudes towards the role of government were conducted by the International Social Science Programme (ISSP) in 1985 and 1990. Four West European countries are represented in ISSP 1985: Britain, Austria, Germany, and Italy. In ISSP 1990, Norway and Ireland were included as well. Most of the data used in this study are from these two surveys, but supplemented with data from the comparative survey Political Action (1973–6) and from national election surveys for Sweden, Norway, the Netherlands, Britain, and Denmark. But before going on to examine these data, we introduce three approaches to explaining attitudes towards the size of government.

Expansionist or Contractionist Attitudes?

In the late 1970s and early 1980s, theories of fiscal crisis and political overload were common in the scholarly literature. As the discussion in Chapter 1 indicated, neo-conservative scholars, neo-liberal economists, and neo-Marxist critics alike suggested that governments had grown too big. By exceeding the limits of what services can be provided, governments had engendered negative evaluations of government performance. A rather different perspective is suggested by Inglehart's (1990: 9) hypothesis about the marginal utility of the welfare state. The very success of welfare policies, Inglehart argues, has had the effect of reducing support for the further extension of welfare. A third approach is suggested by Sears and Citrin (1982: 65–6), who show, empirically, that attitudes towards government are negative at the general level but positive with regard to specific policy programmes. Let us consider what these approaches lead us to expect about attitudes towards the size of government.

According to the general overload argument (King 1975; Brittan 1975; Offe 1980; Habermas 1975), the expansion of the public sector in the 1960s created high expectations about the ability of governments to solve all problems. If these expectations are disappointed, the result will be a serious decline of public confidence in government. In the 1970s, the oil crisis and declining levels of economic growth allowed governments less opportunity to fulfil demands and obligations. When public demands are not satisfactorily met by public expenditures, or the costs of government activity exceed resources, government overload is expected to result. If government tries to accommodate public demands by maintaining public expenditures at a higher level than public revenue, fiscal overload will result.

In several West European countries, including Germany, Britain, Denmark, and Italy a significant imbalance between public revenues and expenditures was evident by 1975. According to Rose and Peters (1978), political bankruptcy will occur when government erodes the economy, and its own effectiveness, by spending more money than it has. Political bankruptcy undermines the authority of the state, producing a gap between government and the people as well as political indifference. Moreover, when government grows, this may lead to rigid bureaucracy and general inefficiency, which, in turn, leads to more negative evaluations among mass publics. Lane and Ersson (1987: 5) note that Denmark and Italy are cases where inefficiency in government has eroded the legitimacy of the state. Inflexible and unrealistic expectations about government, or political indifference, may reduce support for government activities. The consequences of overload may, therefore, be generally negative attitudes towards government, which, in turn, produce attitudes demanding a reduction in the size of government.

There is no agreement about the consequences of overload, however.

Among neo-conservatives (Bell 1976; Crozier, Huntingdon, and Watanuki 1975), there were worries about the growth of sectional demands leading to constant group conflict over every budget, and thus a general decline in support for political parties and the executive agencies of government (Birch 1984: 137). Lipset and Horowitz (1978) argued that the growth of the public sector weakens the bonds of the family and community, making people even more dependent upon government services. For neo-Marxists, the 'fiscal crisis of the state' threatens the political legitimacy of the liberal democratic state. Liberal democracy legitimizes the capitalist system in the eyes of workers and develops welfare services to keep the disadvantaged from rebelling against the prevailing capitalist order. The fiscal crisis arising from overloading public expenditures in the late capitalist state—reflecting the endemic contradictions of capitalism—produces political overload, which, in turn, erodes support for the parliamentary system, bringing about a legitimation crisis. According to Offe (1980), reducing public expenditure will not solve the problem because people resort to the support systems of the welfare state out of helplessness and dependency, which makes it impossible to cut public expenditure.

Although the dynamics of political and fiscal overload are interpreted differently, their consequences might affect attitudes towards the size of government in much the same way. The general overload argument leads us to anticipate that attitudes towards the size of government were highly expansionist in the early 1970s. With the expansion of government and its attendant problems, we can expect negative attitudes towards government activities in the late 1970s and early 1980s. This may have led to more contractionist attitudes towards the size of government in the early 1980s.

However, it is not certain that negative evaluations do go in a contractionist direction. If people want government to provide a large range of public services but are dissatisfied with the way policies are implemented, attitudes are just as likely to be expansionist and more demanding. The fact that people are not satisfied with how government is performing does not mean they do not want government to provide certain kinds of services: they might simply wish them to do better. So we have to distinguish between general attitudes to government and specific attitudes to particular policy areas. Thus, we would expect attitudes towards the range of government responsibility to show that people want to expand the activities of government, while attitudes towards the power of government might reflect a lack of political support.

A rather different approach is suggested by Inglehart (1990: 248–57), who argues that the marginal utility of welfare explains why, among EC countries, support for the classic economic policies of the left was lowest in Denmark. According to Inglehart, the success of welfare policies has reduced the demand for more of the same. Of course, it is questionable whether the classic policies of the left, such as income equality and the nationalization of industry, have been implemented in West European countries since the early 1970s. Moreover, a general move towards the right in party support has influenced the social democratic parties by moving them towards the political centre.[1] What Inglehart shows, empirically, is a correlation between gross domestic product (GDP) per capita and attitudes towards the traditional policies of the left.

None the less, the concept of marginal utility can be used to hypothesize that attitudes towards the size of government are related to the political direction of the policy implemented, as well as the actual size of government. Valen (1981) has shown that, in Norway, people tend to perceive political parties as more extreme than their own position on a left–right scale. On average, Labour party voters tend to see the party as more to the left than themselves, and Conservative party voters tend to see the party as more to the right than themselves. After a time lag, this can produce a demand for a change of policy. Thus, in due course, parties which expand the responsibilities of government might stimulate protest against expansion, while parties which reduce government spending might provoke protest against contraction.

It could be assumed that conservative parties are generally contractionist in outlook while socialist parties are generally expansionist. This is not true of all social democratic parties, and it is hard to make any such general statements when it comes to Christian democratic (or Christian) and centre parties. Moreover, protest about policy could indicate either—or both—that the marginal utility of retaining the same policy over the years is low, or that, after exposure to a policy, its defects have become clear to the population. It is also difficult to stipulate how long it takes before a policy provokes protest.

While Inglehart claims that attitudes towards a policy can be described according to its marginal utility, other scholars have developed different arguments. Wilensky (1976), for example, argues that welfare backlashes and tax revolts have not been strongest in countries where government spending is highest. They occur both in 'élite' welfare states such as Denmark and in 'laggard' welfare states such as America. To explain tax revolts, Wilensky gives more weight to the visibility of taxes rather than their size. Similarly, Esping-Andersen (1990: 33) claims that 'anti-welfare state sentiments over the past decade have generally been weakest where welfare spending has been heaviest, and vice versa.'

During the 1970s and 1980s, among the countries included in the ISSP data, Britain, Norway, and Germany had a higher GDP per capita than Ireland and Italy (Lane, McKay, and Newton 1991: tables 4.1 and 4.2). In Britain, Norway, and Germany, there was a change from social democratic to conservative governments during the late 1970s and early 1980s, but left parties were still strong in the countries of southern Europe.[2] In general, we would expect conservative governments to be less expansionist than social democratic governments. The marginal utility hypothesis suggests that the utility of the typical policies of the left is lower in wealthier countries or countries with 'big' government. This more or less corresponds to the position in Britain, Germany, and Norway in the early 1980s. Thus, we might expect that attitudes in Britain, Germany, and Norway were less expansionist than attitudes in Italy and Ireland during the 1980s.

However, the problem with relying on levels of economic development and the lagged effects of policy is how to measure the effects of economic development, and how much time it takes before we can expect attitudes to change. By 1990, the Conservative Party had been in government in Britain for eleven years, and the government's final consumption as a percentage of GDP per capita declined from 1975 to 1985 (see Chapter 2). Thus, according to the hypothesis of marginal utility and the likelihood of lagged effects, we might expect a revival of more expansionist attitudes, since the utility of government budgets will have become higher. However, GDP per capita in Britain was still higher than in Italy and Ireland. Thus the hypothesis of marginal utility leads us to anticipate both that attitudes in Britain became more expansionist in the later 1980s and that attitudes in Italy and Ireland are more expansionist than attitudes in Germany, Norway, and Britain.

Finally, as we are examining attitudes towards government, we need to be aware of the distinction between general and specific attitudes. Both the overload hypothesis and the marginal utility hypothesis treat attitudes about the size of government as one dimensional. Sears and Citrin (1982: 65–6), however, show that attitudes towards government are generally negative but specifically favourable. When very general questions are asked, Californians appear to want smaller government and lower taxes; when specific questions are asked, Californians want to maintain or expand services in most areas of federal and state activity. Sears and Citrin tried to explain this paradox by taking into account other beliefs, such as attitudes towards government waste, but without success (1982: 71):

> The simultaneous desire for less government and lower taxes, on the one hand, and current service levels, on the other, were held even among people who felt government operated with minimal waste and among the more sophisticated of Californian voters. Nor could it be explained by assuming that voters wanted to reduce the size of government by cutting out services they were unsympathetic to.

They also found that when respondents were forced to choose between reducing taxes and maintaining current services, most opted for maintaining services. Drawing on Sears and Citrin, then, we may find that general questions about spending produce responses which are more negative than specific questions about spending on particular programmes.[3]

We have now introduced three approaches to explaining attitudes towards the size of government. The overload hypothesis suggests that attitudes towards the range of government responsibility and spending levels are expansionist while attitudes towards the power of government are contractionist. The marginal utility hypothesis indicates that differences in attitudes between countries correspond to levels of economic development: people in countries with highly developed economics are likely to be less expansionist than people living in countries with less developed economies. The marginal utility hypothesis also suggests that attitudes are related to the political colour of the party in power. Finally, we note that we need to distinguish between general and specific attitudes, expecting general attitudes to be more negative than attitudes towards specific government activities.

Attitudes towards Government Responsibilities

In this section we investigate attitudes towards the *range* of government responsibilities. We do not examine these attitudes in terms of specific services or controls, but sum them into attitudes towards government activity as a whole. It is important to remember, however, that our indicators do not represent a comprehensive account of ideas about the size of government. The questions used are principally concerned with the welfare state, so many other government activities are not included. Using these questions is a pragmatic decision, based on the available data. However, the welfare state is the largest part of government activity, and probably, when it comes to government, what people are most concerned about.

The Political Action study and both ISSP surveys include a battery of questions about government responsibility. In Political Action, there are twelve questions: four about traditional welfare state concerns (the elderly, medical care, housing, education); one about job security; one on the equalization of wealth; two on the rights of women and minorities; and four items about other policies (pollution, energy supply, rising prices, and crime prevention). In the ISSP surveys, there are seven questions: three are about government intervention in the economy; three about welfare state concerns; and one about equality. All these items represent important questions about what government should be doing. Moreover, Edeltraud Roller (1991) has shown that all these items load on the same factor in the 1985 survey, and the correlations between the items are so high that we can use them to construct an index measuring attitudes towards the range of government activity.

In Table 4.1, we show the percentage of respondents in seven countries who think it is 'essential' or 'important' that government takes responsibility in the twelve policy areas identified in the 1974 data. Table 4.2 shows the percentage in six countries who think that the government should 'definitely' or 'probably' be responsible for the seven policy areas specified in the 1985 and the 1990 surveys. It is important to remember, however, that the attitudes reported in the two tables are not the same, so they should not be compared according to level. This means that any statement about trends is restricted to the 1985 and 1990 data.

The mean scores in Tables 4.1 and 4.2 show that a large majority of people favour government taking responsibility in all these areas. Attitudes are evidently very favourable towards big government: there are clearly many things people want their governments to do. And none of the figures indicate a widespread wish for a reduction in government responsibility. Thus, people's attitudes are generally expansionist or in favour of the status quo, depending on the actual scope of government

TABLE 4.1. *Attitudes towards government responsibility, 1974*

	GE	GB	NL	AU	IT	SW	FI	Mean
Elderly	93	88	93	89	92	90	96	92
Medical care	94	95	93	94	96	86	95	94
Education	93	92	98	90	93	89	88	92
Housing	88	85	94	81	92	71	77	84
Equalization of wealth	71	52	82	68	72	75	58	68
Job security	94	85	90	94	94	89	94	91
Low prices	96	—	94	92	95	—	94	94
Minority rights	66	59	73	53	—	68	61	63
Equal rights for sexes	76	49	75	63	64	72	63	66
Pollution control	93	85	92	85	89	92	87	89
Crime prevention	97	87	90	94	95	82	96	92
Energy supply	96	—	95	94	91	—	96	94
Mean	88	78	89	83	88	81	84	85
N	1,483	1,483	1,201	1,585	1,779	1,290	1,224	

Notes: Entries are percentages who think it is essential or important that government take responsibility in the policy field stated. Question: 'Now we would like to know how you feel about some of the particular issues and problems that people often talk about these days. We would like to know (*a*) How important these issues and problems are in your view, and (*b*) How far you feel [the] government has responsibility for them.' Codes: Is it something that you feel (1) is essential for government to do; (2) something that government has an important responsibility to do; (3) some responsibility to do; (4) no responsibility at all to do? Entries in the table are categories (1) and (2) from question (*b*).

Source: Political Action (1973–6).

in particular countries. There are some differences between policy areas, however. There are sweeping majorities in favour of government responsibility for welfare concerns such as old age pensions, medical care, health, and employment in both 1974 and 1990 in all the countries. But the equalization of wealth (1974), or reducing income differences (1985 and 1990), and government responsibility for rights (1974) attract somewhat less support than welfare concerns. These differences are examined more closely in subsequent chapters. What we are interested in here are the mean scores which represent the cross-national picture.

In 1974, the highest level of support for government assuming a large range of responsibilities was found in the Netherlands (89 per cent), closely followed by Italy and Germany. Britain had the lowest mean

TABLE 4.2. *Attitudes towards government responsibility, 1985 and 1990*

	GE	GB	IT	AU	IR	SV	NO	Mean
Provide health care								
1985	98	99	100	98				99
1990	95	100	99		99	97	99	98
Provide for elderly								
1985	97	98	100	99			99	
1990	95	99	99		98	97	99	98
Provide for the unemployed								
1985	85	86	85	68				81
1990	78	80	78		91	90	91	85
Provide jobs								
1985	82	72	89	84				82
1990	74	63	85		71	75	84	75
Control prices								
1985	76	93	98	93				90
1990	70	89	96		92	86	92	88
Assist growth of industry								
1985	54	95	84	75				77
1990	52	94	82		90		67	77
Reduce income differences								
1985	67	75	84	78				76
1990	64	74	78		82	74	72	74
Mean								
1985	80	88	91	85				86
1990	75	85	88		89	87	86	85
N								
1985	1,048	1,530	1,580	987	—	—	—	
1990	2,812	1,197	983	—	1,005	1320	1,517	

Notes: Entries are percentages who think it is probably or definitely the government's responsibility. Question: 'On the whole, do you think it should be or should not be the government's responsibility to . . . ?' Response codes: definitely should be = 1; probably should be = 2; probably should not be = 3; definitely should not be = 4.

Sources: Data for Germany, Britain, Austria, Italy, Ireland, and Norway are from ISSP 1985 and 1990. Data for Sweden are from the Research Programme on Comparative Political Culture, G. Gustafsson and O. Johansson, Umeå University.

score (78 per cent). An eleven-point difference between the lowest and the highest mean score suggests a remarkably small variance among the seven countries. We find much the same consensus in 1985 and 1990: the difference between the highest and lowest mean score is 11 percentage points again in 1985 and 14 points in 1990. Moreover, disaggregating the two response categories which have been combined in Tables 4.1 and 4.2 strengthens the general picture: in the 1974 data, more people thought that government responsibility was 'essential' rather than 'important'; in the 1985 and 1990 data, more people thought the government was 'definitely' responsible than thought it was 'probably' responsible. All in all, the similarity among the countries is more striking than the differences.

However, the cross-national differences become somewhat larger when the response categories are disaggregated. Considering only the proportion who think that government is 'definitely responsible', the difference between Switzerland and Italy widens from 7 to 26 percentage points. In Germany, where attitudes were less favourable in 1985 and 1990 than in the other countries, this difference is even greater. Indeed, in Germany, Britain, and Italy, support for government responsibility declines a few percentage points between 1985 and 1990. Although the change is not large enough to conclude that attitudes were becoming contractionist, signs of a trend are evident: the mean score in Britain declines from 88 per cent in 1985 to 85 per cent in 1990; from 80 per cent to 75 in Germany; and from 91 to 88 per cent in Italy.

The most obvious finding from these data is the similarity between the countries. Moreover, although the data are not strictly comparable, they indicate some change from 1974 to 1985 and 1990. This is particularly noticeable in Germany and Britain: attitudes in Germany were more favourable in the early 1970s and less favourable in 1985 and 1990; in Britain, attitudes were less favourable in 1974 and more favourable in 1990. That is, they switched places over the period. Looking at the outcome of elections and the political colour of the government at the time helps us to understand this switch.

In Germany, the Social Democrats were in government from 1969 until 1982. Following the ousting of Helmut Schmidt as Chancellor, the Christian Democrats assumed power, and remained in government through into the 1990s. This changeover is reflected in the data shown in Tables 4.1 and 4.2. When the Social Democrats were in power, attitudes were more favourable to a large role for government; since the Christian Democrats (in coalition with the Free Democrats) have been in power, attitudes towards government responsibility have become less supportive. The further decline of support for wide government responsibility from 1985 to 1990 probably reflects the problems following reunification, especially fears about the costs of reconstruction in the former East Germany.

The situation was rather different in Britain. There was a Conservative government in 1970–4, a Labour government in 1974–9, and a Conservative government thereafter through to the 1990s. That the least favourable attitudes towards the range of government responsibility in 1974 are found in Britain probably reflects the beginnings of resistance to the idea of big government; and throughout the 1980s, Conservative governments made 'rolling back the frontiers of the state' a major feature of their programme. However, recalling our earlier point about lags in public responses, attitudes may have become more favourable by the mid-1980s following the experience of cutbacks in some welfare programmes. It is harder to explain why attitudes towards government responsibility are less positive in 1990 than in 1985.

In Italy, in all three years, attitudes were highly supportive of government responsibility. Throughout the period government expenditures, as a proportion of GDP, were lower in Italy than in Germany and Britain (see Table 2.5) This may suggest a lower correlation between attitudes and policy than in other countries. Although support for the Christian Democracts declined steadily during the 1970s and 1980s, most of the coalition governments of the period were led by a Christian Democratic prime minister. However, attitudes towards government responsibility appear not to have turned in the same conservative direction as in Britain and Germany. Thus, although differences in support levels between the two northern countries and Italy were larger in the late 1980s than in the early 1970s, it is the similarity in attitudes towards government responsibility which is striking.

When attitudes are as similar as shown in Tables 4.1 and 4.2, there is little point in focusing on differences between countries. Moreover, we have too few data points to compute correlations between attitudes and macro-level data such as expenditure levels. However, both the overload argument and the marginal utility hypothesis imply statements about cross-national differences. The overload hypothesis suggests that expectations about government activity had become very high. This is confirmed by the data in Tables 4.1 and 4.2. Furthermore, it was argued that governments were unable to fulfil their obligations and meet rising expectations, so financial or government overload would result. This would lead to a lack of confidence in government which would finally produce less support for government activities. In other words, in countries where the size of government has declined, we should expect attitudes to be less favourable than in countries where government has continued to grow. We can examine this argument by looking at the growth of government receipts over the period.

We can see from Table 4.3 that the countries with the lowest levels of support for government responsibility also had the lowest growth in government receipts from 1975 to 1985. However, whereas the attitudinal data show that the biggest gap is between Germany and the other countries, the dividing line in the growth of government receipts is between Germany together with Britain, and the other countries. Even though the order of countries is the same, the two measures do not vary in tandem. Most obviously, in terms of the overload hypothesis, support for government responsibility is high in Britain although the growth of government receipts was meagre. A similar conclusion would have emerged if we had used pre-unification levels of support for government responsibilities in Germany.

According to the marginal utility hypothesis, attitudes would be favourable towards reducing the size of government in countries with more advanced economies and more highly developed welfare states. Of course, in a world-wide perspective, all these countries have relatively advanced economies and welfare states, and attitudes are still highly favourable to the range of government responsibility. None the less, according to GDP per capita, there are quite big differences between these countries (see Chapter 2). According to the hypothesis, we would expect attitudes in countries with lower GDP per capita to be more favourable to wide government responsibilities than attitudes in

TABLE 4.3. *Attitudes towards government responsibility, 1990, and growth of government receipts, 1975–85*

Country	Support for government responsibilities (mean percentage)	Growth of government receipts 1975–85 (1950=100)
Germany	75	9
Britain	85	9
Norway	86	22
Sweden	87	33
Italy	88	30
Ireland	89	39

Notes: Entries on support for government responsibilities are mean scores from Table 4.2. Entries for the growth of government receipts are the percentage changes in government receipts when the level in 1950 is set to 100.

Sources: ISSP (1990) and Table 2.2 above.

TABLE 4.4. *Attitudes towards government responsibilities, 1990, and GDP per capita, 1985*

Country	Support for government responsibilities (mean percentage)	Real GDP *per capita* (international prices) 1985
Germany	75	10,708
Britain	85	8,665
Norway	86	12,623
Sweden	87	9,904
Italy	88	7,425
Ireland	89	5,205

Notes: Entries on support for government responsibilities are mean scores from Table 4.2. Entries for real GDP *per capita* are from Lane, McKay, and Newton (1991: table 4.2). Prices are given as constant prices (US$1980 at 1980 exchange rate).

countries where GDP per capita is higher. The data shown in Table 4.4 allow us to examine this claim.

The table does, indeed, reveal some tendency for countries with a lower GDP per capita to have the most favourable attitudes about the range of government responsibility, while the countries with a higher GDP per capita have less favourable attitudes. However, again as noted above the only notable difference in attitudes is between Germany and the rest. Attitudinal differences, then, do not appear to correspond to varying levels of GDP per capita.

We can draw two conclusions from the analysis in this section. First, people in Western Europe generally favour government taking responsibility for a large range of activities. Indeed, bearing in mind the general claims of the overload and marginal utility arguments, support levels are perhaps surprisingly high. Secondly, although there are variations among the countries we have examined, neither growth in the size of government nor differences in levels of economic development evidently account for these differences.

Attitudes towards Government Spending

If people generally favour their government taking on a wide range of responsibilities, how do they feel about government spending? This question relates to the *degree* of government activity. In this section we analyse whether people want government to spend more, less, or the same amount on government programmes.

The ISSP surveys include eight questions on government spending: four on health, old age pensions, education, and unemployment benefits; two on law enforcement and defence; and two about the environment and culture. Just as with the range dimension, our focus is not on particular spending areas but, rather, on overall attitudes. However, as attitudes here vary according to the activity in question, and the correlations between some of the questions are negative, we cannot treat the mean scores as an index. Instead, we use factor analysis to uncover the structure of attitudes. As we found similar patterns for each country when analysed separately, the 1985 data for Germany, Britain, and Italy were pooled. We present the rotated factor analysis based on the pooled data in Table 4.5.

Three distinctive factors emerge from the 1985 data. The first is defined by typical welfare concerns: old age pensions, health, unemployment benefits, and education. People who want government to spend more in any one of these fields tend also to want more spent in the other three fields. The second factor combines the desire to see more spent on the environment and on culture and the arts. The third factor

TABLE 4.5. *Attitudes towards spending in eight policy fields, Germany, Britain, and Italy, 1985*

The government should spend more on:	Factor 1	Factor 2	Factor 3
Old age pensions	0.79	−0.08	0.04
Health	0.72	0.07	0.14
Unemployment benefits	0.68	0.12	−0.13
Education	0.64	0.26	0.17
Environment	0.08	0.77	−0.14
Culture and arts	0.12	0.77	0.06
Law enforcement	0.05	0.16	0.84
Military and defence	0.08	−0.30	0.72

Notes: Entries are loadings on rotated factors (varimax rotation). Question: 'Listed below are various areas of government spending. Please show whether you would like to see more or less government spending in each area. Remember that if you say "much more", it might require a tax increase to pay for it.' Categories: spend much more; spend more; spend the same as now; spend less; spend much less.

Source: ISSP (1985).

TABLE 4.6. *Attitudes towards government spending in five countries, 1985 and 1990*

	Germany		Britain		Italy		Austria	Norway	Mean	
	1985	1990	1985	1990	1985	1990	1985	1990	1985	1990
Welfare policies										
Spend more	50	69	83	85	76	81	43	71	70	78
Spend same	45	29	16	14	20	18	52	28	27	20
Spend less	5	2	1	1	4	2	5	1	3	2
N	966	2,635	1,427	1,115	1,463	950	864	1,360		
Order policies										
Spend more	8	6	16	11	13	13	9	8	12	10
Spend same	66	59	71	79	67	68	69	80	68	69
Spend less	26	35	12	10	20	19	22	12	20	21
N	979	2,664	1,436	1,128	1,477	961	862	1,431		
Culture policies										
Spend more	36	50	9	18	36	48	25	17	27	39
Spend same	61	48	74	74	59	49	70	74	65	57
Spend less	3	2	17	8	5	3	5	9	8	4
N	983	2,629	1,345	1,070	1,465	956	868	1,398		

Notes: Entries are percentages. Question: 'Listed below are various areas of government spending. Please show whether you would like to see more or less government spending in each area. Remember that if you say "much more", it might require a tax increase to pay for it'. 1 = spend much more; 2 = spend more; 3 = spend the same as now; 4 = spend less; 5 = spend much less. The variables are: (1) the environment; (2) health; (3) law enforcement; (4) education; (5) defence; (6) retirement; (7) unemployment benefits; (8) culture and arts. Variables (1) and (8) have been added together to form the additive index 'Culture policies' and the categories recoded: 2–4 = spend more, 5–7 = spend same, 8–10 = spend less. Variables (2), (4), (6) and (7) form the additive index 'Welfare policies', and recoded: 4–8 = spend more; 9–14 = same, 15–20 = spend less. Variables (3) and (5) form the additive index 'Order policies' and recoded: 2–4 = spend more; 5–7 = same; 8–10 = spend less. The mean in each case includes only those countries surveyed in both 1985 and 1990 (Germany, Britain, and Italy).

Sources: ISSP (1985, 1990).

identifies people who want more government spending on both law enforcement and defence. In other words, we have three fairly well-defined groups which we might identify as 'welfare seeking', 'culture seeking', and 'order seeking'. In Table 4.6, we can look at the strength and direction of these three types of demands in 1985 and 1990.

With the single exception of Austria in 1985, a majority in each of these countries is 'welfare seeking'. Attitudes were more expansionist in Britain and Italy, less expansionist in Germany and Austria (1985). That spending on welfare became notably more popular in Germany by 1990 largely reflects the relatively low proportion of 'welfare seekers' in 1985. By contrast, 'order seeking' is in a minority in each instance; except in Germany in 1990, a substantial majority want government spending on law and order policies and defence to stay the same. However, a substantial proportion in each country except Britain and Norway (1990) are 'culture seeking'.

In the three countries where we have data for both time points—Germany, Britain, and Italy—attitudes towards welfare spending evidently became more expansionist during the 1980s. Similarly, the proportion of 'spenders' on the environment and cultural policies grew; and only in Germany was there an increase in 'cutters' on order policies. These findings are somewhat surprising, bearing in mind that in these countries, over the same period, attitudes became rather less favourable about the range of government responsibility. One explanation might be that 'spending' was more often associated with national economic problems in public debate in 1985 than in 1990. Also, the 1985 and 1990 ISSP surveys did not include a question about the environment and culture in the 'government responsibility' battery. More interesting, however, is that when people are asked questions about spending rather than government responsibilities, attitudes tend to be more restrictive and to be more variable across policy fields.

Earlier, we suggested that general and specific questions about government responsibilities and spending probably produce a different picture of attitudes about the size of government. Unfortunately, data on general questions are scarce (except in the Netherlands) and confined to countries in northern Europe. None the less, we review the available data in Table 4.7 to get some indication about general attitudes towards government spending and the size of the public sector. Note, however, that the percentages in the table are not comparable; the questions are quite different and the data are from different national surveys.

In all instances, the picture is more negative. Whereas the data in

TABLE 4.7. *Attitudes towards government spending in five countries, various years*

	Negative position	Neutral position	Positive position	*N*
Netherlands				
1975	58	33	9	1,824
1979	39	48	13	4,882
1980	50	41	9	1,875
1981	58	33	9	1,849
1983	63	30	7	1,789
1985	55	37	8	1,817
1986	45	44	11	1,867
1987	45	38	17	1,827
1988	30	47	23	1,830
1989	22	52	26	1,808
Norway				
1985	25	42	33	2,180
Sweden				
1982	41	10	49	3,724
1985	46	10	45	3,873
1988	39	18	43	3,829
Denmark				
1987	39	24	37	1,022
Britain				
1987	46	13	41	3,826

Notes: Entries are percentages. The questions are not comparable between the countries. In Norway, Sweden, Denmark, and Britain the negative position indicates support for reducing government spending, the neutral position indicates a 'does not matter' attitude, and the positive position indicates opposition to reducing government spending. In the Netherlands, the negative position indicates that people favour a reduction in government spending, a neutral position that people want government spending to stay as now, and a positive position that people favour an increase in government spending. Questions: *Netherlands*: 'What do you think of government expenditures: should they be increased, reduced or remain as they are?' *Norway*: 'Are you in general for or against reducing the size of the public sector in Norway? Do you have a definite opinion or are you uncertain about this?' *Sweden*: 'Do you think a proposal to reduce the public sector is good or bad?' *Denmark*: 'In general are you for or against reducing the public sector in Denmark, or don't you have any opinion?' *Britain*: 'Government should or should not reduce spending generally?'

Sources: Cultural Change Study of the Netherlands; Norwegian, Swedish, Danish, and British national election surveys.

Table 4.6 yield a broadly expansionist picture, these data show that almost equal numbers of people support and oppose reducing government spending—including the Netherlands by the late 1980s. Prior to

1988, 'cutters' are particularly evident in the Netherlands, although steadily declining after 1983.[4] More to the point, these data show that attitudes are more negative when general questions rather than specific questions are asked. Although the data are not strictly comparable, we can get some estimate of the difference by comparing the data in this table with the data for Britain in Table 4.6: whereas 83 per cent favoured more spending on welfare policies in response to specific questions (1985), the figure drops to 41 per cent in response to a general question (1987). Clearly, then, support for government spending as a general notion is less widespread than support for spending in particular policy fields, particularly welfare.

Attitudes towards the Power of Government

The power of government is rather different from the dimensions of range and degree. The subject is abstract and belongs to the more general, diffuse end of the continuum of attitudes about the size of government. In other words, it is a more ideological dimension, relating to the constraints imposed by the state and the right of government to interfere in individual lives. We expect attitudes on this dimension to be less favourable than attitudes about the range and degree of government.

According to the overload hypothesis, attitudes about the power of government should be most negative in countries where governments are 'biggest'. However, overload arguments refer not only to the 'objective' size of government, but also to size in a more abstract way. When government grows, people might believe that this leads to bureaucracy and ineffectiveness. This might be unpopular, provoking questions about the authority of government. In Table 4.8, we show the distribution of attitudes about the power of government in six countries. We have two data points for three countries, and one data point for another three. The difference between the percentages of those answering 'too much' and 'too little' is shown in the fourth column.[5] We then consider how these attitudes are related to the 'objective size' of government.

By and large, opinion is divided between those who think government has 'too much power' and those who think that the power of government is 'about right'. Apart from Germany, however, majorities for either position are slim. The only striking deviation from this

TABLE 4.8. *Attitudes towards the power of government, 1985 and 1990*

	Too much power (1)	About right (2)	Too little power (3)	Too much power (net) (4)	*N*
Germany					
1985	30	69	1	29	864
1990	35	61	4	31	2,602
Britain					
1985	52	44	4	48	1,414
1990	50	46	3	47	1,122
Italy					
1985	41	34	25	16	1,440
1990	53	26	21	32	962
Austria					
1985	52	44	5	47	826
Norway					
1990	41	50	9	32	1,361
Ireland					
1990	51	42	7	44	976

Notes: Entries are percentages. Question: 'And what about the government, does it have too much power or too little power? The net figure (column 4) is the difference between the percentage 'too much power' and percentage 'too little power', indicating net dissatisfaction with government power.

Sources: ISSP (1985, 1990).

general picture is the proportion of Italians who think that the government has too little power—probably a reflection of the particular problems of Italian politics. But are these attitudes systematically related to the size of government? In Table 2.5 it was shown that, among the countries examined here, general government receipts as a percentage of GDP were highest in Norway and lowest in Italy. But the net percentage difference in the second last column shows that especially the British, Austrians, and Irish votes tend to be against giving their governments more power. The case of Norway particularly speaks against the overload hypothesis; it has a strong public sector yet a majority thinking that the power of government is about right.

Although about half of all respondents thought government has too much power, our earlier findings indicate that most people want government spending to stay the same or increase, and do not want government responsibilities reduced. One explanation for this apparent paradox, going back to our earlier finding, is the general nature of the question about government power. Even so, it is strange that, in Norway, asking a general question produced only 25 per cent in favour of reducing the size of the public sector but 41 per cent who thought that government has too much power. A rather different explanation may have to do with the political colour of the party in power; supporters of opposition parties are more likely to question the power of government than supporters of the parties in opposition.

In addition to differences on the three analytic dimensions, we expect attitudes towards the size of government to vary between certain social and political groups. In the next two sections, we examine variations in attitudes about the *range* of government responsibilities and the power of government among such groups in Britain, Germany, Italy, Ireland, and Norway based on the 1990 ISSP data. Differences between groups on the *degree* dimension are examined in Chapter 7 and Chapter 8.

Correlates of Attitudes Towards Government Responsibility

We can use two kinds of explanation to account for variations in attitudes towards the range of government responsibilities. The first kind is that people's general political outlook and affiliation to a political party influence their attitudes. Disagreement about the size of government has traditionally been an important source of ideological conflict. The second kind is that different social positions produce different interests in public services; the extent to which people use public services shapes their interest in the range of government responsibilities. We can assume that people of high social status have less need of government services than people of low social status who are more dependent on welfare services. However, as there tends to be a close correlation between social position and political attitudes, both explanations may run together. An example is the gender gap in voting between young women and men (Kenski 1988; Listhaug, Miller, and Valen 1985) and that, generally, women have more interest in public services than men. But the two explanations are sometimes contradictory. For example, we can assume that interest in public services is higher among the elderly than among young people but the elderly are traditionally more conservative than their juniors. What effects do we anticipate from these individual level variables?

Generally, political attitudes change over the life cycle (Abramson 1983), and so does the utility of public services. We can assume that interest in public services is highest among the elderly because they are particularly dependent on welfare provisions whereas middle-aged people carry the major part of the economic burdens of 'big government' through taxation. So we would expect the middle-aged to be less favourable towards big government than old people. However, when using correlation coefficients to examine differences by age, we cannot assume linearity in the relationship between age and interest in government activity. None the less, we expect elderly people to be more in favour of government having a wide range of responsibilities than young people.

We can also anticipate gender differences. Deitch (1988) concluded, in an analysis of US data for 1973–84, that women had become more leftist and generally more favourable towards government activities than men. Similarly, in a study of Norwegian data, Martinussen (1993) found women more supportive towards the welfare state than men. One explanation for this shift highlights the structural changes which have taken place in Western democracies over the last thirty years. The welfare state has made it possible for women to work by providing for the care of the old and children. By contrast, as a result of the growth of public expenditure and the expansion of the workforce, men have experienced larger tax burdens and unemployment. This suggests that men are less inclined to support big government than women.

Attitudes may also vary according to people's social status. People of high social status are conventionally associated with more conservative political attitudes and less interest in public services, usually on account of their high educational attainment and high income. High education might be influential as a political resource—enhancing cognitive competence, political information, and skills—or it may be simply a reflection of social status. Again, as we know from voting studies, both political participation and voting preferences vary by income levels. Thus, we expect differences in education and income to produce differences in attitudes about government responsibility. In particular, we expect people of low income or less education to be more favourable towards government assuming a large range of responsibilities than people with high levels of income or education.

Whether people work in the public or private sector of the economy may also influence their attitudes (Dunleavy 1980). The jobs of workers in the public sector depend on the size of government. When government has a wide range of responsibilities, this usually means a large public sector. Hence, we can anticipate that public sector employees are more likely to support big government than workers in the private sector. On the other hand, many public sector employees are high-earning, well-educated professionals.

As to political groupings, collectivist policies and the expansion of public welfare have been associated largely with socialist or social democratic parties. It is commonly assumed that people who identify with parties of the left are more supportive of the welfare state than people who identify with parties of the right. Thus, we might expect that people who support left-wing parties are more favourable towards big government.

Finally, both the interest and political explanations suggest that social class may influence attitudes towards the size of government. The relationship between class identification and voting has traditionally been very strong, and even though there has been a decline in class voting (Franklin, Mackie, Valen, *et al.* 1992), this relationship has not disappeared. The party affiliation and political engagement of the social classes capture and reflect political attitudes. Class position also indicates people's position in the labour market. People who consider themselves as working class more often work in subordinate positions; people who consider themselves middle class more often work as employers or in positions of authority. Normally it is those without power in the labour market who have an interest in government regulation and government responsibility. Thus, we expect people who perceive themselves as working class to be more favourably disposed towards wide government responsibilities than people who consider themselves middle class.

In all, we expect women rather than men, the old rather than the young, people of low rather than high education, public sector rather than private sector workers, as well as people with low rather than high income, to be favourably disposed towards 'big' government. Additionally, we anticipate that people who identify with parties of the left, and people who consider themselves working class, to be more favourable towards extending government responsibility than people who identify with parties of the right or who consider themselves middle class.[6] In Table 4.9, we show the correlations between social and political groups and attitudes towards the range of government responsibility. The variables were recoded with the expectation that, except for age, all coefficients would show a positive correlation.[7]

Earlier, we found a sweeping majority in favour of big government.

TABLE 4.9. *Social and partisan origins of attitudes towards government responsibilities, 1990*

	Germany	Britain	Italy	Ireland	Norway
Gender	0.08**	0.10**	0.08*	0.05	0.14**
Age	0.00	−0.09**	−0.12**	−0.03	−0.10**
Education	0.15**	0.23**	0.16**	0.22**	0.24**
Family income	0.16**	0.28**	0.16**	0.28**	0.22**
Public/private	−0.01	0.04	0.07	−0.08*	0.11**
Party affiliation	0.18**	0.40**	—	0.15**	0.43**
Subjective class	0.19**	—	0.02	0.22**	0.29**

*$p < 0.05$ **$p < 0.01$

Notes: Entries are Pearson correlation coefficients. The responsibility data are respondent's mean scores on all variables in Table 4.2. For details of codings, see n. 7.

Source: ISSP (1990).

Thus, we might not expect to find large differences in attitudes among these social and political groups. Some of the coefficients in Table 4.9, however, are remarkably strong. Indeed, only seven of the thirty-three coefficients are not statistically significant.

The differences between men and women are significant but fairly narrow. In Germany, Britain, and Norway women are more favourable towards a large range of government responsibility than men, but the differences are insignificant in Italy and Ireland. Similarly, the coefficients for age are not large. However, as we noted earlier, this relationship is probably not linear, so we might expect low coefficients. Even so, the relationship between age and attitudes is significant in Britain, Italy, and Norway. The correlations for education are significant in all five countries, which means that people with relatively little education are more favourable towards government responsibility than the highly educated. Again, the relationship between income and attitudes shows very strong correlations, indicating that favourable attitudes towards government responsibility go along with low rather than high incomes. Employment in the public sector is significant only in Norway; in Ireland, curiously, the relationship is negative.

Party affiliation is undoubtedly important, particularly in Britain and Norway. People who identify with the left in these two countries are decidedly more favourable towards big government than people affiliated with the right. The relationship is significant but of lower magnitude in Germany and Ireland. Unfortunately, we have no data on party affiliation for Italy. Class identification, too, is significant; in Ireland and Germany, subjective social class is a better predictor of attitudes than party affiliation. In all, then, along with education, differences in class identification and party affiliation underlie differences in attitudes towards the responsibilities of government.

Correlates of Attitudes towards the Power of Government

In contrast to government responsibilities, we find that attitudes towards the power of government were generally unfavourable to expansion. However, as before, we might anticipate differences between certain social and political groups. We suggested earlier that people's attitudes might be influenced by the political colour of the party in power. We also have to bear in mind that 'the power of government' is close to the notion of support for the political system. What, then, do we expect?

Historically, liberals and Marxists have been the most trenchant critics of government power. Liberals have argued for limiting government in favour of market-governed arrangements; these arguments have also, more recently, penetrated several conservative parties in Western Europe. The traditional Marxist view of the state as serving the interests of the bourgeoisie remains alive among various political groupings on the radical left. Accordingly, we might anticipate that people orientated to the far left or to the right are likely to question the power of government.

The notion of 'power' is related to political efficacy. Gamson (1968) argues that political efficacy has two dimensions: internal efficacy, or belief in one's own political competence, and belief in the political system. People who feel they have no political power tend to be hostile to any organized accumulation of power; those with little faith in themselves or the political system are often thought to be politically alienated and powerless. Listhaug (1990) claims that internal efficacy varies according to individual resources, especially cognitive competence and gender. Cognitive competence is developed through education, while the traditional role of women implies little motivation to become involved in politics. By contrast, support for the political system depends more on a number of political variables, particularly political distance.

Attitudes towards the power of government are usually analysed in order to examine support for the political system in evaluating political legitimacy. Here, however, we use these attitudes as indicators of support for the party in power and its policies. We expect people's attitudes towards the power of government to be influenced by their political distance from the party in power. In particular, we expect people who support opposition parties to be more negative about the power of government than supporters of the party in power. As political distance is the key variable and the political situation in each country was different in 1990, we have to pose country-specific hypotheses before examining the data.

In Britain, the Conservatives were in power throughout the 1980s; in Germany, a centre–right coalition had been in government since 1982. Thus, according to the political distance hypothesis, we expect people affiliated with left parties in Britain and Germany to be more negative about the power of government than people affiliated with parties of the right. We also expect people of high income and education to be more positive towards the power of government: they tend to support parties of the right, and, moreover, 'their' party was in power. We also expect women to be more negative than men, both because of their lower internal efficacy and, as we noted earlier, because women have become more left-oriented. We also expect the elderly to be less negative than the young: the young are less integrated into the political system and are seldom in positions of authority. Additionally, because of their association with the left, we expect more negative attitudes among working class identifiers than middle class identifiers.

In both Italy and Ireland, the political situation means that our predictions are less clear-cut. In Italy, in 1990, there was a five-party coalition of centre-left and centre-right parties. Thus, according to the political distance hypothesis, we would not expect to find large numbers of people claiming that government has too much power. However, the Communist Party was outside the coalition despite winning about 27 per cent of the votes in the 1987 election. So, both the distance and ideological arguments lead us to expect Communist Party supporters to be quite negative about the power of government.[8] In Ireland, the centre–right coalition—Fianna Fáil and Progressive Democrats—might have led to more people on the left questioning the power of government than people on the right. However, the parties on the left (Labour Party and Workers' Party) have enjoyed only minority support,[9] so we cannot expect their supporters to account for the 51 per cent of the Irish sample who were negative about the power of government. None the less, the political-efficacy hypotheses lead us to expect that women as well as people of low education and income are less favourable towards the power of government than men and those with high education and high income.

In the case of Norway, both the political situation and the data position lead to ambiguous expectations. At the time of the survey, a minority coalition of the conservative and centre parties, which broke up shortly afterwards, was in government. The return to office of the Labour Party reflected both the inability—or unwillingness—of the Conservatives to govern, and the dominance of the Labour Party during the post-war period. Hence, it seems unlikely that people affiliated with the Labour Party felt the Conservative government had too much power. To make matters worse, the question asked in the Norwegian survey was: 'Do you think the Parliament has too much power?' Not only is the power of parliament and government very different, but people who think government has too little power and parliament has too much would give a positive answer. On both counts, therefore, we cannot formulate clear hypotheses about attitudes to government power in Norway.

In Table 4.10 we show the correlation coefficients between attitudes towards the power of government and social and partisan groups. Except for party affiliation in Italy,[10] the variables were recoded in the same way as for Table 4.9. Hence, we expect all the correlations, with the exception of Norway, to be positive.

As the hypotheses are country specific, we examine the results for each country separately. The data confirm most of our hypotheses for Germany. People affiliated with the left are less favourable towards the

TABLE 4.10. *Social and partisan origins of attitudes towards the power of government, 1990*

	Germany	Britain	Italy	Ireland	Norway
Party affiliation	0.22**	0.41**	0.10**	0.10**	−0.21**
Subjective class	0.11**	—	0.00	0.06*	−0.03
Gender	0.05**	0.01	0.13**	0.13**	0.03
Age	0.11**	0.02	0.12**	0.08**	0.03
Education	0.02	0.13**	0.03	0.08*	0.02
Family income	0.09**	0.19**	0.04	0.12**	0.01

*$p < 0.05$ **$p < 0.01$

Notes: Entries are Pearson correlation coefficients. For details of codings, see n. 7.

Source: ISSP (1990).

power of government than people on the right; those who consider themselves working class are less favourable than people who consider themselves middle class; people with low income are less favourable than people with high income. Again, women are more negative than men, and young people more negative than older people. However, education level seems to have no effect on attitudes towards the power of government.

Three of our hypotheses for Britain are confirmed. Party affiliation is clearly very important, with people on the left particularly critical about the power of government. Both income and education are also important; as anticipated, people with little education or low income are more inclined to believe that government has too much power than the more educated or those with high incomes. But we find no differences between the sexes or the age groups.

By contrast, both age and gender are significant in Italy; women and young people are more negative about the power of government than men and old people. Although the party variable is less important in Italy than in Britain or Germany, people who voted for left parties are, as anticipated, more negative about the power of government than people voting for parties of the right. Curiously, however, class differences make no impact. In Ireland, similarly, people who look to left parties are less favourable towards the power of government. Indeed, in Ireland, all our hypotheses are confirmed: women, young people, the less educated, people with low incomes, and people who consider themselves working class, all hold less favourable attitudes towards the power of government. Finally, in Norway, only party affiliation shows a significant relationship with attitudes, indicating that people on the right have more negative attitudes than people on the left. But due to the question asked, we cannot interpret this finding as direct evidence that people on the right are critical of the power of government. However, people affiliated with the right are traditionally less favourable towards government regulation.

Looking for a general pattern among these background variables, the only significant factor common to all five countries is party affiliation. Subjective class is important only in Germany and Ireland; gender and age matter only in Germany, Italy, and Ireland; education makes a difference only in Britain and Ireland; and income level is significant only in Germany, Britain, and Ireland. This suggests that attitudes about the power of government are more country specific than attitudes towards the range of government responsibilities.

Conclusions

We have examined attitudes towards the range of government responsibility, towards government spending in general and in certain policy areas, and attitudes towards the power of government. About the range of responsibility, we found that attitudes were highly favourable in 1974, 1985, and 1990, but attitudes towards spending were more ambivalent. On government spending as a general idea, attitudes fell into two almost equal-sized groups, one favouring cuts and the other the status quo or an increase. When it came to more specific policies, spending on welfare issues was regarded favourably, the status quo was preferred on cultural issues, but attitudes towards spending on law-and-order policies were contradictory. In contrast to the range of government responsibilities, there seemed to be little support for expanding the power of government. Generally speaking, then, people want to expand or retain most government activities but, at the same time, many people felt that government has too much power. However, using several measures to examine attitudes about the size of government makes it difficult to draw general conclusions, especially as attitudes towards the power of government varied according to country. So, to be more specific, we review our findings for each country.

People in Germany, during the 1980s, seemed fairly satisfied about the size of government. Although they were the most restrictive about the range of government responsibility, support for government assuming a large range of responsibilities was widespread. Moreover, with support for more spending on nearly all the policy areas examined increasing by 19 percentage points from 1985 to 1990 (Table 4.6), attitudes became more expansionist during the 1980s. Furthermore, a majority thought that government had about the right degree of power (Table 4.8). In all, then, Germans seemed to favour the status quo on the size of government. The picture seems much the same for Austria. While Austrians seemed not to want more spending on government activities, they were less restrictive than Germans about the range of government responsibility. And although a majority of Austrians thought government had too much power, they were still favourable to the range of government responsibilities. All in all, Austrians seemed to want things to stay much as they are. Thus, even though we have data only for 1985, they do not allow us to classify the Austrians as generally contractionist in outlook.

By contrast, in Britain the size of government seems to have been controversial during the 1980s. There was widespread support for government having wide responsibilities and for more spending on welfare. However, opinion was divided on the general idea of government spending: almost half favoured cuts, almost half were against. Again, half thought government had too much power, the rest thought not. Thus opinion in Britain seems to have been polarized between expansionists and contractionists.

If Italians were not content with government, there was considerable agreement about what they wanted during the 1980s. There was widespread support for government having a large range of responsibility and for more spending on almost all government activities. Unusually, a substantial proportion thought government had too little power. In these respects, Italians seemed to be fairly enthusiastic expansionists. Yet from 1985 to 1990 there was an increase of 12 percentage points in those who thought that government had too much power. This is the only clear contractionist trend in our data. Similarly, the Irish seem to be generally expansionist in outlook. But while very favourable towards the range of government responsibilities, they were more critical about the power of government.

Norwegians, like many others, favoured government having wide-ranging responsibilities. But they were also rather restrictive about spending more on welfare, and not in favour of spending more on the environment and the arts. On the other hand, only 25 per cent wanted to reduce the size of the public sector, and the majority thought that government power was about right. This pattern suggests that Norwegians were broadly in favour of the status quo—except for expanding some welfare services.

In examining differences within countries, we found that social and political influences worked quite differently. Attitudes towards the range of government responsibility are more favourable among people affiliated with left parties, among those who consider themselves working class, and those with low income or little education. However, only party affiliation is a consistent influence on attitudes towards the power of government. We found that in Germany, Britain, Ireland, and Italy people affiliated to left parties held more negative attitudes about the power of government than people affiliated to parties of the right. We explained this in terms of political distance from the parties in power.

We started this chapter by presenting three theories about attitudes towards the size of government. According to the marginal utility and overload hypotheses, we could expect attitudes to be contractionist in countries with more advanced economies, as measured by GDP per capita, and in countries in which government has grown bigger, as measured by the growth of government receipts. Conversely, we could expect attitudes to be expansionist in less-advanced economies and where government is smaller. And according to the distinction between general and specific attitudes, we anticipated that attitudes would be contractionist at the general level but more expansionist on specific policies, especially welfare.

It is difficult to draw firm conclusions about the marginal utility hypothesis, especially as our test was limited to only six countries. Even so, we found that attitudes were more expansionist in countries where GDP per capita is relatively low. Much more striking, however, was the similarity between attitudes at very different levels of GDP per capita. Indeed, the similarities of attitudes towards the size of government across countries were more impressive than the differences in levels of economic development.

As to the overload hypothesis, we found little evidence that attitudes had become more contractionist during the 1980s. The only contractionist trend in attitudes towards the size of government was in the Netherlands during the early 1980s—but even there attitudes turned in an expansionist direction in the late 1980s. In Britain, Italy, and Germany there was widespread support for big government both in the mid-1970s and the mid-1980s, which suggests that attitudes were not influenced by government overload. Thus, what we suggested at the outset seems to hold true: if people have strong expectations about the range of government services, dissatisfaction with government activity does not provoke widespread demands for reducing government activity. Instead, it seems that demands for big government and negative feelings about government exist side by side.

We found the distinction between general and specific attitudes to be very important in accounting for this apparent paradox. While attitudes towards the range of government responsibilities and spending on specific policies, especially spending on welfare, were broadly favourable and expansionist, attitudes towards spending in general and towards the power of government were heading in a contractionist direction. Thus we cannot conclude that attitudes were either expansionist or contractionist. Rather, people appear to want governments to assume a wide range of responsibilities, to increase spending in some areas and to reduce spending in others. Even so, they tend to have rather negative attitudes about the power of government. This rather suggests that the size of government, *per se*, matters less than whether or not people perceive government to be effective.

NOTES

1. A recent example in Norway was the government's action in rescuing the banks and the country's biggest insurance company from bankruptcy in 1991. Two years later the insurance company was returned to private hands and the process of privatizing the banks was started. The Labour government showed no interest in nationalizing these enterprises.
2. In Italy, the Communist Party won some 25–30 per cent of the votes in all the elections during the 1980s.
3. Gans (1988), similarly, argues that one of the traditional paradoxes about American values is that many people want better public services but also lower public expenditure. A survey in 1985 showed 80 per cent of respondents saying they favoured less government spending, while in the very next question 68 per cent agreed that the government should provide more jobs. Gans also shows that this paradox is not new: in 1936 people supported state ownership of the means of production at the same time as they supported cuts in government spending. He argues that this shows that people want 'something for nothing' and that they are ambivalent about the public sector.
4. No other trend data are available. The most obvious explanation for the change in attitudes in the Netherlands is the spending cuts implemented by the Christian Democratic and Liberal coalition governments in power since 1977; by the mid-1980s, the consequences were clear to citizens.
5. The 1990 data for Austria on this question are not available.
6. Unfortunately, the question about subjective social class was not asked in the British version of the 1990 survey.
7. The independent variables were recoded as follows: Gender: female = 1, male = 2. Age: 18–80 years. Education: up to nine years' schooling = 1, 10–12 years = 2, 13–15 years = 3, 16 years and more = 4. Family income: lowest 33 per cent = 1, middle 33 per cent = 2, highest 33 per cent = 3. Employment sector: public sector = 1, private sector = 2. Party affiliation: left = 1, centre = 2, right = 3. Subjective class: working class = 1, middle class = 2.
8. However, we do not have data on party affiliation in Italy, only vote in the last election. But we have voting data only for Germany and Italy. In the other countries, we have to use party affiliation.
9. In the late 1980s, the Labour Party and the Workers' Party garnered between them only 7.9 per cent of the vote; see Lane, McKay, and Newton (1991: table 7.6).
10. In Italy we used vote in the last election, not party affiliation. The coding for the variable is: Left (PCI/PSDI/PSI/PR/Liste Verde) = 1; Right (DC/PLI/PRI/MSI) = 2. Attitudes towards the power of government were coded as: far too much power = 1; far too little power = 5. For the coding of the other variables, see n. 7.

PART II

Taxation and Policy Issues

5

Taxing and Spending: Tax Revolt or Tax Protest?

MARIA A. CONFALONIERI AND KENNETH NEWTON

Taxes are an endless source of political conflict. They are the essential fuel which powers the modern state but they hit citizens where it is said to hurt most. For much of the twentieth century, Western governments have been under pressure to tax more heavily so they can respond to escalating demands for public services but, unlike many matters of political life which have to be taken on trust, citizens have a first-hand experience of taxes and can count their costs. Taxes are also more than an intensely practical matter. They are loaded with political symbolism (Listhaug and Miller 1985). They encapsulate crucial differences between parties and political philosophies, and they raise the timeless issues of liberty and equality, wealth and poverty, fairness and justice, and the relationship of the individual to the state. Taxes are both a means to an end and an end in themselves. Progressive taxation has a rationale of its own justified by egalitarianism and fairness, but at the same time progressive taxes on income and inherited wealth have become such an integral part of Western tax regimes that they are one of the most important sources of government revenue (Rose 1985: 302; see also Ardant 1975: 232–3). This helps to make tax not merely a major battleground of modern politics, but perhaps the major battleground.

Taxes play such a central role in the modern state that it is impossible to separate the issues of government taxing and spending, and impossible to separate taxing and spending from a wide range of other issues of modern government and politics. It is not sensible to ask questions about taxation without, at the same time, asking 'Who pays what for whom to consume how much and why?' Therefore, when examining mass attitudes towards taxation we must also consider attitudes towards service expenditure and towards the welfare state in general.

Perhaps more than any other single indicator, increases in government taxing and spending show how, where, and when government has grown in the twentieth century (see Chapter 2). Perhaps, also, growing resistance to taxation is likely to be the first warning sign of government strain, overload, and the questioning of legitimacy. In other words, hard cash rather than other indicators in the form of trust in government, alienation, or voter turnout rates, may pinpoint the greatest strains in the political system.

Political battles over taxes are the normal state of affairs. As Alt (1983: 208) puts it: 'The history of taxation is to some extent the history of riots, uprisings, and revolution.' From this perspective, the period from 1950 to around 1970 was unusual for its relatively low level of tax conflict. But by the mid-1970s normal conditions were re-established as the Western world entered into a period of 'tax revolt'.

In retrospect, the reasons for such a fundamental swing of public opinion seem to be easily understood. First, the oil crisis of 1973 presaged the end of the long post-war boom in the West. As economic growth slowed, increasing numbers of taxpayers became conscious of what quickly became known as 'the burden on the taxpayer'. Yet during this period citizen demand for public services remained insatiable. Perhaps they were even fuelled by the impact of recession at the end of a long period of economic growth. According to some writers, the gap between the voracious consumption of public services and resentful taxpayers caused overload for governments (Rose and Peters 1978), and the gap caused by taxes rising faster than income caused overload for taxpayers (Hibbs and Madsen 1981).

In the years after the war, ever larger numbers of people became caught in the tax net. In 1938, about one in five employed Britons (3.8 million) paid income taxes. By the 1980s this had risen to 93 per cent of employed people, or some 24 million individuals (Rose and Karran 1987: 85–7). In 1949, a married man with two children in Britain paid no income tax until his earnings were 13 per cent above the national average. In 1993, he paid income tax if his earnings were only 30 per cent of the national average. The story is much the same in the rest of Western Europe. More people than ever had a personal stake in taxing and spending as a political issue. Whereas many people could hope to get something for nothing in the pre-war period (they could vote for parties advocating tax increases they did not pay), this became less and less possible as taxpayers approached 100 per cent of adult citizens. Fiscal drag—the process by which inflation lifts more people into higher tax brackets—added insult to financial injury in the 1970s.

There is also the nature of the tax regime itself. By the late 1960s income taxes were at an historic high; the top rates of income tax, especially, were the subject of widespread public discussion. This is an important litmus test for the politics of taxation. Direct taxes, particularly income taxes, tend to be visible and politically sensitive—a glance at the wages of salary slip is often enough to tell people how much they pay in income and social security taxes. Lump-sum property taxes, often levied by local authorities, have the same characteristic (Sharpe 1981: 9). In contrast, indirect taxes, such as VAT/TVA, are often hidden in commodity or service costs which makes it more difficult to estimate their amount, or, indeed, whether they are paid at all. As a result, indirect taxes, though they tend to be regressive, also tend to be less visible and to provoke less political opposition.

This mixture of social, economic, and political factors seems to have caused what came to be known as the 'taxpayer revolts' of the late 1970s and the 1980s. The best example is probably the anti-tax Progress Party in Denmark. It took 16 per cent of the poll in the 1973 election to become the second largest party in the Danish Parliament, and almost held its position in the elections of 1975 and 1977. A similar party emerged in Norway, which later developed into the anti-tax Progress Party. Finland had its own version in the Small Farmers' Party. In Britain, Mrs Thatcher scored the first of three successive election victories in 1979 arguing strongly for lower taxes and reducing government spending. In Sweden, in 1976, the Social Democrats lost control of government for the first time since the early 1930s, and high taxation was a major election issue. In Germany, an anti-tax Citizens' Party was founded in 1978 by the former chairman of the Tax Officials Association, although it was short lived.

Tax protest did not stand alone as a political issue but, it was claimed, was part and parcel of a more general reappraisal of the modern state. In Wilensky's view there was a 'welfare backlash' in which taxes were symbolic of a deeper alienation from big government, the public sector, and the welfare state (Wilensky 1975: 107–19). It was said that the welfare state had grown to its limits (Flora 1986*a*, 1986*b*), and that public opinion was turning against it (Offe 1984: 157).

Whatever its real or deeper significance, the tax revolt had an immediate and remarkable impact. Many countries in Western Europe (and beyond) reformed their tax systems in a rapid and sweeping manner (Pechman 1988; OECD 1987). The reforms often took a very similar form in different countries in Western Europe. They did not so much reduce taxation as raise revenues from a wider range of sources. Income taxes were generally simplified by, for example, reducing the number of tax brackets and simplifying the rules governing exemptions and deductions. But sometimes the overall nature of the tax system was made rather more complicated by a wider range of taxes. There was a trend away from direct and visible taxes, such as income tax, to indirect and less visible taxes. In many cases the highest rates of income tax were reduced. In Britain they were lowered in steps from 83 per cent in 1978 to 40 per cent. In Sweden, the top rate was cut from 82 per cent in 1984 to 42 per cent by 1989, in Italy from 72 to 50 per cent, and in the Netherlands from 71 to 60 per cent (Kay 1990).

There was also a shift from individual and household taxes, which tended to generate popular opposition, to business and corporation taxes. In some countries the size of the public sector deficit was increased as a way of increasing spending while holding taxes down. In Italy, for example, gross public debt rose to approximately two-thirds of GDP in 1980 and even in Germany it was close to one-third. Since direct taxes, particularly income taxes, tend to be more progressive than indirect taxes, there was a tendency to shift the relative weight of the tax burden between different types of social and economic groups—often from the richer to the poorer. These changes were often introduced by different kinds of government. In Britain, they formed an important part of the economic strategy of a neo-liberal Conservative government, but in Sweden and the Netherlands reforms of a similar kind were introduced by coalition governments of moderate left and right-wing parties.

In this chapter we estimate the strength and nature of the tax revolt in Western Europe. Was it a reversion to 'politics as usual'—a constant grumbling and opposition to taxes? Or was it part of a more serious and fundamental reappraisal of the welfare state and its basic principles of income redistribution, progressive taxation, and egalitarianism? Resistance to paying taxes is as old as the state itself, but resistance to taxes which is part of a fundamental reappraisal of the scope of modern government would be something new and noteworthy. In particular, we examine three general questions:

(1) Is there evidence in the surveys of mass opinion in Western Europe of a widespread and sustained taxpayers' revolt?
(2) Is there evidence that the tax revolt is related to a more general backlash against the welfare state?
(3) Do the survey data support the view that the citizens of the modern state want something for nothing out of the tax and welfare systems in their countries?

Tax Fairness and Tax Justice: Revolt or Protest?

Classical philosophy draws a distinction between fairness, which refers to basic values and goals, and justice which relates to the substantive outcomes of these rules (see Lane 1986: 39). Fairness refers to the principles on which the system is founded; justice refers to the ways in which the basic principles are applied in practice, and to their results (Feinberg 1973: 117). Public opinion about a matter like tax is generally a complex mixture of views about both justice and fairness, but it is useful to make a theoretical distinction between them. Those who reject the fundamental principles of the system are likely to want to change it wholesale. Those who accept the basic fairness of the system but believe it to be unjust in practice are likely to maintain their allegiance to the system while arguing for reform of its operation.

Tax fairness in Western Europe rests on the principles of progressive taxation, income redistribution, and the provision of the basic services of the welfare state (see Chapters 3, 7, and 8). According to the literature on the welfare backlash and the taxpayers' revolt, these principles have been increasingly questioned in recent decades in Western Europe. If this is indeed the case, we can expect the modern state to come under increasing pressure not just to reduce tax levels, but also to reduce spending levels and with them to cut back on the whole scope of government. If, however, the basic principles of equality, service provision, and welfare are still accepted by the general public, then modern 'big government' is likely to be more stable politically. The 'big government' associated with welfare states is more likely to survive public criticism and demands for reform will not necessarily undermine its basic purpose.

A system may be thought fair in principle but, even though the principles are implemented correctly, it may still be thought unjust. In fact anything as delicate and complex as a modern tax system can easily go wrong administratively. Tax evasion, tax avoidance, the black economy, administrative inefficiency, misapplication of rules, or oversight may all help to produce unanticipated and unwelcome outcomes. Consequently, the public may feel the basic aims and goals of the tax regime are fair, but question its justice. In such cases, there is likely to be public pressure for reform, but not for a fundamental reappraisal of the system.

In Figure 5.1 the dimensions of fairness and justice have been dichotomized to identify four types of attitude towards tax regimes. First, those who believe the system to be both fair and just are termed 'tax compliants'. Secondly, those who believe in the fairness of the system but not in its justice are called 'tax protesters'. They do not dispute the stated goals of tax policy, but believe that the way in which it operates means that at least people do not get their just deserts. The third group are those who believe the system to be both unfair and unjust. They reject its basic rules of allocation and its outcomes and are termed 'tax revolters'. Fourthly, and more a theoretical possibility than a real-type, are those who believe the system to be unfair but just. They are not of much concern for present purposes, but may be called 'tax formalists'.

The 1950s and 1960s seem to have been decades of general tax compliance in which both the basic principles and the *modus operandi* of tax regimes were broadly accepted. According to some views, however, the 1970s saw the start of a tax revolt in which public opinion increasingly rejected the basic principles of the welfare state: steeply progressive income tax, redistribution of wealth, guaranteed minimum incomes, and so on. Others argued that the attitude shift was more modest than this—an expression of tax protest rather than revolt. According to Rose (1984: 212), 'To speak of a tax revolt is to substitute hyperbole for analysis' (see also Rose 1983*a*; Coughlin 1980: 154). In the next section we consider the evidence. Was there a 'welfare

		Fairness	
		Fair	Unfair
Justice	Just	Tax compliance	Tax formalism
	Unjust	Tax protest	Tax revolt

FIGURE 5.1. *Attitudes towards the tax system*

backlash' which questioned the fundamental basis of taxes and expenditures, or was there rather a tax protest which accepted the principles of the system, but urged reforms to make the outcomes more acceptable? The evidence and conclusions of Chapters 4, 7, and 8 in this volume suggest that we are likely to find more tax protesters than tax revolters in Western Europe.

Problems of Evidence

Methodological and data problems are commonplace in cross-national and time-series research, but they are more acute than usual in the case of taxation. First, there is rather little evidence available by comparison with other topics such as trust in government, political participation, even attitudes towards welfare provision. With a few exceptions, political scientists have not been much interested in taxation, but have left the topic to economists. Secondly, systematically comparative data are largely restricted to one major survey—the International Social Science Programme (ISSP)—and this did not start until 1985. Moreover, the first survey covered only six West European countries; two later surveys with relevant questions covered only eight countries. Hence, our data base is rather limited. National surveys have been conducted at different times in different countries, but the questions asked and the years covered are rarely comparable.

Thirdly, it is difficult to collect valid and reliable evidence on attitudes towards taxation. A great deal turns on what sorts of questions are asked. A general question will often present one sort of picture, but specific questions about specific taxes or services may yield a rather different picture (see Chapter 4). Most important of all, priced and unpriced questions tend to yield very different responses. Asked if they think taxes are too high, or if government spending should be cut, most people immediately say 'yes': asked if they think more money should be spent on public services a similar proportion say 'yes'. But responses are usually different if people are asked what services they would cut, if any, in order to reduce taxes and spending, or whether they would be prepared to pay more taxes in order to pay for better services, and if so, what services. If particular tax prices are then attached to particular services, the responses may well differ again (Peters 1991: 16; see also Chapter 4).

Finally, there is the problem of a possible gap between attitudes and behaviour; what people say and what they do are sometimes rather different matters. This may be particularly true of taxation where it is sometimes said that some people may say one thing to opinion pollsters, but do another in the privacy of the polling booth. None the less, given the importance of taxation as a political issue, it seems unwise for political scientists to abandon the topic because the data position is not ideal. Rather, we should make use of the available evidence, while keeping in mind its limitations.

A Tax Revolt?

The ISSP surveys for 1985, 1987, and 1990 include questions about attitudes towards taxation. Three of the questions of particular interest to us are as follows:

1. 'On the whole, do you think it should or should not be the government's responsibility to reduce income differences between the rich and the poor?' (1985, 1990)
2. Respondents were asked how strongly they agreed or disagreed with the statement: 'It is the responsibility of the government to reduce the differences in income between people with high incomes and those with low incomes.' (1987, 1990)
3. Do you think that people with high incomes should pay a larger share of their income in taxes than those with low incomes, the same share, or a smaller share?' (1987)

These questions deal with the principles of tax fairness; income inequality, progressive taxation, and the reduction of income differences. There are only minor differences in the wording of the first and second question but, as they cover different years and a slightly different set of countries, we report the results for both in Table 5.1.

A cursory examination of the distributions shows that support for the principles of reducing income differences and for progressive taxation is high in almost every country in all three years. The exception is Switzerland in 1987, but national differences are not the most notable feature of the figures. On the contrary, support for the reduction of income differences by using progressive income tax is a common characteristic of all West European countries—or, at least, of those countries where ISSP surveys were carried out.

This conclusion is entirely consistent with the findings of Beate

TABLE 5.1. *Attitudes towards issues of tax fairness in six countries*

(*a*) Government's responsibility to reduce income differences between rich and poor

	West Germany		Britain		Italy		Austria	Norway	Ireland
	1985	1990	1985	1990	1985	1990	1985	1990	1990
Should be	67	64	75	74	84	78	78	72	82
Should not be	33	36	25	26	16	22	22	28	18
N	1,048	2,812	1,530	1,197	1,580	983	1,580	1,517	1,005

(*b*) Government's responsibility to reduce income differences between those with high and low incomes

	West Germany		Britain		Italy		Austria	Switzerland	Norway	Ireland	Netherlands
	1987	1990	1987	1990	1987	1990	1987	1987	1990	1990	1990
Agree	61	56	64	57	82	70	81	43	56	69	65
Disagree	24	20	23	24	9	15	11	40	25	18	24
N	1,397	2,812	1,212	1,197	1,027	983	972	987	1,517	1,005	1638

TABLE 5.1. Cont.

(*c*) People with high incomes should pay a larger share of their income in taxes than those with low incomes

	West Germany		Britain		Italy		Austria	Switzerland	Norway	Ireland	Netherlands
	1987	1990	1987	1990	1987	1990	1987	1987	1990	1990	1990
Larger	80	87	77	85	79	84	86	82	75	82	73
Same	19	12	22	14	20	15	13	17	24	17	22
Smaller	1	1	1	1	1	1	1	1	1	1	4
N	1,397	2,812	1,212	1,197	1,027	983	972	987	1,517	1,005	1,638

Note: Entries are percentages.

Sources: ISSP (1985, 1987, 1990).

Huseby in Chapter 4 and Edeltraud Roller in Chapter 7. Both find a relatively consistent pattern, across Western Europe, in mass attitudes towards the welfare responsibilities of government and towards questions of equality. They also find that support for public services and for a measure of income redistribution is relatively high across all countries, and that there is rather little evidence of much decline during the 1970s and 1980s, although the desire for greater equality may not have been as strong in 1990 as earlier (Chapter 7). In other words, research on different sides of the taxing and spending coin suggests much the same conclusions: there is a West European pattern in which support for the fundamentals of the welfare state—progressive taxation and reducing income differences—is relatively high, and seems to have remained so into the 1990s.

Evidence of a tax revolt would include either low or declining levels of support for the principles of progressive taxation and income redistribution. It is possible that support had declined by 1985–90 from even higher levels in the 1960s and 1970s. We cannot tell from these data which start only in 1985. For evidence of longer term trends we have to turn to studies carried out over a period of years in particular countries. Fortunately we have data of this kind, but unfortunately it is for only three countries: Denmark, Norway, and Sweden. These data are presented in Table 5.2. Note, however, that we cannot place too much reliance on these figures because they are responses to slightly different questions in different countries and at different times. Nevertheless, they all relate to the principle of progressive taxation. Moreover, whereas the ISSP questions ask simply about attitudes towards the principle of progressive taxation, the Scandinavian surveys go one step further and ask whether income taxes should be more or less progressive than they are already. As all three countries were notorious for their steeply progressive taxes at the time, they are good test cases for evidence of a tax revolt.

Once again the figures present a fairly consistent pattern in different countries and at different times. With the exception only of Denmark in 1990, an absolute majority either opposed less progressive income taxes or were in favour of them being more progressive. There may be a tendency for opinion to move against even more progressive taxation in Denmark and Sweden, but the trend is not strong and it is difficult to draw this conclusion from figures which tend to fluctuate in the short run. If anything, the figures suggest a hardening of opposition to less progressive income taxes in Norway. In short, the figures for the three Scandinavian countries are consistent with the ISSP surveys which

TABLE 5.2. *Attitudes towards progressive taxation in Denmark, Norway, and Sweden, 1971–90*

	Denmark	Norway	Sweden
1971	52		
1973	71	58	
1975	55		
1976			64
1977	57	57	
1979	64		64
1981	50	65	
1982			62
1984	52		
1985		72	57
1990	44		

Notes: The entries are as follows: for Denmark, percentages agreeing that 'High incomes should be taxed more strongly than they are today'; for Norway 1973, percentages disagreeing with tax relief for higher incomes: 'Many people think that tax reliefs should benefit primarily people with high incomes, while others think that people with low incomes should profit from tax reliefs, while others think that tax reliefs should evenly benefit all. What do you think?' For Norway 1977–85, percentages choosing 'bad proposal' in response to: 'Indicate whether you think this is a good proposal which it is important to carry through or a bad proposal and it is important it is not carried through: to reduce taxes on higher incomes'; for Sweden, the percentages disagreeing with the statement, 'We should reduce taxes on upper incomes'.

Sources: Danish, Norwegian, and Swedish election surveys.

indicate underlying support for the basic principle of progressive income tax, and they show little if any decline in such support.

The ISSP surveys ask a series of other questions which reveal why people are so strongly in favour of progressive taxation. Respondents were asked whether they agree or disagree that 'Inequality continues to exist because it benefits the rich and the powerful'; that 'Large differences in income are necessary for . . . prosperity'; and that 'Differences in income . . . are too large'. Large majorities in Germany, Britain, Austria, the Netherlands, Italy, and Switzerland believe that inequality exists because it benefits the rich and the powerful; pluralities or absolute majorities do not agree with the suggestion that large differences in income are necessary for their country's prosperity; and overwhelming majorities, ranging from a low of 66 per cent in the Netherlands to a high of 90 per cent in Austria, believe that income differences in their country are too large (ISSP 1985: 66–93). In short, the evidence from the ISSP data, summarized in Figures 5.2–5.4,

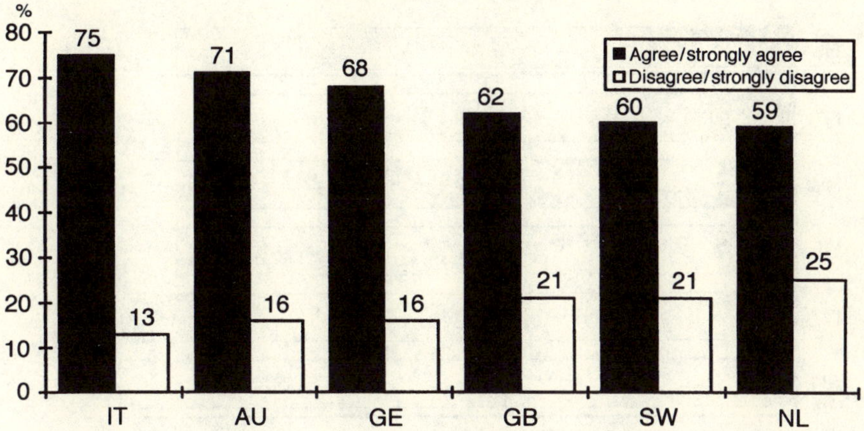

FIGURE 5.2. *'Inequality continues to exist because it benefits the rich and powerful?'*

Source: ISSP (1987).

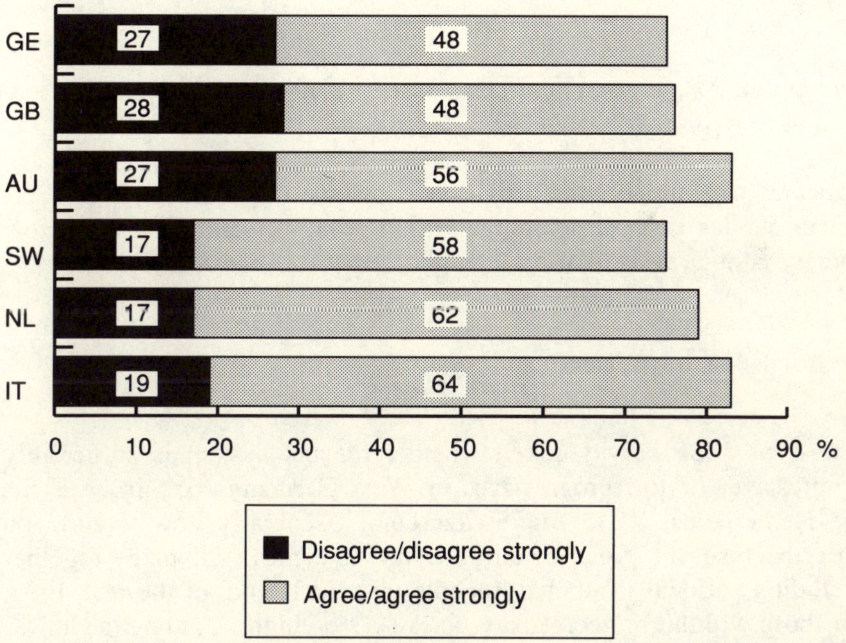

FIGURE 5.3. *'Large differences in income are necessary for [respondent's country's] prosperity?'*

Source: ISSP (1987).

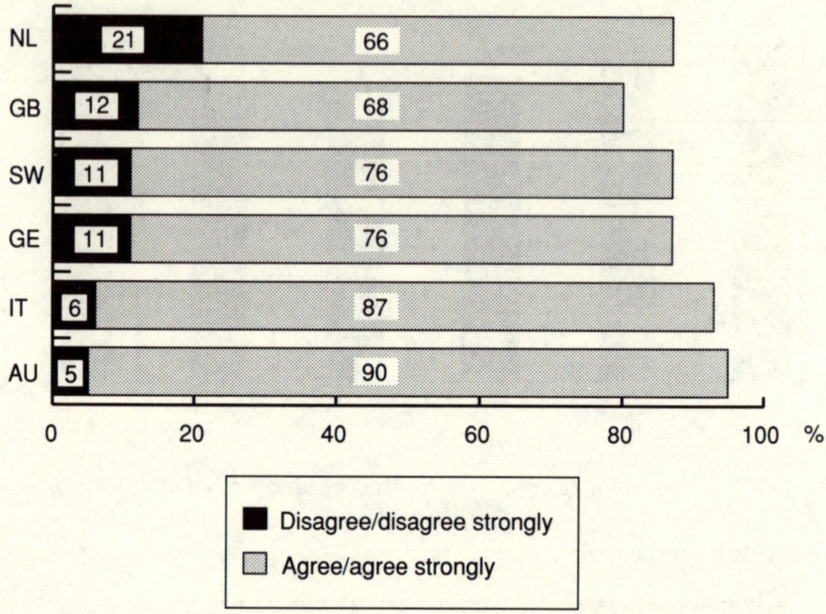

FIGURE 5.4. *'Differences in income in [respondent's country] are too large?'*
Source: ISSP (1987).

indicates that support for progressive income taxes across West European publics is based upon egalitarian principles and the feeling that society is not yet egalitarian enough.

Tax Protest?

The 1987 ISSP survey asked whether the tax system is sufficiently progressive, or too progressive, in West Germany, Britain, Austria, the Netherlands, Italy, and Switzerland: 'Generally how would you describe taxes in [your country] today. We mean all taxes together including national insurance, income tax, VAT, and all the rest. First, for those with high incomes are taxes . . . too high . . . about right . . . too low? For those with middle incomes are income taxes too high . . . about right . . . too low? For those with low incomes are income taxes too high . . . about right . . . too low?'. This question is about the justice of the tax system. Responses are summarized in Table 5.3. Once again

TABLE 5.3. *Attitudes towards the justice of taxation, 1987*

	West Germany	Britain	Austria	Netherlands	Italy	Switzerland
Taxes on high incomes are:						
Too high	13	24	19	27	19	11
Too low	57	41	54	48	61	57
Taxes on middle incomes are:						
Too high	52	41	47	60	62	51
Too low	4	5	4	2	4	8
Taxes on low incomes are:						
Too high	85	87	78	80	85	69
Too low	1	1	5	1	2	1
N	1,397	1,212	972	1,638	1,027	987

Note: Entries are percentages.

Source: ISSP (1987).

the results are clear and consistent across nations. The great majority of people in all six nations feel that taxes on those with high incomes are too low. Overwhelmingly majorities feel that taxes on those with low incomes are too high. There is also a general feeling that taxes on those with middle incomes are too high. National variations stand out less clearly than the consistency of opinion across all six countries.

Spain is not included in the ISSP surveys but it seems to fit the same pattern. In 1985, 1987, and 1988 a survey asked respondents whether or not they thought taxes in Spain were just. A majority in each survey (71, 69, and 64 per cent) said they were not; a much smaller proportion (15, 16, and 22 per cent) thought they were (CIS 1988).

The implications of these figures are clear: most people feel that the principle of progressive income tax is not justly applied; a substantial majority feel that income taxes on the poor are too heavy; a smaller majority feel the same about middle income groups; and most feel that those with high incomes pay too little. In sum, the majority of West European citizens show signs of believing in the basic principles of the tax system—its fairness—but seem not to believe that these are applied in accordance with the principles—its justice. This combination results in tax protest, but not in tax revolt.

Tax and Spending Cuts

Other ISSP data, from the 1985 and 1990 surveys, seem to contradict the conclusion just reached. These data, from which the statistics reported in Table 5.4 are taken, show large majorities in three countries (not Britain) in favour of cutting government expenditure. They also show that most people believe that their household income taxes are too high. And third, they make it clear that pluralities in three out of four countries (not Germany) also believe that taxes on business and industry are too high.

However, as the questions are unpriced, there is good reason to doubt the significance of these figures. It is scarcely surprising that most people say that their own taxes are too high, and that many believe that business taxes are too high. It is no more surprising that many favour government spending cuts. Rather, the question is how they would respond if asked which services they would cut in order to reduce government spending and taxes. Alternatively they might be asked which services they wish to see improved at what sort of tax

TABLE 5.4. *Percentages favouring government cuts and saying taxes are too high*

	Germany		Britain		Italy		Austria	Norway
	1985	1990	1985	1990	1985	1990	1985	1990
Favour government spending cuts	77	76	38	42	68	70	82	71
Consider their household income taxes too high	68		71		71		76	
Consider tax on business and industry too high	18		42		63		65	
N	1,048	2,812	1,530	1,197	1,580	983	987	1,587

Note: Entries are percentages.

Sources: ISSP (1985, 1990).

price to themselves. The 1985 and 1990 ISSP surveys asked one such priced question:

Listed below are various areas of government spending. Please show whether you would like to see more or less government spending in each area. Remember that if you say 'much more', it might require a tax increase to pay for it.

In a sense this question, too, is loaded since it seems to offer the option of 'more spending' without the need to confront possible tax increases. Equally, it may well have discouraged 'much more' responses. More to the point, the answers to the question, reported in Table 5.5, show an interesting pattern.

First, most respondents draw a clear distinction between different services. Large minorities favour 'much more' spending and tax increases for health, the environment, pensions, and education; and absolute majorities favour 'more' or 'much more' spending on these services in most countries and in most years. Between a fifth and a third of respondents were prepared to pay more taxes for health and the environment, between a quarter and a fifth for pensions and education. There was less enthusiasm for increased spending and taxes for the police and unemployment benefit, and only small minorities would pay more for culture and the arts, and for defence. By and large, the priced 'much more' priorities follow the unpriced 'more' priorities. It seems, then, that taxpayers generally have a clear set of service preferences: they know what they want and are prepared to pay for, and they know what they do not want and are not prepared to pay for. The same general point is made in other chapters of this book, but it is worth repeating because it is central to the particular arguments of this chapter.

The figures also show a fairly high degree of cross-national consistency. There are some variations but, in general, respondents across the five nations rank services in much the same order and in much the same proportions. The questions were asked in both years only in Germany, Britain, and Italy. In most instances the proportions favouring increased spending and taxes were higher in 1990 than in 1985. Nor do people's priorities with regard to services change much between 1985 and 1990. Although these data cover only a five-year period and are only for three countries, there is little here to suggest a tax revolt.

The last sentence raises an important point: it is one thing to show high levels of support for the welfare state and for progressive taxation in 1985 and 1990; it is quite another to show that support for these

TABLE 5.5. *Percentage favouring more government spending (by service), 1985 and 1990*

	Germany		Britain		Italy		Austria	Norway
	1985	1990	1985	1990	1985	1990	1985	1990
Health								
Much more	19	36	36	36	32	39	22	25
More	52	73	88	90	79	85	60	83
Old age pensions								
Much more	11	16	25	29	22	26	13	16
More	46	55	75	82	75	81	51	72
Environment								
Much more	43	61	6	15	17	26	34	24
More	83	90	37	63	63	76	73	74
Education								
Much more	10	20	23	27	17	23	9	11
More	40	59	75	79	64	66	36	56
Law enforcement								
Much more	9	12	9	11	12	17	5	13
More	30	43	40	50	49	57	23	62
Unemployment benefit								
Much more	8	9	12	8	15	15	3	4
More	35	37	41	36	56	52	15	19
Culture, theatre								
Much more	2	5	1	2	8	10	3	2
More	14	22	10	13	36	45	12	10
Military defence								
Much more	2	2	5	2	3	2	3	1
More	6	5	18	9	12	12	12	4
N	1,048	2,812	1,530	1,197	1,580	983	987	1,517

Sources: ISSP (1985, 1990).

principles remains as solid and widespread as ever. Perhaps there was virtually universal support for these principles in the tax compliance years 1950–75, and perhaps such support has fallen in subsequent years.

In searching for time-series data on attitudes towards taxation we face difficulties. There are few cross-national data, and what there are makes up a very incomplete picture. But in painting a picture it is as well to follow Picasso's advice: 'If you have no blue paint, then use green paint.' The problem is that since we also have rather little green paint, we will have to make do with patches of different colour. Rather than dignifying the few time-series data with a table we will make the best of their patchy and non-comparable quality by summarizing them.

Feelings against the welfare state in Denmark seem to have hardened in the early 1970s but then softened again towards the end of the decade. For example, an increasing proportion of Danes agreed that politicians were being too lavish with taxpayers' money between 1971 and 1973 (an increase from 85 to 91 per cent), but the figure declined to 84 in 1975 and 77 per cent in 1977. At the same time, there was a decline in the number of Danes agreeing that too many people were receiving social benefits from 87 per cent in 1973, to 61 per cent in 1975, and to 58 per cent in 1977 (Hibbs and Madsen 1981).

In contrast, anti-welfare attitudes—especially against social benefits and taxation—in Sweden seem to have strengthened during the period from the late 1960s to the early 1980s. There was an increase in the proportion of people agreeing that social reforms had gone too far and that benefits should be cut, from 41 per cent in 1968 to a constant 60 per cent in both 1973 and 1976. The proportions agreeing that welfare should be cut increased from 34 per cent in 1976 to 39 per cent in 1978 (Hibbs and Madsen 1981). A further set of questions asked in Sweden in 1968 and 1981 also suggests a movement of opinion against taxes and welfare services. There was a decline in the proportion of the public agreeing that taxes were reasonable, from 43 per cent to 36 per cent, and a fall from 54 to 39 per cent in those rejecting the idea that taxes were not too high. The feeling that marginal taxes are too high gained strength from 70 per cent to no less than 83 per cent over the 1968–81 period. However, in the same period the proportion agreeing that 'taxes must be reduced at all costs' fell by 10 percentage points, from 63 to 53 per cent (Hadenius 1985).

In many ways Britain is the test case, however, because the Conservative governments of the 1980s frequently and loudly claimed success in cutting taxes and services. In the 1960s and 1970s an increasing proportion of the British public seemed to favour tax cuts (Hibbs and Madsen 1981). The percentage favouring tax and service cuts increased from 29 per cent in 1978 to 37 per cent in 1979, the year of Thatcher's first election victory. Thereafter, support for tax and service cuts declined consistently during the 1980s from 22 per cent in 1982 to 11 per cent in 1987. Conversely, those favouring increasing services and taxes fell from 40 per cent in 1978 to 37 per cent in 1979, but then increased steadily from 52 per cent in 1982 to 66 per cent in 1987 (Crewe 1988; see also Lewis and Jackson 1985). In other words, at the start of the Thatcher era a third of the population wanted tax and service cuts, and a third wanted increased services even if it meant increased taxes. Towards the end of the decade, only one in ten wanted tax and service cuts, and almost two thirds wanted extended services even if it meant tax increases.

Not surprisingly the conclusions drawn from these disparate figures vary from one study to another. In their study of Denmark, Sweden, Germany, the Netherlands, and Britain, Hibbs and Madsen conclude that 'disapproval of the scale of taxation, expenditure, and social services seems to have increased between the early and mid-1960s and early 1970s, and to have been higher in Denmark than other countries' (Hibbs and Madsen 1981: 418). Writing five years later, and with the benefit of more up-to-date and more systematic surveys, Hadenius concludes that the 'Swedes have shown a pronounced reduction of tax discontent', and argues that this may have been due to the increased deficit spending in which the Swedish government indulged to finance services. Nevertheless, he points out that dissatisfaction with high marginal rates of tax in Sweden increased during the period 1968–81.

In Britain the surveys present a mixed picture for the 1960s and 1970s. Some indicate a rise in the dissatisfaction with high taxing and spending levels (Hibbs and Madsen 1981: 420–1). Others claim that this fell far short of a 'widespread mass defection of support for the welfare state' (Coughlin 1980: 134). In the 1980s, however, the figures show a clear trend in which public opinion swung against tax cuts and in favour of tax increases, provided these resulted in better health, education, and social services for the young and the old. Crewe (1988: 37) points out that, although Gallup questions are unpriced, they indicate that there were equal numbers of tax cutters and service extenders in 1979 when Mrs Thatcher came to power, but six times as many service extenders as tax cutters in 1987. The public mood favouring services and taxes has been sustained and is as strong in the early 1990s as it was in the late 1980s.

Kosonen quotes Norwegian, Danish, Swedish, and Finnish studies which indicate that, after a period of public frustration and opposition, there was a growing acceptance of the welfare state and its costs by the middle to late 1980s. He observes that people are 'basically satisfied and ready to pay for social security' (Kosonen 1987: 281).

This disparate array of figures and comments suggest three conclusions. First, the figures indicate that the strength of the tax protest varied in different countries, being most pronounced in Denmark and to some extent in Britain. The protest was more muted in Sweden and Norway, and least noticeable in Germany and the Netherlands. Secondly, even where it was strongest, the anti-tax mood did not undermine basic support for the core services of the welfare state. Thirdly, far from being a long-term underlying trend, even less a turning point in history, the protest seems to have been particular to the period of the late 1960s and the 1970s. In Britain where tax and expenditure cuts were deepest, public opinion swung decisively against them and reaffirmed support for a modest increase in taxes in return for better services.

More for Less? Something for Nothing?

Many surveys of public opinion show that most people think that taxes are too high, especially their own, but that more and better public services should be made available. An Italian survey in 1985, for example, shows that 40 per cent of respondents complained that their taxes were too high but in the next breath expressed the view that public spending should not be reduced (Ferrera 1986; see also Taylor-Gooby 1985; Hadenius 1985). These kind of findings have lead some writers to claim that citizens either do not understand the tax-price of services, or, worse, that they want something for nothing (see, for example, Sears and Citrin 1982; Welch 1985). The general public has either foolishly failed to recognize the plain and simple fact that public services come with a large price tag, or else people cynically express their desire not merely for a free lunch, but for a life-time of free lunches on the welfare state.

Some of the evidence presented in this book is entirely consistent with 'something for nothing' interpretation of public opinion. Tables 4.1, 4.2, and 4.5 show strong support for public job creation schemes, services for the old, the sick, the unemployed, poor students, and so on. At the same time, Table 5.4 shows that most people favour cuts in government spending and think their own household taxes and those of business and industry are too high.

In spite of this, there are reasons for rejecting the 'something for nothing' interpretation of people's attitudes. In the first place, when confronted with a trade-off between taxes and services, taxpayers clearly make certain choices (see Table 5.5). They are more prepared to pay for health and pensions, less prepared to pay for culture and the arts, and least prepared to pay for defence (see also Chapter 4). When asked a sensible—priced—question, they give a response which seems to be based on a set of priorities. They may want a better deal from the government for the taxes they pay—who does not?—but they do not seem to expect to get something for nothing. If they are asked appropriate (priced) questions, their responses seem reasoned and consistent.

Secondly, our findings are generally consistent with the findings in Chapter 4 which show that there is widespread support for health care and services for the old. For example, in 1985 the Austrians were least likely to agree that government should provide a decent standard of living for the unemployed (Table 4.2). Consistent with this, the Austrians are also least likely to favour spending 'more' or 'much more' on unemployment benefit (Table 5.5). Conversely, the Italians are most likely to favour government-financed job creation schemes, and more government spending on unemployment. They are also the most likely to favour more government spending on unemployment. The match is by no means perfect, but there are indications that West European publics are generally inclined to pay for what they want. Indeed, Peters argues that 'citizens have demonstrated that they are not really as naïve about public finance as is sometimes assumed. Most citizens appear to recognize that if they want more services they will have to pay for them through taxes' (Peters 1991: 160; see also Welch 1985). The data presented here support this conclusion.

Two questions asked in a Spanish survey add weight to this conclusion. The first asked respondents to agree or disagree with the statement: 'If we want more services like education and health care, we will have to pay higher taxes.' Almost half, 49 per cent, agreed, whereas 38 per cent disagreed. The second question asked people to agree or disagree with the statement: 'The government should offer fewer services, including such things as health and education, in order to reduce taxes.' In this instance, 74 per cent disagreed and 13 per cent agreed (McDonough *et al.* 1986: 457–8).

There is an additional array of evidence and argument which casts doubt on the 'something for nothing' interpretation of taxpayer attitudes, and which helps to make sense of what might otherwise seem contradictory. The figures in Table 5.1 make it clear that the great majority of citizens favour reducing income differences and progressive taxation. At the same time the figures in Table 5.3 show that the great majority think the tax system is not progressive enough; that those with low and middle incomes pay too much, and the rich too little. To this can be added the finding that most people in Austria, Germany, Britain want to reduce the gap between high and low incomes (see Chapter 7; Taylor-Gooby 1993: 96).

In other words, the evidence—patchy and inconclusive though it is—indicates that many people in Western Europe believe that income differences between the rich and the poor are too large, that it is the responsibility of the government to reduce these differences and redistribute wealth to some degree, but that the tax system fails to do this. In short, the tax system is fair but unjust. Given this, it seems reasonable to express the view that more should be spent on some public services and that the rich should pay the extra costs.

A striking piece of information about the Danish anti-tax Progress Party supports this interpretation. Nielsen (1976) points out that 63 per cent of those who supported the Progress Party in the 1973 election wanted *higher* taxes on the rich. In 1975, the figure was 40 per cent. The conclusion is that many Danish 'tax revolters' were not tax revolters at all, but were protesting against the rich paying too little in taxes.

There are yet further considerations which help to explain why people feel that the tax system is unjust and that they should not have to pay extra taxes for the services they want. They may also help to explain why so many feel that taxes on high incomes are too low. In the first place, there is evidence that tax evasion—the use of illegal means to avoid paying taxes—is widespread throughout the Western world (Listhaug and Miller 1985; Trettner 1974; Frey and Weck 1983; Johnston and Wood 1985). Since it is easier for the relatively wealthy and the self-employed to evade taxes than the poorer and the employees who pay taxes at source, it may also be that people feel wealthier income groups are not paying their fair share.

Secondly, the extensive array of allowances and inevitable tax loopholes usually work to the benefit of those with the ability and resources to exploit them. Tax avoidance of this kind is also of greatest financial benefit to those with most to lose. Whether it is actually true that the rich indulge in both tax avoidance and tax evasion, it certainly seems to be the popular opinion that they do. This serves to undermine popular faith in the justice of the tax system, and fuels the idea that others—the tax-dodgers and the rich—should pay more for public services.

A Spanish survey conducted in 1984 provides some evidence for these claims. In response to the statement 'most people pay the taxes they should', 50 per cent of respondents disagreed; 78 per cent agreed that 'There are too many people in this country who don't pay the taxes they owe.' (McDonough *et al.* 1986: 457–8). Thus not only does the population at large feel that inequalities are unacceptably large, but they may also feel that the tax system does not do enough to reduce them, whatever its best intentions.

In sum, there may well be something in the 'something for nothing' argument, but not as originally construed. It is not so much that ordinary taxpayers want something for nothing, but that they believe that upper income groups are already getting something for nothing by virtue of the workings of the tax system and the way it is manipulated by the rich. Alt writes that 'one cannot read the history of taxation without being struck by how common the theme was of shifting the burden onto someone else' (Alt 1983: 194). Our interpretation of the 'something for nothing' debate may throw new light on the age-old political struggle.

Conclusions

Political scientists who study attitudes towards government find Easton's (1965, 320–32) distinction between community, regime, and authority useful. They argue that a growing distrust of politicians may not necessarily be a threat to modern political systems because allegiance to the community and to the regime is more fundamental. The *Beliefs in Government* study produces a wide array of evidence to show that public faith in politicians has declined in some West European countries, but that trust in the community and the regime has not been undermined (see Volume i, Chapters 9 and 11). Our distinction between tax fairness and tax justice is similar in that fairness refers to basic underlying principles, justice to their practical outcomes.

There is little evidence in the surveys to suggest a strong or growing sense of tax unfairness. Most people, amounting to large majorities in some countries, believe in the basic goal of income redistribution through progressive taxes, especially income tax. There is a large measure of agreement about the need to maintain core public services, especially the most expensive ones of health, pensions, education, and housing. Large minorities are willing to pay more taxes in return for improvements in these services. In sum, we have found very little evidence to suggest a tax revolt which would undermine the basic principles of the modern welfare state.

There is, however, a good deal of evidence to show that citizens across Western Europe are not entirely happy about the way their tax systems operate in practice. A large majority feel that the poor pay too much income tax, a majority feel the same about middle income groups, and most feel that taxes on high incomes are too low. This combination of strong attachment to the allocative principles of the system but dissatisfaction with its outcomes suggests that mass opinion in Western Europe may be described in terms of a tax protest, but not a tax revolt.

This may also help to explain why anti-tax protest was limited to certain countries and to a limited period. The feeling against taxes and spending was not a particularly fundamental or deep-rooted resistance, and it had largely subsided in most countries by 1990 or earlier. In Britain where income tax and public expenditure cuts were the deepest, public opinion swung quite strongly in the direction of increased taxing and spending.

We find some evidence to support the 'something for nothing' interpretation of mass attitudes towards taxing and spending. Asked if they want taxes reduced, most people say 'yes'; asked if they want better public services most people say 'yes'. But this is an illustration of how silly questions get silly answers. If asked sensibly worded (priced) questions, most respondents seem to give a reasoned and internally consistent set of answers. In general, people seem to have a notion of public service priorities, realize these cost money, and back them with a willingness to pay taxes—or more taxes—for them. There are also indications in the survey data that, for some people, the injustice of the tax system means that they should get more services and that the upper income groups should pay for them. In short, it is not that most taxpayers want something for nothing, but they feel the wealthier sections of society are already getting something for nothing.

One of the more notable features of many of the figures reported in this chapter is the relative uniformity of opinion in different countries.

In cross-national studies of this kind it is common to find wide variation between countries. Some figures are high while others are low, some increase, some decline, others are constant. This is not the case with attitudes about the principles of taxation, about public services and expenditures, or about the justice of the progressive tax system. What is remarkable about these figures is how similar public opinion is in different countries. In brief, there seems to be something of a common tax culture across Western Europe.

It is also worth noting that governments moved remarkably quickly to implement rather sweeping reforms of the tax systems in many West European countries in the 1980s. This reaction among governments across practically the whole of Western Europe seems to have been sparked off by the 'taxpayers' revolt', even though this was a short-lived expression of a rather superficial mood swing in public opinion. On the one hand, this indicates that public opinion can and does have effects on governments. On the other hand, given that governments seem not to respond to many other swings in public mood, it may be that governments are particularly sensitive to public opinion about taxes.

We end on a loud and clear note of caution. This chapter depends upon time series and cross-national survey data on mass attitudes towards taxation. The data are often thin and patchy, and some are not notably reliable. Given the importance of taxation in mass politics during the 1970s and 1980s, this is odd, and perhaps reflects that political scientists have not generally taken much interest in tax matters. In any case, some social scientists believe there is sometimes a gap between attitudes and behaviour, especially in the case of tax. It is one thing for citizens to tell an opinion pollster that he or she would pay more in taxes, but it may be another to vote for the party which promises to increase taxes, and still a different thing to pay these taxes without protest. The gap between expressed attitudes and actual voting behaviour has been used to explain the fact that British opinion polls got the result of the 1992 general election comprehensively wrong. Although the claim is hotly contested, Britain, it is said, is a 'nation of liars'—after thirteen years of Thatcherite Conservatism, few are willing to admit in public their preference for low taxes and spending cuts, but some may vote for them none the less. The point, however, is not that there may sometimes be an imperfect match between attitudes and behaviour (we can never tell for sure), but that politicians usually pay close attention to opinion surveys, and take them into account when framing policies. It would, therefore, push the argument way beyond its logical limits to conclude that attitude research is undermined by the claim that people may not always do what they say.

This does not detract from the main thrust of the argument presented here, although it makes us cautious about drawing firm conclusions. Therefore, we deliberately couch them in the classic negative form: we have found little evidence of a widespread taxpayers' revolt across Western Europe; we have found little evidence of a deep or sustained mood in favour of a fundamental reappraisal of the core principles of the welfare state across Western Europe; and we have found little conclusive evidence that voters want something for nothing. In this respect, the conclusions of this chapters are entirely consistent with those of other chapters in this volume, especially Chapters 4, 7, and 8. Equally, we have found little to suggest that taxes and public expenditures will not be the subject of fierce political battles to come, as they have been in past decades.

6

Politics, Economics, Class, and Taxation

KENNETH NEWTON AND MARIA A. CONFALONIERI

This chapter examines the economic, political, and social basis of mass support for, and opposition to, the tax regimes of Western Europe. It concentrates on the issue of progressive income tax and the related matter of income redistribution. Both progressive taxation and income redistribution are important principles of modern tax systems and their underlying goals of equality of opportunity. Taxes are often a central issue in modern election campaigns. Most citizens pay income taxes, and most have clear and often strong views about them. For these reasons, the issues of progressive income tax and income redistribution are important topics for political science research and well suited to surveys of mass opinion.

According to Listhaug and Miller (1985), there are two major theoretical models for explaining resistance to taxation. The first corresponds roughly to the rational choice or social choice model in which well-informed individuals calculate the economic costs and benefits of their tax system and act according to their own self-interest. In other words, the approach concentrates on economic explanations. The second model treats tax attitudes as the product of long-term ideological predispositions and core beliefs about society and its political values. In other words, it is mainly concerned with political explanations. To these we add a third model which concentrates less on purely economic or political factors, and more on variables such as class, education, and age. It revolves around sociological explanations. The three are not necessarily distinct in practice, of course, but the distinction is a useful way to start the theoretical analysis of mass attitudes towards taxation.

One of the best-developed examples of economic self-interest theories is developed by Alt (1983). He notes that taxation always involves redistribution and conflict, especially when progressive income taxes are used to fund redistributive social policies. Resistance to progressive income tax will vary according to average rates of taxation and to marginal rates of progressive income taxes. Where the average tax rates are comparatively low and the incidence of high marginal rates falls mainly on upper income groups, then middle and low income earners will tend to support progressive taxation on higher incomes. Thus, opposition to progressive taxation will tend to be pushed up the income distribution. But where the average tax share is high, and marginal tax rates on middle and low income earners is relatively high, the potential for resistance towards progressive taxation will be pushed down the income distribution. In short, at the individual level, Alt picks out income as a major determinant of attitudes towards tax levels, arguing that these attitudes will be the outcome of an interaction between income, average tax rates, and marginal rates of progressive taxation.

Offe (1987) also suggests an explanation of tax resistance which concentrates heavily on economic interests but differs from Alt's in some respects. He argues that opposition to high taxation will be concentrated in the highest and the lowest income groups. The former believe they pay a great deal and get little in return, while the latter believe that the benefits they get are no greater than the social security benefits they would get without making any contributions at all. Offe's hypothesis assumes that benefits are related directly to people's income while working, and that the system is funded by direct contributions. This is the case in most of Western Europe.

The third of the economic explanations involves distinguishing between the employed and the self-employed. While the self-employed are often wealthier than the employed, what is perhaps more important in determining their tax attitudes is that they fill out their own tax forms rather than having taxes deducted at source. As a result they may be acutely conscious of the size of their tax bills. In other words, income taxes may be more visible to the self-employed, who may suffer less from 'fiscal illusion' as a consequence (Pommerehne and Schneider 1978; cf. Downs 1959; Sorensen 1992).

Listhaug and Miller recommend turning attention to political values and attitudes rather than concentrating on economic calculations. Taxes are as much a matter of symbolic politics as of rational, utlility-maximizing self-interest. In their study of Norway, they find that attitudes towards tax cheating are closely tied up with political and religious values, as well as with confidence in government. They find a weaker connection with economic self-interest variables, such as income, and public or private sector employment. This, they say, is consistent with the conclusions reached by Sears *et al.* (1979, 1980), Citrin (1979), and Lowery and Sigelman (1981) in the United States, as well as Kristensen (1982) in Denmark.

Listhaug and Miller concentrate on the issue of tax cheating which is likely to be more of a moral and a symbolic issue than tax paying. It is not clear that attitudes towards progressive taxation and income redistribution will be as heavily political and symbolic. However, British research shows that support for public spending is more closely connected with attachments to political parties than with variables such as gender, class, age, housing tenure, type of employment, trade-union membership, or geographical region. Labour supporters favour the highest spending across a range of selected services, Conservative supporters the least, with Liberal and Social Democratic supporters somewhere in the middle (Lewis and Jackson 1985; see also Lewis 1980; Edgell and Duke 1982).

A third school of thought emphasizes social rather than either political or economic factors. According to Wilensky, reaction against the modern welfare state and its taxes comes primarily from the emerging middle mass of society. The changing economy of modern society creates new and growing social strata consisting of the upper working class—skilled workers and craftsmen—and the lower middle class of office workers, small entrepreneurs, lower level managers, and semi-professionals. Looking up the social scale, the middle mass sees the upper class, which it believes to be educated, liberal, living well, apparently paying little in taxes, and letting its children run riot at college. Looking down the social scale, the middle mass sees the poor whom it believes to be immoral, lazy, unemployed, unpatriotic, living off public assistance, and often outside the law. The middle mass sees itself as respectable, law abiding, and hard working, economically independent, and paying for the children of the rich to play at university, and the idle poor to live off welfare. The welfare state and its high taxes come to symbolize the grievances of the middle mass against society and government (Wilensky 1975: 116–19).

Wilensky suggests that strongest support for the welfare state and progressive taxation traditionally comes from a coalition of the liberal and educated middle and upper class and the organized working class. But it is increasingly difficult to maintain this coalition, because the liberal and educated groups in modern society are becoming more concerned with the 'quality of life' issues of post-industrial society, such as the environment, culture, education, participation, and job satisfaction. As their support for the materialist goals of the welfare state and its taxes weakens, so they become more sympathetic to the welfare backlash and tax protest. Thus, the coalition of the liberal, upper class and the organized working class falls apart, and the new middle mass emerges as a powerful anti-tax and anti-welfare force. In short, class is the main basis of public attitudes towards taxation.

Peltzman's (1980) analysis is similar but not identical to Wilensky's. Based on long-term historical analysis, he suggests that governments grow where two conditions are fulfilled: first, there must be groups which share a common interest in that growth; secondly, these groups must also perceive and be able to articulate their interests. It is not enough for groups to benefit from the growth of the welfare state. They must also see the benefits and be able to press their case. Education is crucial because it helps people to understand what is happening and to act effectively in the political arena. It is the growth of an educated middle class which has fuelled political pressures for increased income redistribution and equality. Peltzman argues the counter-intuitive conclusion that, 'on balance, more equality breeds a political demand for still more income equalization' (Peltzman 1980: 285).

According to Peltzman, the future may well be different from the past. With universal secondary education and the numbers of university students approaching saturation point, the twin forces of equality and education may well begin to lose their power. As they do so, the pressure for government growth and increased economic equality may begin to wane. Peltzman states that, although it would be imprudent to make precise predictions, there are signs of a slowing down of public pressure for government growth in those countries where education has expanded furthest, especially in the United States. For Peltzman, education seems to be the primary causal variable.

Both Peltzman and Wilensky agree that support for the modern welfare state may become weaker among the liberal and educated middle and upper classes. But Wilensky argues that it is the class interests of the middle mass which causes it to lead the tax revolt and welfare state backlash. Pelztman argues that it is not so much class interests as the educational saturation of modern society which is important. Education is also picked out as the crucial variable by Robinson and Bell (1978) in a comparative study of equality, success, and social justice in England and the United States. They argue that the most highly educated will be most familiar with the principles of enlightened Western civilization, and that one of the more important principles is a commitment to equality. Using education as a measure of enlightenment, they find a positive correlation between education and support for equality in England. In other words, Robinson and Bell, and Peltzman, agree about the importance of education in the past, but Peltzman argues that past trends may well be changing so as to bring about a change in tax attitudes among the better educated.

In some ways, Wilensky anticipates Inglehart's theory of postmaterialist value shift. Inglehart argues that material benefits in the Western world have declining marginal utility and that we have reached a point where non-material benefits have become more important for some key social groups. As a result, the educated, the rich, and the young who have been brought up amid the greatest affluence will increasingly turn to postmaterialist goals, such as culture, the arts, the environment, personal relations, equality, freedom, individualism, participation, and job satisfaction.

The implications of postmaterialist values for tax attitudes are ambivalent. On the one hand, taxes and income redistribution are classic material concerns, which postmaterialists might reject as irrelevant. On the other, affluent postmaterialists might attach relatively little importance to their own wealth and favour the redistribution of a portion of it. Self-centred postmaterialists might be inclined to reject progressive taxation on the grounds that lower income groups should not be concerned with material things. Other-directed postmaterialists might welcome progressive taxation because they believe in equality, freedom, and co-operation. Inglehart claims that postmaterialists favour income redistribution for 'the sake of human solidarity', but his own evidence shows they favour redistribution only slightly more than materialists (Inglehart 1990: 302). In short, Inglehart's own evidence does not strongly confirm either hypothesis.

Some Hypotheses

From our brief review of the literature, we can draw up some hypotheses about variations in support for, or opposition to, progressive income tax and income redistribution.

Rational choice and economic explanations suggest, first, that the strongest support for progressive income tax will come from those who benefit from it most, while the strongest opposition will come from those who benefit least. According to Alt, opposition will be concentrated mainly in upper income groups where average tax rates are low and marginal rates are high, and in upper and middle income groups where both average and marginal rates are high. According to Offe, opposition will come mainly from upper and lower income groups in countries where social security schemes are funded from social security payments and where payments are income related. Rational choice explanations also suggest, secondly, that the self-employed will be less inclined than employees to support income redistribution and progressive income taxes.

According to political and symbolic explanations, the strongest support for progressive income tax and the redistribution of wealth will come from people on the political left. Conversely, support will be at its weakest among people on the political right.

Three hypotheses can be derived from social explanations. First, that the middle mass of people in upper working-class and lower middle-class occupations will express the strongest opposition to progressive income taxes. The traditional working class will support the principle most strongly, and support amongst the educated and liberal upper classes will decline as post-industrial values gain strength (Wilensky). Secondly, support for progressive income taxes will be weakest among the educated in those countries where secondary education is universal and where higher education is reaching saturation (Peltzman). Thirdly, support for materialist goals, including progressive income tax and income redistribution, will be highest among the poorer, materialist sections of modern society. It may be either strong or weak among the more affluent and among postmaterialists (Inglehart).

Research Strategy

There are two main ways of approaching these research questions. The first, the macro-level approach, looks at variations in attitudes towards taxes in different countries and explains them in terms of national-level variables such as gross national product (GNP) per capita, the nature of tax regimes, or political traditions. For example, Wilensky suggests that visible taxes tend to generate tax revolts (Wilensky 1976), while Hibbs and Madsen argue that it is not the level of taxation so much as its composition (Hibbs and Madsen 1981). Rose stresses the importance of long-term developments in the tax regimes of different countries (Rose 1985), while Wilensky emphasizes the importance of forms of government and welfare built around left, Catholic, and corporatist traditions (Wilensky 1981). The second approach, using micro-level data, examines variations among individuals or subgroups within countries and tries to explain them in terms of individual properties of the kind already noted.

In principle, the two approaches are complementary. However, although a strong case can be made for concentrating on cross-national and comparative analysis, in practice the macro-level, comparative approach has delivered inconclusive results. This is because good comparative data are hard to come by. Mass attitudes towards taxation have been compared in a systematic manner in only a small handful of countries. As a result, there are more variables to control than cases to study. Time-series data are even more rare and cover only a short span of years. The ISSP surveys form the best time series, but they started only in 1985 and the most recent available survey is for 1990. Besides, the individual level data show that there are not great variations in attitudes towards taxation between countries (see Table 5.1). We cannot conclude from this that macro-level variables are not important, but confidence in the approach would be improved, and the actual analysis made easier, if the differences between countries were greater. But since most countries show roughly the same distribution of attitudes, and since it is possible to compare only a small number and limited variety of countries, the macro-level approach seems of limited use.

To illustrate the point, we review briefly our macro-level results. Our evidence tends to support the conclusion of Hibbs and Madsen (1980) that visible taxes tend to generate tax revolts, but we have only seven observations and the results are not statistically significant. Support for progressive income tax declines as the rate of marginal income tax increases (see Figure 6.1). As the scattergram shows, Italy, Germany, Britain, Norway, and the Netherlands all lie just below the regression line. Ireland and Austria are outliers, showing the strongest support for progressive income taxes but having relatively high marginal rates of tax. The correlation between the two variables, however, is 0.68, which is slightly below the 5 per cent threshold of significance. We could not find as strong a relationship between support for progressive income tax and tax visibility ($r = 0.19$).

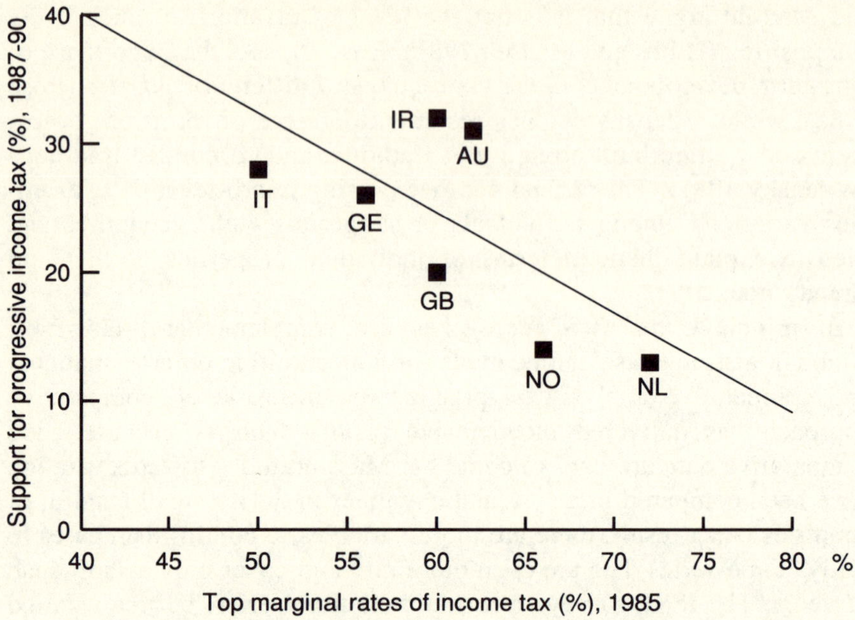

FIGURE 6.1 *Top marginal income tax rates and support for progressive income tax*

Sources: Messere (1993) for marginal income tax rates, 1985; ISSP (1987) for tax attitudes in Austria, Britain, Germany, Italy, and the Netherlands; ISSP (1990) for Ireland and Norway.

All our other attempts to find macro-level explanations for attitudinal differences were unsuccessful. Support for progressive income tax was plotted against equality of post-tax and transfer income, income tax levels of the average production worker, take home pay for the average production worker, and inequality in pre- and post-tax incomes, but with little success. In no case were there more than six countries available for observation, and for some purposes there were only four.

Given the inconclusive and negative nature of the results, we do not report them in detail here. Instead we draw the conclusion that, despite the powerful arguments for the macro-level, comparative approach, it is not satisfactory in practice, and will remain unsatisfactory until the quantity and quality of comparative data improves. The small number of cases available for this study, and others, probably explains the absence of clear and cumulative conclusions: there are too many variables and too few cases to allow firm conclusions to be drawn (Lijphart 1971).

Instead, we turn to micro-level analysis to examine variations between individuals in different countries. The analysis is largely based on ISSP surveys which are the main source of good, comparative data on this topic. *The Role of Government* surveys were carried out in 1985 and 1990, and the *Social Inequality* survey in 1987. Because a thousand or more people were interviewed in most countries, the studies provide a strong basis for statistical analysis.

Each of the ISSP surveys asked a question about support for tax progressiveness, as follows:

> Do you think that people with high incomes should pay a larger share of their income in taxes than those with low incomes, the same share, or a smaller share? [1987]

> Do you think that those with high incomes should pay a much larger proportion [of their earnings in tax], a larger proportion . . . a much smaller proportion? [1990]

The response options for both questions range from 'much larger' to 'much smaller', yielding a five-point scale. Responses to the first question were aggregated at the national level for Figure 6.1, but both questions are used for the individual-level analysis, partly to allow us to check for change or stability over time, and partly to check consistency of responses to different question wordings. The ISSP surveys also provide information about income, employed or self-employed status, political identification and voting behaviour, social class, education, and age. Unfortunately, they do not include any measure of materialism–postmaterialism, so, instead, we use age, class, and education as proxy variables.

Attitudes Towards Taxation

In Table 6.1, we present the results of a correlation analysis between tax attitudes and eight social, economic, and political variables. The picture it presents is clear: although quite a high proportion of the figures are statistically significant, they are generally quite low and of no great substantive significance. As the sample sizes in many countries are about a thousand, or well over in some cases, quite low correlations may be statistically significant but of small explanatory power. There is

TABLE 6.1. *Social, economic, and political correlates of resistance to progressive income tax in eight countries*

	Germany		Britain		Italy		Netherlands	Switzerland	Norway	Austria	Ireland
	1987	1990	1987	1990	1987	1990	1987	1987	1990	1990	1990
Income	0.14**	0.11**	0.12**	0.14**	0.14**	0.13**	0.09**	0.16**	0.13**	0.12**	0.11**
Self-employed	0.08*	0.06*	0.07*		0.11**		0.05*	0.06*			
Subjective class	−0.13**	−0.10**	−0.08*	—	−0.07*	−0.08*	−0.06*	−0.08*	−0.12**	−0.14**	−0.19**
Middle mass									0.12**		0.17**
Age					−0.11*	−0.06*		0.10*		0.10*	
Education					0.10**	0.09**				0.12**	
Postmaterialism						0.14**					0.22**
Party identification	0.21**	0.17**	0.30**	0.24**	—	—	0.23**	0.11*	0.27**		0.06*

$*p < 0.01$ $**p < 0.001$

Notes: Entries are Pearson's *r*. Only significant coefficients are shown. Income is divided into quintiles, 1 = bottom, 5 = top. Self-employed is a dummy variable, 1 = self-employed, 0 = employee. Subjective social class is a dummy variable, 1 = working, 0 = middle class (not asked in Britain in 1990). Age is divided into six groups, 1 = 18–25, thereafter at ten-year intervals until over 65 = 6. Education 0 = less than twelve years in school, 1 = twelve years or more. Party identification 1 = left, 2 = centre, 3 = right (not asked in Italy). Middle mass 1 = middle-class occupations, 0 = working- and upper-class occupations. Postmaterialism is computed as the sum of three dummy variables: 1 = age 18–35, 0 = older than 35; 1 = over twelve years of full-time schooling, 0 = less than twelve years; 1 = middle class, 0 = working class. Resistance to progressive tax is a Likert-type scale, 1 = 'people with high incomes should pay a much larger share of income in taxes', 5 = 'people with high incomes should pay a much smaller share'.

Sources: ISSP (1987, 1990).

a slight tendency for employment status, subjective social class, and income to be related to tax attitudes, but the associations are not particularly noteworthy. The correlations for Germany, Britain, and Italy, in both 1987 and 1990, are roughly of the same order of magnitude. This suggests that changes in question wording in the two surveys do not strongly affect the answers and that there are no great fluctuations in responses over a short period of time. To this extent we can place some reliance in the results, using them for cross-national and time-series analysis.

The strongest correlations in Table 6.1 relate to party identification. The correlations are significant in all countries except Austria and in the two countries for which we have data for both 1987 and 1990—Germany and Britain. These correlations are usually stronger than any of the other social and economic variables shown in Table 6.1. Politics seems to matter more than any social or economic variable in Germany, Britain, Norway, and the Netherlands. In Ireland and Switzerland, the correlations for party identification are statistically significant but substantively weaker. The correlations are insignificant only in Austria. To this extent the figures in Table 6.1 lend support to Listhaug and Miller's approach which suggests that tax attitudes are more closely associated with political orientations than economic or social circumstances.

While party identification stands out from a rather poor field of independent variables in Table 6.1, there is also a suggestion that it may be rather less important in Germany, Austria, and Switzerland than in Britain, Norway, and the Netherlands. This is consistent with the idea that class differences in attitudes towards the welfare state are less sharp in countries which have a Christian democratic tradition than in countries where the social democratic influence is stronger (Wilensky 1981).

However, Table 6.1 does not fully test the Alt versus Offe hypotheses about income. The former suggests a linear relationship between tax attitudes, the exact shape and distribution depending upon marginal and average income tax rates. The latter argues for a U-shaped curve in which opposition to taxes is concentrated among the upper and the lower income groups. These hypotheses are examined in Figure 6.2, using the 1987 data. The results are more in line with Alt's argument, in that they show a general tendency for support for progressive income tax to decline as income rises, and vice versa. The data for 1990 (not shown here) yield virtually exactly the same results.

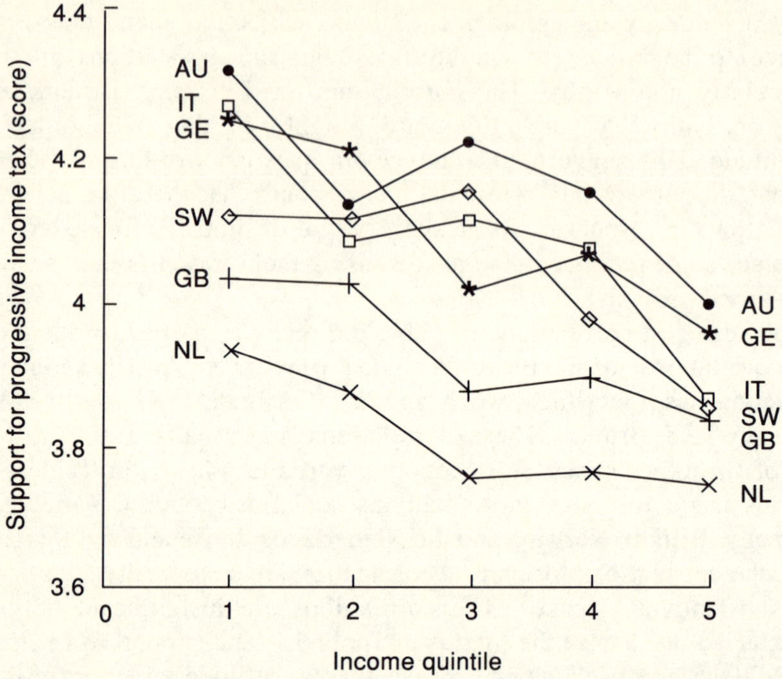

FIGURE 6.2. *Support for progressive income tax by income quintile, 1987*

Notes: On the horizontal axis, 5 = highest income quintile. The vertical axis shows the average score where 5 = those with high incomes should pay a much larger share of incomes in taxes, and 1 = those with high incomes should pay a much smaller share.

Source: ISSP (1987).

The countries covered in Table 6.1, based on ISSP data, may be extended to include Denmark, Sweden, and Norway using election survey data (see Table 6.2). The figures for Norway, which is the one country common to Tables 6.1 and 6.2, are of a similar size, suggesting that the results of the surveys are generally comparable. Once again, although they are usually significant at the 0.001 level, the correlations for income and employment status are not generally impressive. Party stands out by comparison for its relative strength.

Tax Protest and Tax Revolt

Finally, we return to the theme of the previous chapter which centred around the distinctions between tax fairness and tax justice, and between tax revolt and tax protest. Tax revolt is based on the view that the tax

TABLE 6.2. *Resistance to progressive income tax by income, employment status, and party in Denmark, Sweden, and Norway*

	Income	Self-employed	Conservative partisanship
Denmark			
1971	0.15**	0.10**	0.33**
1975	0.23**	0.14**	0.41**
1979	0.07**	0.16**	0.35**
1984	0.25**	0.16**	0.35**
Sweden			
1979	0.01	0.06*	0.37**
Norway			
1981	0.17**	0.14**	0.34**

*$p < 0.01$ **$p < 0.001$

Notes: Entries are Pearson's *r*. Dependent variables: *Denmark*: 'High incomes should be taxed more strongly than they are today' (1 = strongly agree; 5 = strongly disagree). *Norway*: 'I shall read you some proposals some think should be carried through in Norway. For each proposal indicate whether you think it's a good proposal which it is very important to carry through or a bad proposal and important that it should not be carried through: reduce taxes on higher incomes' (5 = very good proposal; 1 = very bad proposal). *Sweden*: 'We should reduce taxes on upper incomes' (6 = very good proposal; 1 = very bad proposal). Income: low = 1; middle = 2; high = 3. Self-employed status: employee = 1; self-employed = 2. Conservative partisanship: socialist = 1; conservative = 2.

Sources: national election surveys.

regime is fundamentally unfair and should be changed wholesale; tax protest is based upon the feeling that although basically fair, the system does not work as it is supposed to, and should be reformed. At the heart of the question of fairness in Western Europe, there lies the principle of using progressive income tax to achieve a degree of equality through the redistribution of incomes. The question of justice involves the extent to which tax regimes actually achieve these goals.

By dichotomizing the two variables 'justice' and 'fairness' and cross-classifying them (see Figure 5.1), we derived four types of tax attitudes:

(1) *Tax compliants* who believe the tax regime to be both fair and just.
(2) *Tax revolters* who believe it to be neither fair nor just.
(3) *Tax protesters* who believe it to be fair but unjust.
(4) *Tax formalists* who believe the tax regime to be unfair but just. This is largely a theoretical possibility.

We hypothesized that most dissatisfaction in Western Europe over the past few decades has taken the form of tax protest rather than tax revolt.

We are now in a position to test this hypothesis using ISSP data for three countries—Britain, Italy, and West Germany. The results are shown in Table 6.3. Clearly, tax protesters easily outnumber tax revolters in all three countries. Indeed, tax compliants also outnumber tax revolters in all three. As one might expect, tax formalism, which is more of a theoretical than a practical possibility, accounts for small, quite trivial proportions of the samples.

The figures in Table 6. 3 are consistent with the theoretical and empirical conclusions of the previous chapter: tax revolters form a comparatively small proportion of citizens, tax protesters a comparatively large proportion. While there is plenty of evidence of dissatisfaction with tax systems, this does not concern the basic issues of progressive income tax, income equality, and income redistribution. Rather, it concerns the failures of tax systems to achieve these goals. Most believe that the rich are taxed too little and the poor too much. Empirically, it is striking that Table 6.3 shows the same distribution of responses across the three countries. This confirms the general picture to be found in many other chapters in this volume which show a relatively high degree of consistency and cross-national uniformity of popular attitudes towards the scope of government and the welfare state.

TABLE 6.3. *Tax fairness and tax justice, 1985*

	Germany	Britain	Italy
Tax compliants	29	25	25
Tax protesters	60	51	61
Tax revolts	8	17	10
Tax formalists	3	7	4
N	864	1,208	1,456

Notes: Entries are percentages. Tax fairness is based on the question: 'Do you think that those with high incomes should pay (1) a much larger proportion, (2) a larger proportion, (3) the same proportion, (4) a smaller proportion, or (5) a much smaller proportion of their earnings in taxes? Those who answered (1) or (2) are classified as believing that the tax system is fair; those who answered (3), (4) or (5) as unfair. Tax justice is based on the question: 'Do you consider that the amount of income tax that your household has to pay is (1) much too high, (2) too high (3) about right (4) too low, or (5) much too low?' Those answering (1) or (2) are classified as believing that the tax system is unjust.

Source: ISSP (1985).

Conclusions

We started by suggesting that explanations of variations in attitudes towards taxation can be divided into those which are primarily economic, primarily social, or primarily political, while recognizing that most explanations mix all three, or assume both of the others. The different claims might be examined at either the macro-level of cross-national comparison or the micro-level of individual analysis, or both. In view of the limitations of the data, we decided to compare attitudes among individuals.

Our analysis suggests that there is weak evidence to support the social and economic models as explanations of mass attitudes towards taxation. Education, age, and employment status seems to have little impact. To this extent, we find rather little evidence to support theories of tax attitudes which dwell upon education. Similarly, there is little to confirm Wilensky's middle-mass hypothesis or Inglehart's claim that postmaterialists support income redistribution.

As we might expect, income is somewhat more closely associated with attitudes towards progressive income tax: the higher the income, the lower the support. If anything, the figures do not support Offe's suggestion of a U-shaped curve in which opposition to progressive taxation is concentrated in the highest and the lowest income groups. Rather, they are consistent with Alt's argument that opposition can be pushed up or down the income distribution according to average and marginal rates of income tax. However, it is not the strength of these tendencies but, rather, the comparative weakness of the association between tax attitudes and personal income which is notable.

Party identification has the strongest association of any of our eight independent variables, and even here the correlations reach only modest levels of strength. There is some indication that left and right party identification plays a rather larger role in countries with liberal-conservative political traditions than in those with Christian democratic traditions.

The evidence strongly supports the suggestion we made in the previous chapter that public opinion leans strongly towards tax protest rather than tax revolt. The great majority of people in Britain, Italy, and Germany accept the underlying goals of income redistribution, greater income equality, and progressive income tax. They do not believe that the tax regime in their country is achieving these goals; the poor are taxed too heavily, and the rich too lightly. As a result, the majority fall into the category of tax protesters. Fewer than one in ten in Italy and Germany are tax revolters, and only one in six in Britain.

Finally, we speculate about why political explanations seem to be more powerful than social or economic explanations, since this seems to be a finding which runs through the *Beliefs in Government* research programme. Tax is, ultimately, a political matter. It is also related to economic and social circumstances, but these must be mediated by political considerations before they can be translated into political attitudes and dispositions. To put it a different way: there is not a direct transposition from the social or the economic to the political, and it is not possible to 'read off' from the social or the economic to the political. On the contrary, it is necessary to place the social and the economic in a political context first. Even though economic considerations enter into tax regimes, tax attitudes are most closely associated with political and governmental factors, such as party identification, and social democracy or Christian democracy. It should not surprise us that tax attitudes are more closely associated with party identification than personal income. What should surprise us is that theorists should have tried to explain attitudes towards taxation primarily in social and economic terms. To change the words of Durkheim: when the political is reduced to the social or the economic, the explanation is likely to be wrong.

7

The Welfare State: The Equality Dimension

EDELTRAUD ROLLER

❖

One of the central questions concerning beliefs about the scope of government is whether trends in these beliefs can be described as expansionist or contractionist. This question has been formulated at a very general level to include all government activities and policies. However, most scholars suggesting the expansion or contraction of beliefs about government at this general level are thinking of those specific policies associated with the welfare state. Most of the specific theories about trends deal explicitly with the welfare state.

Theories suggesting an expansionist trend are usually couched in general terms. Typical of this type are theories of the crisis of legitimacy (Habermas 1973; Offe 1976) or ungovernability (Brittan 1975; King 1975; Douglas 1976). These theories were especially popular during the 1970s, but have never lost their attraction and survive in other forms (Rose 1984). They propose, in common, a general spiral of rising expectations directed towards the institutions of government; and when illustrating their hypotheses, point to economic and social policies (Brittan 1975: 108; Douglas 1976: 485–6; Habermas 1973: 42–54; King 1975: 287; Rose 1984: 182–214). Luhmann's (1990) explicit reference to the welfare state is an example of the second type of theory, suggesting a similar momentum in expectations about the welfare state resulting from the implementation of social rights. Theories anticipating a contractionist trend in beliefs about the scope of government often belong to this second type, suggesting a decline in expectations as a result of value change (OECD 1981: 78) or public debate about the crisis of the welfare state (Offe 1987; Ringen 1987). The popular hypothesis of a 'welfare backlash' (Wilensky 1975) among the middle mass is also of this type. So, too, is the hypothesis that the destruction of collectivities, which results in increasingly selfish orientations, might lead to a loss of support for the welfare state (Offe 1987).

These theories provide the frame of reference for the next two chapters which examine expectations about the welfare state in Western Europe. Our central question is whether these expectations are expanding or contracting. But in order to select appropriate indicators of expectations, we need to define the relevant dimensions of expectations and to define what we mean by the welfare state. Normally, such things would be defined in micro-analytic concepts of attitudes referring, in our case, to citizens' attitudes towards the welfare state. However, previous research on attitudes towards the welfare state, even the few comparative studies available (Coughlin 1980; Haller, Höllinger, and Raubal 1990; Shapiro and Young 1990), does not provide us with such a concept. Rather, researchers frequently, often indiscriminately, rely on questions containing stimulus objects which they regard as simply 'belonging' to the welfare state. One of the main reasons cited (Almond 1980: 27; Shapiro and Young 1990: 144) is that attitudes about the welfare state, along with attitudes about public policies in general, lack a well-defined research tradition.

We make good this lacuna by outlining, in the next section, an analytic concept of attitudes towards the welfare state. The concept was originally developed for a national study in Germany (Roller 1992), but analyses using comparative data demonstrated its utility for comparative studies also (Roller 1991). One of the main characteristics of the concept is that it relies on a definition of the welfare state drawn from macro-analytic research on the development of welfare states (Flora, Alber, and Kohl 1977; Flora and Heidenheimer 1981), in which the welfare state is defined as a set of policies aiming at socio-economic security and equality. That is, in contrast to previous analyses which distinguish between specific policies, such as social security, old age assistance, employment, medical care, and the like (Shapiro and Young 1990: 156–70; Coughlin 1980), we distinguish between policies according to the goal of socio-economic security and the goal of socio-economic equality. In this chapter, after the conceptual discussion, we concentrate on attitudes towards policies for socio-economic equality. Attitudes towards socio-economic security as a goal of the welfare state are examined in the following chapter.

An Analytic Concept

Our concept of attitudes towards the welfare state (Roller 1992), like comparable micro-analytic concepts (e.g. Almond and Verba 1963: 14–15), has two dimensions: the objects of an attitude and the modes of an attitude. According to widely accepted definitions of policies, the concept distinguishes between three objects of attitudes: the goals, the outputs (means or instruments), and the outcomes of policies (Almond and Powell *et al.* 1978: 15–16, 287). Since we are analysing expectations about government, our objects are the goals of policies—defined as the desirable conditions for which the government is responsible. Attitudes about goals are normative, which is why expectations about government can be located there.

Goals can be further differentiated along the dimensions of *range* and *degree*. As we noted in Chapter 3, range refers to the number of policy goals or policy areas for which the government is responsible. Indicators measuring this dimension ask whether the government, in principle, should be responsible for achieving a specific goal. The degree dimension refers to the intensity of government activity within a policy area, and is closely connected to the quality of policy outcomes. Indicators measuring this dimension ask for the preferred level of government activity within a policy area. It is assumed that attitudes about range are more fundamental than attitudes about degree (Roller 1992: 46). Thus, on the basis of this concept, we can suggest a distinction between the range and the degree of expectations. This analytic screen is applicable to all policies.

What, then, are the specific features of the welfare state? According to Flora and his colleagues (Flora, Alber, and Kohl 1977; Flora and Heidenheimer 1981), the welfare state is constituted in those policies which have as their goal socio-economic security and socio-economic equality. They arrive at these two goals by interpreting the welfare state as an answer to developmental problems emerging in the modernization process. First, the demand for socio-economic security followed from the industrialization process, which led to a loss of the security functions of the household. Secondly, the demand for socio-economic equality is a consequence of the democratization process with its stress on political equality; effective political equality can be realized only under the condition of socio-economic equality (Marshall 1964).

From this general framework, it follows that all specific policies referring to these twin goals should be analysed as matters relating to the welfare state. Such policies are security of income, health, housing, job security, education, the reduction of differences between the rich and the poor (Flora, Alber, and Kohl 1977: 725–6; Zapf 1986: 389–91). At the same time, however, a distinction between two kinds of policies is suggested. On the one hand, there are policies like pensions which aim primarily at socio-economic security. On the other hand, policies like the redistribution of income aim primarily at socio-economic equality. Because of the ambiguous character of 'equality' in Western societies (cf. Lane 1986), we suggest that policies designed to achieve socio-economic security win more support than policies designed to achieve socio-economic equality.

There are two further distinctions to make. Since equality has different meanings (Bell 1979), Flora *et al.* (Flora, Alber, and Kohl 1977: 722–3; Flora and Heidenheimer 1981*b*: 24–5) distinguish between equality of result and equality of opportunity. They also suggest, moreover, an additional distinction in order to differentiate between policies aiming at the provision of national minima and redistribution in a more strict sense. Establishing national minima, for instance, is the goal of poor relief, a minimum wage, national pensions, compulsory education, and certain social services, whereas progressive taxation is an example of redistribution in the stricter sense. By contrast, comprehensive secondary education, for example, is an attempt to realize equality of opportunity. The main difference between equality of result and equality of opportunity is that equality of opportunity is compatible with social inequality but equality of result is not. Based on the work of Flora *et al.* (Flora, Alber, and Kohl 1977: 723), it can be assumed that policies aiming at equality of opportunity enjoy higher support than policies aiming at equality of result.

Our analytic concept, then, implies hypotheses about the relationship of attitudes to different objects. But bear in mind that the range dimension of beliefs about the scope of government is assumed to be more fundamental than the degree dimension, which implies that beliefs about the degree of government activity are more susceptible to fluctuations in specific situations. Keep in mind, too, that policies aiming at socio-economic security are likely to enjoy more support than policies aiming at socio-economic equality; so also are policies aiming at equality of opportunity rather than equality of result. A summary of the objects of the attitudes to be measured by our indicators is set out in Table 7.1.

As to types of attitudes, our analytic approach also distinguishes

TABLE 7.1. *Types of relevant indicators*

	Range	Degree
Socio-economic security	(*a*) It should be or should not be the government's responsibility to provide health care for the sick.	(*a*) More or less government spending for old age pensions.
Socio-economic equality		
Equality of opportunity	(*b*) The government should provide more chances for children from poor families to go to university.	(*c*) The government should increase or reduce spending for schooling of very young children from poor families even before they reach the usual school age.
Equality of result		
National minima	(*b*) The government should provide everyone with a guaranteed basic income.	The government should increase or reduce the level of guaranteed basic income.
Redistribution	(*a*) The government should reduce the differences in income between people with high incomes and those with low incomes.	Taxes on those with high incomes should be increased or reduced.

Note: Items (*a*) and (*b*) are from ISSP (1985 and 1987), respectively; item (*c*) is from Free and Cantril (1967: 12).

between interest orientation and value orientation (Roller 1992: 48–54). This distinction has been suggested in several studies of attitudes towards the welfare state (Whiteley 1981: 465–6; Taylor-Gooby 1983*b*: 175; Pöntinen and Uusitalo 1986: 7; Haller, Höllinger, and Raubal 1990: 23)—although using different, and not very precisely defined, terms. Following the work by Sears *et al.* (1980) on self-interest and symbolic politics, we can define these two types of attitudes. Interest orientation is an instrumental orientation referring to the attainment of material needs for oneself, and is short term in character. Value orientation refers to long-term fundamental predispositions of a universal moral character which have been acquired through socialization. Thus, support for the welfare state can be based on an instrumental orientation because it satisfies personal material needs, such as security in the case of ill health, or it can be based on a moral orientation because it creates social justice by, for example, reducing the differences between the rich and the poor. It is assumed that value or moral orientations are more important for the long-term functioning of the welfare state than an interest or instrumental orientation, because interest orientations are more susceptible to change (Roller 1992: 52).[1]

The conceptual distinctions we have drawn allow us to divide our examination of attitudes towards the welfare state into two parts: beliefs about policies aiming primarily at socio-economic security, and beliefs about policies aiming primarily at socio-economic equality. As we noted earlier, this distinction diverges from previous approaches. Thus, with this help from analytic tools developed in policy research, we can see that the distinction between social security and old-age assistance, employment, redistribution and the like, which is drawn by Shapiro and Young (1990), is settled at different analytical levels. For example, whereas 'old-age assistance' refers to an instrument or a programme, 'redistribution' refers to a goal, and 'employment' to a domain of life.

In this context our main difficulty with previous research is that it lacks clear analytic criteria, which leads to doubts about the conceptual or empirical usefulness of the results. A possible alternative to our distinction according to types of goals might be a distinction based on instruments (cf. Coughlin 1980). However, one of the major findings of macro-level research on the welfare state is that national welfare states use different policy instruments, or programmes, to secure similar goals. Thus, focusing on programmes is not appropriate for a comparative study. The advantage of our approach, with its more abstract level of differentiation, is that the fundamental goals identified by Flora *et al.* are conceptually tied to major developmental processes. Thus they have a theoretical rationale. Moreover, macro-level research demonstrates that the distinction based on goals is empirically fruitful in describing various welfare policies and welfare states.[2] Furthermore, by taking into account the findings of value research on support for security and different types of equality, the distinction according to goals implies hypotheses about levels of support for welfare state policies.

One problem with our approach, however, is that specific policies are seldom aimed exclusively at only one goal. They often aim to achieve socio-economic security and, at the same time, socio-economic equality. Pension programmes, for example, aim at socio-economic security by setting a national minimum. We resolve this problem by classifying specific policies according to their primary goal.

We now turn to focus on the main purpose of this chapter, which is to examine support for policies to secure socio-economic equality. Our parallel concern with support for policies to achieve socio-economic security is discussed by Per Arnt Pettersen in the next chapter.

Hypotheses and Data

We have pointed to the central position of the welfare state in theories relating to the development of beliefs about the scope of government. However, in applying the distinction between socio-economic security and socio-economic equality policies, we find that most of these theories concentrate on social benefits and social services; that is, socio-economic security policies. However, there are some theories which deal with questions about equality. First, there is Wilensky's (1975: 117) hypothesis about the welfare backlash of the 'middle mass'—the upper working class and the lower middle class. According to this hypothesis, members of the middle mass are dissatisfied with the redistributive effects of taxation because they consider themselves to be the financiers of poverty, a situation from which they have happily escaped. This hypothesis suggests declining support for socio-economic equality policies. We can derive, secondly, a contrary development from Luhmann (1990: 42) who points out that both goals of the welfare state—security and equality—are open principles which only provide guidelines for government activity. The implementation of these principles starts up a continuous process of identifying new inequalities which have to be compensated for by the government. Consequently, expectations about government activity with respect to socio-economic security and equality increase automatically.

In addition to these specific hypotheses, there is at least one more general theory from which we can deduce hypotheses relating to the development of beliefs about socio-economic equality policies. This is the theory of value change in Western democracies, especially Inglehart's (1977) arguments about the political consequences of value change. According to Inglehart, materialist goals have declined in importance since the late 1960s while postmaterialist goals have become more important. In general, socio-economic equality policies cannot be assigned to either materialist or postmaterialist goals. Some policies, such as the redistribution of income, have been identified as embodying materialist goals (Inglehart 1984: 25), while others, for example women's equality and the equal treatment of minorities, are considered to reflect postmaterialist goals (Baker, Dalton, and Hildebrandt 1981: 141). If value change theory is correct, expectations about materialist equality policies such as redistribution should decline while, at the same time, expectations about postmaterialist equality policies—what adherents of value change theory call 'new' equality policies (Baker, Dalton, and Hildebrandt 1981: 136–59)—should increase.

However, there are plausible grounds for suggesting a different development. The 'old' and 'new' equality policies are closely related to each other, even among mass publics (Farah, Barnes, and Heunks 1979: 416). Furthermore, according to some commentators, the political actors of the postmaterialist left have picked up the 'old' materialist goals of socio-economic equality and integrated them into their thinking (Goodin 1992: 197). Therefore, as a consequence of postmaterialist value change, we might assume an expansion of expectations about all socio-economic equality policies.

In a nutshell, although socio-economic equality policies have not been central in the debate about attitudes towards the welfare state, there are some hypotheses which can guide the analyses of beliefs about socio-economic equality policies. These hypotheses arrive at contradictory predictions, some stating that expectations about socio-economic equality policies are increasing, while others posit that expectations are declining. Even so, they have in common the suggestion of a continuous trend in one direction or another.

The course of development in beliefs about the scope of government in Western Europe is central to our study. However, the data situation presents some difficulties; in particular, there are few comparable studies measuring expectations about socio-economic equality. The first Political Action study (Barnes, Kaase, *et al.* 1979) includes two items referring to equality policies, but they were not replicated in the 1980 follow-up study (Jennings, Van Deth, *et al.* 1989). Likewise, three Eurobarometer surveys—Nos. 11 (1979), 16 (1981), and 19 (1983)—include only one item on the redistribution of income. The only exception to this patchy record is the International Social Survey Programme (ISSP), which conducted a comprehensive study on social inequality in the 1987 survey (Alwin *et al.* 1990). Additionally, the 1985 and 1990 ISSP studies, focusing on the role of government, included some items on socio-economic equality. Thus the data record restricts our opportunities for longitudinal analysis.

The data situation is also responsible for another limitation. Earlier, we distinguished between beliefs referring to the *range* of government activity and beliefs referring to the *degree* of government activity. However, the available indicators ask only about government responsibility for socio-economic security; that is, they measure the range dimension. There are no questions asking about the degree of government activity in this area. Hence, our analysis is restricted to the range of beliefs about socio-economic equality policies.

Support for Socio-Economic Equality Policies

According to our approach, support for socio-economic equality policies should differ according to the type of policy. Policies aiming at equality of opportunity should show higher support than policies aiming at equality of result. But we have not yet specified what we expect of the two aspects of equality of result—that is, policies of national minima and redistribution. According to Flora *et al.* (Flora, Alber, and Kohl 1977; Flora and Heidenheimer 1981), policies for redistribution have more radical consequences than national minima because they aim at overall equalization, whereas national minima are confined to equalizing minimal starting points. Hence, we anticipate that support for redistribution policies is lower than support for national minima policies.

Before looking at the data, we should clarify the relationship between support and expectations. Up to now we have used the terms almost interchangeably, but there are significant differences. Support is defined 'as an attitude by which a person orients himself to an object either favourably or unfavourably, positively, or negatively' (Easton 1975: 436). Thus support is a very general notion. Expectations, however, are more specific: they take the form of statements that an action should or should not be undertaken by someone who is responsible for it. An expectation in the sense that an actor should do something can be interpreted as support for the fact that an appropriate actor performs a certain kind of action. Expectations about government action in the field of socio-economic equality are therefore a specific expression of support for the welfare state. There are other aspects to support, for example satisfaction with the performance of the welfare state (Roller 1992: 38–

54). But we are examining beliefs about the scope of government, thus we are interested only in expectations as a specific feature of support.

The 1987 ISSP survey covered six West European countries—Austria, Britain, Germany, the Netherlands, Switzerland, and Italy—and includes questions asking respondents whether they agree or disagree with government responsibility for various socio-economic equality policies. Equality of opportunity is measured by the item 'providing more chances for children from poor families to go to university'. Equality of result referring to national minima is measured by 'providing a job for everyone who wants one' and 'providing everyone with a guaranteed basic income'. Equality of result referring to redistribution is measured by 'reducing the differences in income between people with high incomes and those with low incomes', and whether 'people with high incomes should pay a larger proportion of their earnings in taxes than those who earn low incomes'. Assigning the item 'providing a job for everyone' to equality of result and not to equality of opportunity deserves an additional comment. According to Bell (1979: 263), the decisive difference between equality of result and equality of opportunity is that the second refers to 'equality of access to the means of securing unequal outcomes'. For example, there are no restrictions on access to means such as public positions, participation in the market, or education. Equality of result, however, refers to equal outcomes such as income, status, and authority (Bell 1979: 264). At first glance, a job can be regarded as a means of bringing about unequal outcomes, such as income differences. But providing everyone with a job does not mean equal access to the means which characterize equality of opportunity. Instead, it signifies an equal distribution of a minimum level of means. Therefore, we assigned providing a job to the national minima aspect of equality of result.

The distribution of expectations about socio-economic equality policies, shown in Table 7.2, reveal that they enjoy strong support. With the exception of two policies in Switzerland, 50 per cent and more of respondents agree that the government should engage in these policies. Several values are above 80 per cent. However, distinguishing between types of policies, support for equality of opportunity policies is higher, on average, than support for equality of result policies. But the difference is not uniform. There is relatively weak support, across these countries as a whole, for guaranteeing national minima in the form of a guaranteed basic income (56 per cent) and for redistribution by reducing income differences (66 per cent). But support for the other two

TABLE 7.2. *Support for different socio-economic equality policies, 1987*

Dimension	Item	AU	GB	GE	NL	SW	IT	Average
Equality of opportunity	The government should provide more chances for children from poor families to go to university	80	84	87	85	81	90	85
Equality of result								
National minima	The government should provide a job for everyone who wants one	80	59	77	75	50	82	71
	The government should provide everyone with a guaranteed basic income	57	61	56	50	43	67	56
Redistribution	The government should reduce the differences in income between people with high incomes and those with low incomes	81	64	61	65	43	82	66
	People with high incomes should pay a larger proportion of their earnings in taxes than those with low incomes	86	77	80	73	82	79	80
Means index		77	65	71	66	51	83	69
N		972	1,212	1,397	1,638	987	1,027	

Notes: Entries for 'The government should . . . ' items are percentages of respondents who agree strongly or agree. Entries for the second-taxes item are percentages of respondents who say much larger proportion or larger proportion.

Source: ISSP (1987).

policies—providing national minima in terms of a job (71 per cent) and redistribution by progressive taxation (80 per cent)—is almost as strong as support for an equality of opportunity policy (85 per cent). But this general pattern does not prevail in each of the six countries. There is particularly strong support for reducing income differences and providing everyone with a job in Austria and Italy but much weaker support for these policies in Switzerland and, in some measure, in Britain.

Thus the picture is not as clear as we expected. Certainly, the equality of opportunity policy is strongly supported, but the redistribution policies do not lack support. Instead, it is the national minima policy of a guaranteed basic income which gets the weakest support in all countries. However, the fact that the data do not confirm our hypothesis—that redistribution policies enjoy less support than national minima policies—should not be overemphasized. This unexpected result could be due to the moderate terms of the redistribution item, as we know from other research that there is weak support for radical proposals to reduce income differences (Verba *et al.* 1987: 99). We can conclude that redistribution policies enjoy support insofar as they do not mean equalizing results but only some narrowing of inequalities.

A second important finding is the variation in support for different policies which belong to the same type of policy. This is especially true in the case of national minima: support for a guaranteed income is weaker than support for a guaranteed job. This suggests that people differentiate between the type of goods being distributed, giving less support to the distribution of financial rather than non-financial benefits. Support for socio-economic equality policies, then, not only depends on the type of equality being aimed at, but also on the type of goods being distributed. We come back to this point later.

Cross-National Differences

We have noted nation-specific differences in support for socio-economic equality policies. To point up the differences, a summary index based on mean levels of suppport was computed covering all five policies included in the 1987 ISSP data.[3] The values of the means were rounded according to the four original response categories. This index, shown in the bottom row of Table 7.2, reveals some variation between the six countries. Italy displays the strongest support for these socio-economic equality policies (83 per cent), followed by Austria (77 per cent), Germany (71 per cent), the Netherlands (66 per cent), and Britain (65 per cent). Support is weakest, and notably weaker, in Switzerland (51 per cent).

Several explanations for these cross-national differences can be derived from the literature. Following Inglehart (1990: 248–57), for example, we can suggest that the differences are a consequence of diminishing marginal utility, or, as he puts it, 'as a society moves closer to an equal income distribution, the political base of support for further redistribution becomes narrower' (Inglehart 1990: 252). Arguing that economic development goes together with a reduction in economic deprivation, he identifies economic development as the independent variable, using the gross domestic product (GDP) per capita as the indicator of development levels. Haller, Höllinger, and Raubal (1990: 34), in trying to explain national differences in support for the role of the government in general, also refer to levels of national prosperity as a central determinant. They argue that people in economically less advanced countries compare their standard of living with those of prosperous countries; since they think the government can directly influence economic development, they are more supportive of government intervention than people in the prosperous countries. Although the specifics of these arguments differ, both assume that standards of living have an effect on national levels of support for socio-economic policies. Haller, Höllinger, and Raubal (1990: 35–7) also refer to cultural and political variables as determinants. But these additional variables produce little significant variation between the countries studied here, so they seem to be fairly unimportant. Moreover, variations in standards of living seem to be the most popular explanation for national differences in support for the socio-economic equality policies of governments.[4]

Drawing on these arguments, we explore whether national differences in support for socio-economic equality policies are determined by different standards of living. Obviously, in this respect, the relevant indicator is the degree of socio-economic equality within a country. But there are also good reasons for taking account of the wealth of a country. Inglehart (1990: 250) argues that the reduction of inequality goes along with growing wealth. Another argument can be derived from research specifically on social inequality. Here, scholars such as Beck (1992) try to explain the growing irrelevance of inequality in public debate by arguing that sensitivity about inequality declines with the growing wealth of a country.

The most widely used indicator of socio-economic equality is the Gini index, relating the number of wage earners to income share, which yields a measure of the equality of incomes. Unfortunately, there are problems with the data for this index. The published data (see Lane, McKay, and Newton 1991: 22) do not cover all the countries we are examining. Moreover, comparisons between countries are made more difficult by variations in the time points and the measurement concepts (O'Higgins, Schmaus, and Stephenson 1989: 20). Faced with this situation, we used the Gini index calculated by Bornischer in 1978 which covers most of our countries (see Lane *et al.* 1991: 22). This index measures, principally, the equality of the pre-tax distribution of incomes in the late 1960s.[5] The other determinant—the wealth of a country—was measured using 1985 GDP per capita in US dollars from the OECD National Accounts (Lane *et al.* 1991: 48).

In Table 7.3, we show the rank order of several West European countries according to levels of support for socio-economic equality policies, the Bornischer Gini index, and GDP per capita. Looking at the first two columns, there is clearly little agreement between the rankings for levels of support and the Gini index. We would expect to see the lowest levels of support in countries with the highest level of income equality. This is not the case. However, looking at the first and third columns, the expected relationship does seem to exist for GDP per capita. Italy, the country with the highest level of support for socio-economic equality policies, has the lowest GDP per capita, while Switzerland, which shows the weakest support for socio-economic equality policies, has the highest GDP per capita. Even so, this pattern is clear only for the extreme cases; there is no obvious structure to the relationship in the other four countries.

A more systematic analysis of these relationships using regression analysis confirms these impressions. The relationship between the Gini index and support for socio-economic equality policies is not significant, but the relationship between GDP and levels of support, shown in Figure 7.1, is significant. The adjusted R^2 is 0.57, which is significant at the 5 per cent level. Thus, in the six West European countries covered by the 1987 ISSP study, the wealth of a nation is more relevant than standards of living as a determinant of beliefs about socio-economic equality policies.[6]

To check whether the results based on the 1987 ISSP data are of a general character, we also analysed the data from the three Eurobarometer surveys. These were carried out earlier, between 1979 and 1983, in

TABLE 7.3. *Support for socio-economic equality policies by equality of income and national wealth*

	Percentage of respondents agreeing with socio-economic equality policies		Gini index (Bornischer)		GDP per capita	
	1987				1985	
Switzerland	51	(6)	0.401	(6)	16,642	(1)
Britain	65	(5)	0.346	(1)	10,337	(5)
Netherlands	66	(4)	0.393	(4)	12,249	(3)
Germany	71	(3)	0.392	(3)	14,198	(2)
Austria	77	(2)	0.369	(2)	10,936	(4)
Italy	83	(1)	0.397	(5)	8,647	(6)
	1979–83				1980	
Denmark	71	(10)	0.365	(2)	12,941	(2)
Britain	72	(9)	0.346	(1)	9,495	(7)
Netherlands	77	(8)	0.393	(4)	11,970	(6)
Germany	80	(7)	0.392	(3)	13,216	(1)
Luxembourg	83	(6)	—		12,489	(3)
Belgium	87	(5)	—		11,985	(5)
Italy	88	(4)	0.397	(6)	8,081	(8)
Ireland	90	(3)	—		5,656	(9)
France	93	(2)	0.421	(7)	12,335	(4)
Greece	95	(1)	0.394	(5)	4,164	(10)
	1973–6				1975	
Britain	52	(7)	0.346	(1)	8,763	(5)
Finland	58	(6)	0.463	(7)	9,455	(4)
Austria	68	(5)	0.369	(2)	8,573	(6)
Germany	71	(4)	0.392	(3)	11,165	(2)
Italy	72	(3)	0.397	(5)	6,809	(7)
Switzerland	75	(2)	0.401	(6)	14,600	(1)
Netherlands	81	(1)	0.393	(4)	10,893	(3)

Notes: The Gini index is from Lane, McKay, and Newton (1991: 22). It ranges from 0 to 1, with 0 being maximum equality and 1 maximum inequality. In most cases the data used are for the late 1960s. GDP per capita is from Lane, McKay, and Newton (1991: 48). The 1987 data are based on support for different socio-economic equality policies; see Table 7.2, means index. The 1979–83 and 1973–76 data are based on support for redistribution of income. In the Eurobarometer data, *N* is approximately 1,000 for each country but about 300 for Luxembourg. In the Political Action data, *N* varies between 1,201 (Netherlands) and 2,307 (Germany). For the ISSP data , see Table 7.2. Respondents are 18 years and older. Weighted data.

Sources: ISSP (1987); Eurobarometer, Nos. 11, 16, and 19; Political Action (1973–6).

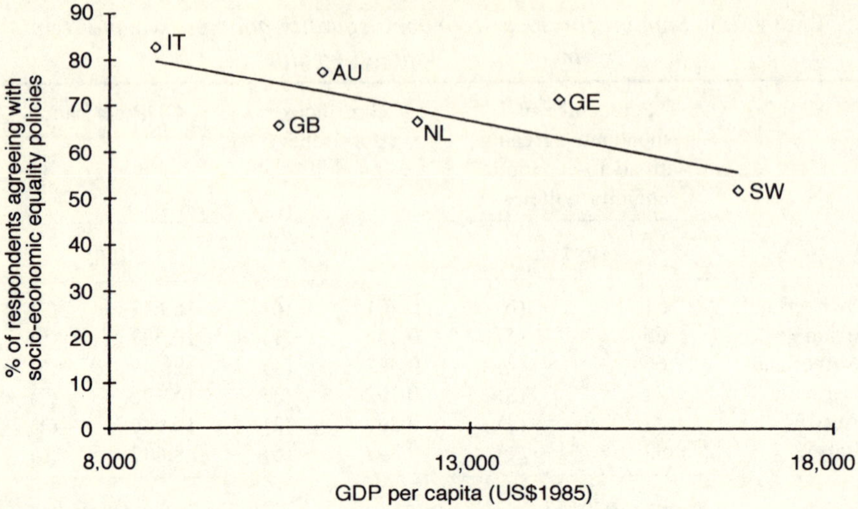

FIGURE 7.1. *Support for socio-economic equality policies by national wealth, 1987*

Source: ISSP (1987).

ten West European countries. In this instance, the indicator of socio-economic equality policies is the redistribution of income, which we measured using a means index and including all three time points (1979, 1981, 1983) for each country. The results are shown in the second part of Table 7.3. Comparing the rankings for levels of support and the Gini index—our measure of income equality—we find that the countries with the lowest levels of inequality show the lowest levels of support for the redistribution of income (Denmark, Britain), while the countries with the highest levels of inequality show the highest levels of support (Italy, France, Greece). However, no such systematic relation exists for GDP per capita.

Again, these impressions are confirmed by the results of a regression analysis. The relationship between support for income redistribution and GDP per capita was not significant, but, as shown in Figure 7.2, the relationship with the Gini index is significant. The adjusted R^2 is about 0.57, which is significant at the 5 per cent level. This finding supports the hypothesis about a relationship between standards of living and support for socio-economic equality policies. In this case, however, the relationships rest on the distribution of income, not the wealth of a country.

Data from the Political Action study, conducted even earlier in the 1970s, also allow us to test the relationship between standards of living

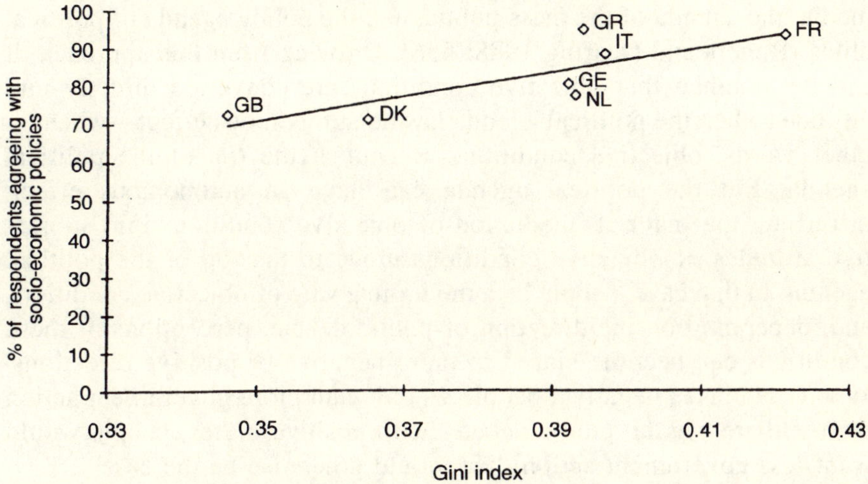

FIGURE 7.2. *Support for socio-economic equality policies by equality of income, 1979–83*

Sources: Eurobarometer, Nos. 11, 16, and 19.

and beliefs about socio-economic equality. The results, shown in the last section of Table 7.3, clearly refute the hypothesis that standards of living are determinants of beliefs about socio-economic equality policies. The rank orderings for both the Gini index and GDP per capita indicate that no relationship exists between support for socio-economic policies and either the distribution of income or levels of national wealth. To sum up: in the mid-1970s, in Western Europe, there was no clear relationship between national standards of living and support for socio-economic equality; in the 1980s, some systematic relationship did exist. How can this change be explained?

The undeclared premiss of our hypothesis—that standards of living influence levels of support for socio-economic equality policies—is that there is a direct translation of objective conditions into (subjective) attitudes. This is a simple model which leaves out any intervening variables that might mediate or 'disturb' this process. According to models of political communication (McQuail and Windahl 1981), public debate is an important intervening variable which can have autonomous effects on attitudes among mass publics. Public debate can be analysed with the help of the concept of political agenda, defined 'as issues or events that are viewed at a point in time as ranked in a hierarchy of importance', and which includes the agenda in the media, the agenda of the mass public, and the policy agenda of political élites (Rogers and Dearing 1988: 556). Drawing from this approach, it can be assumed that objective conditions are converted directly into attitudes when the political agenda has no autonomous effect—when, in other words, objective conditions are not at the top of the political agenda. But the political agenda can have an autonomous effect, disturbing the 'natural' mediation of objective conditions into subjective attitudes, if objective conditions move to the top of the political agenda. In that case, people become more aware of objective conditions and, depending on the direction of public debate, perceptions of these conditions can become biased in more negative or positive directions. When the bias is negative, people would want more government action than if there was no public debate; with positive biases, people would want less government action than would otherwise be the case.

Following this more complex model, the central question is whether socio-economic equality had been on the political agenda in the 1970s but disappeared in the 1980s. Research on inequality (Beck 1992) has demonstrated just this pattern: socio-economic equality had been at the top of the political agenda in the 1970s as a result of the wave of political protest starting in the 1960s but the issue faded away in the 1980s. Indeed, our data give some hints on this changing political agenda. As we can see from Table 7.3, those countries which show strong support for income redistribution in the early 1970s, such as the Netherlands and Switzerland, tend to show weak support later on in 1979–83 and 1987. However, Austria, for example, shows lower support in 1973–6 and higher support in 1979–83 and 1987. From the 'political agenda' perspective, the direct link between standards of living and support for socio-economic equality policies is missing in the mid-1970s because socio-economic equality had been a popular issue in political debate. This link was re-established in the 1980s when socio-economic equality disappeared from the political agenda. Thus, based on concepts drawn from political communication research, we can offer a plausible explanation for the contradictory results of our analysis of the relationship between standards of living and support for socio-economic policies. Unfortunately, we are not in a position to verify the explanation empirically.

Development of Support

What about developments in support for socio-economic equality policies during the 1970s through to the 1990s? Due to the data problems we noted earlier, we can only give some hints about the late 1970s and the 1980s. We can examine support for the redistribution of income in the late 1970s and early 1980s based on the three Eurobarometer studies. The ISSP data allow us to look at the developments in beliefs about three policies aiming at equality of result during the second half of the 1980s. However, given the differing composition of the studies, the ISSP data are available only for Britain, Germany, Italy, and Austria. The data are presented in Table 7.4.

The Eurobarometer data on support for income redistribution indicate a decline between 1979 and 1983, except in Britain and Germany. But this decline, averaging some 5 percentage points, follows no general linear trend. In Denmark, Belgium, Germany, and Ireland an initial fall between 1979 and 1981 is followed by a minor recovery between 1981 and 1983. In Britain, support levels remain stable between 1979 and 1981, but they increase rather sharply in 1983. Although the ISSP data for the later 1980s include questions about the redistribution of income, the indicators in the Eurobarometer and the ISSP studies cannot be compared directly. However, between 1985 and 1987, we can see an upward trend, averaging some 11 percentage points in support for narrowing income differences. But between 1987 and 1990 the trend moves downwards again by an average of some 8 percentage points. The general impression on the issue of redistribution, then, is that there was no general trend in the 1980s. There are fluctuations up and down, but varying within a restricted range.

Besides the distribution of income, the ISSP studies include two policy items relating to equality of result: progressive taxation,[7] which belongs to the redistributive aspect; and providing a job for everyone seeking work, which belongs with the provision of national minima. As we can see from Table 7.4, support for progressive taxation declined in Germany and Italy between 1985 and 1987, but increased again between 1987 and 1990. In Britain, however, support levels stayed almost steady between 1985 and 1987, but then rose fairly sharply in 1990. In the case of national minima for jobs, only the data for 1985 and 1990 are strictly comparable. They show a decline in support between 1985 and 1990, and some indications of recovery in 1990.

To sum up: the available longitudinal data on beliefs about socio-

TABLE 7.4. *Development of support for different socio-economic equality policies: eleven countries*

Dimension/item	DK	AU	BE	GB	GE	IR	LU	NL	FR	IT	GR	Average
EQUALITY OF RESULT: NATIONAL MINIMA												
Provide a job for everyone												
1985[a]	—	84	—	72	82	—	—	—	—	89	—	81
1987[b]	—	80	—	59	77	—	—	—	—	82	—	73
1990[a]	—	—	—	63	74	—	—	—	—	85	—	74
EQUALITY OF RESULT: REDISTRIBUTION												
Reduction of differences in income												
1979[c]	78	—	89	70	81	93	93	79	96	94	—	86
1981[c]	66	—	86	70	78	88	79	78	93	85	95	80
1983[c]	68	—	87	77	82	89	78	74	89	85	95	81
1985[d]	—	66	—	52	56	—	—	—	—	67	—	58
1987[d]	—	81	—	64	61	—	—	—	—	82	—	69
1990[d]	—	—	—	57	57	—	—	—	—	70	—	61
Progressive taxation												
1985[e]	—	—	—	76	90	—	—	—	—	86	—	84
1987[e]	—	—	—	77	80	—	—	—	—	79	—	79
1990[e]	—	—	—	85	87	—	—	—	—	84	—	85

Notes: Entries are percentages. The average includes only countries for which complete longitudinal data are available. The items are: [a] 'The government definitely or probably should provide a job for everyone who wants one'; [b] 'Agree strongly or agree that the government should provide a job for everyone who wants one'; [c] 'Agree strongly or agree that greater efforts should be made to reduce inequality in income'; [d] 'Agree strongly or agree that the government has the responsibility to reduce the differences in income between people with high incomes and low incomes'; [e] 'People with high incomes should pay a much larger proportion or larger proportion of their earnings in taxes than those who earn low incomes'. Respondents are 18 years and older. Weighted data.

Sources: Eurobarometer, Nos. 11, 16, and 19; ISSP (1985, 1987, 1990).

economic equality show no pattern of continuously increasing or declining levels of support. This applies to socio-economic equality policies as a whole and to specific types of equality policies. Thus, theories predicting a continuous trend, whether of increasing or declining support for socio-economic equality policies, are not supported by these data. Rather, the data reveal varying ups and downs which seem to be situation specific. However, since these variations occur in several countries at the same time, they appear to have a broad West European character.

Political Cleavages

We now turn to variations within countries, examining group-specific levels of support for socio-economic equality policies. Here the concept of political cleavage is central. The welfare state was a major issue in the class cleavage between labour and capital (Pappi 1977). It is assumed that this conflict eased with the expansion of the welfare state in the 1950s and the 1960s, but revived in the 1970s as a result of public debate about the crisis of the welfare state. Additionally, we hypothesize that the welfare state is an issue in the context of what Inglehart (1984) calls 'the emerging new value cleavage'. But we also assume that the attitudes of the carriers of the new cleavage, the postmaterialists, are ambiguous: they do not support bureaucratic organization but, simultaneously, they favour goals such as social security and social justice (Inglehart 1984: 55–6).

Political cleavages are defined as stable coalitions between socio-structural groups and parties (Lipset and Rokkan 1967). Additionally, a cleavage is interpreted and mirrored at the level of ideology (Bartolini and Mair 1990: 215). Therefore, we examine political cleavages at the social-structural level, the ideological level, and at the party level. However, whereas the 'old' class cleavage can be identified at all three levels, there is continuing debate about the social-structural basis of the 'new value cleavage'. Since some researchers suggest that an essential conceptual element of a cleavage is its basis in structurally rooted conflicts (Bartolini and Mair 1990: 215; see also Chapter 18 in Volume iv of this series), the question arises whether or not the emerging new value conflict can be legitimately characterized as a cleavage. The asymmetry between the class cleavage and the so-called new value cleavage is reflected in the indicators. The class cleavage can be measured at all three levels: at the structural level by occupational status, namely whether or not people are workers and whether they are self-employed or employees; at the ideological level by left–right self-identification; and at the party level by a preference for parties of the left or the right. The 'new value cleavage', however, can be measured directly only at the ideological level, using Inglehart's (1977: 27–9) materialism–postmaterialism index.[8]

Why should we differentiate, in our empirical analysis, between the three levels of a cleavage? Pappi (1977: 244) examined attitudes about the welfare state in Germany using data from a study conducted in 1968. His main finding was that there have been conflicting attitudes at the socio-structural level—between self-employed people and employees—but the differences did not exist in terms of party preference. Pappi interpreted this result as a situation of latent conflict: no party picked up this conflict and placed it on the political agenda. If the discussion about the crisis of the welfare state starting in the 1970s (re)activated the welfare state as an issue, we would expect growing differences at all three cleavage levels between the 1970s and 1980s.

Two surveys were used to test this hypothesis. The Political Action data cover seven West European countries in the early 1970s, and the 1987 ISSP data cover six of these seven countries.[9] Both studies contain two items on policies aiming at equality of result: national minima with respect to jobs, and redistribution by reducing income differences. Note, however, that complete information is not available for all dimensions of the political cleavages. The 1987 ISSP indicator for class measures only whether or not the respondent is a worker, and the materialism–postmaterialism index is included only in the Political Action data. We use Pearson's *r* as a measure of controversy; high correlation coefficients indicate large group-specific differences in support for socio-economic equality policies, and vice versa. The results of our analysis are set out in Table 7.5.

First, we look at the class cleavage. Starting with 'providing jobs', we can see that in the early 1970s there were almost no differences in terms of the structural basis of the class cleavage—although here only weakly measured by differences between the self-employed and employees. In some countries there were rather more differences at the ideological level in terms of left–right identification. This is also the case with party preference. However, the differences are not large. Only in Finland do we find significant conflict at both the ideological level and the party level. With the second item, 'redistribution of

TABLE 7.5. *Support for different socio-economic equality policies and levels of political cleavage, 1973–6 and 1987*

Dimension/item	Groups	FI	AU	GB	GE	NL	SW	IT
EQUALITY OF RESULT: NATIONAL MINIMA								
Provide a job for everyone								
1973–6	Self-employed *v.*	−0.01	0.00	−0.02	−0.05*	−0.04	−0.06	−0.01
1987	employee	—	−0.02	−0.15**	−0.03	−0.08**	−0.05	−0.14**
1973–6	Worker *v.*	—	—	—	—	—	—	—
1987	non-worker	—	0.16**	0.29**	0.12**	0.18**	0.12**	0.08
1973–6	Materialist–	0.03	0.01	−0.02	0.05**	0.01	0.09**	0.03
1987	postmaterialist	—	—	—	—	—	—	—
1973–6	Left–right	0.18**	−0.02	0.06*	−0.01	0.08**	0.08**	0.06*
1987		—	—	—	—	—	—	—
1973–6	Party preference	0.18**	0.09**	0.08**	0.01	0.02	0.11**	0.10**
1987		—	0.04	0.42**	0.13**	0.35**	0.12**	—
EQUALITY OF RESULT: REDISTRIBUTION								
Reduction of income differences								
1973–6	Self-employed *v.*	−0.13**	0.01	−0.07*	−0.06*	−0.07*	−0.02	−0.06*
1987	employee	—	0.01	−0.15**	−0.08**	−0.13**	−0.10**	−0.09**
1973–6	Worker *v.*	—	—	—	—	—	—	–
1987	non-worker	—	0.11**	0.21**	0.19**	0.20**	0.14**	0.09*
1973–6	Materialist–	−0.10**	0.00	−0.07**	−0.04	−0.09**	0.07*	−0.05*
1987	postmaterialist	—	—	—	—	—	—	—
1973-6	Left–right	0.35**	0.04	0.25**	0.12**	0.26**	0.11**	0.20**
1987		—	—	—	—	—	—	—
1973–6	Party preference	0.32**	0.07*	0.30**	0.16**	0.27**	0.15**	0.21**
1987		—	0.11**	0.37**	0.27**	0.50**	0.15**	—

$*p < 0.05$ $**p < 0.01$

Notes: Entries are Pearson's *r*. Respondents in the Political Action data are 18 years and older.

Sources: Political Action (1973–6); ISSP (1987).

income', a rather different pattern emerges. Here, in almost all countries, there were only minor differences between the self-employed and employees, but there were significantly larger differences at the ideological level and at the party level. Thus, according to these data for the 1970s, it depends on the specific type of policy whether or not socio-economic equality policies are a matter of controversy at any level of the class cleavage. Only redistribution of income was an issue within the class cleavage. However, this controversy only existed at the ideological level and the party level—that is, in the political sphere.

What is different in 1987? Using the ISSP data, we can examine the relationship between the class cleavage and socio-economic equality policies at only two of the three levels: at the structural level of occupation and the level of party preference. Fortunately, the 1987 data allow us both to distinguish between the self-employed and employees, and between workers and non-workers. On the policy of 'providing jobs', in some countries things had changed by 1987. In Britain and Italy, where controversy between the self-employed and employees increased significantly, whether or not government should provide jobs was a source of conflict at the structural level of the class cleavage. Also, conflict had increased at the level of party preference in Britain, Germany, and the Netherlands; unfortunately, data for Italy are missing. But no changes at the structural or the party level developed in Austria or Switzerland. Hence, compared to the early 1970s, by 1987 'providing jobs' was on the political agenda in most of these countries and divided supporters of different parties. However, although this conflict also had a structural basis, in Britain and the Netherlands the conflict was more serious at the political level than at the structural level. Developments on the policy of redistributing income were similar to those on providing jobs. With the exception of Austria, conflict gained momentum at the structural level. At the party level, conflict increased in all countries except Switzerland.

Summarizing these developments in the class cleavage during the 1970s and the 1980s, note first that controversy about socio-economic equality policies extends to bring in more policies (including the provision of jobs) and more groups. Secondly, there was increased intensity in the conflict about the equality dimension of the welfare state, both within different types of policies and at different levels of the cleavage. Therefore, the hypothesis about increasing conflict on socio-economic equality policies can be confirmed for the class cleavage—

but with the exception of Austria and Switzerland. However, this controversy is most clearly located in the political sphere.

We noted earlier that the data for the so-called new value cleavage, or value conflict, are restricted to the 1970s. Here, only in a few countries do statistically significant—but small—differences exist regarding the provision of jobs and the redistribution of income. Even so, note that the signs of those small coefficients, indicating the direction of group differences, vary. Most likely, postmaterialists disagree with providing jobs but agree with the redistribution of income. Evidently the ambiguous orientations of this group are manifest in varying support for different socio-economic equality policies.

Although the 1987 ISSP data do not include the materialist–postmaterialist measure, four of these countries (Britain, Germany, the Netherlands, and Italy) are included in Eurobarometer, No. 16 (1983) which has data on both the redistribution of income and materialism–postmaterialism. These data (not shown here) indicate increasing conflict in Germany (Pearson's r, -0.17) and the Netherlands (Pearson's r, -0.13). Hence, there are some weak signs of an increase in conflict on the 'value cleavage', at least in those countries where the new value conflict shows signs of becoming established.

Other hypotheses on group-specific differences have been specified in research on the welfare state. In particular, it has been argued that the welfare state itself has created new conflicts at the structural level. One of these conflicts centres on the distinction between the financiers of the welfare state—the gainfully employed—and the recipients of welfare benefits (Alber 1984: 228–30). Furthermore, the public sector has been identified as the beneficiary of the welfare state (Sears and Citrin 1982: 115; Pöntinen and Uusitalo 1986: 7), giving rise to conflicts between public and private sector employees. Thus, we might anticipate new or intensifying conflicts between the employed and welfare recipients, and between private and public sector employees. We tested these hypotheses, using the same data sources. The results are presented in Table 7.6.

These results are fairly clear. In the early 1970s, conflict between the employed and welfare recipients—examined only indirectly by comparing employees and different categories of people not in employment—existed only in the Netherlands and, to a lesser extent in Italy, on providing jobs. In 1987, in most cases, the differences between these groups had become somewhat larger, but only occasionally is the correlation (Pearson's r) significant at the 1 per cent level. As for

TABLE 7.6. *Support for socio-economic equality policies and welfare-state conflicts, 1973–6 and 1987*

Dimension/item	Groups	FI	AU	GB	GE	NL	SW	IT
EQUALITY OF RESULT: NATIONAL MINIMA								
Provide a job for everyone								
1973–6	Employed *v.* recipients of welfare benefits	−0.00	−0.01	0.02	0.00	−0.13**	−0.06	−0.06*
1987		—	−0.09*	−0.12**	−0.09*	−0.09*	−0.06	−0.11**
1973–6	Private *v.* public sector	—	—	—	—	—	—	—
1987		—	−0.09*	0.08**	−0.04	−0.06	0.05	0.01
EQUALITY OF RESULT: REDISTRIBUTION								
Reduction of income differences								
1973–6	Employed *v.* recipients of welfare benefits	0.00	−0.02	0.02	−0.01	−0.05	−0.01	−0.03
1987		—	−0.08	−0.07*	−0.10*	−0.09**	−0.08*	−0.08*
1973–6	Private *v.* public sector	—	—	—	—	—	—	—
1987		—	−0.06	0.12**	−0.05	−0.03	0.09*	0.02

*$p < 0.05$ **$p < 0.01$

Notes: Entries are Pearson's *r*. Recipients of welfare benefits cover retired, disabled, and unemployed people in 1973–60; in 1987 they cover only unemployed people. Respondents in the Political Action data are 18 years and older.

Sources: Political Action (1973–6); ISSP (1987).

differences between public and private sector employees, which can be examined only in 1987, Britain alone shows significant conflict on both policies.

The welfare state, then, appears not to have generally created new conflicts at the socio-structural level. In the 1970s, only the Netherlands showed signs of such conflicts; in the 1980s, these conflicts became evident in some other countries as well. But the differences between employed and non-employed people, as well as between people employed in the private and public sectors, are so small that we are justified in speaking only of the initial signs of such new conflicts.

Interest- or Value-Based Orientations?

Our analytic concept of attitudes towards the welfare state distinguishes between interest and value orientations as generalized attitudes towards the welfare state. Interest orientation is instrumental, referring to the attainment of material needs for oneself. Thus, it is characterized as a short-term orientation. Value orientation refers to long-term fundamental predispositions of a universal moral character. Since interest orientation is more susceptible to change, we assume that a condition for the long-term functioning of the welfare state is that attitudes engage some value orientation. We now go on to examine whether support for socio-economic equality policies is based on interest orientations or value orientations. Because socio-economic equality *per se* is a moral objective, we anticipate that support for policies aiming at the goal is based on a value orientation rather than an interest orientation.

Most research hitherto has studied types of orientation about the welfare state empirically, via the determinants of attitudes about the welfare state (cf. Pöntinen and Uusitalo 1986: 53). In this research tradition, value orientations have been measured by concepts such as party identification or left–right self-placement, which have been characterized as fundamental predispositions, whereas interest orientations have often been measured by demographic variables, such as occupation, income, and education (Pöntinen and Uusitalo 1986: 53). However, Sears *et al.* (1980: 671–2) have pointed out that demographic variables are only indirect measures of interest orientations compared, for example, to attitudinal measures. Moreover, they argued that demographic variables can stand for fundamental value orientations as well as interest orientations. Consequently, they proposed treating demographic variables as variables in their own right, and looking, instead, for attitudinal indicators to tap interest orientations.

Following these considerations, we specify a regression model which includes value orientations, interest orientations, and demographic characteristics. To measure value orientations, we use party identification, placement on a left–right scale, and materialism–postmaterialism. Life satisfaction, although an indirect measure, is the only indicator available for measuring subjective interest orientations. For the demographic variables, we have to rely on income and education as measures of socio-economic status. However, because of our reservations about the demographic variables, we focus on comparing the coefficients of the attitudinal variables. The empirical analysis is based on Eurobarometer, No. 19 (1983) which covers the broadest range of indicators needed to test the model. Our dependent variable is support for reducing income differences. The results of the regression analysis are presented in Table 7.7.

The analysis yields a clear picture. Value orientations display significant effects in nine of the ten countries whereas interest orientation—measured by life satisfaction—has a significant effect in only three countries. Moreover, comparing the beta coefficients reveals generally larger effects for value orientations than for interest orientation. Belgium is the only exception to this pattern, although neither value orientations nor interest orientation are important in Ireland. On this comparison, then, value orientations dominate over interest orientation—which is borne out in the overall picture shown in the last column. Nevertheless, because our data do not provide direct measures of interest orientation, we cannot confidently conclude that support for socio-economic equality policies owes more to value orientations than interest orientation. But if we accept that party identification, left–right placement, and materialism–postmaterialism are valid indicators of value orientations, then the result of our analysis is that support for socio-economic equality policies is predominantly value based. The attitudinal conditions for the long-term operation of socio-economic equality policies are clearly in place.

The results of the regression analysis are interesting from another perspective. Comparing the explained variances, it is striking that the independent variables explain some sizeable proportion of the total variance in only two countries (Denmark and the Netherlands). Although reaching 20 per cent in those two cases, and rather more than 10 per cent in another two (Germany and France), in most

TABLE 7.7. *Types of orientation and agreement with redistribution of income, 1983*

	DK	BE	GB	GE	IR	LU	NL	FR	IT	GR	All
Value orientation											
Party preference	−0.17**	−0.09	−0.14**	−0.05	−0.03	−0.17*	−0.16**	−0.20**	−0.08	−0.10	−0.13**
Left–right	−0.28**	0.11*	−0.11**	−0.18**	−0.07	−0.00	−0.22**	−0.18**	−0.11*	−0.15*	−0.17**
Materialist–postmaterialist	0.07	0.15**	0.05	0.18**	0.06	0.12	0.09**	0.02	0.00	0.08	0.04**
Interest orientation											
Life satisfaction	0.03	−0.21**	−0.11**	0.03	−0.09	−0.02	−0.06	−0.07*	−0.05	−0.03	−0.09**
Demography											
Income	−0.15**	0.05	0.07	−0.18**	0.02	−0.03	−0.09**	−0.04	−0.05	−0.04	−0.09**
Education	−0.11**	−0.14**	0.04	−0.13**	0.06	−0.16*	−0.14**	−0.09*	−0.09*	−0.02	−0.05**
Adjusted R^2	0.23	0.07	0.07	0.11	0.01	0.05	0.20	0.14	0.04	0.05	0.11
N	568	417	670	374	374	176	681	599	599	463	5,464

$^{*}p < 0.05$ $^{**}p < 0.01$

Notes: Entries are beta coefficients. Respondents are 18 years and older. Weighted data. The independent variables are coded from left to right for party preference; from materialist to postmaterialist; and from low to high for life satisfaction, income, and education.

Source: Eurobarometer, No. 19.

instances the total variance accounted for by the model is low. This finding reveals the high consensus prevailing in West European countries with regard to socio-economic equality policies. It also means that the increased intensity of conflicts about socio-economic equality policies noted in the previous section is not as problematic as it might have seemed—at least not in 1983. Conflicts over socio-economic equality policies reached a significant level only in Denmark and the Netherlands, and to a certain degree in France and Germany.

We do not try to explain national differences in the consensus we have found. However, it is interesting to note that the four countries in which conflict about socio-economic equality policies intensified all belong to the group of countries with the highest GDP per capita (Table 7.3). Does this mean that, with growing wealth, support for socio-economic equality policies declines? At first glance, this explanation seems plausible. However, Luxembourg and Belgium—both high consensus countries—also belong to the group of wealthy countries. Hence, improvements in standards of living are perhaps a necessary but not a sufficient condition for growing dissent on socio-economic equality policies.

Conclusions

Since ordinary understanding and most scientific definitions of the welfare state are restricted to security policies such as pensions and health care, systematic studies of attitudes about the equality dimension of the welfare state are rare. A further consequence of these one-sided definitions is that surveys, above all comparative surveys, include few indicators on socio-economic equality policies. Due to these limitations in the data, we could answer only some of the theoretically relevant questions on beliefs about socio-economic equality policies.

Although research on values and beliefs about inequality has always stressed that support for socio-economic equality is low, the data available to us clearly show that there is considerable support for some types of equality policies. This might be because many scholars think of equality as a radical equality of result. Instead, we have examined policies aiming at a moderate equality of result and, thus, those types of equality policies which are common among the West European welfare states. Overall, West European citizens show strong support for these moderate or 'tamed' socio-economic equality policies.

Nevertheless, the data also indicate the limits of support for such moderate policies. It is the provision of a guaranteed income—a policy aiming at establishing national minima—which gets the weakest support among West European publics. The essence of this policy is that it entitles people to financial benefits without doing anything for them. However, the related policy of providing jobs gets more support. But in this case people are not provided with financial goods, only the wherewithal to earn financial rewards. Guaranteeing a minimal level of income, it seems, offends more against the widely accepted achievement principle than guaranteeing people a job. According to this argument, support for moderate socio-economic equality policies reaches its boundaries when national minima policies leave no space for the achievement principle to operate.

Despite generally widespread support for socio-economic equality policies, there are, however, obvious differences between West European countries. Macro-level analyses hint that these differences are due to national differences in standards of living. While one survey conducted in the 1980s reveals a significant negative relationship between levels of support for socio-economic equality policies and levels of income equality, another survey, also for the 1980s, reveals a negative relationship with the wealth of a country. These relationships indicate that, with increasing equality of income and the increasing wealth of a country, support for socio-economic equality policies declines. A logical consequence of this empirical relationship is that evidence of weak support for socio-economic equality policies cannot, *a priori*, be judged negatively. Weak support can be an expression of the fact that citizens no longer consider such policies necessary, due to the levels of income equality or wealth already attained. It follows, therefore, that a comprehensive evaluation of levels of support for socio-economic equality policies is only possible if one knows how people perceive and evaluate inequality in their society.

The comparative data for the mid-1970s show no systematic relationship between standards of living and support for socio-economic equality policies. We suggested that the absence of such a link is due to the emergence of socio-economic equality at the top of the political agenda during the 1970s, whereas it disappeared during the 1980s. In future analyses, our model of standards of living as determinants of support for public policies has to be modified to include the political agenda as an important factor mediating between conditions and levels of support.

The poor data record did not allow us to provide a definitive answer to the central question of how support for socio-economic equality policies has developed over time. But the analysis of group differences based on political cleavages revealed an interesting aspect of developmental processes: the consensus on socio-economic policies declined between the 1970s and the 1980s. As we can probably assume high consensus in the 1960s, it seems that the public debate about the welfare state which started in the 1970s undermined some of this consensus. But this conflict is carried out largely at the party level; that is, in the political sphere. In comparison, there is less dissent at the socio-structural level.

Finally, our analyses reveal that support for socio-economic equality policies is stronger than we might have expected. However, the analyses of socio-economic security policies reveal significantly stronger support for this other dimension of the welfare state (see Chapters 4 and 8). This means that, although socio-economic equality policies receive relatively high support, they are, none the less, the less popular part of the welfare state.

NOTES

1. For a comparable argument about different types of support for the political system, see Easton (1975).
2. Using these analytical distinctions, Heidenheimer (1981), for example, demonstrated that the main difference between the West European and North American welfare states is that West European welfare states emphasize social security programmes, whereas equality of opportunity through education is emphasized in North America.
3. Factor analysis revealed that all beliefs about these five types of policies form one factor.
4. This hypothesis is also prominent in research on determinants of well-being; see Campbell, Converse, and Rodgers (1976).
5. The following analyses were also carried out with the other Gini indices for the 1970s compiled in the *Political Data Handbook* by Lane, McKay, and Newton (1991: 22). None of the analyses show fundamentally different results.
6. Further regression analyses using not the means index covering all five policies but relying only on the policy of reducing income differences produced the same results. With respect to wealth, the relationship is somewhat stronger (adjusted $R^2 = 0.74$; significant at the 5 per cent level), but somewhat lower for equality of income.
7. The 1987 Austrian data on the progressive taxation item are not shown as this question was asked in only one survey.
8. In some West European countries the 'new value cleavage' also exists at the party level. However, it is only directly measurable where specific parties, such as green

parties, have emerged. Since no such parties existed in 1973–6, we restricted the analysis to the ideological level using the materialism–postmaterialism index.

9. The latest survey, the 1990 ISSP study, covers only three of the seven European countries included in the Political Action study. Thus we relied on the 1987 ISSP survey for our second data point.

8

The Welfare State: The Security Dimension

PER ARNT PETTERSEN

❖

Whatever the historical origin and nature of the welfare state, there are programmes to protect people against misfortune, especially loss of income, ill health, or unexpected expenditure. These are some of the means of pursuing the goal of social equality, which was analysed in the previous chapter. Among the most common and visible programmes are old age pensions, public health services, and unemployment benefits. The most expensive, but also probably the most popular, include the various systems of old age pensions and health services. These two programmes are the cornerstones, and the least contested aspects, of the welfare state. Old age comes to everyone (who does not die young) and sickness is fairly randomly distributed through a population, so no one can be certain that they will not need these services at some stage in their life. Hence, the widespread support for old age pension schemes and health services found in most studies of the welfare state.

Still, even for these two programmes, there is not universal agreement that the government should be the sole provider. Some feel that private savings and private insurance should provide economic security in later life; some prefer the real costs of health services to be paid for by individuals or private insurance within a health services market. However, the basic legitimacy of old age pensions and health services is derived from the universality of ageing and the risks of illness.

Unemployment, by contrast, is distributed in a systematic way. The young and old, the less educated and unskilled, people living in areas of declining economic activity—all have higher than average risks of unemployment. However, for people who work, unemployment benefits might be viewed as an alternative to wages and salaries, as another form of income. If their earnings are low, the employed might even question whether they are better off than those living on the 'dole'. They may wonder if all the unemployed are deserving individuals compared to wage earners. These kinds of doubts may reduce support for unemployment benefits.

The basic question for analysis in this chapter is whether people prefer to see state pension schemes, public health services, and unemployment benefits expand, continue as they are, or reduced. Is spending to be increased or are services, pensions, and benefits considered adequate? These questions concern 'how much', or the *degree* dimension of the scope of government. The *range* dimension of attitudes towards social security was discussed in Chapter 4.

In the next section, we analyse *how* preferences for increased security and protection have developed and varied from the economically confident period of the 1960s, which saw the maturing of the welfare state, through the economic stagnation of the 1970s, and the fiscal austerity of the 1980s. The second section deals with *who*—which demographic and social groups—is more likely to support or oppose the expansion of the programmes for old age pensions, public health services, and unemployment benefits.

Developmental Theories

Two theoretical traditions are explicitly committed to explaining developments in popular support for the welfare state. One we might call 'resistance among the well-to-do', the other 'new values theory'. Both positions argue that the original support which the welfare state enjoyed during the maturing years of the 1960s is fading away.

Typical of 'resistance' arguments is Rose and Peters's (1978) claim that support for welfare programmes will decline as economic recession produces falling real disposable incomes for wage earners. Although varying in severity, economic recession is a common experience in West European countries; indeed, an important factor in the growth of welfare expenditure. The burdens on the wage earners are increased by the 'invisible hand' of inflation and progressive taxation which together reduce the purchasing power of incomes (Rose and Peters 1978; Rose 1984)—or, at least, obstruct expectations about rising real incomes. Rose and Peters predict common trends of reduced support for the expansion of public spending in every West European country, with opposition being most prominent where economic stagnation has been most apparent, as in Britain, or where taxation levels have been most extravagant, as in the Scandinavian countries. Thus, if Rose and Peters's developmental theory is correct, a reduced willingness to expand spending on welfare programmes should be evident among the employed, especially among the more heavily taxed upper income groups. These trends should be apparent regardless of how support is measured.

One version of the 'new values' theory is suggested by Wilensky (1975), who argued that the advanced welfare states were heading for a 'welfare backlash'. Rather than the impact of economic recession, Wilensky was concerned with the impact of economic growth on the transformation of modern society. The message was that education, new industries, and economic development breed individualistic values. An increasingly complex division of labour multiplies the number of occupations requiring specific skills, necessitating individual and discriminating compensation. Specialization is produced through education and occupation, which subsequently promote social mobility. Since this evolution affects mostly the young, Wilensky argued that—in particular—the well-educated younger generation will abdicate as supporters of the welfare state. But even the working-class, often the original target group of welfare programmes, will eventually forsake the welfare state; career patterns and salaries are bound to become individualistic, leading to the abandonment of collective wage negotiation between labour unions and employer's organizations. The 'new' social category, according to Wilensky, is the 'middle mass', which will refuse to pay the necessary taxes, since they perceive no benefits from the welfare state. In common with Rose and Peters, Wilensky suggests continuously falling support for welfare arrangements, including old age pensions, but, by contrast, he suggests that wage earners, especially as income increases, will lose faith in the welfare state. Some may argue that the 'yuppies' of the 1980s precisely fit with Wilensky's predictions of 'economic individualism' (Wilensky 1975: 32–9).

Another version of the 'new values' theory, similarly predicting falling support for the welfare state, can be derived from Inglehart's theory of generations (Inglehart 1977). A simple and direct interpretation of Inglehart's arguments implies that people who grew up before the Second World War—in societies suffering from unemployment, precarious wage agreements, and sparse welfare arrangements—were the advocates of the welfare state and, later, its most reliable defenders. Thus, Inglehart predicts, people of those generations will tend to be more materialist in outlook than the generations who grew up after the war. By contrast, the post-war generations have known material security and moved towards giving priority to postmaterialist values which emphasize the quality of life (Pöntinen and Uusitalo 1986). Even though the implications of 'postmaterialist' values are not entirely clear, it is hard to avoid the conclusion that they imply a continuous decline in support for the welfare state as 'materialist' generations are replaced by new cohorts of 'postmaterialists'.

For Wilensky, too, changing levels of support are related to generations: younger people are less inclined to support the welfare state than pre-war generations. Inglehart also concurs with Wilensky in suggesting that education promotes a new value system. But postmaterialist values are rooted in socialization experiences and encouraged by an awareness of new problems and inventive priorities, not by current occupational opportunities (Inglehart 1977). However, an alternative to the two generation thesis is a 'three or four' generation classification: the pre-war generation, the early post-war generation, the generation which saw the welfare state mature, and the youngest 'post-welfare state' generation. The latter two, or just the last generation, is thought to oppose welfare programmes (Svalfors 1989). However, whatever the details, the predictions made by Wilensky and Inglehart, and the classification offered by Svalfors, agree in focusing on the impact of generational differences; in brief, that the expansion of the modern welfare state is opposed by the young and well educated. Thus, the successive replacement of old cohorts by new young cohorts will lead to declining support for the welfare state.

Note that these theoretical positions, although they rely on different assumptions, are not exclusive. Rather, they may reinforce each other and simultaneously yield accurate predictions. Rose and Peters's assumption that taxpayers constitute an opposition to welfare state expansion may be correct in itself and be in agreement with the predictions of both Wilensky and Inglehart that well-educated younger people oppose expansion. Moreover, such findings might be consistently related to changing value systems. It is even possible that part of the new generation adheres to the values of 'economic individualism' while others have become 'postmaterialists'.

A quite different theoretical position argues that looking for linear trends in support for the welfare state is futile (Downs 1972). The assumption is that people's attitudes on political issues, including the welfare state, are cyclical, both with regard to issue attention and support. The opinion formers and leaders in a society are politicians and the mass media in juxtaposition (Lazarsfeld, Berelson, and Gaudet 1948). The key condition for popularity cycles is the introduction of political novelties, new ideas, or the revival of old ones. Exciting personalities, dramatic presentation and campaigning, conflicts and fierce struggles seize the attention of the mass media. This is reinforced by the tendency of the mass media to concentrate on those with unconventional convictions. Yet political ideas compete for attention, and even the most charismatic individuals and fascinating ideas lose their impact when constantly repeated. Downs's theory of 'issue attention cycles' seems appropriate to analysing attitude change during the 1970s and 1980s when the 'new right' movement was initiated and grew in vitality.

Operationally, this kind of argument suggests that disapproval of the welfare state increases as conservatives celebrate their political victories. We might even anticipate that attitude fluctuations were exposed suddenly, abruptly, and most visibly as the conservative moods of the 1970s and 1980s broke through in various countries. Moreover, it may be the case that stable attitudes have been preserved best where no neoliberal party (or party leadership) emerged or where no conservative parties won increased support from the electorate. This position, of course, implies that as the conservative mood fades away, so does opposition towards welfare state expansion.

Finally, we might consider that, even if predictions of a linear decline in support should prove to be wrong, there might be tendencies which would save at least parts of these positions. Inside every wave of conservative mobilization, the front runners in opposing welfare state expansion, and the last to drop their opposition as the political mood changes again, might be Wilensky's 'middle mass', Inglehart's 'postmaterialists', or Rose and Peters's 'abused tax-payers'. None the less, the hypotheses implied by these theories engage the assumption that particular groups will become more pronounced opponents of the welfare state as we move from the economic growth of the 1960s, through the stagnation of the 1970s, and the crises of the 1980s.

Support for the Welfare State

The theories discussed so far have been concerned with declining support for the welfare state, and predictions about *who* constitutes the opposition. Other theoretical approaches suggest that large segments of the citizenry have acquired strong and lasting confidence in the welfare state. If this is so, the welfare state has the necessary political strongholds to survive and even to develop.

Pöntinen and Uusitalo (1986) argue that at least three groups in society have vested interests in the cultivation and expansion of the welfare state. The consumers, or prospective consumers, of welfare transfers are obvious candidates; the oldest cohorts, in particular, are most likely to support the expansion of old age pensions.[1] Secondly, people who perceive that they incur high tax burdens without consuming any services or receiving transfers, now or in the future, are likely to develop negative attitudes. This implies that people in middle and lower income groups would offer firm support for welfare programmes if the perceived protection and benefits were to surpass tax burdens. This assumption is linked to Rose and Peters's theory of linearly declining support but is distinct in so far as levels of support are expected to hold fairly constant, as between income categories, over the thirty-year period under study. Thirdly, those employed in the public sector, often in welfare state occupations, are likely to develop positive attitudes, because the growth of the welfare state enhances their employment prospects and occupational prestige (Kolberg and Pettersen 1981; Dunleavy 1989). In addition, it is reasonable to assume that public sector employees identify with the values associated with welfare state institutions (Edgell and Duke 1991; Dunleavy and Husbands 1985).

Next, we suggest that people identifying with the lower or working class are most inclined to support the expansion of the welfare state—if only because they are influenced by political rhetoric about the welfare state and on account of patterns of political support among the working class. In most countries, the working class has been thought to be the target group for welfare state reforms, even though empirical evidence suggests that the better off often derive greater benefits from many public services (Olson 1990). Where the connection between the working-class vote and welfare state expansion has been close, we expect class differences in support to be most apparent. Obviously, this also implies that supporters of socialist parties, perceived as the designers of the welfare state, constitute the cornerstone of political support for the welfare state. The Scandinavian countries have been identified as paradigms of the close ties between the working class, labour and social democratic parties and support for the welfare state (Korpi 1981; Esping-Andersen 1985). Britain should fit this picture as well. But evidence of the weaker association between class and party preference over the last thirty years (Worre 1980; Franklin and Mughan 1978) suggests that variation in welfare state support among voters for different parties might have disappeared.

Suggestions that women have increasingly benefited from welfare state programmes have also been advanced (Hernes 1987; Waernes 1987). Women's traditional obligations to family care have been relieved by welfare arrangements, and welfare programmes have reduced women's dependence on their husband's income, especially in cases of divorce and widowhood. Simultaneously, the welfare state has become a major arena for women's employment. We anticipate that all these factors promote positive attitudes towards welfare programmes among women in general. However, the major programmes benefiting women, as well as the advancement of women in the labour force, have appeared only during the last twenty years or so. Thus, we assume that younger women are more favourably disposed to the welfare state than their mothers and grandmothers. This tendency should increase as we move from the 1960s to the 1980s. Yet younger or working women may have higher expectations of the welfare state, leading them to be less satisfied and more critical than older, and possibly less demanding, women.

Analytic Strategy

Our theoretical assumptions focus on who opposes or supports welfare state expansion. However, some of our questions are implicitly concerned with why some people support and some people oppose welfare state expansion. We can say little about this because we do not have comparable survey data on attitudes towards the welfare state which might be correlated with opinions about welfare state expansion. A broader picture of the attitude structures which underpin support or opposition has to wait until we have a series of surveys over several years which ask the appropriate opinion and value questions.

Comparing popular opinions towards welfare state programmes at one specific time point, let alone over time, involves a multitude of obstacles and possibilities for misinterpreting the data. Survey questions are not identical, or even similar, between national surveys; question and answer categories in national surveys are modified over the years. The specific character of national welfare programmes also means that we have to be cautious about interpreting findings since institutional variations may lead people to react differently even when the survey questions are similar.

Even so, although the survey questions are not identical and programmes differ, we may still assume that the different preferences of various social groups about expansion are sufficiently robust and stable to be revealed by multivariate analysis. Drawing on the theoretical arguments outlined above, we consider similarities of support and opposition across a number of countries. In the next section, we focus on similarities in the development of attitudes across countries, starting by introducing trends in Britain as a comparative baseline. The British Election Study and the British Social Attitudes surveys constitute the longest time series available. Even more to the point, Britain has endured the economic, social, and political changes most relevant to our theoretical propositions.

Development of Preferences

Longitudinal data about the evolution of popular support for old age programmes are available for six countries: the four Nordic countries, Britain, and the Netherlands. There are two basic variants of the relevant question; both of them are included in the British data. One concerns preferences for increasing old age pensions, which has also been asked in Finland and the Netherlands. In Britain and the Netherlands, the wording of the question is virtually identical. The second, and comparable, question relates to programmes of social security. A question of this kind has been asked in Denmark, Norway, Sweden, and Britain. As transfers to the older generation constitute the major part of the programme in these countries, respondents are likely to associate the questions with old age pension schemes. However, this kind of question is, in fact, more general in nature than those specifically about old age pensions.

Overall, we consider these questions as functional equivalents—in the sense that they should reveal the same tendencies. That is, according to our initial theoretical arguments, we anticipate either a linear decline in support or politically based cycles of support. We also assume that the differences in question formulation are of minor importance when analysing social variation in the structure of preferences.

First, then, we examine the moods of the British over the last twenty years. The period was marked by major political shifts, from the Conservative government of the early 1970s, the Labour government of the mid-1970s, through the landslide victories of Margaret Thatcher and towards her less popular years of the late 1980s. This gives us both a preliminary overview of developments in attitudes, and an initial test of the theoretical arguments. In Table 8.1 we show, for four elections, whether people in Britain thought that social services and benefits had gone too far and should be cut back, should stay as they are, or be expanded.

Three main trends are evident. First, there is a basic stability over the period in the proportions who prefer expansion; approximately 30 per cent preferred an increase in social services and benefits in 1974, 1983, and 1987. But, secondly, in 1979 the proportion who preferred expansion fell to less than 20 per cent. The 1979 election was the first of Mrs Thatcher's victories, when the Conservative Party won its largest share of the vote since the 1950s (44 per cent). The notable corollary is the increase in the proportion of the electorate wanting a reduction in services and benefits. The balance of opinion did not shift from expansion to the status quo, but exhibits almost a 20 percentage point increase in the proportion of people preferring reduced levels of services and benefits. Thirdly, by 1983 the proportion wanting to

TABLE 8.1. *Support for expansion or reduction of social services and benefits in Britain, 1974–87*

	1974	1979	1983	1987
Expansion	31	19	28	34
As now	33	26	49	39
Reduction	32	50	19	24
Don't know	4	5	4	3
N	2,431	1,859	3,933	3,810

Notes: Entries are percentages. The questions are formulated similarly for 1974, 1979, 1983, and 1987: 'Now, we would like to ask what you think about social services and benefits. Which of these views comes closest to your own view: social services and benefits have gone too far and should be cut back; social services and benefits have gone somewhat too far and should be cut back a bit; social services and benefits should stay as they are; more social services and benefits are needed?'

Sources: British Election Study (1974, 1979, 1983, 1987).

reduce provision fell to a lower level than in 1974. Whereas 32 per cent opted for reductions in 1974, this figure dropped to 19 per cent in 1983, then climbed back to 24 per cent in 1987. This pattern implies that over the years an expanding proportion felt that the level of benefits and services was adequate and satisfactory. Note also that the proportion preferring expansion peaks at the 1987 election, while opposition to expansion is lowest at the 1983 election.[2]

The only explanation which fits this pattern of fluctuations within basic stability is political preference cycles stimulated by political campaigns. The breakthrough of the right wing of the Conservative Party in the late 1970s stimulated a general feeling of dissatisfaction with the over-expansion of social policies in Britain. Neither the generation theories of Wilensky and Inglehart, nor the tax burden theory of Rose and Peters—all predicting a linear decline in preferences for expansion—contain the possibility of generally stable support along with opposition cycles. Whether the specific groups predicted by these theories constitute the new opposition will be analysed later. Now we look to see if the same pattern holds for support for old age pensions in Britain and our other West European countries.

Comparing support for old age pensions in Britain, shown in Table 8.2, with general preferences for the expansion of benefits and services (Table 8.1), immediately reveals that schemes specifically related to old age pensions are more widely supported. The only real disagreement is between those who want expansion to continue and those who feel that provision is satisfactory. Hardly any opposition exists.

However, popularity cycles are again evident. In the early 1960s in Britain, 77 per cent wanted spending on old age pensions to increase, the figure drops to 55 per cent in the mid-1960s, and to 43 per cent in the late 1960s. Then a slight increase occurs in 1970. Unfortunately, the British Election Study did not include the question about old age pensions in 1974 and 1979, so we cannot tell if support for increasing old age pensions fell in the 1970s as it did for benefits and services. But the increase in support for old age pensions during the 1980s is clear, reaching the same levels as in the early 1960s.

The Netherlands, too, shows declining support for increasing old age pensions through the 1970s, followed by a resurgence of support during the second half of the 1980s. That is, support for expansion followed a cyclical pattern. The low proportion of expansionists in 1980 coincided with increased support for the liberal parties and a drop in support for the socialist parties.[3] In the following election, support for the liberal

TABLE 8.2. *Support for social security and old age pensions in Britain and the Netherlands, 1964–87*

	Expansion	As now	Reduction	Don't know	*N*
Britain					
1964	77	20	—	3	1,769
1966	55	41	—	4	1,874
1969	43	44	8	5	1,114
1970	57	36	4	3	1,334
1983	81	16	—	3	3,941
1985	74	23	2	1	1,474
Netherlands					
1970	59	28	—	13	1,901
1975	33	58	1	8	1,975
1980	22	65	1	12	1,977
1985	33	54	1	12	1,954
1986	35	49	1	15	2,012
1987	37	47	1	15	1,985

Notes: Entries are percentages. The British question for 1964, 1966, 1969, 1970, and 1983 is: 'Do you feel that the government should spend more on pensions and social services, or do you feel that spending for social services should stay as it is now?' For 1985: 'Do you think that the government should spend more or less on old age pensions?' The Dutch question is: 'Now, I mention some social services. Will you please tell me for every one of them whether it is, in your opinion, sufficient or insufficient at the moment? What is your opinion of old age pensions?'

Sources: British election studies; British Social Attitudes Study (1985); Cultural Change in the Netherlands.

parties dropped back again, accompanied by a revival of support for more spending on pensions, although not reaching the same levels as in the late 1960s. Finally, it is particularly striking that there was virtually no support for reducing old age pensions in either Britain or the Netherlands during this period.

Does support for social security follow the same pattern in the Nordic countries? These are often portrayed as consensus nations, where there was negligible conflict among parties and voters about the development of the welfare state. The common picture is also of basic similarities in their welfare state institutions. This picture reflects both self-perceptions among the Nordic peoples, as well as descriptions provided by foreign observers (Graubard 1986; Kolberg 1992).

The distributions in Table 8.3 reveal similarities as well as differences in the evolution of attitudes towards social security schemes and reforms. As in Britain and the Netherlands, none of the Nordic countries reveals basic and long-term preferences for reducing old age pensions. However, the proportion in favour of expansion varies considerably over time and between the four countries.

The pattern of support in Denmark and Norway conform nicely to the popularity cycles revealed in Britain and the Netherlands. These tendencies are less obvious in Sweden, but they are not at all visible in Finland. Indeed, only Finland fits the assumption of a linear decline in support. However, as we have few data-points for Finland, interpretations have to be cautious. Although after 1975 there was altogether a 20 percentage point decline in the proportion supporting the expansion of pensions, there was still, in 1985, close to a majority preferring expansion. Moreover, as these were Finland's most prosperous years, economic recession or fiscal crises do not provide credible explanations for the decline. Again, Finland is neither among the most heavily taxed countries, nor did Finland experience any major increases in the level of taxation during this period (Lane, McKay, and Newton 1991: tables 5.1–5.4). At face value, it looks as if either Wilensky's or Inglehart's generation theory might fit the pattern of attitudes in Finland. However, closer inspection of the data reveals that it is actually among the younger generation that the welfare state enjoys most popularity, even if the differences are rather modest (Pöntinen and Uusitalo 1986: 54).

The popularity cycle is most visible in Denmark. During the 1960s, at least 60 per cent supported the expansion of social security; in the early 1970s, this proportion dropped to around 40 per cent; by the late 1970s, there was again a majority preferring expansion; and by the 1980s firm majorities for expansion, reaching 80 per cent in 1987, had returned. By 1990 there was decline again, with 66 per cent supporting expansion. The ups and downs of the Danish popularity cycle are closely related to the rise and fall of the populist—anti-tax and anti-government—Progress Party. The Progressives had an immediate and surprising success during the 1970s, garnering around 15 per cent of the votes in three elections. In 1984, however, support dropped to a meagre 3 per cent.

In Norway, preferences for expanding social security peaked with the National Insurance Scheme, introduced in 1966 by a non-socialist government. The first major drop follows closely after 1973, when, as in Denmark, the Progress Party was established and won its first seats in parliament.[4] Ties to the cycles of political popularity are clear again in 1981, when there was a further decline in support, but this time linked to the victory of the Conservative Party, which achieved its highest

TABLE 8.3. *Attitudes to social security, social reforms, and old age pensions in the Nordic countries, 1960s–1990s*

	Expansion	No opinion	No expansion	Don't know	*N*
Sweden					
1960	33	8	49	10	1,466
1964	33	—	63	4	2,849
1968	51	—	42	7	2,866
1970	35	—	59	6	2,743
1973	32	—	60	8	2,421
1976	32	—	61	7	2,683
1979	27	—	67	6	2,674
1980	25	—	68	7	1,449
1985	30	—	62	8	2,671
1988	30	—	61	9	2,529
1991	24	—	68	8	2,478
Denmark					
1964	62	—	22	16	3,104
1969	67	5	23	5	707
1973	42	—	58	—	1,850
1974	39	7	47	7	3,915
1978	55	7	32	6	2,085
1979	56	7	31	6	1,973
1984	63	6	24	7	1,029
1987	80	4	15	1	1,022
1988	73	4	20	3	670
1990	66	5	26	3	1,002

	Expansion	As now	Reduction	Don't know	*N*
Norway					
1965	42	36	9	13	1,619
1969	(68)	—	(25)	(7)	1,162
1973	18	49	22	11	1,218
1977	33	38	7	22	1,727
1981	22	51	16	11	1,596
1985	38	39	5	18	2,180
1989	27	56	11	6	2,195
1993	21	63	10	6	2,194
Finland					
1975	68	23	4	5	1,011
1980	58	37	2	3	976
1985	47	46	4	3	961

Notes: Entries are percentages. 'No opinion' in the Swedish and Danish data means that the responses are not classifiable according to the categories used. The Swedish question, formulated similarly for each year, is: 'Social reforms have gone so far in this country that the government should reduce rather than increase social support and benefits in the future. What is your opinion on this issue? Do you entirely agree, agree somewhat, have an ambivalent position, disagree somewhat, or disagree entirely?' The ambivalent category was used only in 1960. The 'entirely' and 'somewhat' responses are collapsed in the table. The Danish question varies. In 1964, the question was: 'What do you think of the current size of the old age pension?' In 1969, 1974, 1978, 1979, and 1984, the question was: 'Which of these statements fits your own opinion: (*a*) Social reforms have gone too far, people should manage without social support and benefits from government; (*b*) The social reforms which have been introduced in Denmark should at least be maintained at the present level. Which do you agree with?' In 1973, 1987, 1988, and 1990, the question is similar to that asked in Sweden. The Norwegian question, except in 1969, is: 'Many people think that by now we have more than enough social security benefits, and that we should attempt to limit them in the future, while others claim that we should maintain our social benefit programmes and if necessary extend them. Do you have an opinion on that? What is your opinion?' In 1969 the question was: 'Social reforms in this country have come so far that the government must reduce social payments and support to people instead of increasing them.' Those disagreeing are classed as expansionists; those agreeing wanting reduction. The Finnish question is: 'In the following I list some cash benefits mainly financed by taxes. Please tell me, in each case, whether taxes should be used more than now, the same as now, or less than now to finance these benefits.' (Pöntinen and Uusitalo 1986).

Sources: national election studies.

post-war vote: from 17 per cent in 1973, Conservative support rose to 32 per cent in 1981. The 1985 election was virtually an election on the welfare state, which revitalized the popularity of social security expansion. The drop yet again in 1989 is associated with the best ever result achieved by the Progress Party. However, both the Conservatives and Progressives did rather poorly in 1993, while support for expanding social security dropped even further. But this decline is more than compensated for by the highest ever proportion expressing satisfaction with the current level of provision, while opposition remained stable.

Sweden reveals more stable patterns, although some variation is evident. Swedish support peaked during the late 1960s, when about 50 per cent of the electorate preferred increased social support and benefits. This corresponds to the best ever electoral result for the Social Democrats, who won more than 50 per cent of the vote. Thereafter, during the 1970s, support fell back to the levels found in the early 1960s, and, in parallel, opposition to expansion grew until, in 1980, expansion was supported by only about a quarter of the electorate and opposed by about two-thirds. This pattern broadly continued through to 1991, when the Conservative vote increased to 23 per cent (from 18 per cent in 1988) and New Democracy—a neo-liberal, populist party similar to the Progress Party in Denmark and Norway—won almost 7 per cent of the vote in its first election. Even so, note that the variation in support for expanding social security is only slightly above 20 percentage points (based on the deviant case of the 1968 election), whereas in Denmark the variation was about 40 percentage points. Generally, Swedish support levels have stayed at around the 30 per cent level for a period of twenty-five years, with the exception of the electoral successes of the Conservative Party in 1980 and 1991. This pattern clearly supports the theory of popularity cycles.

The overall picture reveals some common patterns in support for pensions and social security. During the 1960s, when most countries introduced major social reforms, their popularity seems unquestionable. This conforms to our initial theories about attitudes towards the welfare state. During the 1970s, welfare systems continued to enjoy support, but with growing division between those wanting continued expansion and those wanting only to preserve, or even dismantle, what had been established. This mood of non-expansion or opposition seems to be shared in a number of West European countries from the 1970s through to the 1990s. These changes in attitudes are closely linked to the political campaigns of either new populist, neo-liberal parties, or changes in the ideology and policies of old liberal or conservative parties. Common to their campaigns was opposition to welfare state expansion, even proposals to dismantle established programmes in some cases. In Britain and Scandinavia, where these shifts have been most evident, shifts in attitudes have also been most pronounced. Yet, according to our evidence, bouts of opposition to the welfare state were short-lived exceptions. During the 1980s, as economic recession became evident, the popularity of the welfare state was revitalized—except in Finland.[5]

Another major finding is the lack of hard core opposition to the welfare state. Where the survey question explicitly offers the option, the proportions preferring a reduction in social security are largest in Norway. However, over the entire period for which we have data, Norwegians were quite satisfied with the levels of social security provision. This was also true for the Dutch and the Swedes. By contrast, the demand for expansion was pronounced in Britain and Denmark, perhaps because, for most people, pensions are not income related.[6]

Finally, we examine the popularity profiles of three major programmes relating to the security dimension of the welfare state. From the ISSP surveys in 1985 and 1990 we have identical questions about whether or not the government should spend more on old age pensions, health services, and unemployment benefits. For Germany, Britain, and Italy the questions were asked in both years, but only in 1985 for Austria and 1990 in Norway. The distributions are presented in Table 8.4. Before embarking on this analysis, however, we should keep in mind Beate Huseby's finding (Chapter 4) that people tend to respond negatively to general questions about increasing government spending but to react more positively to questions about spending in specific policy areas such as pensions and health services.

As we noted earlier, in Britain and the Netherlands, with unambiguous questions about which programmes to expand, support for both old age pensions and health services is relatively high compared to general support for social security and benefits. Nowhere do we see any sizeable opposition to government spending on either programme. In every country, except for pensions in Germany in 1985, support levels for increased spending on pensions and health services are well above 50 per cent. There is no sign of reduced willingness to spend on either programme; on the contrary, although small, the changes between 1985 and 1990 show the increasing popularity of both programmes. This is most prominent in Germany, where there is a ten-point increase in support for spending more money on pensions, and a twenty-point increase in favour of spending more on health services. The same tendencies are evident in Italy; the changes are smaller but preferences for more spending in 1985 are much higher than in Germany.

Unemployment benefits, on the other hand, do not enjoy the same level of popularity. Austria even demonstrates that in 1985 a majority favoured less spending on unemployment benefits. Still, in countries where the question is repeated, the basic profile is one of stability. Only in Britain do we find a noticeable change, a drop of five points among those who want to spend more.

An intriguing pattern is revealed, however, when we compare these countries. Only in Italy is there a majority—just—in favour of more government spending on unemployment benefits. In Germany and Britain, this proportion drops to 35 per cent. In Norway, it drops to less than 20 per cent; one in four even wants unemployment benefits cut. This clearly undermines the idea that the Scandinavian welfare states are rooted in stronger and more stable popular support than in less affluent countries which spend less on welfare. This is even more striking since unemployment, which was of no social or economic significance in Norway during the 1960s and 1970s, had become one of its political embarrassments by the late 1980s.

TABLE 8.4. *Support for increased spending on old age pensions, health services, and unemployment benefits in five West European countries, 1985 and 1990*

Programme	1985			1990		
	Old age pensions	Health	Unemployment	Old age pensions	Health	Unemployment
Austria						
More	55	62	13			
As now	41	32	35		n.a.	
Less	4	6	52			
N	1,471	1,474	1,475			
Germany						
More	46	52	35	55	73	37
As now	50	41	52	43	24	50
Less	4	7	13	2	3	13
N	1,021	1,019	1,006	2,724	2,756	2,719
Britain						
More	75	88	41	82	90	36
As now	24	11	40	17	9	47
Less	1	1	19	1	1	17
N	1,484	1,497	1,465	1,167	1,172	1,144
Italy						
More	75	79	56	80	85	52
As now	21	14	26	17	11	31
Less	4	7	18	3	4	17
N	1,539	1,551	1,511	969	976	959
Norway						
More				72	83	19
As now		n.a.		27	16	57
Less				1	1	24
N				1,447	1,461	1,416

Notes: Entries are percentages. The question is: 'Listed below are various areas of government spending. Please show whether you would like to see more or less government spending in each area. Remember that if you say "much more", it might require a tax increase to pay for it.'

Sources: ISSP (1985, 1990).

Social Protection and Social Position

Our next question concerns who supports the welfare state, and what differences we find between expansionary periods for the welfare state and recessionary times. The comparisons across countries and years are made using the variables and definitions described in the Appendix. The questions are from the British election studies (Table 8.1), the Cultural Change Study for the Netherlands (Table 8.2), and several national election studies for Denmark, Norway, and Sweden (Table 8.3). For Norway and Sweden, we can examine the demographic correlates of support for expanding social security as far back as the 1960s. Denmark, Britain, and the Netherlands provide such evidence for the 1970s and 1980s. The results are shown in Tables 8.5 and 8.6.

In both Norway and Sweden support for expanding old age pensions is clearly class related. From the 1960s to the 1980s people who identify with the working class are invariably more in favour of increased spending on pensions and benefits than almost any other group. No other variables have such consistently significant correlations. However, close inspection of the relationship indicates that the effects are weakening: there is a steady fall in the size of the coefficients as we move from the 1960s to the 1980s. But age, surprisingly, has an opposite impact in the two countries. Elderly people are more favourable towards expansion in Norway, although the relationship is significant only in 1973. In Sweden, it is the younger generation which supports expansion, and the impact seems to grow over the years. Also, contrary to our initial assumptions, education tends to induce support for spending. Indeed, in the mid-1970s the well educated are among the most positive about expanding social security.

Two other groups show a similar willingness to support spending. People employed in the public sector are more favourable to expansion than those working in the private sector, which fits with the assumption of socialization in 'public policy' values. Again, employed people are consistently more hostile to social security expansion than those not in the labour force, which conforms with Rose and Peters's expectations. However, there is not the anticipated opposition as income increases. In view of the strong relationship between income and pensions in Norway and Sweden, few Scandinavians would be surprised that the well-to-do are rather satisfied. Lastly, note that Swedish women tend to be more positive about increasing pensions than men, although the relationship is statistically significant only in 1968.

TABLE 8.5. *Support for old age pensions in Norway and Sweden, and for increased social benefits in Denmark*

	Norway: old age pensions			Sweden: old age pensions			Denmark: social benefits			
	1965	1973	1985	1968	1973	1988	1979	1981	1984	1987
Gender	−0.006	0.032	−0.028	−0.090**	−0.038	−0.013	−0.008	0.058	−0.018	0.012
	0.004	0.028	−0.011	−0.067**	−0.038	0.039	−0.013	0.058	−0.006	0.030
Age	0.017	0.106**	0.008	−0.076**	−0.043	−0.171**	−0.120**	−0.128*	0.058	−0.056
	0.010	0.086**	0.015	−0.041	−0.016	−0.106**	−0.096**	−0.129*	0.038	−0.053
Income	−0.010	−0.020	0.044	−0.039	—	−0.007	−0.040	−0.042	−0.109	—
	−0.036	−0.042	−0.023	−0.032	—	−0.071*	−0.037	0.014	−0.086	—
Education	0.007	0.093**	−0.015	0.048*	0.094**	0.028	0.130**	0.117*	0.096	0.017
	−0.050*	0.015	−0.044	−0.004	0.065**	0.045	0.059	0.040	0.008	0.041
Employed *v.* non-employed	−0.018	−0.023	−0.090**	−0.060*	−0.057*	−0.169**	−0.068	0.015	0.063	−0.052
	0.002	−0.042	−0.066**	−0.028	−0.029	−0.022	0.014	0.055	−0.004	−0.005
Publicly employed	0.075**	0.028	0.055*	—	—	0.168**	—	—	0.034	0.076*
	0.063**	0.025	0.050*	—	—	0.129**	—	—	0.028	0.065
Working-class identification	0.170**	0.129**	0.124**	0.207**	0.155**	0.101**	0.246**	0.286**	0.159**	—
	0.156**	0.105**	0.118**	0.192**	0.130**	0.076**	0.207**	0.238**	0.136**	—
R^2	0.028	0.021	0.019	0.049	0.028	0.049	0.065	0.081	0.020	0.004
N	1,334	1,058	2,023	2,398	1,917	1,811	930	453	465	993

$^*p < 0.05$ $^{**}p < 0.01$

Notes: Entries in the upper line are beta coefficients; in the lower line, Pearson's *r*. A dash indicates that relevant data are not available. The definition of variables is given in the appendix. The dependent variable is based on questions reported in Table 8.3. R^2 is adjusted.

Sources: national election studies.

Looking at support for social benefits in Denmark reinforces the picture of a common pattern in Scandinavia. Again, identification with the working class is consistently the best predictor of support for spending, and during the late 1970s and early 1980s education has a positive impact on willingness to spend. Moreover, as in Sweden, it is the younger generation which wants to expand benefits, even if this inclination fades during the 1980s. We also find public sector employees consistently more supportive than those employed in the private sector. But, in contrast to the other Scandinavian countries, Denmark reveals no differences between the employed and people not in work. Note also that, again, there is no significant relationship to income. Considering that Scandinavians are among the most heavily taxed in Western Europe, this suggests that the Scandinavian model of income-related pensions and benefits does not provoke opposition to tax-financed social security systems.

Britain's social benefits are basically flat rate payments; any additional benefits come from private insurance or employers' schemes. Thus, there is not the direct connection with income—the higher the earnings, the higher the benefits—as in Scandinavian systems. Looking at Table 8.6, Rose and Peters's assumption about the effect of income appears to have some merit. Although data on family income are available only for 1979 and 1987, the negative relationships are quite striking. For those years for which we lack data on income there are negative relationships with education, although weaker than for income. Given the strong relationship between education and income in Britain,[7] this suggests less willingness to fund social benefits among the well-to-do. The consistently negative attitude among tax payers in general, with the employed being more sceptical than those not in the workforce, reinforces an image of the British as reluctant taxpayers so long as they perceive that benefits are distributed to the less fortunate. This patterning of attitudes is well in line with the tax burden assumptions of Rose and Peters.

However, these preferences are consistently challenged by the younger generation. Contrary to the theories of both Wilensky and Inglehart, the young are not abandoning the welfare state, but, rather, demanding its expansion. Together with the young, and in opposition to the well-off and well educated, the British working class look for larger pensions and benefits. This portrays British welfare politics as even more related to class differences than is the case among Scandinavians.

The data for the Netherlands reveals a third and new picture. For the

TABLE 8.6. *Support for increased social benefits in Britain, 1974–87, and old age pensions in the Netherlands, 1970–85*

	Britain: social benefits				Netherlands: old age pensions			
	1974	1979	1983	1987	1970	1975	1980	1985
Gender	−0.022	−0.035	−0.008	−0.023	−0.052	−0.027	−0.004	0.085*
	0.023	0.017	−0.022	0.001	0.063*	−0.018	−0.001	0.062
Age	−0.167**	−0.098*	−0.197**	−0.205**	−0.004	−0.050	−0.054	0.008
	−0.101**	−0.013	−0.135**	−0.120**	−0.020	−0.049*	−0.028	0.007
Income	—	−0.149**	—	−0.159**	−0.033	−0.094**	−0.061	−0.051
	—	−0.180**	—	−0.120**	−0.045*	−0.081**	−0.071*	−0.105**
Education	−0.054*	−0.039	−0.038*	—	−0.044	0.037	−0.051	0.027
	−0.055**	−0.077*	−0.039*	—	−0.012	0.005	−0.063	−0.050
Employed *v.*	−0.134**	−0.080*	−0.106**	−0.048*	—	−0.009	0.042	0.000
non-employed	−0.069**	−0.106**	−0.145**	−0.034	—	−0.018	0.035	−0.011
Publicly	—	—	—	—	—	—	—	—
employed	—	—	—	—	—	—	—	—
Working-class	0.115**	0.078**	0.154**	0.055**	0.057	0.015	0.004	0.114**
identification	0.123**	0.114**	0.160**	0.095**	0.054*	0.036	0.054*	0.127**
R^2	0.041	0.044	0.055	0.048	0.005	0.007	0.006	0.018
N	2,215	1,418	3,450	3,084	1,345	1,324	1,380	1,238

$^*p < 0.05$ $^{**}p < 0.01$

Notes: See notes to Table 8.5.

Sources: British election studies; Cultural Change in the Netherlands.

Dutch, there is little discrimination regarding preferences about spending on pensions. Indeed, for nearly all the variables, the relationships are less consistent and weaker than for both the Scandinavian countries and Britain. The upper-income groups are reluctant about spending more, but the association tends to drop to non-significance as we introduce statistical controls. Social class is significantly related to expansion only in 1985, the last year for which we have data. In that year, however, we find gender emerging as significant, with women being slightly more in favour of expansion than men. On the whole, the Netherlands seem to be without persistent tension in the field of old age policies. At the same time, no social group emerges as the political stronghold of welfare state support.

Expanding the Security Dimension

So far we have analysed only the structure of support for old age pensions, or policies which include social security as a major part of the programme. The three questions in the 1985 and 1990 ISSP surveys which we looked at earlier (Table 8.4) allow us to extend the analysis. The question about spending on pensions enables us to validate the inquiry so far, by bringing our data for Britain and Norway up to 1990 and introducing three additional countries: Austria, Germany, and Italy. Moreover, as the questions are identical in each country, the data allow us both to examine within-country group differences and to compare such differences across countries. In Table 8.7 we report the structure of support for old age pensions in Germany, Britain, Italy, and Austria in 1985; and for Germany, Britain, Italy, and Norway in 1990. The multivariate results (beta coefficients) are shown in the upper row of each entry, the bivariate results (Pearson's *r*) in the lower row.

Some common trends are evident among these countries in 1985. Although the relationships are sometimes weak, they correspond broadly with generation theory as well as theories of tax frustration. In each country, older people are more likely to support pensions, especially in Britain; in Germany, only the bivariate relationship is significant. The positive impact of age in Britain, compared to Table 8.6, is best explained by the change from a general question about support for 'social benefits and services' to explicit support for 'old age pensions' in Table 8.7.

At the bivariate level, increasing education and income induce

TABLE 8.7. *Support for old age pensions in Western Europe, 1985 and 1990*

	Austria	Germany		Britain		Italy		Norway
	1985	1985	1990	1985	1990	1985	1990	1990
Gender	0.041	−0.003	0.042	−0.008	−0.032	0.027	0.046	0.086*
	0.068	0.035	0.067*	0.020	−0.016	0.072*	0.068	0.113**
Age	0.117**	0.038	0.059*	0.147**	0.106**	0.105**	0.080**	−0.089*
	0.160**	0.080*	0.120**	0.222**	0.193**	0.155**	0.133*	0.047
Income	−0.047	−0.012	−0.088**	−0.073*	−0.174**	0.034	−0.068	−0.083*
	−0.112*	−0.080*	−0.170**	−0.252**	−0.243**	−0.090*	−0.139**	−0.139**
Education	−0.066	−0.071	−0.084**	−0.120**	−0.080*	−0.100**	−0.060	−0.012
	−0.098*	−0.138**	−0.186**	−0.263**	−0.182**	−0.173**	−0.131**	−0.072
Employed *v.*	−0.057	−0.079	−0.021	−0.031	0.003	−0.065*	−0.015	−0.076*
non-employed	−0.144**	−0.115**	−0.109**	−0.177**	−0.135**	−0.130**	−0.072*	−0.115**
Publicly	—	−0.045	0.003	−0.004	0.021	—	0.049	−-0.002
employed	—	−0.085*	−0.063	−0.050	−0.007	—	−0.008	−0.040
Working-class	−0.005	0.091*	0.132**	0.141**	—	0.089**	0.075*	0.126**
identification	0.051	0.139**	0.206**	0.214**	—	0.143**	0.132**	0.158**
R^2	0.034	0.032	0.067	0.114	0.072	0.049	0.034	0.047
N	793	885	1,975	1,230	967	1,224	855	853

$*p < 0.05$ $**p < 0.01$

Notes: See notes to Table 8.5.

Sources: ISSP (1985, 1990).

scepticism about the continued expansion of pensions, although education is significant only in Italy and Britain after statistical control. And in Britain income remains important for support. Furthermore, in line with Rose and Peters, we find that in all four countries employees are more opposed to expanding pensions than people not in work. Except in Austria, social class is relevant but gender has almost no impact. Where we have data on occupational sector, there is not the anticipated support among public employees towards public pension schemes.

Much the same pattern is reproduced when we analyse the corresponding set of variables for 1990. Increasing age continues to have an impact in all four countries. Note, however, that in Norway, after controlling for other variables, the impact changes, with younger generations being the most supportive of pensions. Increasing education and income continue to induce opposition to expanding pensions. Both variables are significant in Germany and Britain. Norway conforms to the other countries in exhibiting opposition from higher income groups. Lack of employment, of course, correlates with low income and—except in Norway—is significant only at the bivariate level. Moreover, for the second time, gender makes a difference in Norway where women are slightly more favourable towards spending on pensions than men. Finally, belonging to the working class continues to stimulate preferences for increased spending on pensions.

Some comments on our initial theoretical propositions are appropriate here. No single theoretical position alone can explain the pattern of support we found. Rather, several theoretical positions have to be taken into account, but all of them with weak explanatory capacity, as revealed by low correlations and rather low R^2 values. For some countries, the consistent connection with age, income, and/or education, gives some indication that both generational differences and tax frustration may be involved. So does the bivariate relationship for support among the employed—'the general tax payer'. Both the correlations with age and employment could be explained by an 'interest' argument: people not in work receive the smallest pensions, whether the system is income related as in Scandinavia, work related as in Germany, or is a flat rate system, with insurance adding to pensions, as in Britain.

The correlations between class and spending preferences are obviously the strongest and most consistent, which supports the theoretical arguments about welfare politics as a matter of class differences. When gender is significant, Norway and the Netherlands being the clearest cases, women are slightly more supportive than men. Being employed in the public sector makes the least impact, which leaves Scandinavia (see Table 8.5) as the only case giving credibility to the theory that people who work in public agencies have distinctive values and preferences.

Public health services provide security against unexpected, and sometimes very large, costs. In most countries, relying on public health services means free or inexpensive services, but traded off against a waiting period for treatment other than in emergencies. This is often thought to encourage people who can afford it to prefer private health services, and they are likely to be less concerned with continuous growth in the public sector. Our analysis of support for public spending on health services, presented in Table 8.8, tends to confirm this.

In 1985, both increasing income and education reduces support for spending on health services. Both variables have a significant impact in Austria, whereas education is the more prominent factor in Germany and Italy, while income is the better predictor in Britain. Social class continues to be related to support for public spending on health, but only in Germany and Britain does the relationship hold up in the multivariate analysis. In Britain, people employed in the public sector were rather more in favour of public health services, but in Germany these attitudes were more characteristic among employees in the private sector.

Five years later, in 1990, a very similar attitude structure persists. Income continued to hold back support for public spending on health services in Britain, while education had the same effect in Germany and Norway. Class identification has much the same impact as in 1985 in Germany, but rather less in Italy. Unfortunately, there are no data for class identification for Britain in 1990. The only new trend, which was just visible in 1985, is that women are more in favour of public spending on health services than men. This was most evident in Germany and Norway.

While the security problems related to old age and health affect everyone, unemployment involves only fractions of the population. Thus, attitudes towards unemployment benefits constitute a test of solidarity, since most people neither wish nor expect to be a beneficiary. The social profile of support for unemployment benefits in 1985 and 1990 are shown in Table 8.9.

In 1985, the most striking difference compared to support for pensions and health services is that the impact of age has changed completely. Now it is the younger generation in Britain and Austria which prefer increased spending. Another new aspect is the stronger and more

TABLE 8.8. *Support for public spending on health in Western Europe, 1985 and 1990*

	Austria	Germany		Britain		Italy		Norway
	1985	1985	1990	1985	1990	1985	1990	1990
Gender	0.030	0.039	0.075**	0.028	0.058	0.028	0.032	0.137**
	0.056	0.074*	0.086**	0.044	0.070*	0.049	0.044	0.144**
Age	−0.033	0.053	−0.015	−0.044	−0.077*	−0.037	−0.018	−0.116**
	0.007	0.067	0.043	−0.019	0.034	0.015	0.010	−0.058
Income	−0.086*	−0.045	−0.009	−0.085*	−0.148**	−0.037	−0.066	−0.035
	−0.103**	−0.105**	−0.074**	−0.117**	−0.105**	−0.096*	−0.081*	−0.085*
Education	−0.081*	−0.162**	−0.136**	0.004	−0.012	−0.147**	0.002	−0.115**
	−0.092*	−0.230**	−0.170**	−0.068	−0.047	−0.165**	−0.026	−0.098*
Employed *v.*	−0.043	−0.026	−0.017	0.006	0.038	0.006	−0.029	−0.033
non-employed	−0.070*	−0.045	−0.042	−0.047	−0.018	−0.052**	−0.032	−0.074*
Publicly	—	−0.041	0.042	0.080**	0.054	—	0.047	0.001
employed	—	−0.096*	−0.007	0.056	0.037	—	0.014	−0.018
Working-class	−0.050	0.086*	0.087**	0.166**	—	0.031	0.043	0.017
identification	0.004	0.175**	0.146**	0.189**	—	0.105**	0.065	0.070*
R^2	0.014	0.059	0.039	0.042	0.018	0.027	0.003	0.036
N	804	885	2,000	1,242	970	1,231	862	863

$*p < 0.05$ $**p < 0.01$

Notes: See notes to Table 8.5.

Sources: ISSP (1985, 1990).

TABLE 8.9. *Support for unemployment benefits in Western Europe, 1985 and 1990*

	Austria	Germany		Britain		Italy		Norway
	1985	1985	1990	1985	1990	1985	1990	1990
Gender	−0.022	0.029	0.020	−0.029	−0.005	−0.005	0.111**	0.039
	0.027	0.075*	0.044	0.035	0.047	0.051	0.165**	0.048
Age	−0.106**	0.007	−0.122**	−0.107**	−0.113**	−0.031	−0.067	−0.121**
	−0.015	0.016	−0.062*	0.004	0.009	0.026	0.019	0.080*
Income	−0.097*	−0.067	−0.047	−0.197**	−0.179**	−0.007	−0.207**	−0.044
	−0.132**	−0.118**	−0.130**	−0.290**	−0.198**	−0.102**	−0.216**	−0.116**
Education	0.009	−0.008	−0.004	−0.025	−0.047	−0.033	−0.024	−0.061
	−0.048	−0.074*	−0.075*	−0.166**	−0.107**	−0.107**	−0.081*	−0.117**
Employed *v.*	−0.120**	−0.037	−0.079**	−0.109**	−0.096*	−0.117**	−0.127**	−0.027
non-employed	−0.111**	−0.084*	−0.074**	−0.206**	−0.145**	−0.137**	−0.129**	−0.059
Publicly	—	−0.011	−0.011	0.063*	0.075*	—	0.144**	0.025
employed	—	−0.052	−0.055	−0.004	0.041	—	0.032	0.060
Working-class	0.098**	0.094*	0.195**	0.194**	—	0.119**	0.007	0.203**
identification	0.117**	0.112**	0.209**	0.292**	—	0.148**	0.089*	0.240**
R^2	0.031	0.017	0.059	0.134	0.050	0.032	0.076	0.068
N	784	872	1,972	1,217	948	1,202	846	838

*$p < 0.05$ **$p < 0.01$

Notes: See notes to Table 8.5.

Sources: ISSP (1985, 1990).

consistently significant difference between the employed and non-working population. In all four countries, those who work are less inclined to support increased spending on unemployment benefits. The impact of income and education is much the same as for old age pensions and health services: support for spending declines as income and education increases. But in each case, support is related to social class; working-class self-identifiers are more willing to support spending on unemployment benefits than those identifying themselves as middle class.

As we move to 1990 little changes. Including Norway in the analysis only confirms that the younger generation is more inclined to support unemployment benefits. But, in contrast, there is no such tendency in Italy in either year. We also continue to see a lack of solidarity towards the unemployed among the employed. Income and education are still negatively related to support in all four countries at the bivariate level, but at the multivariate level they are significant only in Italy and, as usual, Britain. Finally, class endures as an important determinant of welfare state support, although the impact in Italy weakened between 1985 and 1990. However, Italy reveals some exceptional impressions in 1990: women seem to be more in favour of unemployment benefits than men, and so are people employed in the public sector compared to those working in the private sector.

Considering our initial theoretical arguments, the generational explanations proposed by Wilensky and Inglehart cannot account for the patterns of support for unemployment benefits. On the contrary, the youngest age groups are the most concerned about security against unemployment, as well as those who—on circumstantial evidence—seem to have a sense of solidarity. However, Rose and Peters's arguments about tax burdens and frustration accord well with the general patterns of attitudes for both 1985 and 1990. As for other welfare programmes, social class seems to be the most consistent catalyst in generating support for increased spending. This tendency is evident from the mid-1960s through until 1990 for at least three different policy areas related to the security aspects of the welfare state.

Welfare Politics

Today the welfare state is a common political project. Conflicts about the welfare state rarely relate to basic principles but to priorities about which needs have to be met and the extent of coverage. However, historically the welfare state was associated with political parties which were concerned to protect workers against the fluctuations of markets, the dangers of the work place, and illness or infirmity. These were generally socialist, social democratic, or labour parties. Even if welfare programmes have been supported by other parties, and liberal as well as conservative parties have introduced welfare reforms, the notion of the welfare state as primarily a project of democratic socialism is well established.

Our final analysis is concerned with the relationship between party support and attitudes towards the welfare state: are supporters of social democratic—or labour—parties still more in favour of public spending on welfare than supporters of centrist or conservative parties? For this analysis, we divided voters into three groups: conservatives, including supporters of populist, 'new right' parties; centrists, which consisted of supporters of liberal, Christian, centre, and agrarian parties; and left voters, which embraced supporters of social democratic, socialist, left socialist, labour, and communist parties. This party preference variable was then introduced into the regression equations used for the ISSP 1985 and 1990 data. The results are shown in Table 8.10.[8] Only the effect of party adherence is entered in the table since the effects of controlling for the other independent variables are displayed in the two previous tables.

Three main findings emerge. First, the effect of party politics is more important in some countries than others. The strongest relationship between party preferences and willingness to spend more on welfare programmes appeared in Britain, but there are similar effects in Germany. In Norway and Austria, party adherence is relevant only for spending on health services and unemployment benefits; supporters of different parties seem to agree about spending on old age pensions. Secondly, the importance of party politics varies across different welfare programmes. Support for unemployment benefits is most clearly connected to party preferences in all four countries. Then follows support for health services, and lastly backing for old age pensions.

Thirdly, whereas the earlier models resulted in fairly small R^2s, the introduction of party preference increases the explained variance quite substantially—even after controlling for class identification and social stratification variables such as income and education. Most prominent is the increase in the R^2 for Britain, especially on support for unemployment benefits in 1985 where the explained variance exceeds 20 per cent.

TABLE 8.10. *Party adherence and support for increased spending on old age pensions, health services, and unemployment benefits, 1985 and 1990*

	Austria	Germany		Britain		Norway
	1985	1985	1990	1985	1990	1990
Pensions						
Beta	0.065	0.165**	0.069*	0.166**	0.211**	0.024
Pearson's *r*	0.074	0.176**	0.166**	0.225**	0.228**	0.060
R^2	0.027	0.056	0.075	0.141	0.111	0.055
N	619	689	1308	1094	846	667
Public health						
Beta	0.085*	0.187**	0.148**	0.279**	0.258**	0.090*
Pearson's *r*	0.094*	0.192**	0.159**	0.324**	0.278**	0.122**
R^2	0.018	0.084	0.069	0.114	0.084	0.045
N	624	668	1323	1104	850	673
Unemployment						
Beta	0.137**	0.232**	0.170**	0.306**	0.309**	0.165**
Pearson's *r*	0.142**	0.239**	0.162**	0.390**	0.334**	0.242**
R^2	0.053	0.061	0.085	0.207	0.139	0.102
N	609	661	1,304	1,083	832	655

*$p < 0.05$ **$p < 0.01$

Notes: The beta coefficients are controlled for gender, age, education, family income, employed *v.* non-employed status, public employment *v.* private employment, and subjective class. The definition of the party adherence variable is given in the appendix. R^2 is adjusted.

Sources: ISSP (1985, 1990).

This suggests some conclusions relevant to our theoretical arguments. Even if class politics and political preferences do not present us with a single and conclusive explanation of support for the welfare state, this dimension—often overlooked in the last decade of political science analysis—is clearly the best predictor of welfare preferences, although still fairly modest.

Finally, we investigate whether the impact of party adherence has changed since the 1960s. Here, we have to go back to the questions asked in national election studies, so we have to allow for the slight variations in the questions asked. Not surprisingly, the countries for which we have the appropriate data are those where class politics and class parties have been most prominent: Britain, Denmark, Norway, and Sweden.[9] Interestingly, these countries have all experienced some attenuation of the relationship between class position and party preference (Worre 1980: 318; Franklin and Mughan 1978: 523–34). Among voters who would be classified as working class—according to their education, income, and occupation—fewer were voting for left-wing parties by the late 1980s. However, socialist parties are often supported by young and well-educated middle-class employees in the public sector. The impact of party adherence over time is shown in Table 8.11.

Norway and Sweden provide the longest time series, and reveal slightly different patterns. In both countries, voting for left socialist or social democratic parties increases support for spending on old age pensions, but much more so in Sweden than in Norway. Indeed, there is remarkable stability in the relationship between party adherence and support in Sweden. If anything has changed it is towards the more pronounced importance of party adherence. This is explained by the fact that Social Democratic governments have introduced the major

TABLE 8.11. *Party adherence and support for increased spending on old age pensions in Denmark, Britain, Norway, and Sweden*

	Beta	Pearson's r	R^2	N
Denmark				
1979	0.315**	0.348**	0.141	824
1981	0.349**	0.401**	0.186	392
1984	0.413**	0.380**	0.144	414
1987	0.268**	0.276**	0.074	857
Britain				
1974	0.287**	0.306**	0.113	1,878
1979	0.297**	0.317**	0.120	1,186
1987	0.330**	0.364**	0.149	2,599
Norway				
1965	0.191**	0.207**	0.044	1,023
1973	0.043	0.045	0.029	655
1985	0.197**	0.214**	0.045	1,256
Sweden				
1968	0.334**	0.347**	0.138	2,314
1973	0.306**	0.286**	0.096	1,684
1987	0.366**	0.344**	0.162	1,605

*$p < 0.05$ ** $p < 0.01$

Notes: See notes to Table 8.10.

Sources: national election studies.

welfare reforms in Sweden, while in Norway the major programme—the National Insurance Scheme—was carried through by a non-socialist coalition which included centrist parties (Liberal, Christian, and Agrarian) and the Conservative Party. In Norway, the impact of party is non-significant in 1973 as the political consensus on welfare policies still existed. By 1985, however, as conflicts over welfare spending or tax relief became salient issues, political polarization reappeared.

Exactly the same picture emerges for Britain and Denmark for the 1970s and 1980s. Party adherence encourages welfare support, and there is no sign of the relationship weakening, except at the 1987 election in Denmark. And even then, the relationship is much stronger than most of the significant relationships revealed in this chapter. Although several theoretical arguments suggest hypotheses on the processes which determine expansionist or restrictive attitudes towards the welfare state, the results shown in Tables 8.10 and 8.11 indicate that welfare policies have been and remain a matter of ideological and political preferences. The conflicts and their solutions depend on party strength among the electorate and the popularity cycles of ideological positions.

Conclusion

At the outset of this chapter we presented a number of theories which have enjoyed prominence in attempting to explain the development of support for the welfare state. These theories allowed us to anticipate who are the supporters and the opponents of welfare programmes. One of our main conclusions is that no single theory alone provides reliable explanations or interpretations of the support patterns revealed. All the theories have some merit, and some findings are consistent with more than one theory. These observations suggest caution about accepting those arguments uncritically. We have to be aware of the shifting relevance of different theories as a consequence of national politics and the changing nature of the welfare state.

None the less, several conclusions seem indisputable. First, there is no evidence that welfare states, or specific welfare programmes, are generally losing support over time, as some theories predict. Rather, there are ups and downs in their popularity. The 'downs' seem to be connected to general changes in the national political mood. Vigorous conservative campaigns, sometimes leading to electoral victories, are accompanied by a decline in the proportion of the public demanding expansion of the welfare state, or even an increase in the proportion supporting reductions in spending. But such campaigns appear not to create lasting opposition. Rather, the opposition created by conservative politicians tends to fade away as the novelty of their messages becomes yesterday's news and the public have direct experience of poorer services.

Secondly, to explain which groups promote or contest the welfare state, a complex relationship has to be considered. Several of the theoretical arguments are relevant but each explains only part of the process leading to different attitudes. Certainly, theories predicting a continuous decline in support for the welfare state failed when confronted with our evidence. None the less, the groups which are supposed to be primarily responsible for challenging the welfare state—the well educated and the rich—are, indeed, among the most sceptical about the expansion of old age pensions, public health services, and unemployment benefits.

The younger generation is also more sceptical than the older generation about old age pensions and health services, which accords with generation theories. But this pattern of support is also consonant with an interest interpretation: the older generation is particularly supportive due to their vested interests in old age pensions and 'free' health care. We also noticed that the young behaved quite differently over unemployment benefits, where they might be thought to have vested interests.

Finally, class identification and party adherence are stronger correlates of attitudes towards social security than any other variables. There is no substantial and systematic reduction in the impact of class identification on attitudes as we move from the mid-1960s through to 1990. This indicates that welfare policies continue to be a matter of class politics, suggesting that theories of class formation provide a superior explanation for people's spending preferences on welfare programmes over the entire time period analysed. This conclusion is reinforced by the impact of party adherence. Electors who vote for leftist or working-class parties are more inclined to support spending on welfare programmes than those voting for centrist or conservative parties, even after controlling for class position. This relationship, too, is remarkably stable from the 1960s until the early 1990s, and is by far the best predictor of spending preferences. In people's minds, there are differences in the welfare policies pursued by parties of different political colour, and their preferences among the parties reflect their preferences about the development of the welfare state.

APPENDIX

The variables used in Tables 8.5–8.11 were coded as follows.

Dependent variable

The dependent variable differed slightly according to the data set used. For the ISSP data, the question is: 'Listed below are various areas of government spending. Please show whether you would like to see more or less government spending in each area. Remember that if you say "much more", it may require a tax increase to pay for it.' Three items were used: more or less spending for old age pensions; more or less spending for public health services; more or less spending for unemployment benefits. The codings are: spend much more = 4; spend more = 3; spend the same as now = 2; spend less and spend much less = 1. In national elections surveys, if possible an approximation to the four-value classification in the ISSP is used. In some cases only a three-fold classification was possible. The questions shown in the notes for Tables 8.1–8.3 indicate the codings used in each case.

Independent variables

Gender: Women = 1; men = 0.

Age: 18–24 years = 1; 25–34 years = 2; 35–44 years = 3; 45–54 years = 4; 55–64 years = 5; 65 years and older = 6.

Income: The income distribution is divided into quartiles. Family income is used, except for Germany where only individual respondent's income is available.

Education: The education variable in the ISSP data is specific to each country. To allow cross-national comparisons, three broad categories were imposed: basic education and incomplete secondary education = 1; secondary education completed and all other post-school education, excluding a degree = 2; degree level = 3. The education data from the national election studies were recoded keeping as close as possible to the ISSP categories: basic education = 1; more than basic education but no college or university education = 2; college or university education = 3.

Employment status: Employed = 1; unemployed or pensioners, housewives, students = 0.

Employment sector: Works for the government or nationalized industries = 1; other occupations and unemployed = 0.

Class identification: In the ISSP data, the coding was: upper middle class and upper class = 1; upper working class and middle class = 2; working class and lower middle class = 3; lower class = 4. In Italy, class position is based on an estimation of the socio-economic position of the respondent by the interviewer. In the national elections studies, the coding was: self-reported middle class = 1; forced-answer middle class = 2; forced-answer working-class = 3; self-reported working-class = 4.

Party adherence: In the ISSP data, the question is: 'If there were a general election tomorrow which party do you think you would most likely support?' The national election studies ask for vote intention just prior to the election or actual vote just after the election, depending on whether the survey is a pre- or post-election survey. The coding is: parties classified or named as conservative or neo-liberal/populist = 1; as liberal, Christian, agrarian or peoples parties = 2; as left-socialist, socialist, social-democratic or leftist = 3.

NOTES

1. With synchronic survey data it is difficult to discriminate, empirically, between theories claiming increased opposition among the younger generation and theories advocating increasing support among the oldest generation. The distribution of support would look similar if one or both sets of theories are correct. Only if genuine panel surveys were available could changes in individual attitudes be followed through different life-cycles and circumstances.
2. The opposition to expansion at the 1979 election is confirmed by a slightly different question. The 1974 (October) and 1979 British Election Study included a question asking people if they thought social services had gone too far, were about right, or if welfare reforms had not gone far enough. In October 1974, 34 per cent thought that social services had gone much too far or a little too far (Taylor-Gooby 1985: 27). In 1979, the responses were: 'much too far' and 'a little too far', 49 per cent; 'about right', 32 per cent; 'not quite far enough' or 'not nearly far enough', 17 per cent; don't know, 3 per cent. *N* = 1,864.
3. Support for the liberal parties increased by 5 percentage points to reach 28 per cent; support for the two socialist parties fell from 35 to 30 per cent. See Lane, McKay, and Newton (1991: tables 7.6 and 7.10). Note that the Netherlands does not have a conservative party in the British or Scandinavian tradition, but rather a multitude of religious, liberal, and socialist parties.
4. The very low level of support for expansion in 1973 was linked to a major debate about the abuse of social security rights. This debate also revealed strong suspicions inside the Labour Party that the disability pension scheme was being inappropriately used (Kolberg and Pettersen 1981).

5. However, we only have three data points for Finland. In view of the fluctuations over time in the other countries, we would have to be cautious about interpreting the 10 percentage point drop every fifth year between 1975 and 1985 as establishing a clear trend.
6. Except for people employed by the government in the public sector, state pensions are not income related in Britain and Denmark.
7. According to the ISSP data, the Pearson correlation between education and income in Britain is 0.45 in 1985 and 0.46 in 1990.
8. Italy is not included in Table 8.10 as the question about voting was not asked.
9. Finland is not included in the analysis as we were unable to secure the Finnish election survey data. The Netherlands is not included because the nature of the Dutch party system makes it difficult to use data from the Dutch Cultural Change Study to classify the parties in a way comparable to the other countries.

9

Government Intervention in the Economy

OLE BORRE AND JOSÈ MANUEL VIEGAS

❖

State management of the economy is the classic issue of economic liberalism. From its origins, in the writings of Adam Smith and Jeremy Bentham in the late eighteenth century, liberals argued against mercantilist thinking that it was the responsibility of government to initiate and regulate a nation's economy. Liberals believed that the greatest benefits for all would materialize in a society where government refrained from interfering with market forces, leaving production and prices to untrammelled competition among firms and individuals.

During the nineteenth century, these ideas were directed against conservatives who sought to protect the domestic economy for national reasons. During the twentieth century, liberalism has been opposed by socialists who have argued that a liberal economy generates inequality and social misery. The success of early welfare policies in transforming the old liberal state entailed that, from a radical, or left, position in politics, liberalism has gradually shifted towards the right. This shift has not been accomplished without repercussions in party systems. In many countries, the liberal parties were in crisis between the two world wars, as in Britain and the Weimar Republic—although the outcomes were widely different.

The forces opposed to liberalism can be seen in state ownership policies. In many countries, nationalization resulted from the coming to power of political forces based on socialist ideology and intent on transforming the economy and society. In opposition to a market logic, certain enterprises in important sectors of some national economies were put under state control—to be guided by social purposes, not profit. This happened in France during the Popular Front government in the 1930s and more recently under the Common Programme of the Left in the early 1980s. Similar nationalization policies were implemented in Britain, mainly by the post-war Labour government, as well as in Portugal after the 1974 revolution.

The expansion of the state into the economy, however, has not always been accomplished by nationalization. In many cases, the state assumed control of certain enterprises or took shares in their capital for pragmatic reasons: to restructure an economic sector; to act against a monopoly; to create financial institutions for development, due to the lack of private capital. In other cases, the state intervened for nationalistic reasons, usually to keep strategic economic activities under national control. Thus, several governments of the right have coexisted with large sectors of the economy under state control and have even expanded their involvement.

In Italy, the public enterprises created by the Fascist governments, such as AGIP (Azienda General Italiana dei Petrolii) in 1926 and IRI (Instituto per la Ricostrucione Industriale) in 1933, were reorganized and developed by post-war Christian democratic governments. They also created other enterprises, for example, ENEL (Ente Nazionale per l'Energia Elettrica) in 1962 for the management of the fuel sector and EFIM (Ente Participazione Finanziamento Indústria Manifatturiere) in the financial and industrial sectors. Similar developments took place in Spain, Greece, and Portugal, mainly during the 1940s and 1950s. In Spain, large public holdings were created, such as INI (Instituto Nacional de Industria) and the ICO (Instituto de Crédito Oficial). State participation in some enterprises has also taken place in Germany under governments of the right. But this has been under special conditions, namely the acceptance of competition between these businesses and private firms. Among government firms there was a tradition of autonomy and decentralization, so these enterprises were the responsibility of the federal authorities and also the commune and the *Land*.

The process of nationalization and the expansion of state control in the economy developed over time and for strategic purposes. By contrast, privatization policies developed rapidly in the late 1970s and during the 1980s had an important place on the political agenda of several West European countries. The policies were integrated in a revival of liberal ideology which marked the Reagan presidencies in the United States and the Thatcher governments in Britain. Furthermore, neo-liberal privatization ideas, which first affected the more developed countries, have also been adopted in less-developed countries—witness the drive towards privatization in Eastern Europe.

In a strict sense, privatization consists of the transfer of state-run enterprises into private ownership. But in a larger sense, privatization also represents the acceptance of a market logic in state-run sectors; for example, by maintaining competition in these sectors, or managements operating autonomously, or by subcontracting activities to the private sector.

Although there are similarities in the privatizations carried out in West European countries, two different forms can be distinguished. First, there are the paradigmatic privatizations in Britain after 1979, France after 1986, and in Portugal after 1990. In these cases, the transfer of public enterprises into private ownership required parliamentary ratification of specific laws. In Portugal, it required constitutional reform. In other instances, the state took shares in the capital of the enterprises to be privatized, without special legislation. In these instances, the position of the state is the same as for a private investor. This second arrangement reflects developments in most West European countries.

These two forms of privatization are different in both their legal aspects and their ideological underpinning. The statute of a public enterprise under special legislation has the underlying purpose of serving the community, its integration in a political strategy being more important than market logic. The transfer of these enterprises to private ownership is therefore a major change in economic policy. When, on the other hand, the state merely shares in the capital of an enterprise as a private investor, the company is subject to competition and a market logic, although it is also subject to the strategic orientation of the state. Privatization by this means has more limited political implications.

Thus, neither nationalization nor privatization have had the same institutional characteristics, nor the same impact, in all West European countries. In contrast to the extension of state ownership, however, privatization policies have been introduced at about the same time in much of Western Europe but with different political significance in each country.

Some Hypotheses

The questions to be addressed in this chapter deal with the attitudes of West European publics towards economic liberalism and economic interventionism during the past few decades. We can infer from the history of nationalization that attitudes towards government intervention in the economy depend neither on the size of the public sector, nor the means by which the public sector has grown. Hence, instead, we focus on the impact of economic growth, or relative economic standing, and the perceived need for regulation.

A hypothesis which may guide our exploration, at least part of the way, is that attitudes towards economic regulation are tied to the success or failure of the capitalist economic system. It was the success of capitalism in promoting economic progress which made liberal ideology popular during the nineteenth century. The First World War, however, both fomented a nationalism which was alien to liberal thinking and made economic regulation necessary. But liberalism reigned again during the 1920s when the general idea was a return to 'normalcy'. The failure of capitalism during the 1930s again made interventionism popular, although, ideologically, it was advocated in the name of socialism in some countries, conservatism in others, and fascism in yet others. And from the 1950s onwards, amid the growth of welfare states, economic liberalism remained a forceful set of ideas, stimulated particularly by the success of the American and German economies.

There are, of course, many twists to such a general hypothesis which cannot be elaborated in advance. We shall discuss them as we explore different sets of data. But our general hypothesis is that support for public ownership and government regulation is highest in economically less-advanced countries. One reason is that in these countries people think there is insufficient private capital for the investment necessary for economic development. Another reason is that social inequality is greater in these countries, and the ideologies which advance working-class interests advocate state intervention to correct such distortions. Thus, government regulation is identified with the welfare state. In the economically advanced countries, by contrast, the market system is usually credited with generating high standards of living; interference with the market is thought to lead to inefficiencies. By repeating and extending policies which have proved successful in the past, people expect growth to continue.[1] To test our hypothesis, we compare West European countries using data from the Eurobarometer series.

As to the long-term trend, economic growth should be accompanied by more liberal attitudes, whereas economic recessions should lead to more interventionist attitudes. However, it is often claimed that the tide turned towards neo-liberalism around the mid-1970s. Certainly, in the more economically advanced societies, the 1980s witnessed liberal policies which were almost unthinkable during the 1960s and early 1970s. Where possible, we compare survey data from the 1980s with earlier data to investigate this claim.

The economic liberalism of the 1980s, of course, presents a problem for our hypothesis because of the setbacks in living standards arising from the energy crises in 1973 and 1979. Such setbacks should have made interventionist measures more popular. However, it is doubtful whether people felt these difficulties were due to a failure of the capitalist system. Indeed, conservative and liberal parties have argued that they followed from economic management by socialist governments under the influence of trade unions during previous decades.

Beliefs about state intervention in the economy are central to modern political ideologies. Normally, we would expect people who identify with the left, or support social democratic, socialist, or communist parties, to be more favourable towards public ownership and economic regulation than people on the right. However, in countries such as Germany and Ireland, where state ownership has been initiated by governments of the right, and not supported by parties of the left, the correlation between left orientations and support for nationalization may not exist. In other words, the beliefs and attitudes of most people towards state intervention are not necessarily incorporated in an ideology in the way Converse (1964) conceptualizes ideology. State regulation of the economy, and even an expanding public sector, are deeply rooted in some people's minds. But these ideas are not necessarily organized and articulated in a systematic way.

Indeed, we expect to find liberal principles existing side by side with demands for economic intervention. When a market economy fails to deliver the goods, liberal ideas are not abandoned, although interventionist policies may be accepted as a practical necessity. Examining the ways in which this conflict is resolved lead us to more general questions regarding the structure of beliefs about economic management. The 1985 and 1990 ISSP surveys contains a series of items about different forms of economic management. These data allow us to examine whether people's attitudes towards one interventionist policy are related to their attitudes on other policies. As we shall see, it is highly doubtful whether interventionism and liberalism constitute opposite positions in the public mind. Some forms of intervention are more widely acceptable than others, and they tend to be popular even among those attracted to liberal principles.

Along with economic and ideological factors, a third theme is the social bases of attitudes towards economic management. We investigate whether there are systematic differences in these attitudes, across countries and over time, between social groups in West European societies. In particular, differences between workers, salaried employees, and the self-employed are theoretically interesting in relation to our hypothesis that liberalism is associated with the success of capitalism. Certainly, it has been more successful for some groups than for others. Capitalists ordinarily want the state to protect their property but not to interfere with their business. Their position is often echoed by many of their employees, although workers have often supported government intervention to maintain jobs and living standards. In most Western societies, however, manufacturing workers are a shrinking group, and for that reason a trend towards less interventionist attitudes might be anticipated.

Finally, age or generational groups as well as gender groups are relevant for our analysis. In the first place, government intervention in the economy has different consequences for different age and gender groups; indeed, it may be argued that, in general, it is middle-aged men who have most to lose from government intervention. In the second place, generational differences may suggest a value change towards more liberal values and away from socialist values.

Levels of Economic Development

The tendency of the public sector to expand faster than the national product in wealthy societies, or Wagner's Law, was noted many years ago. This tendency does not apply to all government activities. Some forms of administering the nation's economy, such as providing loans for private industry, require few government personnel. Others, such as regulating production, prices, and distribution, engage huge bureaucracies. Thus Wagner's Law operates at those stages of development when the economy generates more social problems than it solves. As production, labour, and markets expand, traditional sectors are left behind and new forms of social inequality emerge, so the need for economic regulation is likely to grow. The growth is at first slow, as the liberal climate which stimulated growth remains dominant. Then interventionist pressures accelerate for a period, and lead to demands for institutional control. But gradually the expansion of government activity approaches a natural limit where demands ease off because interventionist policies have been implemented and there is less inequality. Thus government regulation is assumed to be an S-shaped development over time.

In order to stimulate such a development, public demands for regulation should follow the slope of the S-curve; in the latter stage, as the standards of living in a society rise, the demands should decline. In comparing the national economies of Western Europe, we expect the less advanced countries to exhibit pressure for more regulation, whereas the most advanced countries should exhibit growing scepticism about further regulation. We can test this proposition with data from Eurobarometer, No. 11 (Spring 1979) and No. 16 (Fall 1981), which included one item about government management of the economy and another about the expansion of public ownership.

In Figure 9.1 we show the relationship, in 1981, between the gross domestic product (GDP) per capita on the one hand, and support for more government management of the economy and more public ownership on the other.[2] The upper line indicates support for more economic management. The decline in support with increasing average income is evident (r = 0.91). Greece, Ireland, and Italy show the highest levels of support among the nine countries, and rank lowest in average living standards. Denmark and Germany show the lowest levels of support for extending economic management, and rank highest in living standards. Belgium and Britain occupy intermediate positions on both variables. Only France tends to deviate from the pattern: there is a higher level of support for economic management than would be expected from the level of average income.

The lower line in Figure 9.1 concerns attitudes towards expanding nationalization. Again, the fit with the regression line is satisfactory (r = 0.84). Ireland and Greece are distinctive in displaying widespread support for the expansion of public ownership along with the lowest GDP per capita. We might note that this relationship is not readily explained by the influence of socialist ideology: whereas post-war nationalization in Greece was underpinned by a radical tradition, such a tradition is absent in Ireland.

It would appear, then, that demands for government economic management and for public ownership decline with increasing economic development. This is contrary to some accounts of modern

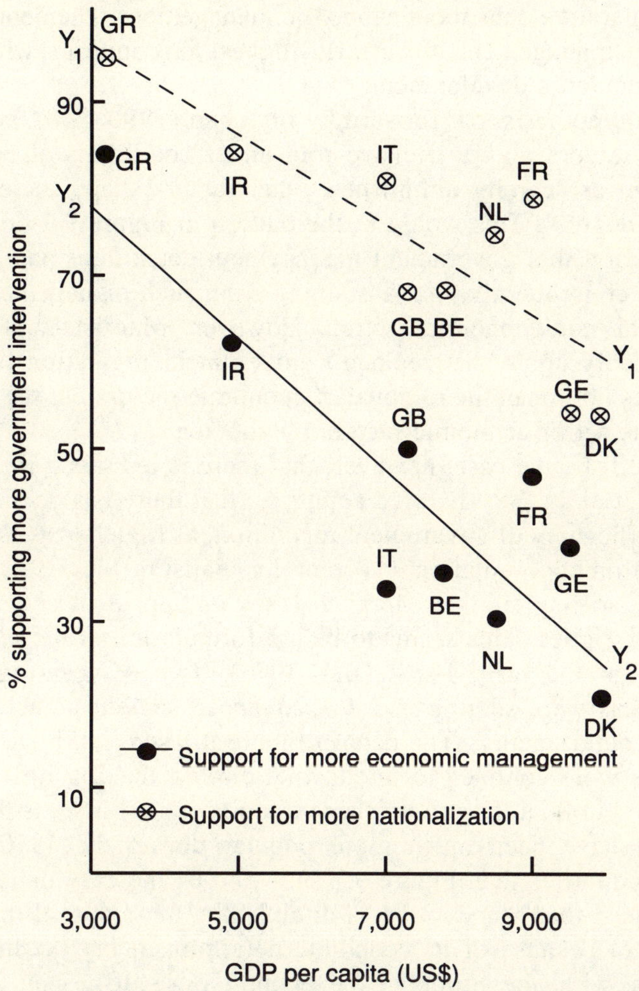

FIGURE 9.1. *Support for more economic management, support for more public ownership, and average income in EC countries, 1980*

Notes: Support is measured as percentage in favour of more government management of the economy. Average income is measured as GDP per capita.

Sources: Eurobarometer, No. 16, and OECD statistics.

polities which point to the danger of government 'overload' (cf. King 1975; Birch 1984), when expectations about what the government should do rise beyond the capacity of governments to fulfil them. This hypothesis may be valid for other policy fields, but it does not fit our comparative data about economic management. The demands for government management are clearly highest in countries with lower levels of economic development.

Another hypothesis, put forward by Inglehart (1990: 248), holds that 'economic factors play a decisive role under conditions of economic scarcity; but as scarcity diminishes, other factors shape society to an increasing degree'. This would fit the pattern in Figure 9.1 only under the assumption that government management constitutes an economic factor, and consequently, that abstaining from such management paves the way for non-economic factors. However, Marxists and liberals could probably agree that replacing government regulation by a free market does not mean the removal of economic factors but the replacement of one set of economic factors by another.

It may still be the case, however, that there is less need for government regulation in the advanced countries; that there is a decline in the marginal efficiency of government regulation, as Inglehart puts it. In so far as government regulation is a central socialist or Marxist idea, such a decline also implies that Marxism loses its appeal in economically advanced societies. This seems to be a reformulation of the postindustrial thesis of the early 1970s (Bell 1973). Twenty years ago, when Marxist ideas were soaring in many advanced societies, such a thesis appeared counterfactual. The data in Figure 9.1 suggest, however, that these ideas were confined to intellectual circles, making little impression on the public at large. Another possibility, of course, is that these ideas may have been much more popular during the 1970s in the advanced countries than Figure 9.1 shows to be the case in 1981.

We suggest that Marxism has a diminishing mass appeal in wealthy societies not because of its economic determinism but because of its connection with the struggle for economic security and equality. Government regulation of business has traditionally been seen as one strategy for furthering that goal; the structure of taxation and the welfare system, examined in previous chapters, represent alternative strategies. The diminishing appeal of government regulation in advanced societies stems, we suggest, mainly from the greater equality in these societies and the relatively smooth functioning of their welfare institutions.

The Liberal Trend

There are two major obstacles to interpreting Figure 9.1 as evidence of a secular decline in public support for economic management and public ownership. One is that the data are for only one time point, so the evidence is static. This is discussed in this section. The other has to do with people's understanding of economic management, which is taken up in a later section.

For some countries, there are time-series data which throw light on changes in public opinion about economic management. These data, which come from the Scandinavian countries, are used to plot the trends presented in Figure 9.2. We have data reaching back to the 1960s for the Swedish item: 'The leaders of banks and industries get far too much influence if society has no possibility of controlling private enterprise.' The graph shows the proportion who agreed with the statement. The trend line suggests that although attitudes have fluctuated over the period, the climate in favour of interventionism was much the same in the late 1980s as in the late 1960s. The graph for Denmark shows the proportion who agreed with the statement: 'The state has too little control over private investments.' It exhibits a very ragged course, including a sharp drop of 25 percentage points between the 1979 and 1981 elections. Although the trend conforms with our expectations, such dramatic fluctuations should warn us against drawing rigid conclusions from a relatively short time series. The Norwegian I series measures reactions to a proposal to reduce state control of industry. The proportion who thought this unimportant or were against the proposal—that is, they favoured state control—declined from 57 per cent in 1977 to 51 per cent in 1989. The Norwegian II series uses the same item as in Sweden, and shows a slight reduction from 1969 to 1981. Thus, the overall impression of Figure 9.2 does not support the hypothesis of a long-term decline in public demand for economic management in advanced countries. The erratic mood in Denmark, and the revival of support for government intervention in Sweden during the 1980s, mean that no predictions are safe.

With respect to nationalization, we have additional data for the Netherlands. However, the data refer only to the last two decades. The time series for these data are shown in Figure 9.3. The Swedish and Norwegian items, almost identical, were a proposal to nationalize big enterprises. The graphs show the proportion who thought the proposal was bad or rather bad, as against those thinking it did not

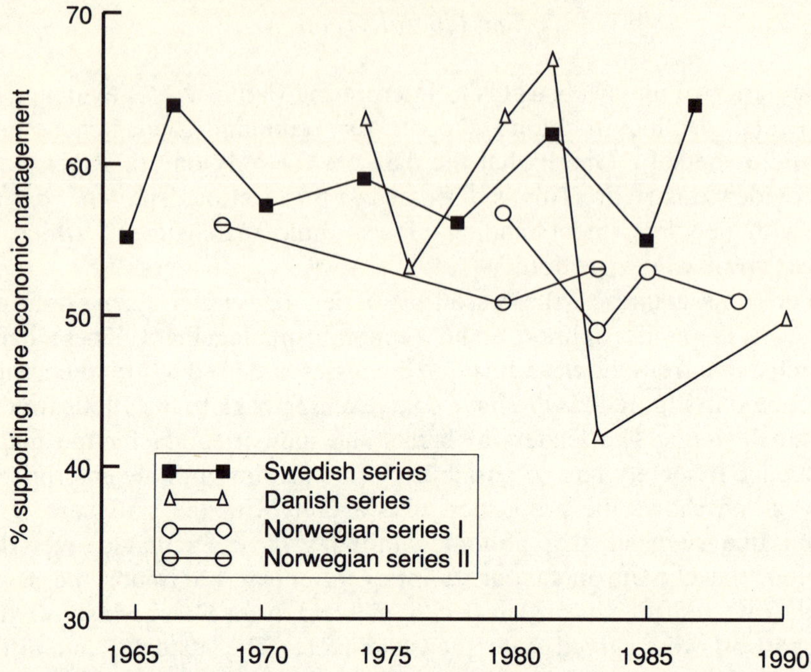

FIGURE 9.2. *Support for government regulation of private business in three Scandinavian countries, 1965–90*

Notes: Danish statement: 'The state has too little control over investments.' Entries are percentage agreeing. Swedish statement: 'The leaders of banks and industries get far too much influence if society hasn't got any possibility of controlling private enterprise.' Entries are percentage agreeing. Norwegian series I data are responses to a proposal to reduce state control of industry; Norwegian series II statement was the same as the Swedish item. Entries for both series are percentage agreeing.

Sources: Danish election surveys; Norwegian election surveys; Sweden: Holmberg (1981: 250); Holmberg, Gilljam, and Oskarson (1988: 52); and Gilljam, Holmberg, and Bennulf (1991: 48).

matter or that it was good or rather good. The Danish item asked respondents to choose between (*a*) the state taking over the banks and big industry, and (*b*) the banks and private industry continuing to be privately owned. The graph shows the proportion agreeing with (*b*) as against those agreeing with (*a*) or refusing to take sides. The Dutch item asked respondents to agree or disagree that the government should nationalize big industries and enterprises. The two responses expressing disagreement are combined in the graph.

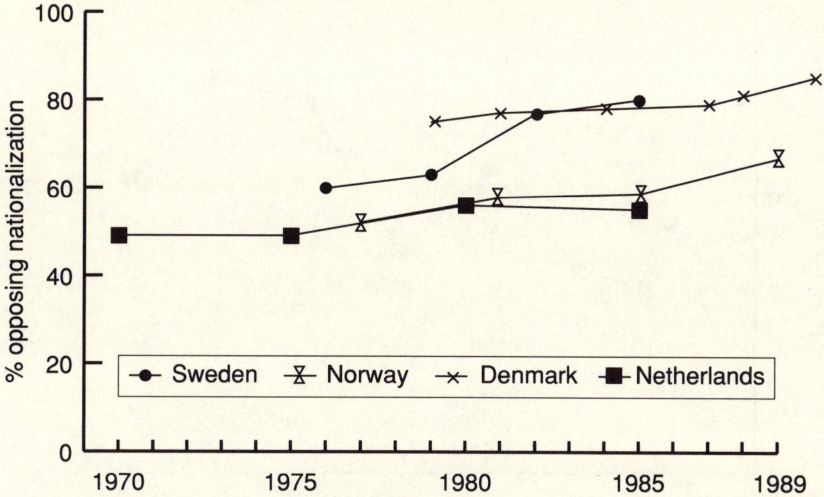

FIGURE 9.3. *Opposition to nationalization in Scandinavia and the Netherlands, 1970–90*

Notes: The Swedish and Norwegian data are based on almost identical questions asking respondents to evaluate a proposal to nationalize big enterprises. Danish question: respondents were asked to choose between (*a*) 'Parliament should decide that the state takes over the banks and big industry' and (*b*) 'The banks and big industry should continue to be in private ownership'. Except in 1981, the entries are the percentage selecting option (*b*); in 1981, when this option was not posed, the entries are the percentage disagreeing with option (*a*). Dutch question: respondents were asked if they agreed or disagreed with government nationalizing big industry and other big enterprises; entries are percentages disagreeing or disagreeing strongly.

Sources: Swedish election studies; Norwegian election studies; Danish election studies; Cultural Change in the Netherlands.

Figure 9.3 may be supplemented by Figure 9.4, which shows the development of support for privatization in Britain. The question asked respondents to choose among four options: (*a*) nationalize many more enterprises, (*b*) a few more, (*c*) no change, or (*d*) privatize some enterprises. The graph shows the proportion choosing (*d*). Because of the different question and scale used, Britain can be compared with the countries represented in Figure 9.3 on the development of beliefs but not on absolute values.

In a first analysis, we can see a tendency towards declining support for nationalization from the mid-1970s through to the middle and late 1980s. In Sweden and Britain there is a turning point in this change between the late 1970s and the early 1980s but the trend in Norway and

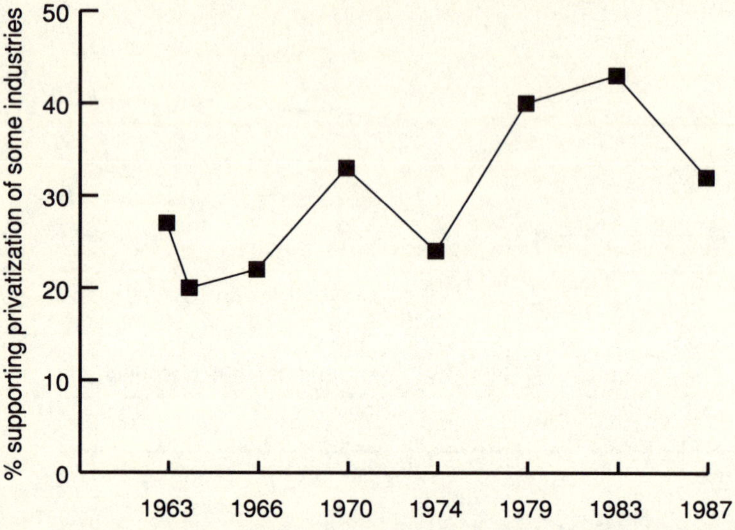

FIGURE 9.4. *Support for privatization in Britain, 1963–87*

Notes: Question: 'Which of these statements comes closest to what you feel should be done: Nationalize a lot more; Nationalize a few more; No change; and Privatize some.' Entries are percentages selecting last option.

Sources: British election studies.

the Netherlands is more steady. A high level of resistance to nationalization is evident in Denmark since the late 1970s.

Attitudinal development in Sweden and Norway during the 1980s, however, has led to convergence among the Nordic countries. There is a strong tradition in these countries of the state assuming direct responsibilities for social security, health, and education but without extensive nationalization. The political left in Scandinavia has traditionally advocated the regulation of employment and welfare, with less interest in the state ownership of industrial and financial enterprises.

The situation is rather different in Britain. During the early 1970s, the public sector was extended to absorb the car manufacturers British Leyland and Rolls Royce, due to their weak performance in a general context of economic crisis. But the 1979 Conservative victory broke the post-war consensus about public ownership, opening the way to a vigorous neo-liberal programme. Thus, the increased support for privatization evident by 1979 can be understood as a reaction to the previous economic malaise. But the rapid progress of a liberal programme, which involved the privatization of monopolies providing essential services, together with fears that this policy would generate more social inequality, might explain the change in attitudes towards privatization during the later 1980s.

Crisis and Policy Effects

Although the Eurobarometer data do not allow us to track long-term trends in attitudes towards economic management, they permit us to go back to spring 1979 and autumn 1981 to examine whether short-term changes fit the presumed trend. Figure 9.5 shows how support for more economic management developed during this period of two and a half years.

The average for the nine countries is 68 per cent in 1979, rising to 70 per cent in 1981. Although small, the increase fits with the hypothesis that failures in the market economy generate demands for economic management, for it was precisely the 1979–81 period which was characterized by recession as a consequence of the second oil crisis. The average change across the countries shown in Figure 9.5 warns against the general thesis that demands for economic management are more or less automatically declining over time.

The change in interventionist attitudes differs considerably between countries, however. In Britain, there was a rise of 10 percentage points in support for more intervention but in Belgium a drop of almost 13 percentage points. These short-run changes fit neither the static nor the long-run pattern that demands for economic management decline as living standards rise. France, Britain, and Denmark did not suddenly become poorer, nor Belgium become richer, over this period. Nor do the changes fit with the idea of an S-shaped curve. If they did, the demand for more intervention should decline, particularly in the richer countries. But as Figure 9.1 shows, the three countries in which support for economic management declined between 1979 and 1981—Belgium, Italy, and Ireland—were not leading the field in GDP per capita.

To explain these short-run changes we might attempt to relate them to policy changes. In Britain and Denmark, governments became markedly less interventionist, but Figure 9.5 shows large increases in the demand for more economic management. Thus some of the change in attitudes might be construed as reactions against policy changes. However, policy did not change to the same extent in Germany and Italy. Moreover, the swing in Denmark here is hard to reconcile with the swing in the opposite direction in Figure 9.2. And to account for the

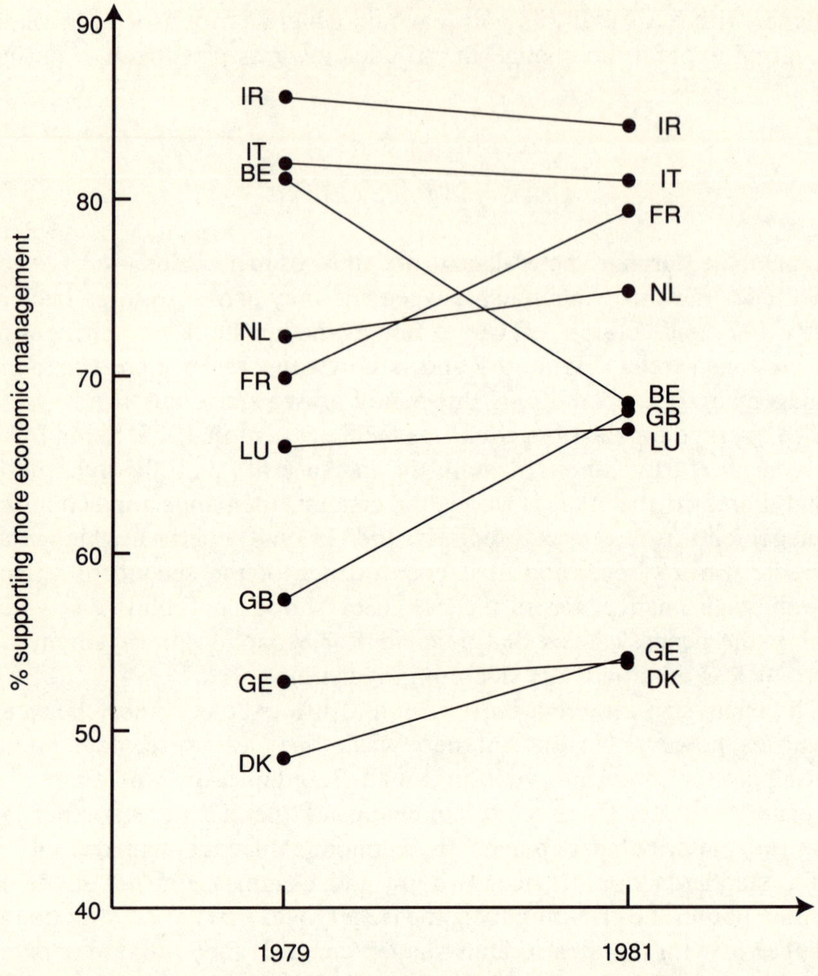

FIGURE 9.5. *Support for more economic management in nine West European countries, 1979–81*

Notes: Question: 'Do you favour or disfavour more government management of the economy?' Entries are percentages in favour.

Sources: Eurobarometer, Nos. 11 and 16.

large increase in France compared with the even larger decline in Belgium seems to call for specific hypotheses and additional evidence beyond the scope of this chapter.

The theory that short-run changes in support for economic management are a reaction against actual policy must also explain how the policy acquires support among the majority of voters. It is often held that an international swing towards neo-liberalism took place around 1980, citing in support the electoral victories of Margaret Thatcher in Britain in 1979 and Ronald Reagan in the United States in 1980, both on a programme of economic liberalism. In our data, however, the British case is especially puzzling; in the very country seen as paradigmatic of the new liberal trend, public attitudes shifted toward interventionism.

One explanation might be that the Thatcher and Reagan victories were not related to changing attitudes about economic management but, rather, resulted from the failure of previous governments to secure high employment and stable prices. This would mean that the arrival of the Conservative government in Britain was due not so much to its liberal stance as to rising unemployment and the desire for tax reductions. The sharp rise in demand for economic management in Britain 1979–81 could then be accounted for as the reaction against a policy which, although not desired by a majority of the public, could be carried through by a government with a large majority. It is tempting to press this explanation a bit further, to suggest that such a reaction would be particularly manifest among supporters of opposition parties. In the British case, the increase in interventionist demands should be especially evident among Labour voters. As we shall see in the next section, however, the evidence points in a different direction.

Attitudes towards nationalization also underwent dramatic changes during the 1979–83 period. As is evident from Figure 9.6, declining support for the expansion of public ownership was common among the EC countries, except in Germany and especially Britain. The decline in support for public ownership in France and Belgium was particularly steep. But political developments in these two countries were very different. In France, an extensive nationalization programme was implemented in 1982, affecting large parts of the industrial and financial sectors. Difficulties with the management of these enterprises, together with opposition from much of the political and economic élite, led to increased opposition among the public.[3] But there was no attempt to extend nationalization in Belgium, and there has been less ideological controversy over state intervention (Debbasch 1989).

The Netherlands, Germany, and Italy reveal a similar pattern of attitudes, without large fluctuations, over this period. In spite of the importance of state ownership in these countries, especially in Italy, state intervention occurred in a market context, not as the result of a nationalization programme carried out by the left. In Italy, Christian

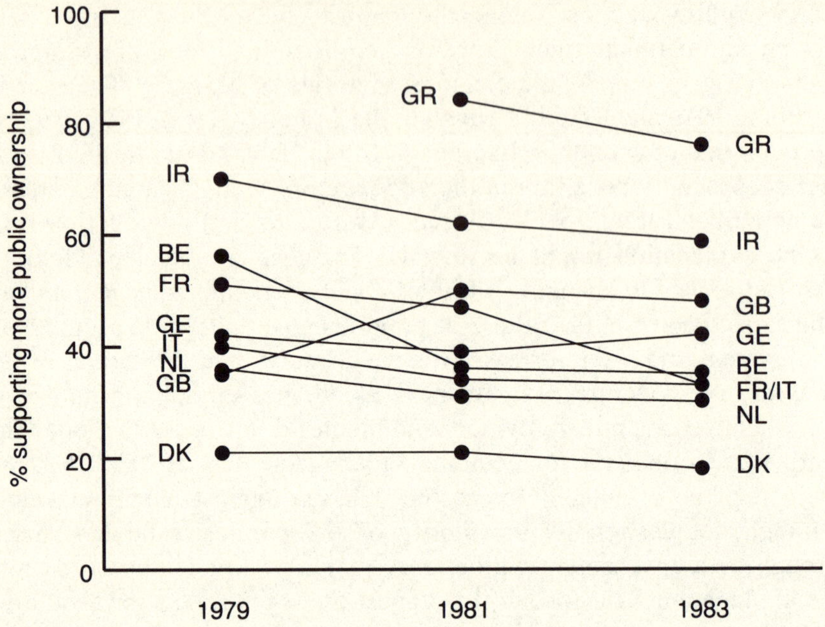

FIGURE 9.6. *Support for more public ownership of industry in nine West European countries, 1979–83*

Note: 'Public ownership of enterprises should be expanded'; entries are percentages agreeing and strongly agreeing.

Sources: Eurobarometer, Nos. 11, 16, and 19.

Democratic governments expanded state intervention in business, distributing the management of enterprises among the parties according to the *lottizzazione* system. The Italian Communist Party, however, in command of the left, was not (then) as reconciled to private ownership as many of the social democratic and labour parties of Western Europe. Clearly, beliefs about public ownership must be more complicated than we can see from these Eurobarometer data. We pursue this point further in a later section.

Differentiating Economic Policy

Until now we have proceeded as if terms such as 'management of the economy', 'public ownership', and 'economic liberalism' are readily understood and have the same meaning in all societies. This may not be so. Hence, before we analyse the sources of attitudes towards economic policy, we need to look into the content of these terms. As we cannot do this with the Eurobarometer questions, we turn to the 1985 and 1990 ISSP surveys. On the issue of economic management, these surveys identify eight policies which are presumed to 'help the economy'; on public ownership, the 1985 survey distinguishes between five branches of the economy. The drawback of the ISSP surveys, however, is that they cover only five countries. None the less, it is still possible to make comparisons with the findings from the Eurobarometer data.

In Table 9.1, we show the aggregate level of support, in 1985 and 1990, for eight policies by which government might help the economy.

TABLE 9.1. *Support for eight economic policies, 1985 and 1990*

1985 Survey	Germany	Britain	Italy	Austria	Average
A. Wage control	28	32	72	58	48
B. Price control	56	60	90	87	73
C. Cut government spending	77	38	68	82	66
D. Finance new projects	71	88	91	72	81
E. Less government regulation	41	54	41	47	46
F. Support new technology	75	90	74	66	76
G. Support declining industry	58	50	74	46	57
H. Reduce working week	50	49	63	36	50
Average *N*	1,033	1,492	1,580	960	
1990 Survey	**Germany**	**Britain**	**Italy**	**Norway**	**Average**
A. Wage control	31	36	72	46	46
B. Price control	51	55	88	66	65
C. Cut government spending	76	42	70	71	65
D. Finance new projects	72	83	90	84	82
E. Less government regulation	37	43	43	53	44
F. Support new technology	70	89	75	86	80
G. Support declining industry	62	60	76	46	61
H. Reduce working week	53	42	53	24	44
Average *N*	2,759	1,174	960	1,436	

Notes: The question wording is: 'Here are some things the government might do for the economy. Circle one number for each action to show whether you are in favour of it or against it. A: Control of wages by legislation. B: Control of prices by legislation. C: Cuts in government spending. D: Government financing of projects to create new jobs. E: Less government regulation of business. F: Support for industry to develop new products and technology. G: Support declining industries to protect jobs. H: Reducing the working week to create more jobs.' Entries are percentages in favour.

Sources: ISSP (1985, 1990).

Three of the four countries appear in both years, the fourth is Austria in 1985 and Norway in 1990. Of the eight policies, six are interventionist and two (items C and E) are anti-interventionist.

Among the interventionist policies, we find some to be consistently more popular than others. For example, price controls are more popular than wage controls in all eight instances. Even more popular is government financing of new projects to create jobs. The popularity of these two items corresponds well with the findings in Table 4.2 shown earlier in this volume, which revealed a widespread tendency to assign to governments the responsibility for keeping prices low and providing a job for everyone who needs one. When it comes to government help for industry, we find far more positive attitudes towards support for new technology than for declining industry—except in Italy. In Britain, support for new technology surpasses all other policy measures. In view of these positive attitudes, then, it is odd to find that the proposal to cut government spending is also widely popular—except in Britain. The three least popular proposals are wage controls, less government regulation of business, and reduction of the working week.

It would be interesting to know how support for different forms of economic management changes over time. In our data, this is possible for Germany, Britain, and Italy, but only for a five-year period. Most changes from 1985 to 1990 are small, suggesting that the popularity of different policies in different countries tends to be relatively fixed. There is, generally, a common ranking of policies, but there are also interesting national variations. For example, people in Britain seemed to have had enough of spending cuts under the Thatcher regime; people in Italy, unusually, want wage control as well as price control.

On the issue of public ownership, our earlier analyses referred to attitudes towards large enterprises, irrespective of sector. However, we believe that people's attitudes differ according to the type of enterprise in question: in particular, that people are relatively reluctant about the privatization of natural monopolies, such as telecommunications and water supplies; or enterprises providing essential services, such as public transport; or enterprises with environmental implications, such as the electricity industry. They more readily support the privatization of enterprises and services which operate in a competitive market and have fewer implications for the quality of life. Levels of support for state ownership in five different economic sectors are shown in Table 9.2.

The distributions in Table 9.2 largely confirm our expectations. In 1985, across the four countries, the average level of support for state

TABLE 9.2. *Support for state ownership in different economic sectors, 1985 and 1990*

	Electricity	Public transport	Steel industry	Banks and insurance	Automobile industry	Average *N*
Germany						
1985	19	25	9	5	2	952
1990	16	—	—	7	—	2,387
Britain						
1985	26	19	19	10	9	1,363
1990	30	—	—	7	—	1,077
Italy						
1985	36	33	22	24	15	1,375
1990	28	—	—	21	—	900
Austria						
1985	26	33	25	16	9	757
Norway						
1990	28	—	—	7	—	1,347

Notes: The question wording is: 'What do you think the government's role in each of these industries should be: (1) Own it, (2) Control prices and profits but not own it, or (3) Neither own it nor control its prices and profits?' Entries are percentages selecting option (1).

Sources: ISSP (1985, 1990).

ownership is 27 per cent for electricity and public transport, 19 per cent for the steel industry, 14 per cent for banks and insurance, and 9 per cent for the car industry. That is, support for state ownership declines as we move from sectors providing essential services, or have environmental implications, to sectors which operate competitively. In Italy, however, there is a relatively high level of support for state ownership of the two latter sectors—confirming our earlier finding of widespread support for state intervention, including public ownership, in Italy. Next to Italy, Austria has the highest level of support for state ownership whereas Germany shows the lowest overall support for nationalization. The contrast between Austria and Germany is more marked for the competitive industries, less marked for the monopolies. This tendency is also evident in Britain and Norway.

The Structure of Beliefs

Classical economic liberalism advocates that the state refrains from controlling prices or wages, supporting industries or penalizing them with corporate taxes, all of which interfere with market forces. But can we expect to find a liberal dimension in public attitudes in Western Europe? Although liberalism has been with us for two hundred years, we cannot assume a strong dimension. Management of the economy is nowadays accepted as a practical necessity by many who adhere to liberal principles. As we may anticipate from Chapter 3 and Chapter 4, in most countries even liberals tend to hold the government responsible for unemployment and inflation. The levels of support we saw in Table 9.1 point in the same direction: when something between 50 per cent and 90 per cent of people in several countries advocate price controls, and at least 70 per cent in those countries advocate government job-creation projects, it leaves little room for viable liberal policies. And the popularity of government support for new technology suggests that even liberals are inclined to believe that, at least for a time, some industries have to be protected against foreign competition.

Free and Cantril (1967) introduced a useful distinction between ideological and operational attitudes. The former deal with abstract principles, the latter with concrete matters. They found that there is often a gulf between the two, such that many people are liberal in principle but turn interventionist when it comes to practical proposals where they stand to lose from an application of liberal principles. Thus, interventionist measures are often introduced on the pretext that they are exceptional and will be removed when the situation improves. In this light, widespread support for liberal principles may look rather like the hypocrisy of free-riders.

In order to validate such a distinction, we carried out a factor analysis of the items in Table 9.1. We could anticipate three different results. One was the absence of any clear belief structure, for Converse (1964) has shown the low 'constraint' between beliefs among the mass public. Another possibility is that, despite the inconsistencies we pointed out, we find a reasonable one-dimensional structure with the six interventionist items loading positively and the two liberal items loading negatively on the same factor. Thirdly, we might find one interpretable factor capturing some but not all of the items, thereby identifying certain elements of an economic policy. This turned out to be the actual outcome. The loadings on the first unrotated factor are shown in Table 9.3.

We find a fairly similar belief structure in all five countries. Demands for wage and price controls along with government projects to create jobs, government support for declining industry, and a reduction of the

TABLE 9.3. *Structure of attitudes towards eight economic policies, 1985 and 1990*

1985 Survey	Germany	Britain	Austria	Italy
A. Wage control	0.70	0.47	0.69	0.60
B. Price control	0.79	0.66	0.74	0.60
C. Cut government spending	0.24	−0.01	0.07	0.18
D. Finance new projects	0.62	0.67	0.49	0.70
E. Less government regulation	−0.32	0.21	−0.21	0.22
F. Support new technology	−0.14	0.55	−0.02	0.58
G. Support declining industry	0.69	0.56	0.63	0.74
H. Reduce working week	0.41	0.50	0.44	0.49
1990 Survey	**Germany**	**Britain**	**Norway**	**Italy**
A. Wage control	0.61	0.56	0.69	0.58
B. Price control	0.74	0.70	0.73	0.54
C. Cut government spending	0.31	0.34	−0.28	0.16
D. Finance new projects	0.58	0.56	0.62	0.69
E. Less government regulation	−0.02	0.15	−0.46	0.31
F. Support new technology	0.16	0.42	0.22	0.53
G. Support declining industry	0.68	0.62	0.66	0.73
H. Reduce working week	0.53	0.51	0.53	0.57

Notes: Entries are loadings on the first factor derived from factor analysis. For question wording, see Table 9.1. The responses have been coded from 1 = strongly in favour, through 5 = strongly against.

Sources: ISSP (1985, 1990).

working week, all load highly on the first factor. We call this factor 'pragmatic interventionism', or simply interventionism. Interventionists demand that their government regulates prices and wages, creates jobs by either initiating public works or supporting declining industries, and reduces the length of the working week.

In order to examine support for interventionism, we summed the five policy positions (items A, B, D, G, and H) into an index. As all the items deal with government action to protect the jobs and incomes of ordinary people, they constitute a logically consistent series. Demands for government support for new products and new technology (item F) are positively correlated with this factor in Britain and Italy, but not in Germany, Austria, or Norway. Thus, as we cannot say that, in general, interventionists also want their government actively to promote innovation, item F is not included in the index.

The two remaining items, C and E, are worded as liberal statements and embrace ideological liberalism. To enter them as items in a single interventionist–liberal dimension they would need to have high negative loadings on the same factor. For government expenditure, only Norway shows a negative loading. For reducing government regulation of business, there are negative loadings only in Norway, Germany, and Austria, and they are not of the same magnitude as the loadings of the other items.

The three items which are not part of the interventionist factor (items C, E, and F) present interesting internal relationships. In the 1985 data, 'less government regulation of business'—the core item of liberalism—is correlated with 'cuts in government spending' (average $r = 0.17$ in the four countries). It is even better correlated with 'support for industry to develop new products and new technology' (average $r = 0.21$). But the two latter items are uncorrelated (average $r = 0.04$). To overstate our case slightly, it seems that respondents who want less government regulation of business also want either cuts in government spending or government support for industrial innovation—but not both.

The interventionist factor calls to mind Free and Cantril's operational attitude. Their ideological attitude might have been represented by items C and E, but this emerges in only a rudimentary form. One reason why the items are not included in the interventionist attitude is that they are worded in the opposite direction to the five interventionist items. An acquiescent response effect may have played some part in removing the expected negative correlation between the five interventionist items and the two liberal items. But that does not explain why the latter two are so weakly correlated, since their relationship should be strengthened by response setting. Thus the low correlation between items C and E makes it difficult to claim the existence of Free and Cantril's ideological attitude. We can safely conclude only that an attitude of pragmatic interventionism can be identified among the publics of these five countries.

We now turn to the items in the 1985 ISSP survey on public ownership, shown in Table 9.2. For each type of enterprise, respondents chose between three positions: (*a*) the state should own it; (*b*) the state should control but not own it; (*c*) the state should neither own nor control it. A factor analysis of the responses (not shown here) revealed two factors in Germany and Austria, the first comprising banks, the steel industry, and the automobile industry, and the second comprising electricity and public transport. A one-factor solution emerged for

Britain and Italy, but neither electricity nor public transport load as strongly on this factor as the other three enterprises.

We therefore constructed two indices, one dealing with attitudes towards the ownership of the 'competitive' industries (banks and insurance, steel, automobiles), the other dealing with the 'natural monopolies' (electricity, public transport). In Table 9.4 we show the Pearson correlation coefficients for the relationship between these two indices, the interventionism index, and the liberal item 'less government regulation of business'.

The first column shows that the correlation coefficients between the interventionism index and the liberal item 'less government regulation of business' in 1985 varied from −0.19 in Germany and −0.11 in Austria to an insignificant 0.03 in Britain; in Italy it is a significant 0.07 but with the 'wrong' sign. Just as we expected from the factor analysis, there is no clear belief structure where ideological liberalism is concerned. Moreover, the table does not show that in 1990 the correlation dropped to an insignificant −0.04 in Germany, or that only in Norway did the liberal item merge into the interventionist index ($r = -0.28$).

In the second column of the table, fairly strong correlations (r between 0.34 and 0.47) emerge between the interventionism index and ownership of the competitive industries. Demands for state ownership of these

TABLE 9.4. *Intercorrelation of attitudes towards economic intervention, liberalism, and state ownership of natural monopolies and competitive industries, 1985*

	Int/Lib	Int/OwnC	Int/OwnM	Lib/OwnC	Lib/OwnM	OwnC/OwnM
Germany	−0.19**	0.47**	0.22**	−0.14**	−0.11**	0.33**
Britain	0.03	0.34**	0.15**	−0.13**	−0.07*	0.55**
Austria	−0.11**	0.37**	0.25**	−0.21**	−0.14**	0.45**
Italy	0.07**	0.35**	0.14**	−0.02	−0.11**	0.47**

$^*p < 0.05$ $^{**}p < 0.01$

Notes: Entries are Pearson's r. For question wording, see Tables 9.1 and 9.2. Interventionism (Int) is an additive index of responses to items A, B, D, G, and H in Table 9.1, ranging from 5 to 25. Liberalism (Lib) is the score on item E in Table 9.1, ranging from 1 to 5. Attitude to state ownership of banks, steel, and automobile industries (OwnC) is the additive score of the last three items in Table 9.2, ranging from 3 to 9. Attitude to state ownership of public transport and electricity (OwnM) is the additive score on the first two items in Table 9.2, ranging from 2 to 6.

Source: ISSP (1985).

kinds of enterprises appear to constitute the hard-core of interventionism. The third column shows that the correlations between interventionism and state ownership of public transport and electricity are smaller (*r* between 0.14 and 0.25) than those in the second column; evidently, some non-interventionists believe that these natural monopolies should be state owned.

The fourth and fifth columns of Table 9.4 show that the ownership indices and the liberal item 'less government regulation' are negatively but rather unsystematically correlated (*r* between −0.21 and −0.02). Private ownership of competitive enterprises without government control would seem to be logically consistent with less government regulation of business; hence, fair negative coefficients could be expected in the fourth column. However, this is the case only in Austria. The last column shows that the correlation of the two control/ownership variables is rather strong, with *r* between 0.33 and 0.55. Therefore, although we identified two factors for Germany and Austria, these two factors are by no means independent of one another. Strong polarization between the adherents of private and public ownership is still evident.

To sum up. Our analysis of the belief structure reveals that economic interventionism is a consistent attitude but the notion of a 'liberal attitude' is much less clearly founded. Apparently it is one thing to adhere to liberal principles, quite another to denounce interventionist measures. A particularly familiar creature is the voter who combines pragmatic interventionism with liberal principles. That much was already clear from Table 9.1, which showed that four out of five respondents want their government to start new job-creation projects, yet two out of three want the government to cut spending. Since these two demands are not voiced by opposite camps among the electorates but are practically unrelated to one another, we know that roughly half the electorate support both policies at the same time—signifying considerable inconsistency in public attitudes.

Sources of Interventionist Attitudes

In the rest of this chapter we use the ISSP data and the Eurobarometer data to examine the attitude 'economic interventionism', including attitudes towards public ownership. To what extent interventionism is also reflected in responses to the economic management item in the Eurobarometer data, we cannot test directly. Nor can we tell whether support for the public ownership of competitive industries is related to the Eurobarometer item on demands for more public ownership. Our strategy is to employ both sets of items to test the general hypothesis that interventionist attitudes are fuelled by failures in the functioning of capitalist systems, and to eliminate alternative hypotheses.

One alternative hypothesis would be that interventionism, being a philosophy of the deprived, is fed by general discontent with the political system. People who have lost their jobs, been hurt by inflation, or workers in small firms struggling to remain competitive, may well turn against the political system. Thus, interventionism could be related to political distrust. Such a relationship might be expected among Italians: we found four-fifths of Italians to be interventionists compared to roughly one-half in the other three countries. Since we know that political distrust is widespread in Italy (see Chapter 12), we might suspect that interventionism is influenced by negative feelings about the political system rather than any particular ideology.

In testing such an explanation, however, we found only weak evidence. Four items in the ISSP 1985 survey were used to divide the respondents in Germany, Britain, and Italy into five groups according to their level of distrust in government.[4] The Pearson correlation between interventionism and political distrust turned out to be very low: $r = 0.04$ in Germany, 0.05 in Britain, and 0.09 in Italy. Clearly, we cannot conclude from these values that the demand for government action springs from resentment against the political system.

Next, we are interested in interventionism among people on the left and the right of the political spectrum. The left tradition of state intervention, particularly nationalization, still persists. However, as we noted earlier, there are left traditions in Western Europe which led to state regulation of the economy but not to public ownership. We also know that governments of the right or centre-right have expanded the public sector or coexisted with a large public sector, at least until the late 1970s. Of course, the term 'government management of the economy' tends to be associated with socialism, even though economic management was deeply ingrained in classical conservatism. But during the 1980s, many governments, socialist as well as conservative, found it necessary to keep their economies on a tight rein. Therefore, we need to probe the association between economic management and socialism. The counter-hypothesis is that the meaning of economic management varies across countries and over time as a result of programmes initiated by governments of both the left and the right.

TABLE 9.5. *Correlations between attitudes towards more or less government management of the economy, attitudes towards more public ownership of industry, and respondents' left–right location, 1979–83*

	Management ownership	Management/ left	Ownership/ left
France			
1979	0.34**	0.00	0.39**
1981	0.39**	0.24**	0.39**
1983	−0.15**	−0.27**	0.33**
Belgium			
1979	0.44**	0.04	0.15**
1981	0.38**	0.02	0.20**
1983	0.07	0.08	0.10*
Netherlands			
1979	0.38**	0.09**	0.33**
1981	0.30**	0.13**	0.28**
1983	−0.07*	−0.07	0.32**
Germany			
1979	0.30**	0.08*	−0.05
1981	0.33**	0.08*	0.02
1983	0.01	−0.10**	0.07**
Italy			
1979	0.38**	0.21**	0.30**
1981	0.26**	0.06	0.20**
1983	−0.03	−0.16**	0.07
Denmark			
1979	0.33**	0.21**	0.37**
1981	0.30**	0.20**	0.37**
1983	0.03	0.01	0.41**
Ireland			
1979	0.23**	0.00	0.04
1981	0.12**	0.01	0.05
1983	0.17**	0.07*	0.01
Britain			
1979	0.35**	0.20**	0.27**
1981	0.14**	−0.04	0.23**
1983	0.10**	0.05	0.20**
Greece			
1979	—	—	—
1981	0.31**	0.14**	0.37**
1983	−0.06	−0.17**	0.40**

*$p < 0.05$ **$p < 0.01$

Notes: Entries are Pearson's *r*. The question wording in Eurobarometer, Nos. 11 and 16, is: 'Do you favour or disfavour more government management of the economy?'; in Eurobarometer, No. 19: 'Do you favour or disfavour less government management of the economy?'; in Eurobarometer, Nos. 11, 16, and 19: 'Do you favour or disfavour more public ownership of industry?' The variables are: Management = favours more government management of the economy (1979 and 1981); favours less government management of the economy (1983); Ownership = favours more public ownership of industry; Left = left self-placement. The variables Management and Ownership have four codes, running from 1 = favour strongly to 4 = disfavour strongly; Left has ten codes, from 1 = extreme left to 10 = extreme right.
Sources: Eurobarometer, Nos. 11, 16, and 19.

The association between attitudes towards economic management, public ownership, and placement on the left is examined first with data from Eurobarometer, Nos. 11, 16, and 19, which we looked at earlier. In Table 9.5 we report the intercorrelations between the items on public ownership and economic management, and their correlations with left–right self-placement.

In the 1979 and 1981 data, support for more economic management correlates with support for expanding public ownership (column 1) with an average Pearson's *r* of 0.34 in 1979 and 0.28 in 1981. The decline in 1981 was caused by a drop in the correlations for Britain (0.14) and Ireland (0.12). It appears that in these two countries attitudes towards economic management became disconnected from attitudes towards nationalization. If we combine this observation with the previous observation that economic management became, overall, more popular in Britain between 1979 and 1981 (cf. Figure 9.5), then support for economic management must have increased among non-socialist voters. This point will be substantiated in the next section.

The correlations between attitudes towards economic management and respondent's position in left–right terms (column 2) are weaker, averaging 0.10 in 1979 and 0.09 in 1981. They vary considerably between countries and over time; only in Denmark is there a fair correlation in both years. Thus attitudes favouring economic management are not, generally, firmly located on the left side of the political spectrum.

In the 1983 survey, the item on economic management was reversed, asking whether the government should play a smaller rather than a larger role in the economy. Consequently, we expect the correlations for 1983 (columns 1 and 2) to turn negative. However, this happens only in some of the countries, notably France. The average of the correlations in both columns is practically zero. In Britain and Ireland the correlations in the first column remain positive and significant even after the item has been reversed! Although it is hard to draw substantive conclusions from changed item wording, at least we might speculate why support for public ownership suddenly becomes consistent with support for less, not more, economic management. Our guess is that, according to the discourse of the British Conservative government and Irish Fianna Fáil government, the connotations of 'managing the economy' are positive whereas for 'public ownership' they are negative. Evidently, Thatcherism did not mean that government should play a smaller role in managing the economy, but a different role. On the whole, then, the call for more economic management is only vaguely associated with a left position, and when the item is reversed into a call for less economic management, its meaning evaporates in most countries. Evidently, 'economic management' is a term with many and rather vague meanings.

As to the relationship between left identification and support for public ownership (column 3), significant positive correlations are observed in all countries except Germany and Ireland. The lack of correlation in Germany reflects the fact that state intervention occurred during a period of relative consensus about public ownership which was integrated into a logic of private enterprise and market competition. In Ireland, the weak relationship probably follows from the absence of a radical left tradition along with state intervention by right-wing governments.

Two countries, France and Denmark, show especially high correlations (*r* equal to 0.39 and 0.37 respectively) between support for public ownership and left self-placement. In the case of Denmark, where overall support for public ownership is very low, this correlation implies that only voters on the far left support public ownership. However, note also that in most of these countries, the correlation between left identification and support for the expansion of the public sector tends to decline between 1979 and 1983.

Finally, we examine attitudes towards power centres generally associated with the execution of economic policy. In Table 9.6 we display the correlations between interventionism and whether respondents think that (*a*) trade unions have too much power, (*b*) business and industry have too much power, and (*c*) the government has too much power. The first item was assumed to represent a conservative belief, the second item to express a socialist belief. In these two columns the coefficients come out with the expected sign, confirming that our interventionism index is, indeed, related to a socialist outlook. So far, these results fit with those in the previous table.

The third column, however, contains a surprise: it shows that in Germany, Britain, and Italy, interventionists tend to think that the government is too powerful! The correlations are significant at the 1 per cent level, ruling out simply a casual relationship. This apparent inconsistency is most evident in Britain, which also suggests how the inconsistency arises. During the 1980s, all three countries were governed by parties of the right which were perceived by opposition parties of the left as an obstacle to more interventionist policies. This perception was especially well founded in Britain, where the Conservative government used its powers to combat the trade unions. However, such a perception was not well founded in Austria where, at the time of the survey, a Social Democratic prime minister headed a coalition government, or in Norway, where government shifted between the Labour Party and the bourgeois parties. Thus Austria and Norway present the expected positive sign.

The attitudinal correlates in Tables 9.5 and 9.6 do not directly confront our thesis that interventionism stems from the failures of the capitalist economy. However, Table 9.5 weakens the alternative hypothesis that interventionism is confined to left-wing or socialist ideology, while Table 9.6 weakens the hypothesis that interventionists favour a strengthening of central government.

TABLE 9.6. *Correlation between interventionism and attitudes towards power centres*

	Trade unions	Business	Government
Germany			
1985	0.26**	−0.19**	−0.13**
1990	0.19**	−0.12**	−0.15**
Britain			
1985	0.12**	−0.14**	−0.18*
1990	0.02	−0.07*	−0.18**
Italy			
1985	0.09*	−0.07	−0.10*
1990	0.10*	−0.09*	−0.09*
Austria			
1985	0.27**	−0.17**	0.13**
Norway			
1990	0.33**	−0.18**	0.10**

$^*p < 0.05$ $^{**}p < 0.01$

Notes: Entries are Pearson's *r*. For the definition of interventionism see Table 9.4. Questions: 'Do you think trade unions have too much power in this society?' 'What about business and industry, do you think they have too much power?' 'And do you think government has too much power?' Of the five responses, 'Definitely not' was assumed to be the most positive, 'Yes definitely' the least positive.

Sources: ISSP (1985, 1990).

Economic Policy and Party Systems

The liberal trend we observed in Figure 9.3 and Figure 9.4 might be expected to cause problems for socialist parties in the economically advanced countries. If they retain a policy of expanding the role of government as manager of the economy, their electoral support would be eroded; if they abandon interventionism, they would compromise their ideology and might lose credibility. In practice, there seem to be several processes at work in the party systems. First, socialist parties have tended to follow the trend in public opinion, with the result that in the advanced countries they are to the right of even the conservative parties in the less advanced countries. This tendency among supporters of left parties is evident from Table 9.7, which shows how different are voters for the left from country to country. For example, in 1979, only 66 per cent of Danish leftist voters favoured more government management while 91 per cent of Italian leftist voters did so.

An even greater difference is seen between voters for parties of the right. Only 49 per cent of Danish rightist voters favoured more economic management, whereas over 90 per cent of Irish and Greek voters did so. Evidently rank and file conservative voters in the less advanced countries are far removed from liberal thinking. Hence, along with the ideological crisis in the socialist parties, there may be a crisis within the conservative parties as they abandon their role as protectors of small entrepreneurs.

Actually, as the table suggests, conservative voters in some countries are more inclined towards economic management than are voters for the political centre. Of course, the distinctions between left and centre, and between centre and right, have to be drawn differently in different countries. Relying on the classification in the Eurobarometer surveys, we see that voters for centre parties are not always in an intermediate position between voters for the left and the right. Especially in Germany and Italy, comparatively small centre parties with liberal traditions survive, and their voters tend to agree with conservative voters about economic management. As a simple average for the six countries with centrist parties, 73 per cent of left voters, 61 per cent of centrist voters, and 60 per cent of right voters supported a greater role for government in economic management in 1979. In 1981 the corresponding figures were 75 per cent, 62 per cent, and 63 per cent.

In terms of change from 1979 to 1981, British Conservative voters underwent a metamorphosis—as we anticipated from Table 9.5. Their

TABLE 9.7. *Party preference and support for more economic management in nine West European countries, 1979 and 1981*

	Left	Centre	Right
Germany			
1979	71	57	65
1981	77	59	63
	(209)	(70)	(347)
Italy			
1979	91	66	88
1981	90	63	88
	(373)	(37)	(331)
Belgium			
1979	89	90	91
1981	89	77	85
	(120)	(139)	(176)
Britain			
1979	82	73	57
1981	77	71	73
	(344)	(97)	(262)
Denmark			
1979	66	64	49
1981	73	60	58
	(313)	(57)	(245)
Netherlands			
1979	86		76
1981	87		80
	(389)		(416)
France			
1979	78	75	77
1981	91	83	78
	(407)	(85)	(186)
Ireland			
1979	88		91
1981	90		86
	(285)		(326)
Greece			
1981	98		93
	(449)		(113)

Notes: Entries are percentages in favour of more government management of the economy among voters for parties of the left, centre, and the right. The distinction between parties of the left, centre, and right is made according to the Eurobarometer file, variable 51. Average *N* in parentheses.

Sources: Eurobarometer, Nos. 11 and 16.

support for more economic management rose from 57 per cent in 1979 to 73 per cent in 1981; among Labour voters it declined from 82 per cent to 77 per cent. Thus, in just over two years, the difference between the two big partisan camps declined from 25 percentage points to a mere 4 points. But it would be facile to conclude that economic management ceased to be a controversial issue; a much more plausible conclusion is that 'managing the economy' came to mean very different things in the two camps. Far from releasing control of the economy, the new Conservative government in Britain was concerned with creating a strong and autonomous centre from which to exercise its statecraft (Bulpitt 1986).

In general, the Eurobarometer data on government economic management exhibit modest partisan differences. But because of the low validity of the measure, we cannot conclude that during the late 1980s there was a general consensus about economic policy. At least, such a conclusion should be cross checked against the ISSP data. Our interventionism index can be used to examine the extent of support for economic intervention among partisans in Germany and Britain for both 1985 and 1990, Austria in 1985, and Norway in 1990.[5] The proportion of interventionists among partisans is presented in Table 9.8.

The parties in each country have been arranged in the table roughly from left to right. In Germany, the most interventionist voters are the Greens, the least interventionist are the Free Democrats. This corresponds exactly to the Eurobarometer data in Table 9.7, which also showed the disinclination for economic management among Free Democrats. In Britain, the difference between Conservative and Labour voters on interventionism is 22 percentage points in 1985 and 19 points in 1990, and interventionism declined among both Conservative and Labour voters. Finally, in Austria and Norway, voters for left parties are more interventionist than voters for parties of the right. In all, we find partisan differences of around 20 per cent in Germany, Britain and Austria, and 35 per cent in Norway.[6]

Are attitudes towards public ownership differentiated in much the same way? Here we return to the Eurobarometer data, which also allow us to observe the extent of change over the 1979–83 period. In Table 9.9, we show the levels of support for extending public ownership among supporters of the most representative parties of the left and the right in four West European countries.

In all countries we observe large differences between supporters of different parties in their attitudes towards public ownership. We also

Table 9.8. *Support for interventionism by party preference, 1985 and 1990*

	1985	*N*	1990	*N*
Germany				
Green	54	37	66	134
Social Democrat	52	322	51	813
Free Democrat	29	38	32	75
Christian Democrat/Social	35	363	35	651
Britain				
Labour	59	518	50	440
Green	—		46	37
Social Democrat/Liberal	44	137	44	95
Conservative	37	476	31	396
Austria				
Socialist	70	333	—	
People's Party	50	313	—	
Norway				
Socialist Left	—		58	137
Labour	—		54	324
Centre Party	—		51	65
Christian Party	—		42	81
Right Party	—		23	223
Progress Party	—		32	180

Notes: Entries are percentages of interventionists among party supporters. Interventionists are defined as those scoring 5–12 on the interventionism index, which ranges from 5 to 25 (see Table 9.4).

Sources: ISSP (1985, 1990).

observe rapid change in attitudes among partisan groups. In France and Italy, support for public sector expansion declined among Communist and Socialist supporters after quite high levels in 1979. On the other hand, support for public ownership fell sharply among Gaullists and Giscardians in France but increased among Christian Democrats in Italy. But these differences among right-wing voters in France and Italy correspond to different political realities: in France, the Socialist government expanded nationalization in face of intense opposition, but in Italy relatively right-wing governments coexisted with a large public sector.

In Britain, there are evident differences between Labour and Conservative supporters, with Liberal supporters holding an intermediate position. However, between 1979 and 1981, support for expanding public ownership increased among all partisans, including Conservatives. It is particularly interesting to find that, by 1983, support among

Liberals almost matches support among Labour supporters. We have already suggested reasons for these changes but, in view of the short time series, we should not make too much of them. By contrast, in Germany, developments diverged: among Social Democrats there was increasing support for public sector expansion but declining support among Christian Democrats.

We can see, then, that public ownership and government intervention in the economy continue to be issues of partisan conflict in Western Europe. Although in some countries the trend towards non-intervention and private ownership—which we might anticipate from rising productivity in private sectors—is duly reflected in the attitudes of some partisan groups, this does not mean that a consensus on the state's economic role is gradually replacing traditional ideological divisions. At least, our data do not permit such a conclusion.

TABLE 9.9. *Support for more public ownership by party preference in four countries, 1979, 1981, and 1983*

	1979	1981	1983
France			
Communist	86	81	63
Socialist	85	62	51
Ecologist	48	34	36
Gaullist	32	21	19
Giscardian/Liberal	30	21	12
Germany			
Social Democrat	38	38	48
Christian Democrat/Social	41	39	38
Free Democrat	37	34	20
Green	67	59	53
Italy			
Communist	68	50	51
Socialist	42	30	31
Christian Democrat	29	31	35
Republican	9	15	17
Britain			
Labour	57	66	67
Liberal	31	37	52
Conservative	23	42	39

Note: Entries are percentages favouring public ownership among party supporters.

Sources: Eurobarometer, Nos. 11, 16, and 19.

Belief Systems and Social Structures

There are multiple theoretical possibilities for analysing the relationship between social structure and political outlooks. In reductionist versions, attitudes and beliefs are identified with political ideologies, and adherence to them results from the interest maximization of each social class. Empirically, however, the relationships are more complex.

The experiences of social agents are, of course, intrinsically associated with the social class to which they belong. However, social structures define not only different economic interests, but also different meanings, which are integrated in values and belief systems (Michelat and Simon 1985; Schemeil 1985). They are not necessarily conscious, since they result partly from institutionalized routines which are accepted as natural (Bourdieu 1977, 1980). Thus, the belief system of individuals cannot be explained only by economic structures but depends also on socialization (Easton and Dennis 1967; Sears 1974; Percheron 1971; Inglehart 1977), shared social identities (Tajfel 1981), and the predominant cultural context (Elazar 1970).

The literature in this area invokes social and economic structures, especially in the analysis of social classes, but also social and cultural structures, stressing education and religion, and the effects of political structures. In this section, we single out for analysis respondents' occupation, education, gender, and age as indicators of their positions in the social structure.

First, we look at the effects of social class. Economic liberalism was the ideology of the nineteenth-century entrepreneurial class. It carries the image of freedom and progress, but also the stamp of social misery and uprooted masses. Modern forms of interventionism grew up in the working class, which needed the state as a bulwark against capitalism and social injustice. Such images are not easily effaced, especially when encapsulated in class subcultures, as they have been in many West European societies.

Today, the working class is shrinking as new generations receive education and move into the ranks of salaried employees. Small-scale independent farmers and artisans, traditionally sceptical about the benefits of the free market, are also declining in number. These trends may account for some part of the long-term development of support for economic liberalism and interventionism. In its later stages, the success of capitalism, which according to our hypothesis leads to economic liberalism, becomes expressed not only in higher living standards for ordinary people, but also in the gradual elimination of the traditional working class and the petty bourgeoisie.

We deal first with economic management. Class differences alone do not explain the large variations among West European countries which we witnessed in Figure 9.1. In Table 9.10, we use data from Eurobarometer, No. 11 (Spring 1979) to present an overview of support for more government management of the economy among the self-employed, non-manual employees, and manual workers.

As the average for these eight countries shows, support for economic management is lowest among the self-employed and highest among manual workers, with non-manual employees closer to the self-employed than workers. A few countries deviate from this general pattern; in Italy, especially, there is widespread support for increasing economic management among the self-employed. The differences in attitude between the occupational groups, however, are small compared with the differences between countries. On average, only 10 percentage points separate the level of support among the self-employed and workers, but in Denmark, for example, manual workers are far less supportive of more economic management than the self-employed in most countries.

One is tempted to conclude from these data that, generally, class or occupational position is not a major factor in attitudinal differences on economic management. However, data from Sweden and Denmark

TABLE 9.10. *Support for more economic management by occupational class in eight countries, 1979*

	Self-employed	Non-manual employees	Manual workers
Denmark	55	54	60
Germany	60	66	71
France	73	72	85
Netherlands	66	81	86
Britain	63	64	77
Belgium	77	85	87
Italy	89	81	93
Ireland	86	89	86
Average	71	78	81

Note: Entries are percentages supporting more economic management among occupational groups.
Source: Eurobarometer, No. 11.

indicate that class position is an important factor in Scandinavia. In Table 9.11 we show the proportions in the three occupational groups giving a liberal response to a question on economic management which was repeated in several Swedish and Danish electoral surveys.

Among workers around 20 per cent gave a liberal response, a figure which has not changed significantly over the years, except for a drop to 12 per cent in Sweden in 1968 and Denmark in 1979. Among salaried employees, approximately twice that proportion gave the liberal response, and among the self-employed the proportion rises to above 50 per cent in some years. Support for the liberal position comes especially from the 'old' self-employed middle class and, to a lesser extent, from the 'new' middle class of salaried employees—but in only small measure from the working class.

As to public ownership, we noted earlier that in some countries nationalization was designed to produce a new economic and social order to favour the working class. But socialists and social democrats have not always advocated public ownership. In many cases, their objectives have been pursued by state regulation of employment, wages, and working conditions. Moreover, expansion of the public sector has also had other strategic purposes, such as promoting economic development or national interests. There are other reasons, too, for people to support government intervention in the economy. We have

TABLE 9.11. *Opposition to government regulation of private enterprises by occupational class: Sweden and Denmark, 1960–84*

	Workers	Salaried employees	Self-employed
Sweden			
1960	19	42	53
1964	20	39	43
1968	12	27	38
1976	22	42	52
1979	21	37	43
Denmark			
1971	18	32	48
1975	18	35	52
1979	12	21	39
1984	20	35	59

Notes: Entries are percentages opposed to government regulation of private companies among occupational classes. For question wording, see notes to Figure 9.2.

Sources: Swedish and Danish election surveys.

in mind the rational management of natural resources, and state control over activities with implications for the quality of life. This kind of reasoning is related to a change in values which, although advocated by a minority, is supported by new social strata with increasing importance in developed societies (Inglehart 1977).

The analysis here is confined to examining attitudes towards expanding public ownership among occupational classes in France, Germany, Italy, and Britain, the four largest EC countries in Eurobarometer, Nos. 11, 16, and 19. The distribution of support is shown in Table 9.12.

Support for expanding the public sector declined over the period among the working class in France and Italy. In Germany and Britain, however, support increased among all three groups. In France, there was an abrupt decline in support for more public ownership among the liberal professions and top managers between 1979 and 1981, just before the nationalization programme was introduced. In Germany, however, support for public sector expansion increased among the liberal professions and top managers from 1981 to 1983.

TABLE 9.12. *Support for more public ownership of private industry by occupational class in four countries, 1979–83*

	Professionals managers	Non-manual salaried	Manual workers
France			
1979	50	54	66
1981	10	54	56
1983	19	27	45
Germany			
1979	29	42	34
1981	26	33	58
1983	45	43	39
Italy			
1979	18	35	49
1981	21	29	43
1983	8	28	39
Britain			
1979	14	22	42
1981	26	39	53
1983	30	42	58

Note: Entries are percentages among occupational groups who support more public ownership of private industry.

Sources: Eurobarometer, Nos. 11, 16, and 19.

Next, we consider the effects of education. The results above suggest a shift towards state intervention during the last decade among the well educated and professionally qualified. This tendency, associated in some countries with higher levels of economic development, seems to arise from dissociating state intervention from social equality but, instead, linking interventionism to a new logic about the global functioning of the economy. Our hypothesis is that state intervention is not intended to apply to the entire economy, nor is there any intention to abandon the rules of market competition. Rather, the aim is selective state intervention in sectors concerning natural resources, the environment, and the welfare of citizens.

To understand this shift in beliefs, we have to disaggregate attitudes towards the public sector to consider separately beliefs about enterprises which are natural monopolies, or with strong implications for the quality of life, and those functioning under competitive, market conditions. We can test our hypothesis by examining attitudes towards different economic sectors in the ISSP data for 1985 and 1990. In Table 9.13, we display the correlation coefficients for the impact of education on attitudes towards public ownership in different economic sectors.

We find that in Germany, Austria, and Ireland there is no correlation between education and support for state ownership of the electricity industry or public transport. In countries where the correlation is significant—Britain (electricity), Italy (electricity and public transport, 1985) and Norway (electricity, 1990)—it is positive. That is, support for public ownership in those sectors increases in accordance with educational level, which is contrary to the results obtained when analysing the public sector as a whole. However, for banks and insurance companies, and the automobile industry, the correlations are significant but negative, indicating that support for public ownership is low among those with higher education.

These results reveal that in some countries and at some time points, people with higher levels of education believe in state intervention as a regulatory activity which can lead to state ownership of monopolies. But, at other times, there is no relationship between educational level and attitudes towards state ownership. However, when it comes to the competitive sector of the economy, the more highly educated are almost invariably negative about state ownership, preferring private enterprise and market regulation.

New social and cultural purposes may be implied by this shift in

TABLE 9.13. *Correlation between education and attitude towards government control and ownership of different sectors of the economy*

	Electricity	Public transport	Steel industry	Banks and insurance	Automobile industry
Germany					
1985	−0.01	−0.02	−0.24**	−0.17**	−0.23**
1990	0.02	—	−0.13**	−0.08**	—
Britain					
1985	0.12**	0.01	−0.03	−0.05	−0.16**
1990	0.08**	—	−0.09**	−0.09**	—
Italy					
1985	0.08**	0.08**	−0.10**	−0.07**	−0.11**
1990	0.00	—	−0.11**	−0.04	—
Austria					
1985	0.00	0.01	−0.19**	−0.16**	−0.18**
Ireland					
1990	−0.01	—	−0.14**	−0.07**	—
Norway					
1990	0.08**	—	−0.20**	−0.10**	—

*$p < 0.05$ **$p < 0.01$

Notes: Entries are Pearson's *r*. For question wording, see notes to Table 9.2. The codings used here are: own it = 3; control prices and profits but not own it = 2; neither own it nor control its prices and profits = 1.

Sources: ISSP (1985, 1990).

beliefs, namely welfare and environmental concerns. The relationship between education and scope of government beliefs about welfare and environmental protection is discussed in Chapters 7 and 8 and in Chapter 11 respectively. With regard to state intervention, we hypothesize that well-educated people do not have the same interest in protecting their jobs and income by means of government support as the less well educated do. But we must also bear in mind educational differences when it comes to attitudes towards the nationalization of different economic sectors. The results of our analysis seem to confirm our hypothesis that this form of state intervention reveals new values and political objectives. Traditional left ideology which seeks to alter the economic order for egalitarian purposes is not involved. Rather, the aim seems to be to secure significant state regulation in those economic areas with important social and environmental implications.

Finally, what are the effects of gender and age? As we have identified the attitude, economic interventionism is generally associated with economically dependent people, and people who look towards the state as the vehicle for changing situations which they think are wrong. This applies not only to social classes but also to age and gender groups. The relative strength of interventionism among these groups is shown in Table 9.14. Our measure of interventionism is the index we computed earlier using the five indicators from the ISSP data (see Table 9.3).

Since women are generally more economically dependent than men, we expect to find more support for intervention among women. This is borne out in the first two columns of the table. As an average across these eight national samples, 59 per cent of women as against 51 per cent of men are interventionists.

Differences in support for government intervention may also be expected to exhibit an age pattern, but what we expect depends on which model we adopt. On the one hand, according to a 'value' model, the new generation will typically be the bearer of modern values which gradually replace the traditional values of older generations. Since the most developed countries have the least interventionist public (cf. Table 9.1), according to this model we expect the young to be less

TABLE 9.14. *Support for interventionism by gender and age, 1985 and 1990*

	Gender		Age				All
	Male	Female	18–24	25–44	45–64	65+	
Germany							
1985	40	47	55	33	44	53	43
1990	39	51	56	46	43	41	45
Britain							
1985	48	48	43	39	55	65	48
1990	35	45	41	35	41	53	41
Italy							
1985	77	88	87	80	83	86	83
1990	76	82	80	77	80	84	79
Austria							
1985	57	60	58	57	59	58	59
Norway							
1990	36	51	50	38	39	51	43
Average	51	59	59	51	56	61	55

Notes: Entries are percentages of interventionists. For definition of interventionists, see Tables 9.3 and 9.8.

Sources: ISSP (1985, 1990).

interventionist than the old. On the other hand, according to an 'interest' model, both the young and the old tend to depend on government for support, whereas the middle-aged are more likely to enjoy financial independence. Hence, we expect to find the lowest level of interventionism among those in their active years.

The third and following columns of Table 9.14 display the level of support for interventionism among four age groups. Except in Austria, the pattern tends to be U-shaped, with interventionism reaching its lowest level among those aged 25–44 years. Just as predicted from the 'interest' model, the young and the old tend to be more interventionist than the middle-aged. It is more difficult to fit the pattern into a 'value' model when old and young generations share the same attitude. However, for those having reached their mid-twenties, and usually established in work, one might still argue that the figures are consistent with a trend towards liberalism. Even so, we need data over a longer period before deciding between the two models.

Conclusions

We began this chapter by pointing to the historical association between liberalism and capitalism. From that, we derived the working hypothesis that public support for liberalism would depend on the success of the capitalist system. Assuming that the high living standards in some European countries are mainly due to the application of liberal economic policies, it is consistent with this hypothesis that we found support for more government management of the economy and more public ownership to be weakest in countries with, on average, a high standard of living (Figure 9.1). With regard to nationalization, there is a downward trend in support in some countries with high living standards (Figures 9.3 and 9.4).

Support for government management of the economy increased between 1979 and 1981, when the energy crisis threatened living standards in most Western countries (Figure 9.5). This accords with our working hypothesis, as it suggests that demands for government intervention thrive on failures of the capitalist economy. The fact that a neo-liberal government came to power in Britain in 1979 could be explained differently. However, large national deviations not predicted by the hypothesis suggested that economic management may mean different things depending on political circumstances. This was confirmed when we found that support for economic management was not always associated with socialist preferences, and bore no systematic relationship with left–right position (Table 9.6). A closer study of eight policies of economic management in eight national samples revealed that economic liberalism is far from being a distinctive attitude in the public mind, except possibly in Scandinavia. What does exist is an attitude, positive or negative, towards concrete forms of government intervention (Tables 9.1 and 9.3). Hence we prefer the term economic interventionism.

In examining attitudes towards state ownership, we found state ownership of competitive sectors to be less popular than state ownership of monopolies such as electricity and public transport (Table 9.2). Support for state ownership of competitive sectors was characteristic of hard-core interventionists, so may, thereby, be viewed as a component of interventionism (Table 9.4).

The main motivation for interventionism seems to be the immediate interest of ordinary people in protecting jobs and the buying power of wages or, for the petty bourgeoisie, business incomes. Such interventionism is practically unrelated to liberal ideas. Some plausible types of intervention, such as price controls and job-creating projects, are also popular among middle-class groups and voters for bourgeois parties. Conversely, liberal principles of cutting government spending and regulation are accepted by large sections of the working class and voters for parties of the left. None the less, middle-level and hard-core interventionists tend to be socialist in outlook and party preference (Table 9.8). Under bourgeois governments, demands for intervention are tempered by the feeling that such policies hand over power to the 'wrong' government (Table 9.6).

Our working hypothesis is a fair guide to the social correlates of interventionism. Applied to the individual level, the hypothesis implies that individuals or groups who tend to lose out under the capitalist system are likely to support demands for government intervention in the economy. Consistent with this, we found that blue-collar workers are more interventionist than white-collar workers and the self-employed (Tables 9.10–9.12). In analysing support for state ownership, we found that people of low education tend to support state ownership of competitive sectors, whereas support for state ownership of monopoly sectors is either unrelated or positively correlated with higher levels of education (Table 9.13). Lastly, that women are more interventionist than men, and the young and elderly more interventionist than the middle-aged (Table 9.14), can be explained by the fact that, on the whole, it is middle-aged men who tend to profit most from the capitalist system.

In general, however, differences in attitudes within countries are less impressive than differences between countries. For example, Social Democrats in Germany and Denmark are, on average, far less interventionist than Italian Christian Democrats (cf. Tables 9.7 and 9.8). It is tempting to claim that average standards of living in a society are more important than individual economic positions in discouraging interventionist attitudes. But we incline to the view that these national differences go back to political traditions dating from the early phases of industrialization. In Italy, Austria, Spain, and Portugal economic interventionism, particularly nationalization, was promoted by parties of both the left and the right, opposed only by minor liberal parties in the centre. In northern European countries, nationalization was confined to the programmes of socialists on the far left. It requires a longitudinal study based on a much longer time series than is available from the data record to corroborate our hypothesis that interventionism is undermined by the success of the capitalist system in generating high living standards. Our data offer only a glimpse of developments during a period, from around 1975 to 1990, which comes late in the industrialization of these countries.

NOTES

1. One may think of this as an application of the principle of reinforcement, which has a long tradition in behavioural psychology (Thorndike 1911).
2. Luxembourg is omitted here and throughout the chapter as there are too few cases for analysis.
3. These Eurobarometer data do not include Portugal, but there is some evidence of a similar evolution there. Agreement with the statement 'The big economic activities should be state owned'—an indicator included in an inquiry into political culture in 1988 —reached 39 per cent in 1988 but had fallen to 22 per cent by 1991.
4. Some of the items were not asked in Austria.
5. In Italy, partisan preference was not asked.
6. It might be added that such ideologized differentiation seems characteristic of Scandinavian party systems. In Denmark, the statement 'The government should co-ordinate and control private enterprise', was endorsed by 58 per cent in the socialist camp as against only 22 per cent in the bourgeois camp (Danish Election Survey 1979). With regard to Sweden, Gilljam and Holmberg (1993: 125) demonstrate a high correlation between party choice and attitudes towards controlling

banks and industry, but the correlation declined after 1979. However, responses to an even more ideological item, proposing 'a society with more private initiative and a market economy', retained its high association with party choice into the election of 1991.

PART III

The Cultural and Natural Environment

10

Government, Communications, and the Media

PETER GOLDING AND LEO VAN SNIPPENBURG

The state has always been involved in the regulation of communications, from the early licensing of printers through to the establishment of public service broadcasting systems in the mid-twentieth century. Communications institutions straddle both industrial and cultural policy, and state intervention has been extensive because of this twin function. For the same reasons, state intervention has also frequently been confused and contentious.

In recent years, communication systems in Western Europe have been subject to two contradictory pressures. On the one hand, economic change and technological developments have provided the occasion for substantial deregulation, affording new market spaces especially in the field of broadcasting. In many countries the traditional public service broadcasting organizations have found both their ideological and fiscal props suddenly vulnerable to new commercial imperatives. On the other hand, many countries have witnessed renewed demands for cultural regulation, restricting the free flow of material considered socially undesirable or morally damaging. The juggling act required of the state in meeting these contrary demands has reflected the considerable inconsistency in public opinion.

Many of the debates on these issues have occurred within national boundaries. However, the international character of many cultural goods has promoted a growing sense that cross-national policy is required in this area. One of the problems, reflected in uncertain public opinion, is that the harmonization of regulation can be seen as contradicting free market demands for unimpeded cultural flows. This is especially the case for smaller states (Trappel 1991). Efforts to attune interference in, or control of, public communication by the governments of different countries concern not only the organization and the content of the mass media. They also stretch over all modes of public communication, engaging issues such as the right to free speech and the right to demonstrate.

In this chapter, we review these changes and assess the general character of public opinion about the form and the extent of government intervention in communications. We begin by looking at the dimensions of this aspect of government activity, and then go on to consider the general shifts in media policy in Western Europe over the last forty years. This provides a backdrop to the data we present. These data deal with public attitudes about the proper boundaries between the public and private domains in the realm of broadcasting, and with opinions about the appropriate levels and forms of intervention in communications more generally. This means focusing on the question of censorship.

Dimensions of Policy and Attitudes

Governments regulate communications in two ways. First, governments regulate the structure of media organizations: licensing producers and distributors, controlling access to scarce resources, limiting patterns of ownership and control, setting minimum levels of indigenous investment, and so on. Secondly, governments regulate the content of the media, restricting the availability of material deemed to be harmful, seditious, obscene, or simply damaging to national culture. They may also promote material they believe to be morally or educationally uplifting. In 1993, for example, the British government found itself embroiled in public debate about the role of video and computer games in contributing to an apparent crime wave. At the same time, it confronted hostile public opinion provoked by rapidly growing government intervention in the content, including the language and moral tenor, of the school curriculum.

On issues such as these, governments may be interventionist or *laissez-faire*—although in this area the distinction can be misleading. For example, many countries engaged in the apparent 'deregulation' of broadcasting are, in fact, merely 're-regulating'; they have created a new supervisory regime with clear and well-defined objectives of encouraging particular forms of participation and certain kinds of participants in the new communications arena. The process may also be contradictory. A government anxious to liberate new entrepreneurial forces in communications by reducing statutory intervention, may, within the same complex of ideological or political inclinations, find itself driven to increasing intervention on such matters as public morality and cultural change.

The complexity of regulatory regimes is depicted in Figure 10.1. Of course, no state falls neatly into one of these quadrants, which may be conceived as ideal types. However the figure illustrates possible shifts over time as governments, and indeed public demand, move from one quadrant to another. Hence, it serves as a location chart for some of the hypotheses and findings we discuss in this chapter. The figure also provides a rough map of different positions in conflicts over communications politics. For instance, part of the concern over the content of communications, especially in the media, has been nationalist in flavour. The film industry in many countries receives substantial state subsidy explicitly to compensate for the power and potentially dominant character of Hollywood imports. Even in Britain, where state support has been uneven and restrained, the industry has a history littered with attempts, through import quotas and other measures, to afford a protectionist shelter for national film culture. More recently this concern has taken on a European dimension. The involvement of the EC in regulating television and film flows has provoked much debate and argument, and in some cases furious hostility.[1] Perhaps the most significant attempt so far to evolve a European policy on cultural regulation is represented by *Television Without Frontiers*, published by the Commission of the European Communities (1984).

		Structure	
		Interventionist	Liberal
Content	Interventionist	Authoritarian	Free market-strong state
	Liberal	Regulatory	Libertarian

FIGURE 10.1. *Dimensions of government intervention in communications*

The different strands of government involvement in communications—or, more specifically, the media—can be simply illustrated by comparing the press with broadcasting in most countries. In Western Europe, broadcasting has largely evolved on a basis of public service beliefs and structures, whereas the press has evolved, latterly at least, firmly in the private sector, subject only to variable but limited degrees of support and subsidy in some countries. However, technological changes, notably satellite, video, and cable, are held to have destroyed the 'natural monopoly' which provided the rationale for public service media. In particular, spectrum scarcity has become irrelevant as an argument for close public regulation and national monopoly.

The role of public opinion in these debates is quite problematic. Lord Reith, founding Director-General of the BBC, justified the 'brute force of monopoly' underpinning public service broadcasting with the claim: 'few know what they want, and very few what they need'. His words seem prophetic; policy relating to both the organization of the media and their products appears to have been driven more by technological and economic forces than by any evident shifts in the political or moral climate. However, before examining public opinion data on these issues, we outline the general form of developments in the media policy of West European governments.

Government and Media Policy

The variation in communications policy between different West European states reflects two consistent themes. First, policy has been driven by contradictory imperatives, depending on whether communications is seen as an industry, requiring an industrial strategy to steer its evolution, or as an arm of national culture, requiring statutory regulation to ensure its contribution to the direction of cultural life. Secondly, policy has evolved largely without significant input from public opinion, which has almost everywhere followed rather than led government policy. A brief review of national developments in a selection of countries illustrates the main features of the evolution of policy across Western Europe.[2]

Austria

After initially being divided into four sectors at the end of the war, the national broadcasting system, Österreichische Rundfunk, came into being in 1954 when the country regained full sovereignty. The concentration of the press has been a major concern, to which Austrian governments have responded with subsidies to stabilize the industry. Broadcasting is defined constitutionally as a public service, but easy and widespread foreign reception has driven ÖRF to adopt a more commercial approach to compete with these channels.

Belgium

The structure of the media reflects the linguistic divisions within Belgium. In recent years, the Flemish press has overtaken the Walloon press in circulation. Public service broadcasting was given an absolute monopoly after the war, and in 1960 distinct organizations for the Flemish and Walloon communities were established, followed by a third for the German-speaking sector in 1977. Belgium has an exceptionally high proportion of households with cable television. Due to competition, the monopolies of the public services were ended in the early 1980s, and commercial broadcasting set up in 1987. Statutory supervision of the new stations was transferred to the three communities in 1989, and the success of these new stations has led to changes in the programming and financing of the public service stations. Generally public policy has been relatively non-interventionist.

Denmark

Having operated a state broadcasting monopoly since 1926, the unitary model was broken with the establishment of a second television channel in 1987 which went on air the following year. This change followed from diverse pressures: commercial interests; growing reservations about the monopoly position of Danmarks Radio; and the reception of several foreign stations. Denmark has no party-owned newspaper, and provides less state subsidy to support the press than other Scandinavian countries. As in many small countries, the issues in public debate have been a mixture of cultural sovereignty and commercialization, although broadcasting policy has never been very high on the political agenda.

Finland

The national broadcasting organization, Oy Yleisradio AB (YLE), has enjoyed a monopoly since 1927. Commercial television began the same year as public service television in 1957, but in 1964 the commercial company was incorporated into YLE. The YLE monopoly was only effectively broken with the development of local radio since 1985. As elsewhere in Scandinavia, there is a state scheme of subsidies for the press. Most of the changes in the broadcasting regime have been fuelled by the arrival of foreign media via satellite which has produced pressure for deregulation.

France

In the early 1980s the socialist government initiated a major nationalization of the communications industry and adventurous advances in informatics. But in the mid-1980s, the pendulum swung back towards denationalization under a coalition government of the right. Public service broadcasting has been joined by a growing array of complementary sources, including Canal Plus and La Cinq, but ambitious cable plans have rather fizzled out. Public opinion may have been influential in the continuing pressure for the decentralization of the media, especially in supporting strong regional newspapers and growing demands for regional broadcasting. Télévision Française 1 (TF1) was privatized in 1986 and programming has become increasingly populist.

Germany

The media system in former West Germany was almost entirely the creation of the allied powers after the war. The structure and regulation of broadcasting is based on the *Länder*. Most of the major papers are post-war creations but, despite strong party organizations, there is little in the way of a party press. Policy concern about the press has increasingly addressed issues of press concentration. The main issue has been the challenge to public service networks, arising particularly from the high proportion of households connected to cable networks, and the role of major corporate players, often with Christian Democratic sympathies. Commercial television was introduced—experimentally—in 1985, and has become more widely available via cable and satellite since 1987. In response to those pressures, the two major public broadcasting services—Rundfunkanstalt (ARD) and Zweites Deutsches Fernsehen—have lost audiences, hence the licence fee was raised by 25 per cent in 1992.

Italy

The national broadcasting system Radiotelevisione Italiana was created after the war, and a second channel was introduced in 1961. A third channel was introduced in 1979 to counter the explosion of private local broadcasters unleashed by legislation in the mid-1970s. Italy's broadcasting scene has displayed a more anarchic and fragmented form than almost anywhere else in Western Europe. Underneath the confusion, however, lies a duopolistic pattern of the remnants of public service broadcasting—traditionally the purview of the Christian Democratic, Socialist, and Communist Parties—alongside Silvio Berlusconi's empire. Recent legislation has been targeted at cross-media ownership, the extent of national and European material shown on television, and advertising. The proliferation of channels has stifled the development of cable in Italy.

The media in Italy constitute a quite unique institutional force. Berlusconi's victory in the 1994 general election, at the head of Forza Italia, amounted to an unprecedented transfer from media power to political power. Although Berlusconi's command of both broadcasting facilities and political patronage is unmatched in Western Europe, he represents a concentration of political resources which is causing some alarm among political observers. At this point, however, it is too soon to assess the impact of the 'Berlusconi phenomenon'.

Netherlands

The Dutch term invariably used to describe media structures is *verzuiling*, often translated as 'pillarization'. A more precise translation is not available, but the sectional pluralism which it describes, of a society organized around social movements, parties, and religious communities, is well reflected in the media. These 'pillars' in broadcasting are subsumed under the Nederlandse Omroepprogamma Stichtung, which provides co-ordination and complementary programming of news, along with cultural and educative material. Strong public support for foreign programmes and commitments to EC regulations have propelled recent trends to some deregulation and commercialization. Cable penetration is extensive. As elsewhere, public policy reflects an uncertain defence of existing public service structures, which are being eroded by the obvious popularity of commercial alternatives. Commercial radio and television were legally admitted on cable in 1992, and some terrestrial room has been made available to Dutch commercial radio since late 1993.

The press in the Netherlands has always been organized on a commercial basis, although with the strong involvement of social and political movements. Since the 1960s, concentration has reduced the 'pillarization' of the newspaper industry, provoking government measures—through subsidy and agreements with publishers—to preserve the diversity of the press.

Britain

The dominance of the British Broadcasting Corporation in the spectrum of British broadcasting has been under threat since the introduction of commercial broadcasting in 1954. However, only under the Conservative governments of the 1980s has the centrality of public service broadcasting—a philosophy explicitly shared by the regulated commercial network—been challenged. Moreover, the growth of new media—cable, satellite, video—has brought the future of the BBC increasingly into question. A government consultative paper was published in late 1992. This raised the spectre that the BBC would be much reduced in size by the end of the decade, with only a third of the audience, and concentrating on the types of programmes which are unattractive for the commercial sector. In the event, the government's final proposals, published in 1994, were less Draconian than anticipated. The BBC's charter was renewed for ten years, although funding based on a licence fee is to be reviewed within five years. The Corporation was encouraged to become an 'international multi-media enterprise', and to foster collaboration with private capital.

Public opinion on broadcasting policy is rarely a factor in political debate or electoral politics in Britain, other than periodic flurries caused by pressure groups agonizing over pornographic or violent material. Public policy on the press has been consistently *laissez-faire*, with no subsidy scheme, and only the most tentative anti-monopoly legislation. More recently, concern over the growing prurience and wildness of the popular press has led to some, often contrived, public outrage over privacy. Thus, for the first time there is the possibility that statutory rather than merely voluntary controls over press behaviour might be considered.

As these examples show, throughout Western Europe we can see a rapid shift in recent years towards a more diversified and commercially dominated media system. In general, governments have engaged, whether reluctantly or enthusiastically, in deregulation, allowing the private sector to flourish in both scale and scope. Government intervention has taken the form of providing the enabling framework for this shift to occur, while occasionally engaging in bouts of social engineering to limit the excesses of some of the more extreme material becoming available.

Some Hypotheses

Whereas there is a body of research on public attitudes towards several aspects of the activities of governments, as this volume testifies, there has been relatively little systematic research on attitudes towards public policy relating to the media. Rather, researchers have tended to focus on the impact of the media on, among other things, people's attitudes towards major questions of economic and social policy—and, particularly, their perceptions of parties and politicians. Given that the structure and regulation of the media falls within the scope of government, the limited salience of the issue within the research or policy communities is, perhaps, surprising. The lack of data in this area may itself be symptomatic: where no public opinion is thought to exist, and not to matter if it does, there can be no purpose to opinion surveys. But we cannot assume, thereby, that this reflects a low level of interest among the wider public.

The problem remains, however, that we have little measure of attitudes towards the structure of the media. Indeed, we have few data on attitudes towards the media in general. This means that although we could derive hypotheses from the broad framework, there are few propositions which we can test empirically. However, we can suggest three general hypotheses about the character of attitudes in this area. First, we suggest that an apparent move away from intervention in the structure of communications in recent years has sometimes coincided with a growing trend towards state involvement in the content of the media. This corresponds to a movement upwards and towards the right in Figure 10.1. Secondly, we suggest that there is a salience gradient from structure to content. That is, we anticipate that questions about the content of the media are more likely to evoke public response and concern than questions about the structure of ownership and regulation. Thirdly, inasmuch as there is movement in public opinion, it tends to be in response to policy initiatives. Public opinion is seldom a stimulus to media policy, and opinion among national populations is slower to change and more muted in relation to questions of structure than questions of content. When there is a response, it arises from the development of new media technologies and the changing cultural goods they introduce.

In reviewing the data available to us we have focused on a small number of particularly pertinent themes. In the next section, we review attitudes to the structure of broadcasting. Such attitudes have been triggered, largely, by questions about the balance between public and private sectors in broadcasting, and the nature and degree of government regulation required in increasingly pluralistic broadcasting systems. In subsequent sections, we analyse data on public attitudes towards government intervention in the content of the media. Here, we are particularly interested in three issues:

(1) To what extent has there been a change over the last decade or so in public attitudes towards a more liberal or 'permissive' view of the freedom of action allowed to the media?
(2) To what extent can we detect a common pattern of attitudes, or distinctive national patterns, across Western Europe on matters relating to the media?
(3) Which groups in the population are associated with particular attitudes to the performance of the media and the role of government in regulating them?

Bear in mind that our approach is that attitudes about communications and the media are responsive to, rather than determinants of, technological and political developments. This view would be confirmed if we were to find that there is considerable cross-national variation in the attitudes we examine, especially if these variations are related to different national events or policies. Furthermore, our view would be strengthened if we were to find that period effects reflecting sudden 'shocks' to public opinion are more important than generational effects reflecting glacial drifts in public opinion. These issues are discussed in subsequent sections of this chapter. But, first, we look at attitudes towards the structure of the media.

Public and Private Broadcasting

Whether the ownership of the media should be in the public or the private sector has been an issue in most West European countries. The issue arose, in most instances, around the specific question of introducing commercial broadcasting to supplement, or replace, public service corporations of one kind or another. Although there has often been heated debate between the advocates of public service broadcasting and commercial interests, the views of the public seem to have gone largely unrecorded. Hence, the paucity of data to which we referred.

An exception to this silence is one item in a Dutch survey conducted in 1985, before the introduction of commercial broadcasting in the Netherlands. Respondents were asked whether or not they agreed with the following proposition: 'Everyone who wants to should be allowed to produce and broadcast radio and TV programmes.' Although nothing is stated explicitly about state control or government intervention, the proposition clearly implies questioning the desirability of a state monopoly. Thus, we can treat this question as a proxy for a more direct indicator of attitudes about the ownership and control of the media. The distribution of responses is shown in Table 10.1.

Two aspects of this table are particularly interesting. First, with altogether 63 per cent opposing the proposition, the broad sweep of opinion is opposed to a highly liberal broadcasting environment. Secondly, opinion seems to be fairly clearly structured; only a fairly small minority (15 per cent) had no opinion either way. However, although in every instance there is a firm majority against a 'free for all', opposition is more widespread among some groups. Support for control is more common among older people, the less educated, and among women. Conversely, opposition to control is less widespread among the young, men, and the well educated. Church members supported government control in larger numbers than non-members, an important distinction in a country where some 50 per cent of the population are members of an organized church (Cultural Change in the Netherlands 1986). Again, support for government control is higher among people who are politically to the right or in the centre than

TABLE 10.1. *Attitudes towards media freedom, Netherlands, 1986*

	Agree	Neither	Disagree
Age			
16–25	29	16	55
26–44	24	19	58
45–54	21	12	67
55+	15	8	77
Gender			
Men	26	13	61
Women	18	16	66
Education			
Low	19	13	68
Middle	21	16	63
High	29	16	56
Church membership			
Yes	17	13	69
No	26	16	58
Party preference			
Left	26	16	58
Centre	20	17	64
Right	19	11	70
Total population	22	15	63
N = 1,877			

Note: Entries are percentages agreeing with the proposition: 'Everyone who wants to should be allowed to produce and broadcast radio and television programmes.'

Source: Cultural Change in the Netherlands (1986).

among those oriented to the left. In particular, 36 per cent of the extreme left and 25 per cent of the moderate left agreed with the free production and broadcasting of radio and TV programmes as against about 18–20 per cent of the extreme right, the moderate right, and the centre.

The Dutch survey invited the views of respondents in advance of new services being available to them. However, other evidence suggests that resistance to deregulation may weaken as appealing alternatives become more visible. Commercial broadcasting was introduced in Germany after 1985; a survey conducted in 1984 and 1988 asked the following question: 'Who, in your opinion, should be first of all responsible for radio and TV nowadays?' In 1984, 42 per cent of respondents said 'the state'; in 1988 this figure dropped to 35 per cent (Welfare Surveys 1984, 1988).[3]

Changing Attitudes

Any mention of government control of media content immediately conjures up Orwellian images of Big Brother and Draconian censorship. Yet even the most liberal of regimes expects, and is expected by its citizens, both to control and promote certain kinds of images and ideas. Indeed, liberal regimes have to struggle with the contradictory demands of free speech and what is politically, or culturally, acceptable. How far can a government committed to the light regulation of communications intervene in the free distribution of racist literature, for example? Similarly, is a commitment to limited state intervention compatible with the rhetoric of equal opportunities, or curtailing the circulation of violent, obscene, or inflammatory materials? These dilemmas are central to libertarian thinking, as well as to policy and politics in this area. Inevitably, therefore, they are at the core of complex public attitudes.

The so-called 'cultural revolution' of the 1960s is a hallmark of recent history—or so, at least, is commentary on it by some schools of thought. According to Inglehart (1979, 1990), the populations of Western societies have become more 'postmaterialist' in outlook, mainly as a consequence of the gradual replacement of older generations who experienced the insecurity and scarcity of the war years by younger generations raised in the peace and plenty of the welfare state. This thesis suggests that pre-war generations are less democratic and libertarian in outlook, and less sympathetic to alternative life-styles and culturally controversial ideas (Van Snippenburg and Vettehen 1992), than post war generations. On the basis of these claims, we would expect to find substantial differences in support for censorship and the control of media content as between older and younger generations within every West European country.

Following the same arguments, we might also expect that, at the aggregate level, support for government control of the media has declined since the 1960s. This expectation, however, is open to doubt. Changes in attitudes towards broadcasting often seem to come about because of changed cultural circumstances—as when new media sources become available, such as American style radio during the war or pirate radio stations in the 1960s. Attitudes also seem to change as a result of the implementation of government policy, such as the introduction of commercial television in Britain in the early 1950s (Wilson 1961). In this sense, specific developments in the structure of communications, or, even more specifically, in the structure of the media, might have more influence than more general cultural developments.

With regard to generational differences, however, we are on more sure ground. We can test the argument using data from one item in Eurobarometer, No. 21 (1984), in which respondents were asked whether or not they agreed with the proposition: 'There are some books that should be censored.' The item is restricted in scope, referring only to books, but it provides some general measure of how liberal people are about media freedom. Again, although there is no explicit reference to the government in the statement, government control over the content of books is clearly implied. To examine generational differences in attitudes, the samples for six West European countries were separated into those who were born before 1940 and those born after 1940. The results are presented in Table 10.2.

Before examining generational differences, we comment on the general picture revealed by these data. As we can see from the last column in the table, there is some cross-national variation—and one clear outlier. In Germany and the Netherlands, only some quarter of respondents supported the censorship of books; in Italy, the figure rises to a third; and in Belgium and France it rises to almost two-fifths. But the general picture is clear enough: censorship is not supported by a majority of the public in Western Europe. In Britain, however, in sharp contrast, there was a clear majority in favour of censorship. The very different picture in Britain may have been due to the circumstances of

TABLE 10.2. *Attitudes towards book censorship among pre- and post-war generations in six West European countries*

	Agree		Agree if anything		Disagree		Total agreeing
	Pre-war	Post-war	Pre-war	Post-war	Pre-war	Post-war	
Britain	71	49	7	10	22	41	60
Italy	54	25	15	12	31	63	39
Belgium	47	27	27	20	25	53	37
France	48	20	18	15	34	65	33
Netherlands	39	21	15	17	46	62	28
Germany	37	17	22	24	41	59	27

Notes: Entries are percentages responding to the proposition: 'There are some books that should be censored.' The number of cases is about 500 per generation per country.

Source: Eurobarometer, No. 21.

the time, particularly the moralistic tone of Mrs Thatcher's political rhetoric (Gamble 1988).

As to generational differences, the idea of censoring books is clearly more widely supported among pre-war generations than among post-war generations in all six countries. Consistent with the aggregate level figures, there are cross-national variations in the magnitude of the 'generation gap', ranging between 18 and 29 percentage points in support of censorship and between 16 and 32 points in opposing censorship. But the differences between the two generations in each country are in the expected direction.

These results are consistent with the thesis of generational change. To explore this issue further, we examine four items from the 1985 and 1990 ISSP surveys. The content of these items is rather different, focusing on attitudes towards the regulation of media behaviour. Two of the questions pose trade-offs between freedom of information and national security; the other two are more directly related to questions of minority rights and freedom of expression. Unfortunately, even these data are rather patchy: there are two time points for Germany and Britain only, and the items about controlling the press were not repeated in 1990. None the less, they allow us to go rather further in examining the question of changing attitudes.

As we can see from Table 10.3, people value national security above freedom of information consistently across national boundaries. In Britain, Germany, Italy, and Austria, only about a quarter of the population thinks press freedom can be stretched to include the publication of confidential information about defence. However, when the same question is posed in relation to 'economic plans', a quite different pattern emerges. In this case, almost two-thirds of the population support press freedom. Even so, over a third feel that government censorship of information about economic plans is desirable.

The two questions about allowing revolutionaries and racists to publish books tap classic issues about the limits to liberty and political agitation. As we can see, there is considerable division on both issues, although freedom of expression seems to be more readily extended to revolutionaries than to racists. This is not surprising. Other chapters in this series of volumes have pointed to the high levels of system support and confidence enjoyed by West European political regimes (see Volume i, Chapters 10 and 11)—except Italy—so the ideas of minority or dissident groups probably have low salience.[4] Yet most of the countries represented here have experienced intercommunal strife

TABLE 10.3. *Attitudes about freedom to publish: six countries, 1985 and 1990*

	Britain		Germany		Italy	Austria	Norway	Ireland
	1985	1990	1985	1990	1985	1985	1990	1990
Newspapers should be allowed to publish confidential defence papers	25	—	23	—	23	29	—	—
Newspapers should be allowed to publish confidential economic plans	63	—	63	—	64	56	—	—
Revolutionaries should be allowed to publish books	68	61	75	74	55	75	66	50
Racists should be allowed to publish books	53	36	53	49	41	49	52	34

Notes: Entries are percentages agreeing with the propositions derived from the question: 'There are some people whose views are considered extreme by the majority. First, consider people who want to overthrow the government by revolution. Secondly, consider people who believe that whites are racially superior to all other races. Do you think such people should be allowed to publish books expressing their views?'; 'Suppose a newspaper got hold of confidential government papers about economic plans/defence plans and wanted to publish them: should the newspaper be allowed to publish the papers?' The latter questions were not asked in 1990.

Sources: ISSP (1985, 1990).

stemming from racism, involving, for example, Turkish immigrants in Germany and the Lappish minority in Norway. The notable shift in opinion in Britain over the five-year interval may well be related to the controversy following the publication of Salman Rushdie's book *Satanic Verses*. As this led to the proclamation of a *fatwah* condemning to death both the author and his publisher, it raised the question of free speech in particularly acute form. Unfortunately, due to the form of the questions, we cannot be confident that these responses mean that people look to government to control revolutionary or racist publications.

TABLE 10.4. *Attitudes towards freedom to publish among four age cohorts, 1985*

	Britain	Germany	Italy	Austria
Newspapers should be allowed to publish confidential defence papers				
16–25	38	40	20	31
26–43	31	26	26	34
44–54	19	24	22	28
55+	17	13	20	24
Newspapers should be allowed to publish confidential economic plans				
16–25	74	74	66	61
26–43	64	70	64	58
44–54	63	65	64	46
55+	53	52	62	56
Revolutionaries should be allowed to publish books				
16–25	79	85	71	83
26–43	73	82	62	68
44–54	70	71	48	66
55+	53	66	39	56
Racists should be allowed to publish books				
16–25	55	53	49	60
26–43	58	60	45	53
44–54	54	54	35	55
55+	45	45	33	47

Notes: See notes to Table 10.3.

Source: ISSP (1985).

In the absence of longitudinal data, we can get some measure of changes in attitudes over time by examining differences in attitudes among age groups. In Table 10.4 we show the proportions agreeing with the freedom to publish various kinds of material among young adults, mature adults, the middle aged, and older people in the 1985 data.

In every instance, older people have less permissive attitudes. Indeed, in several instances, the differences are quite striking, reaching well over 20 percentage points between the oldest and youngest. Moreover, the decline in permissiveness, in most countries, is monotonic across the age groups. The only notable exceptions to this pattern are found in Italy: Italians of all ages take a generally restrictive attitude towards newspapers publishing confidential defence documents but are generally relaxed about the publication of economic plans.

Much of the research on public attitudes about censorship relates to specific genres or even titles. For example, there are British data on attitudes about the publication of Salman Rushdie's book. There are also data on attitudes towards violent and pornographic material. However, these data are not suited to our purpose. They are sporadic in coverage and, as the survey items are usually a response to specific events, the question wordings vary widely. Even more to the point, it is often unclear whether the items measure people's views on the role of government in protecting public morals as distinct from the acceptability of the material delivered by the media.

Longitudinal data on many of the issues in which we are interested do not exist. However, there are data from the Netherlands for 1970, 1975, and 1980 about attitudes towards censoring films and banning television programmes. Three propositions were put to respondents: 'Film censorship should be abolished'; 'It is not right to ban certain TV programmes, even if some groups will be offended by them'; and 'TV programmes offensive to public morals should be banned.' Although these propositions make no mention of state or government, again it is clear that they relate to public control and therefore imply government intervention. Freedom of expression is an issue which sets limits to government intervention. Table 10.5 summarizes the results.

These figures indicate that during the 1970s the proportion of the population supporting the abolition of film censorship fell (from 48 to 33 per cent). This suggests that support for government intervention by way of censoring films rose fairly sharply. There was a similar but less sharp decline (from 47 to 42 per cent) in the proportion supporting the proposition that offensive television programmes should not be banned.

TABLE 10.5. *Attitudes towards film and television censorship in the Netherlands, 1970, 1975, 1980*

	1970	1975	1980
Abolition of film censorship	48	42	33
No ban on offensive TV programmes	47	41	42

Note: Entries are percentages agreeing with the propositions.

Sources: Cultural Change in the Netherlands (1970, 1975, 1980).

At best, these findings suggest considerable ambivalence in attitudes towards censorship with perhaps some tightening of attitudes towards media freedom.[5] But, certainly, these results are not in line with the notion of a general cultural shift to postmaterialism, which would seem to anticipate a decline in support for government control of media content. To the extent that there was a shift towards more postmaterialist values among the Dutch during the 1970s[6], this was not followed by a parallel change towards a more permissive view of media content—or that citizens be allowed to decide for themselves what they see on film or television. The broad generalizations implicit in Inglehart's formulation of postmaterialist theory seem, on this evidence, not to capture the complexity of the values at play in this area.

The data in Table 10.5 do not allow us to assess the extent to which changes in attitudes are the consequence of period effects or generation effects. The progressive replacement of older, more restrictive generations by younger, more liberal generations might be overlain by more specific developments, such as periodic 'moral crusades' against changing cultural standards or a concerted campaign to secure cultural liberalization. To shed more light on this question, we examine the distribution of opinion among pre-war and post-war generations. In this analysis, however, the pre-war generation consists of people born between 1920 and 1939, the post-war generation of people born between 1940 and 1949.[7] The distributions are shown in Table 10.6.

We see from the table that during the 1970s, opinion among the pre-war and post-war generations changed to about the same extent and in much the same direction as among the Dutch population as a whole. Such parallel changes across the generations suggest that period effects were at work. However, the post-war generation appears generally more opposed to the control of media content, especially the banning of television programmes which are 'offensive to public morals'. This,

TABLE 10.6. *Attitudes towards censorship among pre- and post-war generations in Netherlands, 1970, 1975, 1980*

	1970		1975		1980	
	Pre-war	Post-war	Pre-war	Post-war	Pre-war	Post-war
Abolition of film censorship	49	57	43	49	34	39
No ban on offensive TV programmes	48	52	40	48	40	44
Ban offensive TV programmes	54	31	58	35	53	35

Note: See note to Table 10.5.

Sources: Cultural Change in the Netherlands (1970, 1975, 1980).

in turn, suggests a generation effect. Evidently, then, changing attitudes engage complex interactions between generational differences in outlook and the impact of more immediate developments. However, we cannot disentangle the differential impact of these effects with the data we have. Even so, we think it is warranted to assume that the period effect is the main factor. In terms of cultural history, the period since 1945, and especially since 1960, has been one of accelerated change—not least because of the massive and intrusive expansion in the range and function of the cultural industries.

We can also assess developments in attitudes towards censorship using Danish data collected regularly over a decade from 1971 to 1981. The proposition put to respondents was: 'Radio and television ought to kill extreme views by silence.' The nature of the extremism was not specified, and the censorship agency is implicitly the broadcasting organization, not government. But at the time Danish television was under tight political control. The findings giving the overall, aggregate, picture are presented in Table 10.7.

Clearly, at this aggregate level, there was some liberalization of attitudes over the period. The proportion agreeing with the idea of censorship by silence declined after 1973 and the proportion rejecting the proposition increased. The extent of the change is fairly modest, but its direction is consistent with a generation effect—and not inconsistent with period effects. So we look again at this issue by comparing the extent of change among the pre-war and post-war generations. As in the Dutch data, the pre-war generation was born 1920–39, the post-war

TABLE 10.7. *Attitudes towards censorship, Denmark, 1971–81*

	1971	1973	1975	1977	1979	1981
Agree wholly	23	27	21	14	15	14
Agree partly	13	15	14	14	13	10
Neither	10	9	11	14	12	10
Disagree partly	13	14	11	16	15	16
Disagree wholly	41	35	43	42	45	51
N	1,302	533	1,600	1,602	1,989	968

Notes: Entries are percentages responding to the proposition: 'Radio and television ought to kill extreme views by silence.' *N* excludes missing data.

Sources: Danish election studies.

generation 1940–49. Generations born before 1920 and after 1949 were omitted from the analysis. The results are shown in Table 10.8.

Among the pre-war generation, there is only a hint of more liberal attitudes in 1979 than in 1971. There was a slight increase in the proportion agreeing with the proposition and a small fall in the proportion disagreeing. But these differences are marginal; overall, the balance of opinion among the pre-war generation was much the same in 1979 as in 1971. Among the post-war generation, however, there was a perceptible shift to more liberal attitudes: fewer respondents agreed with the proposition and more disagreed in 1979 than in 1971. The findings from these data, then, indicate clear, if not particularly strong, generation effects.

Thus the data for the Netherlands and Denmark, the only countries for which we have longitudinal data, suggest rather different conclusions. This should not surprise us. From the outset in this chapter, we have emphasized the specific character of national broadcasting regimes, and we have already seen, in Table 10.2, cross-national differences in attitudes to censorship. This reinforces our general point that attitudes in this area of government activity are best understood in relation to the particularities of policy developments. In other words, whereas attitudes towards the scope of government in several policy fields may have a certain autonomy—in so much as they constitute demands—attitudes towards control of the media tend to be a response to innovations in policy.

We can illustrate this point with data for Britain. A survey by Gallup in 1985 found that, offered the proposition 'A law against violence being shown on TV is not necessary', 58 per cent of respondents agreed

TABLE 10.8. *Attitudes towards censorship among pre- and post-war generations, Denmark, 1971 and 1979*

	1971		1979	
	Pre-war	Post-war	Pre-war	Post-war
Agree wholly	20	17	19	14
Agree partly	13	10	15	9
Neither	9	11	11	11
Disagree partly	15	12	15	15
Disagree wholly	43	50	40	51

Notes: See notes to Table 10.7.

and 31 per cent disagreed. But surveys conducted regularly by the Independent Broadcasting Authority found that the proportion of people saying they had seen anything offensive on television declined during the 1980s (Gunter and McLaughlin 1992). Respondents were then asked: 'How much supervision or regulation do you think there is over what is seen on the four main broadcast channels?' In the 1991 IBA survey just under half (47 per cent) thought there was either 'a good deal' or 'quite a lot' of regulation, while well under a third (28 per cent) thought there was 'only a little' or 'none at all' (Gunter and McLaughlin 1992: 62). These findings also reinforce the point, already emphasized in Chapter 4, that people's responses to general propositions and specific questions can be very different.

Another way of looking at this issue is to ask what is the proper level of government involvement, or 'interference', in broadcasting. This was especially contentious in Britain during the 1980s when a series of highly controversial incidents led the government to take issue with the journalistic independence of broadcasters, especially the BBC. A regular questionnaire administered by the Independent Broadcasting Authority, which supervised commercial broadcasting until 1992, shows a drift in public opinion during the 1980s towards doubting the independence of broadcasting from government interference. Other surveys confirm that audiences increasingly saw the BBC, traditionally valued for its independence, as less adventurous in its dealings with the state (Morrison 1986).

Correlates of Attitudes to Government Intervention

Earlier we found cross-national variations in attitudes towards censoring books (see Table 10.2). Opinion in Germany and the Netherlands lent little support to censorship; at the other end of the spectrum, opinion in Britain was firmly in favour. We now turn to investigate differences within the six countries included in Eurobarometer, No. 21 (1984). We look at groups defined by age, sex, education, and political outlook. The distributions are set out in Table 10.9.

The same general pattern is evident across all six countries. Support for censoring books is more widespread among older people, women, the least well educated, and those orientated to the political right than among the young, men, the well educated, and those of a leftist outlook. Although there are variations in the magnitude of the differences, there are no exceptions to this pattern; moreover, support for censorship declines monotonically across the age range, education levels, and political orienta-

TABLE 10.9. *Attitudes towards book censorship in six West European countries, 1984*

	Germany	Netherlands	France	Belgium	Italy	Britain
Age						
15–25	14	18	17	28	25	44
26–43	21	22	24	29	27	53
44–54	32	30	45	35	52	64
55+	40	46	52	54	57	75
Gender						
Male	25	27	31	34	35	54
Female	29	30	35	40	44	65
Education						
Low	35	43	45	44	50	79
Medium	27	28	36	37	33	56
High	19	21	20	32	23	46
Political tendency						
Left	12	19	26	27	25	49
Centre	27	28	34	39	47	57
Right	39	39	40	42	51	72

Notes: Entries are percentages in each category agreeing with censoring books. See also notes to Table 10.2.

Source: Eurobarometer, No. 21.

tions. Note, moreover, this is the same pattern as we found earlier in the Dutch data on attitudes to 'free broadcasting' (Table 10.1).

Several of our data suggest that the better educated are generally more liberal in their outlook on media content. But to what extent does education affect attitudes to the role of government in controlling media behaviour? To assess this, we return to the four items in the 1985 ISSP

TABLE 10.10. *Attitudes towards media freedom by educational level, 1985*

	Britain	Germany	Italy	Austria
Newspapers should be allowed to publish confidential defence papers				
Low education	25	21	27	31
Medium	25	20	24	29
High	26	37	20	27
Newspapers should be allowed to publish confidential economic plans				
Low education	61	62	62	52
Medium	69	63	69	57
High	58	68	63	62
Revolutionaries should be allowed to publish books				
Low education	59	67	34	58
Medium	71	81	50	67
High	77	89	68	78
Racists should be allowed to publish books				
Low education	45	44	27	47
Medium	51	60	38	54
High	65	71	48	57

Notes: Entries are percentages agreeing with the propositions derived from the question: 'There are some people whose views are considered extreme by the majority. First, consider people who want to overthrow the government by revolution. Secondly, consider people who believe that whites are racially superior to all other races. Do you think such people should be allowed to publish books expressing their views?' 'Suppose a newspaper got hold of confidential government papers about economic plans/defence plans and wanted to publish them: should the newspaper be allowed to publish the papers?'

Source: ISSP (1985).

survey to examine responses according to different levels of education. This analysis is presented in Table 10.10.

On the freedom to publish defence plans, the pattern differs from one country to the next. In Germany, the well educated are the most liberal; in Italy and Austria, the most liberal are the less educated. In Britain, there is no difference. On the freedom to reveal economic plans, the mood is generally more liberal, but the differences between the educational groups are intricate; both in Britain and Italy, it is those with medium levels of education who are the most liberal. When it comes to the freedom of revolutionary or racist groups to publish, however, the differences are very clear: the better educated are far more libertarian. Again, this pattern is consistent across all four countries—although there is considerable variation in the 'opinion gap' between the minimally educated and the highly educated, from 10 percentage points in Austria (racists) to 34 points in Italy (revolutionaries). It might be that higher education leads to a greater scepticism about the judiciousness of government action on these matters, or to a greater regard for freedom of speech generally. But clearly, it is on the classic free speech issues, not the general principle of unregulated media, that education levels have the strongest bearing.

Political inclination may be a better guide to people's views on these matters. Where the issue is not highly salient, or people have no direct involvement in the issue, or have no focused views, they are more likely to apply a broad political disposition in responding to the propositions put to them. To explore this, we examine the same set of responses among people of different political orientation. We use the definitions of left, centre, and right according to party affiliation supplied by the ISSP surveys.[8] This analysis is presented in Table 10.11.

The pattern is fairly consistent across the three countries. In most instances, people on the left are more supportive of freedom to publish than people on the right. In Britain and Germany, people with political affiliations to the left are less sympathetic to the idea of controlling the press than people on the right, but in Austria they share much the same stance. However, even among people on the left, support for allowing newspapers to publish confidential defence documents is much lower than support for publishing confidential economic plans. Generally libertarian attitudes towards freedom to publish appear not to extend to matters of national defence. Such discrimination is also evident on allowing potentially subversive groups to publish: support for allowing revolutionaries to publish their views is high among all political groups

TABLE 10.11. *Attitudes towards media freedom by political orientation, 1985*

	Britain	Germany	Austria
Newpapers should be allowed to publish confidential defence papers			
Left	38	36	30
Centre	20	3	6
Right	10	12	29
Newpapers should be allowed to publish confidential economic plans			
Left	78	75	53
Centre	67	51	68
Right	41	50	55
Revolutionaries should be allowed to publish books			
Left	71	76	65
Centre	71	81	62
Right	65	70	63
Racists should be allowed to publish books			
Left	52	53	49
Centre	57	62	52
Right	54	54	50

Notes: See notes to Table 10.10.

but notably lower for racists. Here, the anti-racist inclinations of the left seem to be in conflict with generally libertarian instincts regarding government regulation.

To collate these analyses, we calculated the strength of association between these attitudes towards freedom of the media and the social and political variables for both the 1985 and 1990 ISSP data. To reflect the findings in Table 10.9, the variables were recoded so that we anticipate positive coefficients for older people, women, low education, and right-wing political affiliations. Our results, for both the 1985 and 1990 ISSP data, are presented in Table 10.12.

Several striking observations emerge from this table. First, in Britain and Germany attitudes about restricting what newspapers and revolu-

TABLE 10.12. *Correlates of attitudes towards media freedom*

	Britain		Germany		Italy	Norway	Austria	Ireland
	1985	1990	1985	1990	1985	1990	1985	1990
Newspapers should be allowed to publish confidential defence papers								
Age	0.19**	—	0.19**	—	0.03	—	0.06	—
Gender	−0.03	—	0.07*	—	−0.00	—	−0.03	—
Education	−0.01	—	−0.11**	—	0.07**	—	0.03	—
Party	0.30**	—	0.28**	—	—	—	0.01	—
Newspapers should be allowed to publish confidential economic plans								
Age	0.15**	—	0.17**	—	0.02	—	0.16**	—
Gender	−0.02	—	0.01	—	−0.02	—	0.03	—
Education	0.02	—	−0.04	—	−0.00	—	−0.07	—
Party	0.35**	—	0.26**	—	—	—	−0.02	—
Revolutionaries should be allowed to publish books								
Age	0.24**	0.16**	0.18**	0.22**	0.24**	0.17**	0.24**	0.22**
Gender	0.03	0.08**	0.07*	0.06**	0.07*	0.02	0.10**	0.14**
Education	−0.21**	−0.16**	−0.26**	−0.20**	−0.31**	−0.24**	−0.17**	−0.19**
Party	0.09**	0.19**	0.12**	0.17**	—	0.00	0.02	0.08*
Racists should be allowed to publish books								
Age	0.12**	0.02	0.07*	0.02	0.12**	0.02	0.14**	0.14**
Gender	0.07**	0.15**	0.05	0.04*	0.04	0.11**	0.06	0.13**
Education	−0.19**	−0.12**	−0.24**	−0.11**	−0.18**	−0.12**	−0.08*	−0.14**
Party	−0.02	0.02	0.00	0.01	—	−0.17**	−0.02	0.02

*$p < 0.05$ **$p < 0.01$

Note: Entries are Pearson's r.

Sources: ISSP (1985, 1990).

tionaries publish are strongly correlated with party affiliation. This suggests that the general principle of free speech, along with the more specific question of press freedom, is a highly partisan issue in some countries. But this is not the case in Austria and Norway, and is of lesser importance in Ireland—reinforcing our earlier evidence of cross-national variations. On the other hand, except in Norway, party affiliation has no impact on attitudes towards allowing racists to publish. As we indicated earlier, this probably reflects the conflict between free speech values and anti-racism experienced on the left.

Secondly, the role of education in supporting the right of dissident or extreme groups to publish is very clear. With only one exception, all the coefficients are sizeable and negative, indicating a strong association between higher education and readiness to allow revolutionaries and racists to publish their views. Thirdly, significant differences between the attitudes of men and women are generally less evident than differences between young and older people. This confirms our earlier finding that, for whatever reason, younger people tend to be more averse to government intervention in the media than older people.

Conclusion

Governments intervene in the communications arena, and always have. The evolution of broadcasting in the twentieth century has created communications institutions of unprecedented power and social significance. Thus, it is not surprising that governments perceive them as major objects of policy and intervention. The creation, and subsequent degradation, of the 'public sphere' described by Habermas (1962), among others, is the process by which the media play a changing role in providing for the mutual informing of governments and citizens.

The technical and economic changes of recent years have encouraged new thinking about the proper role of government in the communications field. The general drift has been towards a more *laissez-faire* legislative apparatus, bringing broadcasting into line with the market-driven framework of the printed press in many West European countries. But the massive cultural significance of the media leaves governments wrestling with the contradictory demands of freeing the media from regulation in order to encourage their expansion as industries while endeavouring to remain in command of national cultural policy.

In this chapter, we have sought to review the manner in which public opinion across Western Europe has guided, or responded to, new demands in the communications media field generated by economic and technological change. We have suggested that, in the same way that governments intervene in both the structure and the content of the communications media, so, too, do public attitudes respond to these changes. However, the thin data record made it difficult to detect clear trends in public attitudes—both within particular countries or across Western Europe more generally. It would seem that government intervention in the communications field has been primarily driven by technological change and entrepreneurial initiative, with little input from the mass public. Government action has been in advance of public attitudes, which have largely responded to innovation rather than served to direct change. Thus, attitudes in this domain of government activity stand in contrast to several policy fields examined in this volume: people have clear views about how their health should be provided for, the economy should be managed, and the environment be protected, but attitudes towards government intervention in the communications field appear fitful and unfocused. Perhaps it is more difficult for people to have well-formulated views on the organization and control of institutions and technologies which are both remote and rapidly changing, or perhaps the role of government in this field is more obscure to the public—and thus, as the data record suggests, of less interest to social scientists.

Where people do have a clear view about the cultural artefacts distributed by the media, these seem often to be prompted by high profile or short-term examples of controversial provision. Higher education and more liberal political attitudes may tend to be associated with wider acceptance of a broader range of media fare, but not consistently or predictably. Precisely because policy is itself contradictory and inconsistent, being driven at the same time by industrial and cultural objectives, so the attitudes which follow policy innovation are equally inconsistent. Even so, it is one of the higher ironies that as we move into the 'information age', in which communications institutions take an ever more prominent position at the centre of social change, we know so little about public responses to, and demands for, government action in this field.

NOTES

1. The reaction of the British tobacco industry to the European Commission directive banning cigarette advertisements on television is a case in point.
2. Some of this material is drawn from the Euromedia Research Group (1992), which may be consulted for further details.
3. The existence of these data might be seen to contradict the claim that there are few data in this area, and that public attitudes are only formulated in the wake of policy initiatives. In fact, it is not unusual, as in this example, for surveys to be undertaken to test the potential of proposed political or commercial initiatives. However, the initiatives cannot be seen as responses to articulated demands, and we lack data which endeavour to uncover the development of such demands.
4. The relatively low proportion in Ireland supporting the idea of allowing revolutionaries freedom to publish is probably accounted for by the role of Irish nationalists, especially Sinn Fein and the IRA, in Northern Ireland.
5. Moreover, the double negative implied in the questions may have confused respondents.
6. The development of postmaterialism in the Netherlands, as measured by Inglehart's materialist–postmaterialist index, was more marked in the 1980s than the 1970s; see Vol. iv, Ch. 5.
7. The pre- and post-war generations are more strictly drawn in this analysis. Those born before 1920 were excluded because the 1980 survey had an upper age limit of 65; i.e. the oldest respondents were born in 1915. The post-war generation, or, more strictly cohort, is restricted to those born in the ten years 1940–9 in order to include only birth-year cohorts surveyed in all three years. Cohorts born after 1949 would have been too young to be surveyed in 1970.
8. Party affiliation data are not available for Italy.

11

Protecting the Environment

OLOF JOHANSSON

On a Polish stamp from the middle of the last decade (1985) there is a small aircraft spreading chemicals over a forest. What does it mean? Is the Polish government proud of polluting the country's forests, or does the stamp reflect pride in the effective management of Polish forests with no concern for the environmental problems caused by spreading chemicals from the air? The answer is, of course, pride in effective forest management; stamps are almost always designed to demonstrate identity, good performance, and high culture. The Polish example, however, illustrates the familiar association between environmental problems and the modernization process: pollution or destruction of the environment are often the result of economic activity. Moreover, care of the environment is often secondary when compared with concern for economic progress (Andersen 1990). As late as 1985, the Polish government either ranked environmental problems low among its priorities, or else it was not aware of the side effects of modern technology on the environment.

In general, as an economy is modernized, not only is the potential to pollute the environment greater but so also is awareness of the importance of protecting the natural environment. By the early 1970s this awareness had reached the international front stage. The final declaration from the United Nations Conference on the Human Environment (SIPRI 1972: 5) states: 'The protection and improvement of the human environment is a major issue which affects the well-being of peoples and economic development throughout the world; it is the urgent desire of peoples of the whole world and the duty of all governments.'

Expressed in the language of this volume, the UN declaration asserts that protection of the environment comes within the scope of government. In Chapter 3 of this volume, Edeltraud Roller differentiates beliefs about the scope of government along two dimensions, *range* and *degree*. Range refers to government responsibility for policy goals, degree refers to the intensity of government activity within a policy goal or area. These distinctions can be used to classify the survey questions analysed in this chapter. One type of question deals with government responsibility (range) for the protection of the natural environment as a policy area; that is, whether or not the government should intervene on environmental matters. A second type are questions dealing with whether or not the government should spend more or less money on protecting the environment (degree). A third type of question deals with priorities among different types of environmental protection. There are also some survey questions which tap people's evaluation of the performance of government in environmental protection. However, as discussed in Chapter 1, performance questions are not a measure of the scope of government, so this type of question is not analysed here.

Environmental Threats and Public Opinion

At any given time there will be a number of environmental threats, and different people will perceive them differently depending on their level of knowledge, their evaluation and understanding of scientific facts, and their level of trust in decision makers. The difficulty with the large number of different environmental alarms and their complexity is how to assess their combined long-range effect. Which of the alarms will become real environmental dangers and which will not? Effects which, individually, are marginal may add up to a considerable cumulative threat. Environmental problems are often multidimensional, complex, and systemic because of the interdependence and interaction between the different environmental resources of water, air, and soil (Hofrichter and Reif 1990).

The complexity of environmental protection means that it requires international co-operation, and this is often frustrated by the trade-off between environmental and economic concerns in which the latter, almost invariably, dominate. The examples which describe the dominating role of big companies in this policy area mount up to a very long list, ranging from industrial waste to pollution from cars and household refuse. The debates of recent decades have emphasized the necessity of government action both at home and in collaboration with other governments. Private firms, even large multinationals, can seldom solve environmental problems through their private actions or through some form of co-operation. In most instances, there are no economic incentives for firms to protect the environment, and often there is no well-formed public opinion opposed to the activity involved. This does not mean that individuals and non-governmental organizations can do nothing to prevent environmental deterioration. However, it does point to the fact that environmental threats are public problems, to be solved by national governments. Such complex public problems are best solved by national governments or by international co-operation between governments (Vig and Kraft 1990; Young 1989).

The complexity of environmental questions also means that public opinion is inadequate for dealing with them. It is true that some types of interference in nature are visible and obvious; the construction of major roads, clearing large forest areas, and mining activities, for example. But interventions in the environment which cannot be seen, such as acid rain, are often much more dangerous threats. As Rose (1990: 12) observes: 'Acid rain is frightening, but most people believe it falls on foreign countries. The greenhouse effect is global, but it is thought to be gradual and remote. Pesticides and nitrates may already be in your water, but they are invisible.' This points to the fact that most of the serious threats to the environment require sophisticated instruments to be detected; they are not easily uncovered by ordinary people, nor is their impact readily obvious. This is probably one of the reasons why most countries have an environmental protection policy which is reactive to visible disasters of different magnitudes, rather than long-term policy objectives.

The weakness of public opinion is also due to the fact that under normal circumstances, environmental problems tend to have low salience. Few people feel that their daily lives are affected by environmental problems, probably because the dangers are seldom visible before something dramatic happens. Two recent events which sharply raised the level of salience, at least for a time, are the nuclear accident at Chernobyl and the *Exxon Valdez* oil spill. The *Brahe* oil spill along the coast of the Shetland Isles can also be added to the list.

The three accidents had a dramatic impact on people's awareness of environmental dangers (Dunlap 1989). They also illustrate the international character of many environmental threats. After an explosion in a nuclear power station such as occurred at Chernobyl, not only the devastated land but also the large area of contamination, probably stretching across national borders, will be an environmental hazard for many decades to come (Löfstedt and White 1990). Threats of this magnitude can cause major policy changes by parties and governments. For instance, before the Three Mile Island accident in the United States, the Social Democrats in Sweden were very favourably inclined towards nuclear power. They were unwilling to holding a referendum about Sweden's policy of building nuclear power plants for producing electricity, which the Centre (Farmers') Party had demanded for many years. During the subsequent debate, the Social Democrats changed their position and accepted a referendum. The result supported the Centre Party's opposition to nuclear power, and the Swedish parliament decided that the nuclear power plants should be closed down by the year 2010.

Environmental protection is an area in which experts play a prominent role in policy formation. Disasters like Chernobyl often lead to higher government spending and new regulations, and also to new research questions for both natural scientists and social scientists (Brown 1992). There is a new puzzle to solve because the environmental problems are seen in a new perspective and old arguments no longer apply. The Polish stamp described in our introduction reminds us of the rapid change in perceptions which has taken place; the economic achievements of one year can turn out to be the ecological disasters of the next.

Dependence on professional expertise affects the policy formulation process, the visibility of the goals, and the manner in which problems are understood (Weale 1992). This tends to promote new values and set new policy priorities. Some scholars consider environmental goals and policies to be part of the so-called new politics agenda, or the 'new values politics' (Inglehart 1977, 1990; Baker, Dalton and Hildebrandt 1981). On this new agenda we find issues such as protection of the environment, equality between women and men, reducing differences between regions. This new agenda is seen to represent a more value-oriented politics.

On the new agenda, moral values may take precedence over personal interests. Many commentators in this field emphasize the character of environmental problems as questions about the 'public or common good' (Weale 1992; Gerlach 1986). The step between personal interest in, for example, living in 'a healthy environment with clean air' and supporting 'pollution control of the air' as a public good can be very short. Or as Goodin (1992: 173) puts it: 'on environmental questions, like many others, people thus seem to vote on the basis of the common good rather than—and even in contradiction to—their narrow self-interest'. Goodin argues that people can be moved by moral arguments about what is best for the society as a whole, and so rise above narrow self-interest.

Some Hypotheses

The notion of environmental questions being value-laden in nature is important for our understanding of people's attitudes on these issues. A perceived threat to the personal environment is not a necessary pre-condition for a general concern about the environment. One piece of evidence for this can be found in Swedish election data: parties which are most opposed to nuclear power plants have not done better, electorally, in constituencies with nuclear power plants than in constituencies without (Holmberg and Asp 1984).

We should not, therefore, expect to find large differences in people's attitudes towards environmental protection based on social differences. None the less, there are differences in the way people experience the environment, and these differences can affect their attitudes. As Goodin (1992: 175) notes: 'Complain though American steelworkers may that they cannot eat clean air, they have none the less good grounds for complaint in the fact that they virtually can eat the unclean air that they have to breath [in the absence] of clean air policies.' His argument is that the poor and the working class probably benefit more than the middle class from a clean air policy. Different segments of society might have different environmental concerns but, in objective terms, the working-class will gain more from a clean air policy than other groups because, generally, they live and work in more polluted environments than the middle class. Goodin goes on to argue that if the question of willingness to spend money on environmental protection is asked in the 'right way'—as 'What proportion of your income are you willing to spend on environmental quality?'—the poor prove more concerned with the issue than the rich. According to Goodin's calculations (1976: 170–1), for example, people with low incomes are willing to spend a larger proportion of their income on controlling water pollution than those with middle-level or high incomes.

It is difficult to hypothesize a clear relationship between social class and attitudes to environmental protection. There is also a tendency to underestimate the interest of the working class because the most visible people in green political parties are the new middle class of well-educated young people. Andersen (1990: 112), however, argues that private sector entrepreneurs will be more negative about environmental regulation than, for instance, workers who directly benefit from clean air policies. We should not, therefore, expect workers to be less in favour of environmental protection than other social groups—except where their jobs are at risk because of the costs of environmental protection.

Differences in education are a more likely source of difference in beliefs about environmental protection. The hypothesis is that the better educated are more in favour of protecting the environment as a common good than people with less education. This proposition comes close to Inglehart's (1977, 1990) arguments about the impact of postmaterialist values and the relationship he finds between these values and the new middle class. The hypothesis deduced from this kind of relationship is that higher education and postmaterialist values lead to more positive views about protecting the environment.

There is a logical connection between the impact of education and the significance of age differences. Younger people in Western Europe are better educated than ever before. Consequently educational differences should be reflected in differences between generations. In addition, there is reason to believe that being young is, in itself, a factor since the young get a lifelong dividend from investments in a clean and healthy environment. Consistent with this, in many West European countries, voters for green parties are younger than the average voter; Bennulf and Holmberg (1990), for example, show this to be the case for the 1988 Swedish parliamentary elections. So we hypothesize that younger people are more in favour of environmental protection than older people.

It is difficult to arrive at a hypothesis about the impact of gender which is in keeping with the new literature identifying power relations between men and women as an explanatory factor for differences in attitudes (Eduards, Gustafsson, and Jonasdóttir 1989). But one line of reasoning which builds on this distinction is presented by Bernard (1981), who argues that women have remained in a *Gemeinschaft* world after the transition to modern industrial society which is dominated by *Gesellschaft*. Thus women have a closer relationship with nature—and perhaps a looser relationship with technology—so are more likely to support protecting the environment. Another approach might be to point to the evidence that women are more interested in new politics—or value politics—than men (Peterson 1984; Kyle 1989). Our hypothesis, based on this literature, is that women are more interested than men in protecting the environment.

We test these hypotheses in subsequent sections of this chapter. First, however, we review the available data on environmental questions and specify our research questions.

Data and Research Questions

In this chapter we examine the way protection of the natural environment is seen as coming within the scope of government. We analyse the policies and actions of governments based on the questions used in attitudinal studies in West European countries during the 1970s and 1980s. There are very few data available from earlier decades and it is very rare to find attitudinal questions which focus on the international aspect of environmental protection. In examining the data, our focus is on the scope of government as defined earlier; that is, attitudes towards government responsibility, spending, and priorities among different environmental problems. We also examine interventions in specific environmental policy areas.

A major problem in this field is the restricted coverage of much of the data. There are attitudinal data about the salience and strength of attitudes about environmental questions, and about the relationship between economic realities and concern for protecting the natural environment. But most of these data relate to only one country. Indeed, national surveys reveal that social science researchers, particularly political scientists, have looked at the 'environment' as a topic about national problems, and as a matter for government intervention at the national level with little regard to the international dimension.

However, there are some comparative surveys which provide directly comparable data on environmental questions. These are three Eurobarometer surveys (1979, 1981, and 1983), the first Political Action survey (1973–6), and the 1985 ISSP survey. Most of these comparative data focus on respondents' opinions about how important it is for the government to protect the environment against pollution. They also cover the responsibility of governments for environmental protection, and attitudes towards spending levels.

An interesting feature of these surveys is the way the economic aspects of environmental protection are measured. In particular, very few surveys link pollution to industrial processes. The only questions which deal with the relationship between business and the environment focus on the price relationship. Usually, respondents are asked to indicate whether or not they would accept higher prices if the result would be a better environment. Most questions are about government spending on fighting pollution, although some questions make clear that government spending means using tax income. This way of formulating the problem, again, reveals how the policy area is comprehended: responsibility for intervention, regulation, and paying for improvements is placed on the government. No responsibility is attributed to industry or the ordinary citizen.

Four types of research questions were asked at the beginning of this chapter. Comparative data are not available for all four questions. The first question, concerning people's opinions about the responsibility of government for environmental protection and fighting pollution, can be analysed using data from the comparative data-sets. These data allow us to test the hypothesis that people regard environmental protection as very important. The basis for this hypothesis is the earlier argument that protection of the environment can be seen as a common good which all citizens have a moral obligation to protect (Goodin 1992).

The second question was about levels of spending on the environment. This question can also be interpreted as willingness to spend tax income for the protection of the environment. Based on the same argument, the comparative data allow us to formulate the hypothesis that people are willing to pay higher taxes to protect the environment. If people feel a moral obligation to protect nature from pollution, then they also have a responsibility to see that money is provided. Otherwise there is only symbolic support for environmental protection, rather than support for an effective environmental policy (Gustafsson 1987).

There are no comparative data which are reliable enough to analyse questions about the priority of environmental protection relative to other issues or priorities. Nor are there adequate data to examine opinions about specific actions taken by governments. The only reliable data available are from the British Social Attitudes Survey. These data can be analysed over time, but the same type of consistent data are not available for other countries. These problems will be discussed in more detail in the last section of this chapter.

Protection of Nature

One aspect of protecting nature is to lower the level of pollution. In most cases pollution is perceived as a threat that can be solved at once, provided strong measures are taken by the government. Of course, pollution can also be a problem which requires long-term policies, as is often the case with air pollution. This type of pollution can travel from country to country, and in some cases solutions require international action. In the Eurobarometer, Nos. 16, 19, and 21 (1979, 1981, and 1984) respondents were asked to indicate their level of agreement with the statement: 'Strong measures should be taken to protect the environment against pollution.' The statement is too vague to differentiate between short- and long-term solutions for environmental problems but the data give us a measure on how respondents look upon environmental protection. The distribution of opinion in ten West European countries is shown in Table 11.1.

On average, across Western Europe as a whole, about two thirds of the population are wholly in favour of strong measures. Looking at the

TABLE 11.1. *Support for strong measures of environmental protection in EC countries, 1979–84*

	1979		1981		1984	
	Wholly agree	Partly agree	Wholly agree	Partly agree	Wholly agree	Partly agree
Denmark	61	34	56	36	51	33
Belgium	75	21	65	30	52	40
Britain	59	38	47	49	47	50
Germany	50	41	53	40	50	40
Ireland	51	48	43	54	39	57
Luxembourg	81	17	81	15	82	16
Netherlands	76	19	75	20	71	21
Greece	—	—	98	2	98	1
France	71	25	68	28	66	30
Italy	77	22	76	22	74	24
Mean	67	29	63	33	59	35

Notes: Entries are percentages who wholly or partly agree. The data are based on responses to the question: 'Strong measures should be taken to protect the environment against pollution.' Greece is excluded in the calculation of the mean. *N* is around 1,000 for each country and time point.

Sources: Eurobarometer, Nos. 16, 19, and 21.

countries individually, levels of support seem very high in Greece and Luxembourg, and relatively high in Italy and the Netherlands in all three years. In Germany, Britain, and Ireland support levels are, by comparison, rather lower. Several factors seem to be at work here. The high level in Greece, and perhaps Italy too, could be attributed to the high levels of pollution in their cities—or even to the damage done by polluted air to the relics of antiquity. Ireland, on the other hand, has experienced less industrial development while Britain, with the 1956 Clean Air Act, has had a relatively strong policy of controlling air pollution for some time. Moreover, their Atlantic position tends to limit the impact of wind-carried pollution in Ireland and Britain. These explanations, however, are wholly speculative.

Judging from the figures in the 'wholly agree' columns, and with the exception of Germany and Luxembourg, the demand for environmental protection declined between 1979 and 1983 in all these countries. This is clearly a period effect; the environmental movement peaked for the first time in the second half of the 1970s and then subsided until the second half of the 1980s when the Bruntland Report (1986) and the Chernobyl disaster (1987) made their impact. The fact that the decline did not occur in Germany may be attributable to the formation of the Green Party in 1980.

As almost all respondents used only the two most positive response categories—out of a scale of five—on this question, we cannot anticipate large differences on our independent variables. None the less, in accord with our hypotheses, we examine variations among different groups based on gender, age, occupation, and two value orientations. The first is materialism–postmaterialism, measured by the standard Inglehart index (Inglehart 1977: 27–9). The second orientation is self-placement on a left–right political scale. The results of the analyses are presented in Table 11.2.

The dependent variable—support for strong measures of environmental protection—was coded from 1 (agree strongly) to 4 (disagree strongly). Hence, according to our hypotheses, we anticipate negative correlations for gender, age, and occupation. And this is largely what we find. Even so, the differences are generally small. For gender, the differences are both small and in some countries insignificant. None the less, as a rough average across the EC countries, they indicate that women are some 3–4 percentage points more in favour of strong measures against pollution than men. This accords with our hypothesis. As for age differences, only in Greece do we find clear support for

TABLE 11.2. *Support for environmental protection in EC countries among sub groups, 1979–83*

	Gender	Age	Occupation	Postmaterialist	Left–right
Denmark					
1979	−0.06	0.01	−0.07	—	0.07
1981	−0.13	0.04	−0.11	−0.01	0.10
1983	−0.06	0.01	−0.06	−0.02	0.14
Belgium					
1979	−0.04	−0.01	−0.06	0.07	0.09
1981	−0.06	0.02	−0.00	−0.02	0.05
1983	0.01	0.01	0.04	−0.01	0.04
Britain					
1979	−0.01	−0.03	−0.02	−0.02	0.04
1981	0.00	−0.04	0.01	−0.05	−0.02
1983	−0.05	−0.01	−0.03	−0.05	0.01
Germany					
1979	−0.02	0.02	−0.01	−0.02	0.00
1981	−0.08	0.03	−0.12	−0.05	0.08
1983	−0.02	0.06	0.04	−0.09	0.06
Ireland					
1979	−0.06	−0.02	−0.04	−0.02	0.01
1981	0.02	0.01	0.01	−0.05	0.04
1983	−0.05	−0.04	−0.00	−0.01	0.05
Luxembourg					
1979	−0.06	−0.11	−0.08	−0.03	0.08
1981	0.08	0.03	−0.01	−0.04	−0.03
1983	0.02	0.04	−0.02	0.05	0.11
Netherlands					
1979	−0.06	0.10	−0.06	−0.12	0.11
1981	−0.06	0.02	−0.04	0.02	0.08
1983	−0.03	0.02	0.01	−0.12	0.10
Greece					
1979	—	—	—	—	—
1981	−0.12	−0.10	−0.07	0.21	0.11
1983	−0.06	−0.10	−0.05	0.12	0.16
France					
1979	−0.02	0.05	−0.00	−0.05	0.10
1981	−0.01	0.06	−0.03	−0.03	0.06
1983	−0.00	−0.03	−0.05	−0.00	0.10
Italy					
1979	−0.01	0.03	−0.04	−0.08	0.03
1981	−0.01	0.06	−0.02	−0.01	0.11
1983	0.01	0.03	−0.00	−0.08	−0.03

Notes: Entries are Kendall's tau *b* coefficients. Age was recoded in ten-year intervals, occupation from low to high status. For materialism–postmaterialism the Inglehart four-item index was used.
Sources: Eurobarometer, Nos. 16, 19, and 21.

our hypothesis. Perhaps we must qualify our view of older people: their support for strong measures against pollution may be because they are less committed to technological change than the young, or they cherish the values of a golden past with clean air and water. Again, the coefficients for occupation are small and erratic. Negative correlations indicate stronger support for environmental protection in non-manual compared to manual occupations. This is the case for the overall average for EC countries: in 1979 and 1981, those in non-manual occupations were about 4 percentage points more supportive of strong measures than those in manual occupations. In 1983, however, the difference almost vanishes.

Of the two value orientations, postmaterialism turns out to be a poor predictor of support for strong environmental protection measures. For most of the EC countries there is a slightly negative correlation, indicating some support for our hypothesis. Greece, however, spoils the general picture by exhibiting a definite tendency in the opposite direction, especially in 1981. Left–right orientation fares better as a predictor. A positive correlation indicates that a left orientation goes with an inclination for strong measures to protect the environment. Seven of our ten countries emerge with such a tendency for all three time points. So does Germany after 1979, and Italy until 1983. Finally, in Britain, only the 1979 data show the beginnings of a left–right difference on protecting the environment.

Thus, distinctions based on gender, age, and occupation appear to make little difference to attitudes towards the environment. Political differences, as between left and right, are more important—but, even then, not in every country or for each time point. Only in the occasional instance, notably in the Netherlands and Greece, are postmaterialists evidently more in favour of strong environmental protection measures. None the less, even though several effects are marginal, most of them are in the expected direction.

The mean values for the distributions in Table 11.1 showed that, across Western Europe as a whole, the balance of opinion is strongly in favour of environmental protection. But do people think that protecting the environment comes within the range of government responsibility? In the Political Action study respondents were asked about how much responsibility governments have for dealing with these kind of problems. Although these data were gathered much earlier than the Eurobarometer data—between 1973 and 1976—they give some indication of whether or not people see environmental protection as within the scope

TABLE 11.3. *Assignment of responsibility to government for fighting pollution*

	Level of responsibility in fighting pollution				*N*
	Essential	Important	Some	None	
Finland	47	40	12	1	1,224
Austria	51	33	15	1	1,554
Britain	52	33	14	1	1,483
Germany	65	27	7	1	2,307
Netherlands	54	39	6	1	1,201
Switzerland	57	34	8	1	1,274
Italy	56	33	10	1	1,779

Notes: Entries are percentages. The question is: 'How much responsibility do you think the government has for fighting pollution?'

Source: Political Action (1973–6).

of government. The distributions of responses for the seven West European countries in the study are shown in Table 11.3.

Clearly, an overwhelming majority of the population in these countries think that 'fighting pollution' is the responsibility of governments. Combining the 'essential' and 'important' responses, over 80 per cent, consistently in each country, see this aspect of environmental protection as coming within the range of government activity. Yet these data also suggest some equivocation about the priority to be accorded to the environment by government; except in Finland, a majority consider fighting pollution as 'essential', but only in Germany is that majority sizeable.

How do these percentages compare with those for the 1970s shown in Table 11.1? Of the four countries which appear in both tables, in the early 1970s (1974), the Germans were the most prone and the British the least prone to assign essential responsibility to the government. In the later 1970s (1979), the peoples of the Netherlands and Italy were highly prone to demand measures against pollution, whereas people in Germany were the least prone. The position in Germany—in aggregate terms—is interesting: possibly people in Germany do not want stronger measures because they believe their government is already doing a great deal. However, the lack of relation between the two tables indicates that we cannot infer levels of support for strong environmental measures from people's view about the responsibility of government for environmental protection.

Yet a third way of assessing the importance of environmental protection is to examine the relative priority people accord to the issue—that is, how high or low it ranks on people's political agenda. In the Political Action study, the question about the importance of environmental pollution was posed as one item in a battery of issue items. Combining responses to that item with another question on the level of government responsibility to act on pollution problems yields a measure of where the pollution issue ranks in a scale of importance. The scale ranges from 1 to 5, with 5 indicating that, compared to other issues, government action against pollution has high priority. The distribution of scores on the scale are shown in Table 11.4.

Clearly, the place of environmental protection on the public's political agenda, in the early 1970s, was much the same in all seven countries. It was high on the political agenda among half—or close to half—the population in each case except Finland; only a very small minority, of some 2–3 per cent, gives 'fighting pollution' a low priority, and a further 6 per cent or so accord it fairly low priority. There are some differences between the countries: the electorates of Germany and Switzerland, for example, gave fighting pollution a higher priority than the electorates of Finland and Britain. Even so, the differences are narrow. Evidently, then, by the early 1970s, action against pollution was a major concern among West European publics.

Apart from the high priority given to fighting pollution in Germany and in Switzerland, and the lower priority recorded in Finland, the other

TABLE 11.4. *Ranking of pollution on the political agenda*

	Scale of importance					*N*
	Low	2	3	4	High	
Finland	3	6	21	30	40	1,224
Austria	3	6	20	24	47	1,554
Britain	3	8	21	21	47	1,483
Germany	2	4	18	17	59	2,307
Netherlands	2	4	22	22	50	1,201
Switzerland	2	4	17	23	54	1,274
Italy	2	6	22	23	47	1,779
Mean	2	5	21	23	49	

Note: For the method of constructing the scale, see the codebook for the Political Action study.
Source: Political Action (1973–6).

countries are in a very homogeneous middle position. Once again it is the position of Germany which is interesting. Hildebrandt and Dalton (1978) have suggested that 'new politics' had already become important in West Germany around the mid-1970s. This impression is supported by the Political Action data in Tables 11.3 and 11.4, but we would not have guessed so from the Eurobarometer data in Table 11.1.

The Political Action data shown in Tables 11.3 and 11.4 were also analysed controlling for the same individual-level background variables we used in the analysis of the Eurobarometer data in Table 11.2 in the hope of uncovering statistical evidence for, or against, our hypotheses. As the results showed much the same lack of systematic and significant relationships as we saw in Table 11.2, these correlation data are not presented here. Even so, we might note that young people were less likely than old people to place fighting pollution very high on the political agenda. And, again, both value orientations—materialism–postmaterialism and left–right self-placement—were better predictors of environmental concern, especially in Switzerland and the Netherlands, than the demographic variables. But these were tendencies, not statistically significant relationships.

We have noted that levels of concern and demands for government action on environmental protection vary between countries and within countries over time. Perhaps this reflects lower levels of political awareness, or the greater fickleness, of public opinion at large, whereas the more politically involved have a steadier outlook on environmental issues. However, a recently published Swedish time series among party members and supporters suggests otherwise. The series provides data on the ranking, for 1968 to 1988, of the most important questions confronted at election time, and for 1987 and 1990, on the most important problems for society to solve. The ranking is based on whether or not party members and supporters mention 'environment' in response to an open question. The responses clearly show that before 1982 only a small proportion of the respondents, less than 15 per cent, considered the environment an important problem. In 1985 the proportion mentioning environmental problems as important started to grow, and by 1987 it had reached over 50 per cent. The figure remained at that level until 1990, when it started to decline. By 1993 it was down to about 30 per cent (Swedish election surveys and Samhälle Opinion Massmedia surveys). Evidently, even among the politically active, opinion on environmental issues tends to fluctuate.

Broadly speaking, then, during the 1970s and 1980s a majority of the population in most West European countries were in favour of action against pollution and largely agreed that governments are responsible for undertaking such action. In some instances, the majorities are notably large. On analysing the available data, however, we find that differences between social groups are of far less magnitude than we hypothesized. Therefore, in the case of survey questions concerning the importance or priority of environmental issues, and the responsibility of governments for solving these issues, we are compelled to return to our earlier assessment: environmental issues tend to be everybody's concern. They are equally important to men and women, young and old, blue- and white-collar workers. The best predictors of these concerns are people's political values; in particular, people oriented to the left rather consistently ranked these issues higher than people on the right. But even here we noted important exceptions. Germany before 1980 and Britain after 1980 are examples of polities in which people on the political right were as much concerned about the environment as were people on the left.

In essence, then, the high levels of support demonstrated for environmental protection verified our expectations. Whatever their other concerns, people want to live in a clean, healthy environment free of pollution. Whether they are moved by moral arguments about the 'common good' or from personal self-interest, or even some old 'countryside dream', we cannot tell from the data at hand. But there is clear evidence that the environment matters politically: it is high on people's agenda and governments are expected to act on the issue.

Spending on the Environment

Of course, without any costs attached, attitudes towards environmental issues may simply be part of a long list of desirable things. The real test of the political reality of preferences for a clean environment is that people are prepared to meet the costs entailed. Some of these costs might be in terms of jobs, higher prices, or restrictions on certain activities: many cities, for example, restrict access by car; EC member states are required to enforce minimum standards of water quality. We do not have comparative data which would allow us to estimate the impact of costs of this kind on levels of support for environmental protection. However, the 1985 ISSP survey has data about people's attitudes to the trade-off between environmental protection and higher taxation in four West European countries.

The distributions for the ISSP data are presented in Table 11.5. Before examining these data, however, note that they can be interpreted from two perspectives. First, they can be treated as an indication of the robustness of people's preferences for active policies of environmental protection. Secondly, they provide some measure of the extent to which governments should be engaged in environmental protection—that is, the *degree* dimension of the scope of government. But set against both these ways of interpreting the data, we have to bear in mind the extent of environmental protection already in operation in these countries. An endorsement of government spending 'the same as now' has a different meaning in countries with good or poor records of environmental protection.

The first impression from these data is that attitudes are somewhat 'softer' than our earlier data suggested. Whereas very large majorities in these four countries, with the partial exception of Britain, gave 'fighting pollution' a high priority on the political agenda (see Table 11.4), these majorities fade when the prospect of tax increases are introduced. Even so, with the exception of Britain, the balance of opinion still remains firmly in favour of more government expenditure on environmental protection. And certainly there is no constituency for cutting back spending on environmental policies—even in Britain

TABLE 11.5. *Demands for government spending on the environment in four West European countries*

	Level of spending				*N*
	Much more	More	The same as now	Less and much less than now or no answer	
Austria	34	39	25	2	987
Britain	6	31	58	5	1,530
Germany	43	39	16	2	1,048
Italy	17	46	30	7	1,580

Notes: Entries are percentages. The question is: 'Listed below are various areas of government spending. Please show whether you would like to see more or less government spending in each area. Remember that if you say "much more", it might require a tax increase to pay for it . . . More or less government spending for the environment?'

Source: ISSP (1985).

where deregulation and tax reductions were prominent elements in the Conservative government's programme during the 1980s.

Clearly, there are quite large differences between these four countries. Environmental protection became an active concern of governments in Austria and Germany from the early 1970s; in the mid-1980s, there is still the demand for even more intervention. Britain, too, has had a fairly extensive programme, particularly on clean air. Support for expansion, however, is modest. But in Italy, where environmental protection has been relatively weak, there is only the barest majority for further government involvement. From this perspective, it is evident that the almost universal desirability of environmental protection among West European publics is not translated directly into support for extending the degree of government intervention. In other words, although we have data for only four countries, the differences between them suggest that there are different expectations among different publics about the extent of government involvement in environmental policy.

Again, to test our hypotheses about subgroup differences, we look at the effects of our standard independent variables, shown in Table 11.6. However, in this instance, our analysis is confined to gender, age, and education.

Contrary to our earlier finding, we find that men are more likely than women to take a strong stand on environmental protection. In Germany, 47 per cent of men want to see much more government spending on the environment as against 39 per cent of women. About 40 per cent of both men and women agree that more spending on the environment is required, but women (19 per cent) outnumber men (13 per cent) in

TABLE 11.6. *Relationship between demands for government spending on the environment and gender, age, and educational level*

	Gender	Age	Education
Austria	−0.06	−0.11	0.07
Britain	−0.10	−0.05	0.05
Germany	−0.08	−0.20	0.20
Italy	−0.12	−0.09	0.12

Notes: Entries are Kendall's tau *b* coefficients. Age was recoded in ten-year intervals; education in groups from low to high; gender was coded male = 1, female = 2. For question wording, see Table 11.5.

Source: ISSP (1985).

wanting to see spending at 'the same as now'. Much the same pattern is found in the other three countries but at rather different levels. There are also differences between age groups—except in Britain. The general pattern emerging from the cross-tabulations (not shown here) for Germany, Austria, and Italy is that young people are more prone to demand much more spending on the environment than older people. Among the youngest, up to 24 years of age, 61 per cent want to see much more spending; the figure among the oldest, aged 70 years and older, is 33 per cent. However, older people outnumber younger people when it comes to more modest levels of spending—as indicated by support for 'more spending' and 'the same spending as today'. These differences are clearest in Germany, but they are not found in Britain. Finally, in all three countries, the better educated want government to spend more money on the environment.

The difference between attitudes in Germany and in Britain indicated by these tables is confirmed by data from two other studies. Both suggest that the willingness to spend tax income on environmental protection is greater in Germany than in Britain. The findings from the first study, an Anglo-German comparative survey conducted in 1980, are presented in Table 11.7.

The three groups which, in varying degrees, think the government is spending too little on environmental protection constitute about 81 per cent in Germany but only about 61 per cent in Britain. Very few people

TABLE 11.7. *Evaluation of government spending for environmental protection in Germany and Britain, 1980*

		Germany	Britain
Too little spending	1	34	23
	2	26	15
	3	21	23
	4	13	30
	5	4	5
	6	1	2
Too much spending	7	1	2
N		1,122	417

Notes: Entries are percentages. The question wording is: 'Is the amount of tax money that the government is spending on each of the following problems too little, about right, too much?' Respondents were asked to use a seven-point scale.

Source: Fietkau, Kessel, and Tischler (1982).

in either country take the view that there is too much spending on environmental protection: altogether in Germany 6 per cent and in Britain 9 per cent. On the other hand, while responses in Germany tend to cluster around the view that government spends too little, responses in Britain tend to cluster around the mid-point. Again, this testifies to the fact that most Germans consider environmental protection as something important, but British people tend to be rather less decisive on the issue.

The other study is Eurobarometer, No. 21 (1984). Germany and Britain were the only countries in which two questions were posed about government spending on protection of the environment. In the first question, respondents were asked whether they thought there was too little or too much spending on environmental protection. These data are presented in Table 11.8. They tell much the same story as the data in Table 11.7: there are substantial differences in opinion between the two countries, with people in Germany much less satisfied about current levels of spending on the environment.

Examining the data in more detail (not shown here) we find that, again, in both countries, men tend to believe that there is too little spending on the environment whereas women are more prone to think that spending is about right. There is also a tendency among younger people in Germany to want more money spent while older people usually think the present level is about right. However, in both countries we find that education affects attitudes on this question: the longer people have studied the more likely they are to think that the government spends too little on the environment. The association we found earlier with left–right self-placement and postmaterialism is also repeated. The more leftist or more postmaterialist people are in their

TABLE 11.8. *Government spending for protection of the environment, 1984*

Level of spending	Germany	Britain
Too little	59	36
About right	38	56
Too much	2	2
Don't know/no answer	1	6
N	992	1,042

Notes: Entries are percentages. The question is: 'Is the amount of taxes the government is spending on environment too little, about right or too much?'

Source: Eurobarometer, No. 21.

outlook, the more likely they are to want to see more money spent on protecting the environment.

The second question, investigating the willingness to pay more taxes to protect the environment, also resulted in differences between the two countries. Our findings on this question, shown in Table 11.9, are particularly interesting. According to many of our earlier findings, public attitudes towards the environment in Britain have rather lagged behind other West European countries. But contrary to our initial expectation, it is in Britain, not Germany, that we find greater willingness to pay more taxes for environmental protection.

TABLE 11.9. *Willingness to pay more taxes for protection of the environment, 1984*

	Germany	Britain
Yes	26	40
No	52	50
Don't know/no answer	22	10
N	992	1,042

Notes: Entries are percentages. Question: 'Would you be willing to pay more taxes to protect the environment?'

Source: Eurobarometer, No. 21.

In both countries, half the electorate does not want to pay more taxes to fund environmental protection. On the other hand, the preparedness to pay more taxes for environmental policies is not inconsiderable in Germany and quite substantial in Britain. So our hypothesis that people are willing to pay higher taxes to protect the environment is not supported for Germany but we find some support in Britain. Finally, variations according to gender, age, number of years of schooling, political preferences, and postmaterialist values all show the familiar pattern. However, as we found earlier, the associations are relatively weak.

How consistent are people's attitudes on these two questions? Are those who think the government spends too little on environmental protection the same people as those prepared to pay more taxes for the purpose? A cross-tabulation of the two questions yields the results shown in Table 11.10.

After eliminating those who have no opinion either way, and adjusting the percentages accordingly, the marginal distributions reveal that

TABLE 11.10. *Willingness to pay more taxes for the environment and view on the level of government spending for the environment in Germany and Britain*

More taxes	Government spending on environment			All
	Too little	About right	Too much	
Germany				
Willing to pay	41	23	13	(34)
Not willing to pay	59	77	87	(66)
Total	100	100	100	
All	(61)	(37)	(2)	100
N = 770				
Britain				
Willing to pay	61	36	21	(45)
Not willing to pay	39	64	79	(55)
Total	100	100	100	100
All	(39)	(58)	(3)	100
N = 887				

Notes: Entries are percentages. Entries in parentheses are marginal distributions. The number of missing cases for Germany is 222; for Britain, 115. For the question wording, see notes to Tables 11.8 and 11.9.

Source: Eurobarometer, No. 21.

66 per cent of the Germans say that they do not want to pay more taxes for environmental protection, but 61 per cent of them also believe that the government spends too little money on environmental matters. The corresponding figures for Britain are 55 and 39 per cent.

The cross-tabulation shows that, broadly speaking, attitudes are fairly consistent. Among people who thought government spending was 'about right' or 'too much', a high proportion were unwilling to pay additional taxes for environmental protection. Among those who think government spends too little, almost two-thirds in Britain (61 per cent) are prepared to pay more taxes. However, in Germany less than half (41 per cent) of the people who thought the government spends too little on the environment were prepared to pay higher taxes for the purpose. Thus we have something of a paradox: support for government action to protect the environment tends to be higher in Germany than in Britain, but enthusiasts in Britain are more prepared to countenance the costs in terms of higher taxes. These findings reinforce two of our earlier findings: there are considerable cross-national differences in attitudes; and whereas environmental protection is generally considered desirable, positive attitudes towards government action prove rather 'softer' when it comes to funding the costs.

The conclusion drawn from the table is that, in both countries, there is a certain consistency between willingness to pay taxes and demands for government spending on the environment. The covariance is stronger for Britain than for Germany. But there is still a large part of the population in both countries that wants the government to spend more money, although they themselves do not want to pay more taxes. This group (not shown in the table) makes up 36 per cent in Germany and 15 per cent in Britain, leaving aside those without an opinion on one or other of the two questions.

There is one further matter about cost to discuss: the connection between environmental protection and societal cost. How willing are people to bear the costs of environmental protection in terms of standards of living? In the short term, this may mean a readiness to accept higher consumer prices; in the longer term, to settle for environmental protection in a trade-off against economic development. There are data for Britain which address the first question, and data for Denmark which address the second.

The British Social Attitudes Surveys for 1984 to 1987 asked respondents whether industry should be prevented from causing damage to the countryside, even if it sometimes led to higher consumer prices. The results, presented in Table 11.11, show that, consistently over the four years, there is higher public support for environmental protection in Britain than for low consumer prices.

Evidently, people in Britain are overwhelmingly prepared to tolerate higher prices if this means an undamaged countryside. About 80 per

TABLE 11.11. *Environmental protection and higher prices in Britain, 1984–87*

	1984	1985	1986	1987
No damage	77	79	82	83
Keep prices down	22	19	16	13
Don't know	1	2	2	4
N	1,675	1,804	1,548	2,847

Notes: Entries are percentages. The question wording is: 'Industry should be prevented from causing damage to the countryside, even if this sometimes leads to higher prices. Industry should keep prices down, even if this sometimes causes damage to the countryside. Which of these two statements comes closest to your own views?'

Source: British Social Attitudes Surveys (1984–7).

cent favour protection of the countryside even at some cost to their standard of living. Moreover, levels of support increased somewhat during the period. The proportions of the indecisive are low, and similarly consistent, so that change in attitudes seems to be concentrated among those who wanted to keep prices down. This example again points to a willingness to bear the cost of a better environment.

The Danish data are from the 1990 election study. Respondents were asked whether or not they agreed with two propositions, both aimed at measuring people's preferences as between economic development and environmental protection. One statement proposed that economic growth should take priority over the environment, the other that improvements to the environment should not go so far as to impair the competitiveness of Danish industry. The costs of environmental protection implied by the two questions are clearly more long term, and more distant from people's everyday lives, than increases in the cost of living. However, the wording of the first statement—that economic growth should take precedence over the environment—is a fairly radical assertion of the priority of economic growth, whereas the second is more balanced. As we might expect, the distributions for the two statements are notably different: a massive majority (89 per cent) disagreed with the first statement, and half the respondents (53 per cent) agreed with the second. However, of those who rejected giving outright priority to economic growth, almost half (49 per cent) agreed that environmental measures should not hamper the competitiveness of Danish industry. Furthermore, six out of seven (86 per cent) who disagreed with the first statement went on to disagree with the second. A cross-tabulation of these two items, shown in Table 11.12, shows the balance of opinion as between economic growth and protecting the environment.

As we can see in the top left corner of the table, about a fifth of the sample favoured economic growth irrespective of the impact on the environment. The people in the bottom right corner—almost a third of the sample—are committed environmentalists; irrespective of the implications for Denmark's economic competitiveness, they want to see the environment protected. We might see these two groups as polar opposites, both equally unprepared to countenance a trade-off between economic growth and environmental protection. But there is a yet further sizeable group, in the top right corner, who seem to be just such pragmatists: they disagree with the idea of economic growth at the expense of the environment but endorse some limitation on

TABLE 11.12. *Preference for industrial growth at the expense of environmental protection: Denmark, 1990*

	'Economic growth should be secured through industrial expansion even though it is in conflict with environmental interests'		
	Agree (preference for growth)	Neutral	Disagree (preference for environment)
'Efforts to improve the environment should not go so far as to damage the competitiveness of our industry'			
Agree (preference for growth)	19	8	25
Neutral	2	3	8
Disagree (preference for environment)	3	2	30
N = 881			

Note: Entries are percentages of all respondents who answered both questions.

Source: Danish Election Study (1990).

environmental measures if the international viability of the economy is put at risk.

Evidently, then, depending on how the willingness to pay for environmental improvement is measured, we get different answers to our hypothesis that people are willing to pay for environmental protection. When the question is formulated in general terms, people tend to show that they are prepared to bear the costs of improvements. In which case, our hypothesis that people are willing to pay higher taxes to protect the environment is verified. But when the questions are more specific, people tend, as in the Danish case, to prefer economic growth, even if that means industrial development which has environmental implications.

Conclusion

We hypothesized at the outset that environmental protection is considered a highly important problem among West European publics, and that it is considered to fall within the scope of government. In support of the first hypothesis, we found that, on average, almost 50 per cent of the populations we examined ranked environmental protection high on the political agenda (Table 11.4). In support of the second hypothesis, 80 per cent and more thought that environmental protection was the responsibility of their government (Table 11.3). Thus, notwithstanding the complexity and long-range nature of the problems involved, and the competing problems of ensuring economic growth, environmental protection ranks high among beliefs about the scope of government.

We also hypothesized that people would be willing to meet the costs of environmental protection by paying higher taxes. Our conclusion regarding that hypothesis comes mainly from Table 11.9, and is rather disappointing: neither in Germany nor in Britain was there a majority, in the early 1980s, willing to pay for environmental protection by paying higher taxes. We conjecture that the majority would suggest prohibitive laws or higher consumer prices as better alternatives.

As to individual differences in attitudes, we found that the major influences affecting people's attitudes on the environment are their position on the left–right spectrum and their outlook on a lifestyle dimension such as materialism–postmaterialism. These effects have consistently been greater than the effects of gender, social class, and the respondent's situation in the labour market. We also found that age and educational levels are influential. This is consistent with a body of literature displaying a connection between these two variables and ideological standpoints (Gustafsson 1972; Dennis 1973; Ashford and Timms 1992). But primarily it is their ideological outlook, or their value orientations, which affect people's stand on environmental protection.

More importantly, perhaps, our study has revealed some patterns in people's beliefs which enhance our understanding of how people think about policies in this area. The four-fold schema shown in Figure 11.1 provides a simple illustration of the relationship between, on the one hand, values and ideology, and on the other hand, the more specific attitudes which are derived from people's beliefs about the scope of government on environmental protection. We may fit various parties and groups into this figure.

Our data indicate that the majority of people are located in cell 2 and cell 3. People in cell 2 are placed to the right on the political scale and/or are materialists. These people are quite prepared to exploit nature in the interests of economic growth. Opposed to them are people in cell 3 who are on the left on the political scale and/or are postmaterialists. They are concerned to ensure a sustainable ecology and economic expansion in harmony with nature.

However, in a study of Swedish political parties and their opinions about the exploitation of rivers for developing electric power plants in 1970, Vedung (1991) found a pattern which is inconsistent with this distribution of opinion. He demonstrates that our model has more than one dimension. He shows that the Social Democratic Party was in cell 1 while all the bourgeois parties were in cell 4. The only party which was in a cell consonant with majority opinion was the Communist Party,

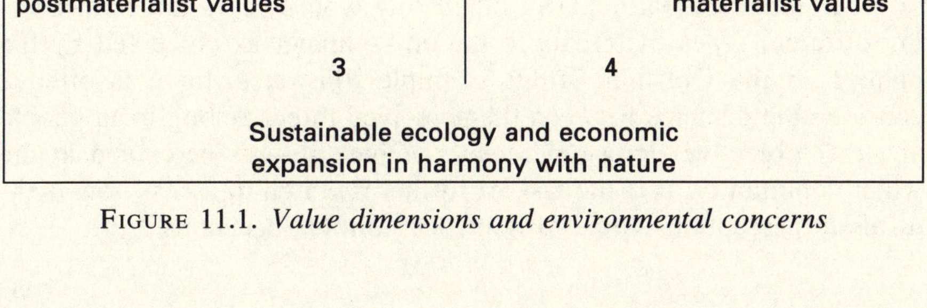

FIGURE 11.1. *Value dimensions and environmental concerns*

which he placed in cell 3. In other words, the main line between the parties went from cell 1 to cell 4 and can probably be explained in terms of electoral politics. In 1970, the Social Democrats were still in government whereas the bourgeois opposition parties had not been in power for almost four decades. To improve their electoral prospects, the bourgeois parties tried in every way to get on the side of public opinion which, in this instance, meant preserving the rivers. The Swedish Communists, however, could take an ideological stance because they did not compete seriously for government with the other four parties. Their opinions were marginal to the political debate and they were likely to gain most support if they followed a clear and consistent ideological line.

Studies of people's opinions about how the scope of government should be defined in relation to environmental problems could be carried out following the model outlined above. For example, several opinion polls have been conducted on the question of the Öresund Bridge designed to connect Denmark and Sweden between Copenhagen and Malmö but mostly they have divided people according to whether they are opponents or supporters. In terms of our model, supporters of the bridge would be placed in either cell 1 or cell 2 and opponents in cell 3 or cell 4. However, if our model were fully applied, and data were also gathered on people's location on the values dimension, a more subtle discrimination of attitudes would be achieved. This greater subtlety might capture some of the complexities, especially the intertwining of scientific, economic, and political arguments, entailed in this environmental issue.

As it is, the process by which people arrive at their position on environmental issues, and the role of government in protecting the environment, is largely unknown. The clearest tendency noted in this study is that people are inclined to take a position which is consonant with their more general orientations—whether in terms of the left–right political spectrum, or materialist–postmaterialist values. Other values or ideological positions might also be relevant, such as Christian values or green ideology. Particularly interesting would be variables measuring different types of threats to the environment as perceived by the public. As the Öresund Bridge example illustrates, there is often a considerable distance between the perceived threat among local people and the 'objective' long-run threat—or benefits—as perceived in the wider community. It is the task of further research to assess how these different perceptions come to influence political decisions.

PART IV

Assessing Scope-of-Government Beliefs

12

Scope-of-Government Beliefs and Political Support

OLE BORRE

❖

Throughout the previous chapters our focus has been on the nature and sources of demands within various policy fields. In our search for the correlates and causes of beliefs about the scope of government, it has been more or less implicitly assumed that such beliefs are important because they guide governments in their policy decisions. But little has been said regarding the consequences of these beliefs. How do people reward their government when they perceive policy to accord with their expectations, and how do they respond when they find themselves at variance with policies in important fields?

The answer provided by democratic theory is that people respond by supporting either the party—or parties—in government, or the parties in opposition, at election time. The consequence, in principle, is that policies are thereby steered in the direction of median public opinion. But experience tells us that this reasoning is simplistic and normative. The entire democratic system, not just the individual parties and leaders, is evaluated in the electoral process. As surveys have revealed, indicators of the public mood such as satisfaction with democracy, trust in politicians and political institutions, the inclination for radical change, and tolerance of unconventional political behaviour, exhibit large variations between countries, over time, and between different groups within countries, notwithstanding the fact that opposition parties are readily available. As the discussion in Volume i demonstrates, the electoral mechanism, in itself, does not ensure a high level of support for the political system.

In this chapter, we explore the consequences of beliefs about the scope of government for political support with a view to explaining the possible loss of political support in advanced democracies. Our main hypothesis is that policy distance—the distance between a voter's policy position and the actual policy of the government—reduces support for the political system. This relationship will be discussed in the first three sections of the chapter. Then, in the following sections, the relationship between policy distance and political support will be elaborated in three directions. First, we introduce controls for party choice. Secondly, we investigate whether the relationship holds for specific policy fields. And thirdly, we examine the hypothesis that, in practice, it is negative policy distance—the tendency to demand 'more' rather than 'less' government—which accounts for the low level of political support in countries with a low aggregate level of support. Finally, some supplementary evidence will be brought in to consolidate our main findings.

Our findings should have a bearing on some of the trends which have been suggested about the development of democratic politics. The overload thesis (King 1975; Rose 1980: 5–23) warned that demands on governments were rising faster than the ability of governments to cope with them, and that this would lead to a loss of political support, thereby endangering the legitimacy of the political system. The loss of support would be evident, for example, in the form of mass dissatisfaction with politics, a decline in the power of government, or indifference among the voters. It is possible that the first part of the argument is incorrect, and the second part is correct only in the sense that the formation of demands can lead to crises of legitimacy for some political systems, or at least to a loss of support among critical sectors of the public.

The overload thesis focused on advanced democracies. Other theoretical arguments, such as those expressed in notions of relative deprivation or rising expectations, suggest that it is in the less advanced societies and in marginalized sectors of the richer societies, where there may be pockets of poverty and problems affecting ethnic minorities, that loss of support for the political system can be observed. Scenarios such as these constitute at least a partial alternative to theories of overload.

Policy Distance

Our main hypothesis postulates a negative relationship between policy distance and political support; or, to phrase it positively, we expect there to be consistency between proximity to policy and political support. The relationship between policy position and trust in politics has been suggested, and investigated, in earlier research. Gamson (1968: 178) suggested that distrust of government can be regarded as a generalization of dissatisfaction with a number of policy decisions. Miller (1974) investigated this relationship with American survey data, in which he found, for example, that the trust score among white respondents in 1964 was higher among those who wanted to maintain the present level of American military activity in Vietnam (75 per cent) than among both those wanting withdrawal (58 per cent) and those who wanted a stronger stand in Vietnam (54 per cent). The pattern was repeated in 1970, although the overall level of political trust had declined during the six years. Moreover, Miller found roughly similar patterns on eight social issues for 1970: in every case those taking some of the moderate positions were more trustful than those taking extreme positions. Since the extreme positions could reasonably be fitted into a left–right dimension, and the moderate positions usually correspond with centrist policies, it was plausible to speak of a political 'cynicism of the left' as well as 'cynicism of the right'. The 1970 data also explicitly showed that the perceived distance to the positions of the Democratic and Republican parties were related to distrust or political cynicism.

Miller and Listhaug (1990) subsequently extended the analysis to Norwegian and Swedish data. Particularly striking are their findings that distrust tends to be correlated with respondent's distance from whichever party is in government—*not* with distance from opposition parties. This suggests that people look at what they believe to be actual policy as implemented by government rather than at the policy stands of the major parties.

According to our hypothesis, the dependent variables should be some operational definitions of political support, while the independent variable should be the degree of harmony or divergence between public opinion and actual policy. Both variables can be conceived at the level of either the nation or the individual citizen. At the national level, a policy which is in accord with the median opinion will be hypothesized to result in a high level of political support, especially if the median opinion is one on which the majority of the public agrees. A policy which does not accord with the median opinion, or with major segments of the population, is hypothesized to result in a low level of political support. In so far as we have indicators of actual policy, public opinion, and the level of support, we can compare nations or follow a nation over time to test the hypothesis.

At the individual level, citizens can be compared with regard to their policy preferences and their attitude to the political system. Policy preferences show up, for example, when a respondent wants the government to spend 'more', 'less', or 'the same as now' in a given policy field. As we have seen from previous chapters, the International Social Science Programme (ISSP) surveys in 1985 and 1990 ask precisely such questions for eight policy fields.

Of course, attitudes towards spending are only part of the whole area of normative beliefs about the scope of government. There are areas of government intervention or state activity which have little to do with the national budget, as is evident from earlier chapters in this volume. However, the classification of beliefs about the scope of government on the basis of 'spending items' shows a striking similarity with the 'new' versus 'old' politics agenda outlined in Chapter 3. Moreover, the strong welfare dimension we found there is in line with our main findings in Chapters 5–10. Thus, an analysis of the spending items in the surveys provides sound grounds for generalizing about the effects of beliefs about the scope of government on political support.

By suitable coding and indexing we are in a position to assess the distance of respondents from the actual policy pursued by the government. By 'actual policy' we mean, of course, policy as perceived by the respondent. The items we use for measuring policy distance come from the ISSP 1985 and 1990 surveys in Germany, Britain, and Italy; Austria was included in the 1985 survey, and Norway in 1990. To assess the distance of respondents to actual policy, in general terms, we coded the categories 'spend much more' and 'spend much less' as 2, and the categories 'spend more' and 'spend less' as 1; the middle category 'spend the same as now' was coded 0. Summing across all policy fields we can obtain a distance index. In Table 12.1 we show the distribution of respondents according to policy distance.

In 1985, the proportion of respondents locating themselves close to government policy was highest in Germany (52 per cent) and Austria (49 per cent), lowest in Italy (30 per cent), with Britain in an intermediate position (40 per cent). Naturally, the distributions in the next

TABLE 12.1. *Distribution of respondents by policy distance in four West European countries, 1985 and 1990*

	Germany	Britain	Austria	Italy	Norway
1985					
Near to government	52	40	49	30	—
At medium distance	37	44	39	49	—
Far from government	11	16	11	21	—
N	907	1,280	781	1,369	—
1990					
Near to government	25	33	—	21	31
At medium distance	51	48	—	49	55
Far from government	24	19	—	30	14
N	2,492	1,017	—	923	1,300

Notes: Entries are percentages. Missing cases on one item are excluded from all items. Policy distance was calculated from eight items asking whether the government should spend much more, more, the same as now, less, or much less than now in each of eight policy fields. For the wording of these items, see Table 4.6. Codes: 'much more' and 'much less' = 2; 'more' and 'less' = 1; 'same as now' = 0. The resulting additive index ranged from 0 to 16; 0–5 were considered near to government, 6–9 at medium distance, and 10–16 far from government.

Sources: ISSP (1985, 1990).

two rows vary the other way. However, it is particularly noticeable that, compared with Germans and Austrians, many Italians feel far removed from their government's policy. In 1990, policy distance was narrowest in Britain (33 per cent near to the government) and Norway (31 per cent), and somewhat wider in Germany (24 per cent near to government) and Italy (21 per cent). It should be noted that, even though the items were exactly the same in the two surveys, fewer people felt near to government policy in 1990 than in 1985. There was a particularly marked increase in policy distance in Germany.

Political Support

Turning to our other main variable, support for the political system can mean many things. Supportive attitudes are illustrated, for example, by the Eurobarometer item on 'satisfaction with democracy', or by some of the items on political distrust which are common in election surveys or political culture studies. The ISSP 1985 survey included a series of items on political support. Three of them seem especially well suited to our purpose, although on the third item, the question used in the analysis is not exactly the same.

(1) 'The public has little control over what politicians do in office.'
(2) 'The average person can get nowhere by talking to public officials.'
(3) 'The government is generally responsive to public opinion' (in Germany, Britain, and Italy). 'The average citizen has considerable influence on politics' (Austria).

In all four countries respondents chose between 'agree' and 'disagree' on each item. Respondents indicating distrust on all three items—by agreeing with the first two and disagreeing with the third—are defined as manifesting low political support.

The first row of Table 12.2 shows the level of distrust in the four countries in 1985. Thus, in terms of distrust, political support tended to be highest in Germany and lowest in Italy, with Britain and Austria in intermediate positions. According to our index which combines responses to the three distrust items, 23 per cent in Germany as against 49 per cent in Britain, 45 per cent in Austria, and 54 per cent in Italy exhibited distrust on all three items.

The second and third rows of the table turn to another attitude which we hypothesize to express political support. Since it can be argued that

TABLE 12.2. *Political distrust and tolerance of protest behaviour in four West European countries, 1985 and 1990*

	Germany	Britain	Austria	Italy	Norway
1985					
Show distrust	23	49	45	54	—
N	681	1,171	527	1,213	—
Tolerate protest	21	29	23	47	—
N	936	1,322	764	1,413	
1990					
Tolerate protest	46	33	—	—	58
N	2,381	1,075			1,277

Notes: Entries are percentages showing political distrust and percentages showing tolerance of protest behaviour. The percentage base excludes missing cases. Distrust was defined by responses to three items in the 1985 survey. Tolerance of protest behaviour was defined as acceptance of 4–6 out of six different types of protest behaviour. Item wordings are given in the text.

Sources: ISSP (1985, 1990).

political trust is sometimes no more than a ritualistic attitude, having no behavioural consequences (Citrin 1974), we might look for an attitudinal indicator of political support which, in a more direct way, takes 'establishment' behaviour as its object. Here, we have tentatively taken the level of tolerance for unconventional behaviour as an indicator of low support. Certainly one should not confuse intolerance with political support but, logically, a preference for policies which are far removed from those pursued by the government and other established parties may well lead the voter to accept unconventional political behaviour as the only remaining channel for influencing the political system.

The ISSP 1985 and 1990 surveys asked which, if any, of six types of behaviour respondents think should be allowed. The six types of behaviour were: (1) organizing public meetings to protest against the government; (2) publishing pamphlets to protest against the government; (3) organizing protest marches and demonstrations; (4) occupying a government office and stopping work there for several days; (5) seriously damaging government buildings; and (6) organizing a nationwide strike of all workers against the government. Respondents chose between 'definitely allowed' and 'probably allowed' on one side, and 'probably not allowed' and 'definitely not allowed' on the other. Counting how many of the six activities respondents thought should be allowed, we defined those allowing between four and six activities as tolerant of protest behaviour.

Table 12.2 shows that, in 1985, 21 per cent of respondents in Germany were tolerant of unconventional behaviour, against 29 per cent in Britain, 23 per cent in Austria, and no less than 47 per cent in Italy. The pattern is roughly consistent with the pattern of distrust, with Germany ranking high in political support, Italy low, and Britain and Austria in intermediate positions. However, as the last row shows, the level of tolerance for unconventional behaviour increased dramatically in Germany between 1985 and 1990—from 21 to 46 per cent allowing four or more unconventional acts. In Britain it increased slightly from 29 to 33 per cent, but the Norwegian respondents (58 per cent) emerged in 1990 as the most tolerant public. Austria did not participate in the 1990 survey, and in Italy the items were not asked.

Policy Distance and Political Support

We can now test our hypothesis of a relationship between policy distance and low political support at the individual level. According to our hypothesis, those locating themselves far from government should exhibit the highest level of distrust in government and the highest level of tolerance for unconventional behaviour. This is investigated in Table 12.3.

The upper section of the table indicates the extent of distrust among people who are near, at an intermediate distance, and far from government policy in 1985. The policy distance model is confirmed in all four countries. In Germany the proportion who gave a distrustful response on all three trust items rose from 16 per cent to 32 per cent as the perceived distance from actual policy increased. In Britain, the corresponding percentages increased from 40 to 64, in Austria from 35 to 57, and in Italy from 51 to 58.

However, the table also shows that policy distance alone does not account for all the differences in political trust between countries. At each distance from government, German respondents are less likely to show distrust than respondents in the other three countries. Even at a close distance, Italians are rather prone to give distrustful responses (51 per cent).

We also hypothesized that distance from government policy leads to greater tolerance of protest behaviour. The middle section of Table 12.3 presents the tolerance score for each country for 1985 among each policy distance group. As we can see, tolerance of protest behaviour varied considerably with distance from government policy. In Germany, only 16 per cent of those near to government policy were tolerant of protest behaviour; this rose to 30 per cent among those far from government policy. For Britain, the corresponding figures are 21 per cent rising to 54 per cent; for Austria, 22 per cent rising to 40 per cent; and for Italy 37 per cent rising to 58 per cent. Again, however, tolerance of unconventional behaviour has a country-specific component which is not explained by policy distance. This is especially evident in the high level of sympathy for unconventional behaviour in Italy, regardless of policy distance.

The lower section of the table shows that the pattern was repeated in the 1990 survey in each of the three countries for which we have data. The rise in tolerance for unconventional behaviour in Germany occurred across the board at each level of policy distance, thus it is not the result of people in Germany having moved away from their government's position.

TABLE 12.3. *Political distrust and tolerance of protest behaviour by policy distance, 1985 and 1990*

	Germany	*N*	Britain	*N*	Austria	*N*	Italy	*N*	Norway	*N*
1985										
Percentage showing distrust who were										
Near to government	16	324	40	398	35	211	51	300	—	
At medium distance	30	219	51	451	53	195	55	543	—	
Far from government	32	68	64	186	57	54	58	254	—	
Percentage tolerating protest behaviour who were										
Near to government	16	444	21	473	22	315	37	376	—	
At medium distance	25	305	31	493	22	254	49	617	—	
Far from government	30	87	54	183	40	77	58	269	—	
1990										
Percentage tolerating protest behaviour who were										
Near to government	35	541	20	309	—		—		51	353
At medium distance	46	1,092	35	459	—		—		59	624
Far from government	58	535	52	170	—		—		68	158

Notes: Entries are percentages showing distrust or tolerance of protest behaviour at each policy distance from government. For definition of policy distance, see Table 12.1. For definitions or political distrust and tolerance of protest behaviour, see Table 12.2.

Sources: ISSP (1985, 1990).

Voting for the Government or the Opposition

The relationship between proximity to policy and political support, or between policy distance and low political support, may be due to various third factors which either intervene between distance and support or exert their impact on both political distance and political support at the same time. For example, structural problems of social inequality, ethnic divisions, or the existence of large minorities may cause both large policy distances and low political support. If we find, for example, that people above a certain income level tend to be more satisfied with democracy, and at the same time in closer agreement with actual policies, than people at lower levels of income, this may explain at least part of the pattern we have observed.

In dealing with background factors which exert an impact on both policy distance and political support, the theoretically most plausible intervening factor is partisanship. Satisfaction with democracy is normally higher among voters for the government party—or coalition parties—than among voters for opposition parties. Even if researchers try hard to make respondents distinguish between support for the incumbent administration and support for their political system, they rarely succeed completely. One can argue that a high level of satisfaction among government voters and a low level among opposition voters is confirmation of our hypothesis, since we can assume that more government voters than opposition voters see themselves as close to actual policy; that is, to perceive their policy distance as quite short. But we do not really know whether policy position is the critical factor producing satisfaction in this instance. It may be the case that government voters are more satisfied than opposition voters simply because their party has the upper hand for the time being—not because their policy preferences are being implemented. Thus, it is critical to control for the allegiance of respondents to government or opposition parties.

Controlling for party allegiance also addresses another intriguing question: why do people whose policy demands are not being met express distrust and support for protest behaviour yet they are still prepared to vote for the governing party? The classical democratic response of citizens with policy preferences at variance with actual policy would be to vote for some opposition party. We should, therefore, test to what extent this tendency comes through in our data, and to what extent it intervenes in the relationship between policy distance and political support.

In Table 12.4 we show the relationship between policy distance and political distrust with respect to some major parties for which our data are sufficiently robust to allow inferences to be made. In Germany we find that voters for the governing Christian Democratic–Christian Social parties vary in political distrust according to their distance from government policy: 10 per cent of those near to government policy are distrustful whereas 27 per cent of those far from government policy are distrustful. Voters for the opposition Social Democrats exhibit a generally higher level of distrust, but they also vary by policy distance, from 22 per cent among those near to government to 39 per cent among those far from government. Thus the relationship between policy distance and political distrust holds after controlling for party affiliation. However, as indicated by the percentage base (shown in parentheses), it is also true that voters for the governing parties feel closer to government policy than voters for the opposition party. Among partisans who feel near to the government, Christian Democrats and Christian Socials dominate over Social Democrats by 146 respondents to 91; among partisans who feel far from the government,

TABLE 12.4. *Political distrust among German, British, and Austrian voters by party and policy distance, 1985*

	Near to government	*N*	At medium distance	*N*	Far from government	*N*
Germany						
Christian Democrat/ Christian Social	10	146	17	65	27	15
Social Democrat	22	91	33	81	39	31
Britain						
Conservative	32	198	39	127	55	22
Labour	41	80	53	173	71	112
Liberal/Social Democrat	48	86	58	84	58	33
Austria						
People's Party	40	72	56	70	56	16
Social Democrat	26	73	48	69	47	17

Notes: Entries are percentages of those voting for a particular party and staying at a particular distance from government who show distrust. The percentage base excludes missing cases. For definition of policy distance, see notes to Table 12.1. On the definition of distrust, see notes to Table 12.2.

Source: ISSP (1985).

Social Democrats dominate by 31 to 15. Such distributional differences apparently go only part of the way in accounting for the hypothesized relationship between policy distance and political distrust.

The British data in the middle section of the table show an even clearer pattern. Among those near to the government, Conservative voters are more numerous than Labour and Liberal/Social Democratic voters taken together; of those far from government, two out of three are Labour voters. Clearly, there is every reason to introduce the control for party affiliation. Having introduced that control, however, we still find that political distrust varies with policy distance—from 32 to 55 per cent among Conservative voters, from 41 to 71 per cent among Labour voters. The Austrian data in the bottom section show (according to the numbers in parentheses) a tie between the two parties at every policy distance. However, voters for the People's Party are less trusting than Social Democratic voters at given levels of policy distance, and voters at a medium or long distance are more trusting than voters near to government.

Thus, for all seven parties, we have found that, no matter whether they support government or opposition parties, voters at a short policy distance express less political distrust than those at medium or long distances. Corresponding data for tolerance of unconventional behaviour are not presented in detail as they do not show such a clear picture as the distrust data. We can illustrate this by means of product-moment correlations between policy distance (ranging from 0 to 16) and tolerance of unconventional behaviour (ranging from 0 to 6). In Britain, there is a significant correlation ($r = 0.24$) between policy distance and tolerance among Labour voters but not among Conservative voters ($r = 0.00$). In Germany, there is a positive but not significant correlation ($r = 0.10$) among Social Democrats, but the correlation disappears ($r = -0.01$) among voters for the Christian Democratic or Christian Social parties.

Welfare, Beauty, and Order

In exploring the relationship between policy distance and support for the political system, we have relied until now on a very general measure of policy distance which cuts across the policy fields covered in Chapters 7–11. Since we have seen from those chapters that a host of different demands are directed towards government from various sections of society, we cannot tell which of these demands are significant in affecting political support unless we break down our measure of policy distance into its components.

In this section we build on the factor analysis of the structure of demands presented in Chapter 4. There it was shown that beliefs about the scope of government with regard to spending in various policy fields could be subsumed into a few types which are common to most West European countries. The partial independence of these factors demonstrated that attitudes towards government spending are not unidimensional. Thus, on the one hand, the 'something for nothing' syndrome is not a uniform pressure on government from all sides; on the other hand, we cannot simply distinguish between a general category of 'spenders' as opposed to a general category of 'cutters'. Rather, there were negative correlations indicating that those demanding one type of expenditure were, to some extent, prepared to give way on other items of government spending.

The factor analysis of the British, German, and Italian data in Chapter 4 (see Table 4.5) showed that three factors emerged in all three countries. The first included the policy fields of old age pensions, health, unemployment benefits, and education. People who want more spent in one of these fields tend also to want more spent in the other three fields. This factor pointed towards welfare policies as the most important field of demand. The second factor combined the desire to spend more on the environment with the desire to spend more on culture and the arts. These are aesthetic demands. We interpret this factor as representing beliefs about protecting the environment and promoting cultural life—or what could be called a 'politics of beauty'. The third factor combined the demand for more government spending on the police and law enforcement with more spending on military and defence matters. That is, the factor dealt with policies of safety or public order.

These three dimensions of policy demands were found—in Chapter 4—not to be entirely independent of each other. By constructing an additive index for each type of demand and looking at the intercorrelations of these three indices in the three countries, it was found that the first two—demands for welfare policies, and for environmental and cultural policies—were positively correlated with coefficients of around 0.3. However, demands for welfare policies and order policies were uncorrelated in Germany and Britain, but positively correlated in Italy. On the other hand, demands for protection of the environment and culture were negatively correlated with demands for order policies in

Germany and Britain, but uncorrelated in Italy. The negative correlations between aesthetic demands and order demands in Britain and Germany suggest that different demands reflect different priorities, which has the effect of compensating across policy areas. By contrast, in Italy there was a stronger tendency towards unidimensionality in people's demands; thus there was a more straightforward divide between 'spenders' and 'cutters'.

When the three countries were compared with regard to the strength of these three types of demand, the hypothesis that it is the wealthier societies in particular which exhibit 'demand inflation' did not receive support (see Table 4.6). While Germany had the highest average standard of living and Italy the lowest, with Britain in a middle position, it was shown that the demand for welfare was high in Britain and in Italy, but Germany trailed far behind. With regard to the maintenance of order, again the level of demand was strongest in Britain and weakest in Germany. Finally, with regard to spending money on environmental protection and cultural policies, Germany and Italy presented the strongest demands, with Britain trailing far behind. To put matters simply: Italy ranked high on demands in all three policy areas, Britain ranked high in two areas (welfare and order), and Germany ranked high in only one area (protection of the environment and cultural policy).

The first question that arises, then, is whether the policy distance model applies not only to the sum total of policies but also to these three policy areas separately. Therefore, we look at the relationship between our two indicators of political support and demands in the three policy areas. The relationships are set out in Figures 12.1–12.3, with respondent's attitudes graded into five positions.

Figure 12.1 deals with demands for spending on welfare. The upper curve shows that the most trustful are those near the middle of the scale, with index values 10–12. These are respondents who think that the level of spending on pensions, health, education, and unemployment benefits is about right. Of course, they may demand more spending on one of these items and less spending on another, a possibility which is not caught by the curve. A higher level of distrust is observed among those who demand less spending, but is found particularly among those demanding more spending on these welfare items. The lower curve in Figure 12.1 shows that the level of tolerance for unconventional behaviour reaches a minimum among those demanding moderate cuts (index values 13–15) in welfare spending. The radical cutters on the left-hand side, and especially the radical spenders on the right-hand side of the figure, are much more tolerant of protest behaviour.

Figure 12.2 deals with attitudes towards spending on environmental and cultural policies. Evidently these attitudes have no systematic relationship with distrust, but their relationship with tolerance of

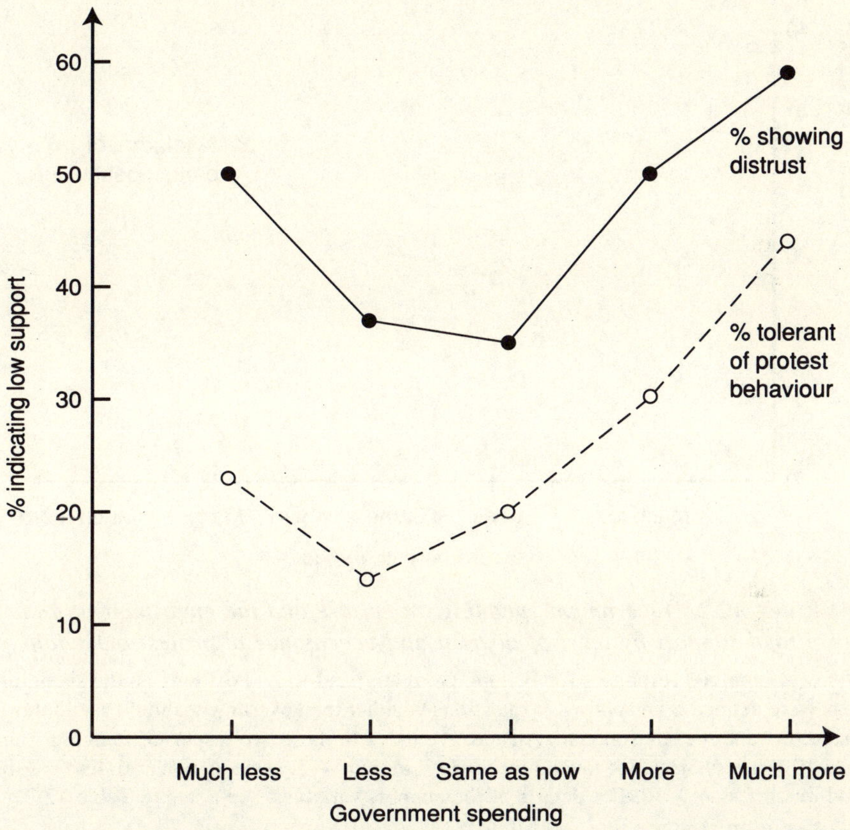

FIGURE 12.1 *Government spending on welfare and political support by level of distrust and acceptance of protest behaviour*

Notes: Combined responses for Britain, Germany, and Italy. Positions on the spending axis were defined by responses to questions whether the government should spend more in four areas: health care, old age pensions, unemployment benefits, and education. An additive index of these four responses, ranging from 4 to 20, was collapsed to: much more = 4–6, more = 7–9, same as now = 10–12, less = 13–15, and much less = 16–20. For details of the support variables, see notes to Table 12.2.

Source: ISSP (1985).

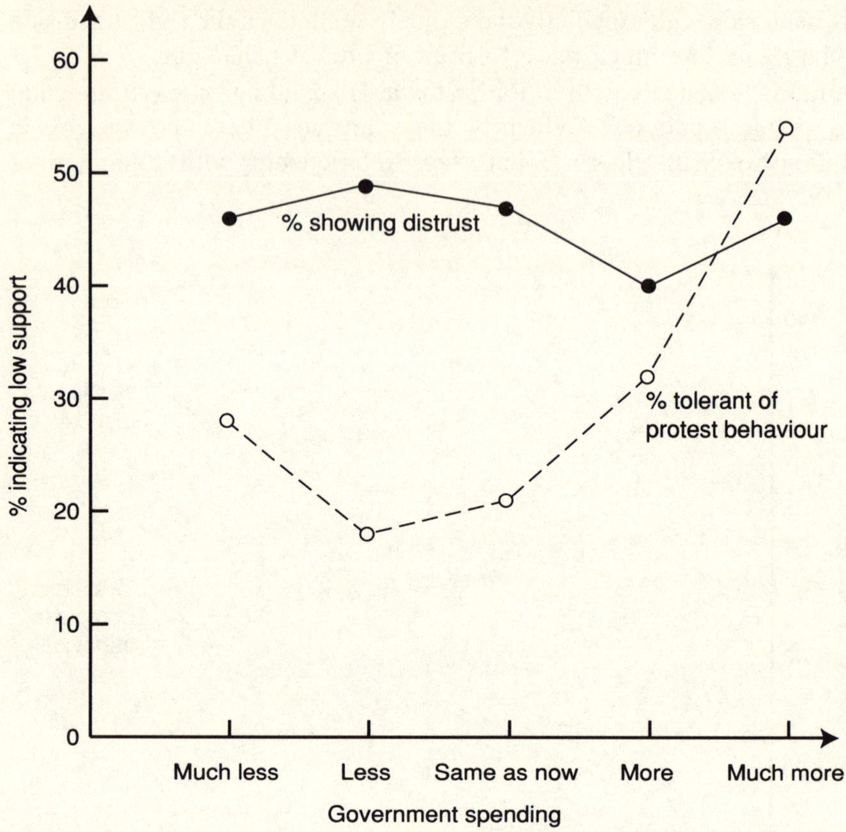

FIGURE 12.2 *Government spending on culture and the environment, and political support by level of distrust and acceptance of protest behaviour*

Notes: Combined responses for Britain, Germany, and Italy. Positions on the spending axis were defined by responses to questions whether the government should spend more on culture and the environment. An additive index of these two responses, ranging from 2 to 10, was collapsed to: much more = 2–3, more = 4–5, same as now = 6, less = 7–8, and much less = 9–10. For details of the support variables, see notes to Table 12.2.

Source: ISSP (1985).

unconventional behaviour is rather similar to that in Figure 12.1. The radical spenders are by far the most tolerant of protest behaviour.

Finally, Figure 12.3 shows the pattern for attitudes towards spending on law and order and defence, or what we term policies of order and security. For political distrust there is a slight V-shaped relationship which accords with the policy distance model. But far more impressive is the relationship with tolerance of protest behaviour, demonstrating that a positive attitude towards spending on order policies goes with a restrictive attitude towards protest behaviour.

So, do beliefs about the scope of government in the form of demands for more spending affect support for the political system? The answer depends on which type of beliefs one is considering, and how one

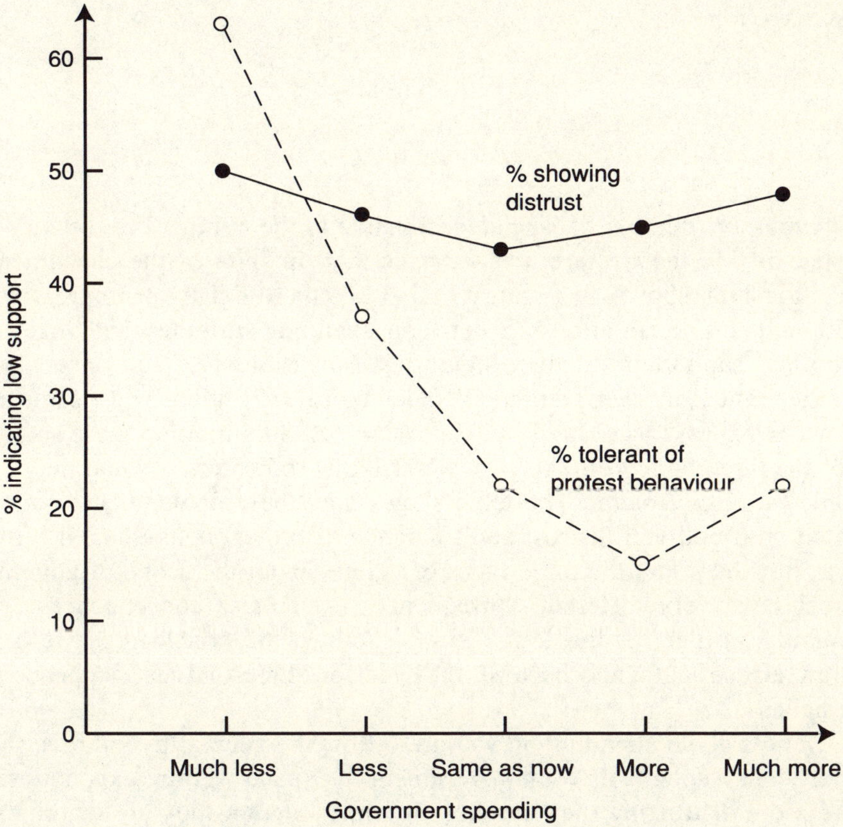

FIGURE 12.3 *Government spending on public order and defence by level of distrust and acceptance of protest behaviour*

Notes: Combined responses for Britain, Germany, and Italy. Positions on the spending axis were defined by responses to questions whether the government should spend more on defence and public order. An additive index of these two responses, ranging from 2 to 10, was collapsed to: much more = 2–3, more = 4–5, same as now = 6, less = 7–8, and much less = 9–10. For details of the support variables, see notes to Table 12.2.

Source: ISSP (1985).

defines political support. In quantitative terms, Figure 12.1 is the more important, both because it encompasses the most costly policies and because it encompasses the largest number of respondents. Very few people have negative attitudes towards these items, therefore the rising right-hand side of the curves in Figure 12.1 tends to overshadow everything else in the field of policy demands. Therefore, it may still be true that the loss of support comes chiefly from the inclination of people to demand more of their government. This is the topic of the next section.

Spenders versus Cutters

The massive number of 'spenders' relative to the number of 'cutters'—especially in the welfare area—means that, in spite of the curvilinear relationships shown in Figures 12.1–12.3, there exists an impressive, although crude, relationship between spending attitudes and loss of political support in all three countries. For Table 12.5, the responses to the eight items were scored as 'much more' = 2, 'more' = 1, 'same as now' = 0, 'less' = −1, and 'much less' = −2. Summing up these scores for the three policy dimensions, we arrive at indicators of what may be called *excess demand*. The table shows how these demands are correlated with political distrust and tolerance of protest behaviour. It turns out, however, that the three types of beliefs about the scope of government have very different consequences—but these consequences are roughly similar for the four countries. Thus, the conclusions we can draw are strengthened because they rest on three or four independent tests.

Beliefs about spending on welfare follow the general hypothesis: the more that respondents want government to expand welfare expenditure, the more distrusting they are and the more tolerant they are of protest behaviour. This is the 'dissatisfied–spender' syndrome in its clearest form. Beliefs about spending on protecting the environment and cultural activity follow the hypothesis so far as tolerance of protest is concerned. That is, people who want the government to spend more on the environment, culture, and the arts—promoting what we call a 'politics of beauty'—accept a higher level of protest behaviour than those who do not want more spending in these areas. But when it comes to political distrust, the pattern disappears in Britain and Italy, and is

TABLE 12.5. *Attitudes in three policy fields, political alienation, and tolerance of protest behaviour*

	Germany	Britain	Austria	Italy
CORRELATION BETWEEN SUPPORT FOR:				
Spending on welfare and:				
Political distrust	0.19**	0.18**	0.17**	0.09**
Tolerance of protest	0.11**	0.20**	0.09*	0.17**
Spending on environment and culture and:				
Political distrust	−0.10*	−0.03	—	−0.02
Tolerance of protest	0.32**	0.24**	0.23**	0.24**
Spending on order and security and:				
Political distrust	−0.11**	−0.09**	—	0.02
Tolerance of protest	−0.37**	−0.37**	−0.23**	−0.22**

*$p < 0.05$ **$p < 0.01$

Notes: Entries are Pearson's *r*. For the definition of political distrust and tolerance of protest behaviour, see notes to Table 12.2.

Sources: ISSP (1985, 1990).

reversed in Germany. Thus, in Germany, spenders on the environment and culture show more trust in government than other people.

Beliefs about spending on order and security present a different pattern again. The negative correlations with political distrust in Germany and Britain imply that people who want their government to spend more on law and order and defence are somewhat more supportive of their government than people who think that enough is already being spent on these activities. The negative correlations with tolerance of protest in the last row indicate that the 'order seekers' certainly do not approve of protest activities as a means of promoting their cause. It would be a strange paradox if they did!

Thus, in broad agreement with the overload hypothesis, we find positive correlations between spending attitudes (especially on the cost-heavy welfare items) on the one hand and political distrust and tolerance of protest behaviour on the other. Our correlations in Table 12.5 assume a linear, or at least monotonic, relationship between 'excess' demand and lack of political support. Although a closer study of our data revealed that the relationship is not monotonic, in so far as extreme 'cutters' also exhibit low support, the crude assumption of the overload thesis—that the loss of political support is due to excessive demands for welfare—still contains a good deal of truth.

A further point to note is that excess demands do not tend to be located in the economically most advanced nations. In an advanced society such as Germany there tends to be a more even balance between 'spenders' and 'cutters' than in a less advanced society like Italy. This might be hypothesized to cause polarization or increased political conflict in the wealthier countries because of more extensive disagreement about policies. In the less advanced countries it would be more precise to say that there is no disagreement but, rather, a common resentment, since almost everybody agrees the government should do more. The lack of consensus in the more advanced countries could be seen as a source of frustration and political instability. Equally, of course, the consensus that the government is not doing enough could be seen as a source of frustration and political instability in the less advanced countries.

A polarization thesis, vaguely identified with Marxist theory, might be interpreted to mean that advanced societies are exposed to a lack of consensus almost regardless of what the government does. To increase government efforts will not be a solution, because at the same time the number of people who claim that government is wasteful or inefficient will increase. The idea that governments produce satisfied and conforming citizens by choosing policies which are in line with majority public opinion—as liberal democratic theory suggests—thereby breaks down. For example, in order to meet demands for social security a government may levy higher taxes, which is likely to annoy taxpayers. Or government may decide to fight inflation at the cost of higher unemployment, thus annoying the unemployed. A government highly committed to solving all its citizens' demands may well solve none of them.

While it is probably true that a large number of 'cutters' would contribute substantially to a low level of political support, this is not a serious threat in advanced countries. As Table 12.1 suggested, the proportion with large policy distances is smaller in these countries than in the less advanced countries; a larger proportion of the public thinks that the level of spending is about right. What counts is that in the less advanced countries almost everybody is likely to engage in 'excess demand', and for that reason the government is robbed of support.

We might conclude, then, that the overload thesis is more correct in pointing towards excess demand as a source of frustration, but incorrectly implies that this situation is especially threatening in advanced countries. Indeed, the theory of relative deprivation seems more relevant in explaining the patterns we found in the tables and figures. The widespread demands for welfare account for much of the level of political distrust and the acceptance of protest behaviour in Italy relative to Germany. Another part of the explanation might focus on faith in the fairness of the political system, which was discussed in Chapter 5, and the quality of political leadership, a dimension which lies outside the domain of this volume.

In comparing the theses of polarization, overload, and deprivation, we have assumed that Germany represents the advanced countries, Italy the less advanced, and Britain an intermediate level. However, since we have dealt with so few countries, our suggestions about the relationship between demand and support, on the one hand, and the level of economic development, on the other, must stand as a crude hypothesis for further investigation.

National Consensus and Satisfaction with Democracy

The policy distance model seems to provide a logically and empirically well-founded approach to the relationship between beliefs about the scope of government and political support. We may, tentatively, explore it further using some data from the Eurobarometer surveys. Although the concept of policy position is not directly applicable in these data, our purpose is to test a 'grand hypothesis' which states that consensus with regard to beliefs about the scope of government is a source of satisfaction with the way democracy works.

For the presentation in Table 12.6, we coded responses to three policy proposals (economic management, efforts to reduce income differences, and efforts to protect the environment) in three Eurobarometer surveys (Nos. 11, 16, and 19) for 1979–83. Since proximity to government policy seemed best indicated by a vague resistance to reform policies, and the greatest distance from government policy seemed to be indicated by a strong desire for reform, we coded 'strongly agree' as distance 4, 'partly agree' as distance 2, 'partly disagree' as distance 1, and 'strongly disagree' as distance 3. These codes were summed for the three items, which resulted in an index of distance ranging from 3 to 12. The index was then collapsed into two categories which, overall, were balanced in size. Those with codes 3–8 were regarded as being near to government policies, and those with codes 9–12 as being far from government. We can then treat the

TABLE 12.6. *Level of consensus and satisfaction with democracy, 1979–83*

	Level of consensus (near to government)	*N*	Satisfied with democracy	*N*
Britain	71	2,446	59	2,897
Germany	66	2,437	78	2,847
Ireland	65	2,418	55	2,727
Denmark	62	2,242	71	2,954
Belgium	42	2,257	48	2,569
Netherlands	41	2,561	63	2,877
France	37	2,413	49	2,691
Italy	37	2,790	18	3,193

Notes: Entries are percentages. Data for the three surveys for each country have been combined. The percentage base excludes missing data.

Sources: Eurobarometer, Nos. 11, 16, and 19.

proportion of respondents with codes 3–8 in a given country as a measure of the degree of consensus in that country. In Table 12.6 we present the level of consensus and the level of satisfaction with democracy in eight West European countries.

The countries are listed according to the level of consensus, as indicated in the first column of figures. There is a gap between the first four countries and the last four. The first group is dominated by consensus, the last group by dissent. Comparing the first column with the second, we find broad agreement with the hypothesis of an association between the two indicators. But the agreement is by no means complete. People in Germany, Denmark, and the Netherlands are more satisfied with their democracies than they should be if judged by their levels of consensus. Italy is at the bottom along with France with regard to consensus, but in terms of satisfaction with democracy Italy is several classes below the other countries. Therefore, all that can be concluded is that an association between the two indicators does exist. For example, computing the raw averages shows that 66 per cent are satisfied in the first four countries as against only 44 per cent in the last four.

Our deviating countries must simply be interpreted to mean that, along with policy consensus, there are other factors affecting satisfaction with democracy. And, of course, our real world experience tells us that this is so. A history of scandals, corruption, and a host of other considerations which have nothing to do with beliefs about the scope of government are likely to affect people's judgements about how democracy works in their country. All we want to demonstrate is that consensus in terms of beliefs about the scope of government also plays some part in those judgements.

It can readily be shown that a similar relationship holds at the individual level. Using the same data, we divided respondents in each country into three groups: the consensus group (codes 3–8), the moderately dissenting group (codes 9–10), and the radically dissenting group (codes 11–12). In Table 12.7, we show the proportion in each group, and in each country, which is near to government, far from government, and in an intermediate position.

As the table shows, our hypothesis that consensus leads to satisfaction with democracy is confirmed in all countries, with only one exception. In Britain, the proportion of those satisfied with democracy is higher among people with policy preferences far from government (53 per cent) than among people at a medium distance (47 per cent). The other countries show differences between the 'near to government' and the 'far from government' groups, ranging from a high of 16 percentage points in the Netherlands to a low of 6 percentage points in Germany.

Our exploration of the policy distance model, or 'proximity model', of political support suggests that it may be rather widely applied. It is

TABLE 12.7. *Policy distance and satisfaction with democracy in eight West European countries, 1979–83*

	Near to government (3–8)	*N*	At medium distance (9–10)	*N*	Far from government (11–12)	*N*
Germany	78	1,556	75	568	72	228
Denmark	73	1,354	70	562	63	271
Netherlands	69	1,028	62	858	53	598
Britain	63	1,652	47	483	53	200
Ireland	57	1,472	52	494	49	316
France	55	826	47	867	43	551
Belgium	51	862	46	690	39	514
Italy	20	1,014	18	917	13	813

Notes: Entries are percentages who are 'very' or 'somewhat' satisfied with the way democracy is working in their country among those at each policy distance from government. The percentage base excludes missing data. Data for the three surveys for each country have been combined.

Sources: Eurobarometer, Nos. 11, 16, and 19.

not restricted to the particular types of data analysed in Tables 12.3–12.5 and Figures 12.1–12.3.

Conclusion

In this chapter we have explored the consequences of mass beliefs about the scope of government in terms of support for the political system. Interpreting attitudinal items of the agree/disagree type as conveying information on policy distance, we have extended the policy distance model. Our findings suggest that such beliefs are related in an ordered and reasonably predictable way to attitudes towards the political system. Assuming that some important beliefs about the scope of government are structured by values, they bridge the gap between needs arising in society and the functioning of the political system. When viewed over a longer time span, advanced societies appear in a better position than the less advanced to bridge that gap. The theories claiming that overload, ungovernability, and demand inflation particularly harass the polities of the economically advanced societies do not hold up against our analysis. In retrospect, they were an overly pessimistic view of the situation in the 1970s and the early 1980s. By comparison, as our data on Italy suggests, fulfilling public expectations and securing public support are likely to be much bigger problems in the less advanced societies.

13

Beliefs and the Scope of Government

OLE BORRE

Most of the previous chapters have been concerned with analysing mass attitudes regarding particular policy fields or suggesting specific consequences for government policy. In this chapter we summarize our questions and findings, and then go on to outline some of their implications for further research. First, we shall argue for the importance of the attitudes we have studied. Secondly, we review the procedures we adopted and the problems we encountered in our research. Finally, we assess our findings on the various issues taken up in this volume.

Our purpose in this study, as we defined it in Chapter 1, was to examine mass beliefs about the scope of government in West European countries since the 1960s. These are beliefs among the mass public about what the government should do, what it can do, will do, or is actually doing. They were taken to encompass knowledge and cognitive expectations about policies as well as normative beliefs about what the government should do.

During the course of our analysis, however, it turned out that survey data for beliefs about the scope of government are deficient in several respects. Few data reach back into the 1960s and the early part of the 1970s, so we lack a backdrop to more recent developments. Hence our findings are largely confined to the comparative surveys of the later 1970s and the 1980s. Moreover, most surveys are concerned with normative statements with which the respondent may agree or disagree. There are few opportunities for studying the cognitive beliefs on which these attitudes may rest. What this means, in practice, is that the concept of beliefs about the scope of government which we employed comes close to the more familiar concepts of policy demands or issue positions.

Even within this rather narrow conceptualization of beliefs about the scope of government, however, it turned out that various typologies could be developed and used fruitfully. The distinction between the *range* and *degree* dimensions of the scope of government, introduced in Chapter 3, allowed us to distinguish between people's beliefs about the extent and the intensity of government activity. Governments may expand in breadth, by taking up new policy areas, as well as in depth, by increasing their activities in established policy areas. This distinction is reflected in our data on mass beliefs: the public assigns responsibility to the government for providing certain services, or assuring certain end-states, and the public increases or reduces demands for government involvement within policy areas. Our data also allowed us to distinguish between issue priorities and issue stands, reflecting the distinction between the salience and the direction of attitudes. In several surveys, data on issue priorities or issue agendas were found along with the more common data on support for specific issue positions.

Therefore, on closer inspection, we found that beliefs about 'what the government should do' could be separated into a number of different variables. This provided us with a framework within which to analyse a rather loose assemblage of data, so enabling us to make much more of what is a rather thin data record. But first, we recapitulate our purpose in studying beliefs about the scope of government.

Purpose of the Study

The most plausible reason for studying beliefs about the scope of government is that they influence government policy, either directly or indirectly. Such beliefs are an important part of public opinion, and in a fairly straightforward way they may induce a government to expand or cut back a welfare programme, introduce or abandon a tax scheme. Perhaps our most general expectation was that as scope of government beliefs become more expansionist, with increasing demands for government action and services over the years, they would contribute to explaining the actual increase in public expenditure which, as we saw in Chapter 2, has taken place since the 1960s. If this is the case, then it would be important to establish whether the demands of the mass public exhibited, overall, trends towards expansion or contraction during, or just before, the period when the scope of government expanded so rapidly and widely. We might even attempt to go further, trying to establish a 'fit' between beliefs about the scope of government and the actual scope of government in various countries at various time points.

Although plausible, and we found empirical support for it in Chapter 3 and Chapter 4, this line of reasoning cannot take us very far. For even if we establish parallel developments in the expansion or contraction of government and beliefs about the scope of government among the mass public, this would tell us little about the mechanism at work in the relationship. It might be that beliefs about what the government should do are influencing government policy, in the classic tradition of democratic theory as we discussed in Chapter 12. Equally plausible but quite different interpretations of the analysis could be that mass beliefs tend to fall in line with actual policy, or, as argued in Chapter 8, that mass beliefs tend to follow the lead given by political élites.

Even so, at the descriptive level, we would expect periods of rapid growth in public expenditure to coincide, if only roughly, with periods of rising demands for government action. Furthermore, we would anticipate finding the largest majorities in favour of public services and large government budgets in those countries where the public sector is largest. In this sense, we would expect there to be some degree of congruence between the actual scope of government and mass beliefs about what the government should do. That is, that there is some 'fit' between the input side and the output side of the Eastonian demand model on which we have drawn. Where the fit is good, we might even talk of the existence of different political cultures: on the one side, societies with a tradition of self-reliance would have fairly limited public budgets and show scant support for welfare programmes; on the other side, societies accustomed to relying on collective measures would have relatively large public budgets and show strong support for welfare schemes.

The second reason for studying these beliefs is their presumed effect on individual political behaviour and, in the aggregate, on mass political behaviour. Rational voters are expected to make their party choices by comparing the position of parties on issues, or by evaluating the government's performance on such issues. Several studies (Franklin, Mackie, Valen, *et al.* 1992) have shown that, over recent decades, voting according to issue positions or the salience of issues constitutes an increasing component of voting decisions compared with traditional party or class loyalties. We expected to find this aspect of politics expressed in the form of plausible relationships between party choice and issue positions.

But voting is not the only type of behaviour which might be affected by beliefs about the scope of government. Those issues or issue preferences which are not identified with any party, and therefore not represented in the legislature, may stimulate protest activity in social movements. Taking this a step further, issue preferences which are perceived to be overruled more or less permanently by the government may give rise to a decline in support for the political system, thereby causing apathy or hostile citizen reactions. A proliferation of unrealistic policy demands may lead to 'government overload', 'ungovernability', or 'legitimacy crises'. Since it is central to the entire Beliefs in Government project, we wanted to deal with this question too. Hence, we examined the systemic consequences of highly divergent policy demands.

In short, beliefs about the scope of government were hypothesized to affect political participation and support in various ways. It might be argued that, in the last analysis, our first two arguments for studying these beliefs coincide, in so far as individual political participation aims to influence policy decisions. The difference is that the first type of analysis, which links policy decisions or their outcomes directly to public opinion, necessarily proceeds at the macro level of the political system, whereas the second type is conducted on the micro level.

The third reason for studying scope of government beliefs is that these beliefs are indicators of social problems and changing social values. It might be expected that a large-scale and longitudinal study of such beliefs would reveal which problems became more pressing during the periods of economic growth and recession experienced in Western Europe over the latest three decades. This might allow us to suggest what kind of problems an approaching post-industrial society would encounter.

Moreover, studying beliefs about the scope of government could be supposed to reveal major value or ideological differences. These kinds of beliefs deal with fundamental questions about the goals of society and the means of furthering those goals. True enough, while these questions nourish political debate and provide the preambles of constitutions and party programmes, they are rarely put to the mass public, nor answered by public opinion. Even so, when presented with survey items listing the tasks of the government, respondents might well echo the ideological debate or suggest which part of that debate is relevant to them. Our hypothesis was that in the economically advanced countries, the ideologies underpinning traditional left–right conflicts are being rivalled by the ideologies of 'new politics'. That is, we asked ourselves whether the functions of the state, as seen by the public, are slowly changing from being mainly a provider of material welfare to becoming a vehicle for enhancing the quality of life.

Combining these three reasons for our study, beliefs about the scope of government are supposed, theoretically, to bridge the gap between social problems and political solutions—between society and politics. Our aim was to find out to what extent they 'worked' as such, given the various limitations encountered in the data record.

Development of Scope of Government Beliefs

A common theme running through our volume is whether demands for government intervention were generally growing in West European societies over the last two or three decades. This is related to the question in the previous section, which dealt with the 'fit' between beliefs about the scope of government and the actual scope of government. If public demands were generally rising, that might explain expanding budgets as a case of public control of policy.

There is a less sanguine interpretation of the same relationship, however. A general and perhaps accelerating rise in demand might be expected from the idea of a 'demand spiral': satisfying demands makes people more dependent on their government and leads to new demands. This interpretation differs from the first by claiming that the process is irreversible and uncontrollable.

Some evidence supporting this latter perspective comes from Chapters 4 and 5, which suggested that demands, in aggregate, exceeded the proposed limits to budgets. Hence, one might conclude that a built-in inconsistency in the form of a public wanting 'something for nothing' exists in all societies. It is true that this inconsistency is markedly reduced when the interview question explicitly tries to make respondents balance the public budget. It is also possible that on closer interrogation the inconsistent voters might turn out to be less inconsistent. As expressed in Chapter 5, silly questions are likely to evoke silly answers. None the less, the spontaneous inclination towards underbudgeting reflected in our data may well be what counts in the eyes of the policy-makers, thus in a crude sense explaining rising public expenditure.

But closer scrutiny of such a hypothesis requires that we observe changes, or differences in the variables. Data on government expenditure, reported in Chapter 2, made clear that in most countries public expenditure has not risen with the same speed in later years as it did during the 1960s and early 1970s. There has been a flattening out of the size of government. It would be interesting to examine whether this development is paralleled with a dampening of demands. In other words, either demands have not spiralled as expected, or else they have become thwarted.

Looking first at demands concerning the *range* of government, we found evidence of a decline in the later period of our study, from 1985 to 1990. The ISSP data permit a comparison of Britain, Germany, and Italy in a number of policy fields for which respondents could assign responsibility to their governments. On average, across these policy fields, the proportion assigning an 'essential' responsibility to government declined from 88 to 85 per cent in Britain, from 80 to 75 per cent in Germany, and from 91 to 88 per cent in Italy. On this score, demands have declined—if modestly.

Moreover, the rank order of these three countries seems to have changed between 1974 and 1985. According to the Political Action data (1973–6), Germany ranked highest in 1974 and Britain lowest. This suggests that, between the 1970s and the 1980s, assignment of government responsibility has been on a downwards course in Germany, on an upwards course in Britain, but remained constantly high in Italy. That is, that the 'demand spiral' was largely confined to the British experience between the 1970s and the 1980s.

However, when we look at demands concerning the *degree* of government, developments during the 1985–90 period were the reverse of what we find for the range of government. On this score, demands did indeed increase in the three countries which we can compare directly. The proportions demanding 'much more government spending' on the environment, the health service, old age pensions, education, and on law enforcement were all significantly higher in 1990 than in 1985. Unfortunately, however, we do not know what the situation was before 1985. Thus, the evidence is not strong enough to support the idea of spiralling demand.

Comparing our evidence with other types of evidence, we incline to the view that the demand changes we observe are reactions against short-term policy changes and not part of a long-term trend. The attempt to roll back the welfare state, most explicitly pursued in Britain, has succeeded in cutting welfare expenditure markedly. This has led to a large and increasing majority being opposed to the cuts—or, at least, to further cuts. As the Conservative Party has managed to stay in power, however, one of the assumptions behind the demand spiral hypothesis seems to be invalidated. This is the assumption that a government which fails to satisfy the demands of a majority of the population will soon be replaced by another which is more willing to do so.

British policy during the 1980s, however, may well have been inspired by public opinion in the preceding period. For example, attitudes towards the provision of social services were strongly contractionist in Britain in the second half of the 1970s, but the public mood was quick to turn around once the Thatcher government began executing its policies (Table 8.1). Consistent with this turnaround, demands for cutting personal taxes were high during the 1970s but almost vanished during the 1980s (Chapters 5 and 6). Thus, Britain could be seen as a case in which exceptionally low demands during an earlier period lead to a shrinking public sector in the next.

The example of Britain is not unique. Even more telling is the case of Norway, where demands for tax reductions soared in 1975 under the Labour government, then declined during the period of Conservative government, only to rise again in 1987 when the Labour government was back in power. France is an example where the pressure to cut taxes was stronger during the 1960s than during the 1970s, although it had little effect. In all of these cases one notices a tendency for the public to (over)react against policies of expansion or contraction. To the extent that governments pay heed to these opinion shifts, we get a cyclical pattern in public opinion. The opposition, being frustrated in its reach for government, may regain its spirit from having the majority of the public on its side.

On specific policy items, moreover, we find simultaneous changes in demand in different directions in different countries. Demands for old age pensions, analysed in Chapter 8, are rather typical of such changes. These demands declined in Britain between 1964 and 1969 but rose again between 1969 and 1983 (Table 8.2). In the Netherlands, however, they declined between 1970 and 1980, rising again during the second half of the 1980s (Figure 8.1). Going on to Scandinavia, we observe that Sweden follows the Dutch downwards trend from 1968 to 1980, while

Denmark and Norway follow the British upwards trend up to the mid-1980s (Table 8.3).

The most likely explanation for these different trends is probably to be found in the different policies pursued. The majority of the public tend to react against policies which curb, or threaten to curb, welfare expenditure. Thus, these changes are not properly trends but, rather, short-term fluctuations caused by the very experience of change or the affront to expectations entailed in policy change. They do not follow the demand-spiral hypothesis; if anything, they suggest the inertia of demands.

Complementing the theory of a demand spiral, bleak prospects have been held out for democracy because of the tendency of welfare states to accommodate demands coming from all quarters of the electorate. These baleful predictions have not materialized, and seem unlikely to do so. (See also Volume i in this series, Chapter 11.) Western democracies have not succumbed to predictions of a 'crisis of legitimacy'; indeed, they seem to be well able to manage periods of political instability.

In a slightly different version, the demand spiral hypothesis may be based on the heavy assignment of responsibility to West European governments (Table 4.1). However, even government responsibility—in the eyes of the public—does not seem immune to downwards adjustment. Table 4.3 suggested that where government receipts had increased little from the mid-1970s to the mid-1980s, the public assigned less responsibility to its government. This was the case in Germany and to some extent Britain, whereas Ireland was the prime example of the growing size of government concomitant with a heavy assignment of responsibility among its citizens. But the German case is evidence that, in certain circumstances, an ethos of self-reliance can take hold also in mature welfare states. Thus, the whole idea that demands are insatiable and constantly rising should be questioned.

The theory of the declining marginal utility of economic policy leads to predictions quite opposite to those of the demand spiral theory. According to the marginal utility hypothesis, every extension of a policy of levelling incomes and regulating industry beyond a certain point, will have a steadily smaller effect. Thus, demands tend to decline as they get satisfied. And, indeed, the direction of policy demands on some welfare and economic policy goals seems to have been downwards, at least during the 1980s. For example, Chapter 7 indicated that social equality as a goal of the welfare state became less pressing between 1979 and 1990; and for a few countries where time series are available, Chapter 9 suggested that demands for economic management have been declining since the 1970s.

Changing Social Problems and Policy Agendas

Thus, the idea of a declining marginal utility of, and support for, policies seems a promising avenue for further research. We may speculate a bit further along the same lines.

We argued earlier that examining beliefs about the scope of government is important because these beliefs reflect underlying social problems and values. The marginal utility hypothesis provides an opportunity to substantiate this claim. Such a hypothesis cannot logically (although perhaps ideologically) be stretched to apply to government activity in its entirety. Rather, it should apply to policies which belong to the older functions of government: as demands for these forms of government activity become satisfied, they should, according to the marginal utility hypothesis, gradually move down the political agenda, giving way to other and newer problems. Therefore, we need to distinguish between the different functional forms of government activity and observe whether people's beliefs about the scope of government reflect such distinctions. For those issues which are rising in importance, marginal utility should not decline; rather, we should expect to find innovative policies and new arenas for government activity. One can also speculate that the first primitive applications of a new policy are often less successful and efficient than fully fledged policies undertaken at a later stage. In the transition between the first and second stages, marginal utility should rise.

Due to the scarcity of time-series data, we do not have direct evidence of this process. However, the first condition for the process to operate seems to be met, as there is solid evidence that beliefs about the scope of government are structured into issue agendas. In Chapter 3, respondents from the EC countries were found to translate their concerns into three types of policy demands: decentralization combined with economic equality; external security; and security against rising prices and unemployment. However, those who saw one type of policy as important tended to neglect or downgrade the other types. This suggests that people, or the aggregated majority of people, shift their demands from one government function to another—thereby taking the wind out of a very broad application of the marginal utility hypothesis.

In identifying such agendas we also set the stage for examining whether different groups attach priority to different types of policy, and whether these agendas showed contrasting trends—as postulated by the 'new politics' and postmaterialism theses discussed, especially, in Chapters 3 and 4. Our assessment of these theses largely confirmed the 'new politics' thesis in that external security seemed to belong to a different dimension from the quest for material security. We were also able to show a tendency for West European citizens to group according to the main functions they assign to the state. While Chapter 3 identified three political agendas in the data on the importance, or priority, of political problems, Chapter 4 and Chapter 12 used other data to arrive at much the same typology of beliefs in terms of government functions. In particular, the 'welfare' dimension was distinguished from, on one side, the 'order' dimension and, on the other side, the 'culture and environment' dimension.

Compared with welfare and economic intervention, demands for maintaining the security of citizens—both in terms of ensuring order in society and protection against foreign powers—is of secondary importance in most West European societies. Moreover, their priority in the hierarchy of importance seems to have declined (although the period since around 1990 may tell a different story). By contrast, demands for government intervention for the purpose of enhancing people's quality of life belong to a comparatively new agenda and seem to be rising in importance. Although, again, time series data are not at hand, we can make tentative inferences from data grouped by age and education; the old agenda prevails especially among older people and the less well educated whereas the new agenda prevails among the young and well educated.

We are well aware, however, of the many problems of validating and forecasting trends in government policy, even in such broad terms. In addition to period effects which may disrupt projected trends, we are also faced with the unknown impact of the way the survey items are worded. When respondents have to rank issues in terms of their importance, they are automatically excluded from rating every issue as highly important.

Levels of Economic Development

Since time-series data occur only sporadically in our study, a number of conclusions have to rest on inference from cross-national but single-wave surveys. In the case of some hypotheses, this gives rise to problems of validity in making inferences from a given pattern to causal mechanisms, from structure to process.

Theoretically, among the most interesting findings in the comparative surveys are those indicating systematic differences in scope-of-government beliefs as between economically advanced countries and the less advanced. Fortunately, the hypotheses in this field can be tested also on comparative data showing the relative position of countries on key variables. We investigated whether, first, the richer societies generally assign more or less responsibility to their governments than the poorer societies, and, secondly, whether it is true that, in the richer societies, demands for policies for economic equalization and the regulation of industry are less relevant than in poorer societies.

Concerning the range of activities for which the government is held responsible, Table 4.1 showed a characteristic difference in 1974 between, on one hand, the Netherlands, where expectations are high, and on the other hand, Britain or Switzerland, where they are low. Such a difference cannot be attributed to different levels of economic development, but must have its roots in traditions or ideologies about government intervention. The difference might also be influenced by transient public debates about whether government has gone too far, or, conversely, whether government is being negligent. Moreover, by 1985 people in Britain seemed to have increased the range of their demands relative to people in Germany (Table 4.2). Evidence of this kind does not support the hypothesis that high or rising demands is a feature of poorer rather than richer societies.

Concerning the second hypothesis, which deals with the degree dimension of government, among the eight nations included in the Political Action study the demand for a policy to reduce economic inequalities was strongest in Italy and weakest in Switzerland. This pattern dovetails with the average income level (Figure 7.1). However, other pieces of evidence suggest that the critical factor is the level of inequality rather than general standards of living. In the Eurobarometer surveys of 1979–83, the demand for greater equality was seen to be slightly positively related to actual or objective inequality (Figure 7.2).

In a slightly different version, the same thesis holds with regard to economic management and nationalization, discussed in Chapter 9. People in societies at a high level of economic development are less inclined towards increasing the extent of state control of the economy than are people in societies at low levels of development. Although it is not too clear what people associate with economic management, and we have no way of documenting that economic regulation is stricter in rich countries than in poorer countries, at least it appears that with rising living standards, fewer people feel the need of further extending regulation.

We also investigated whether the second thesis holds for particular welfare items. Central to the welfare state is the citizen's security during illness, old age, and unemployment; these concerns everywhere seem to appeal to the public in this order of priority, as Table 8.4 showed. The same table showed the desire for expansion to be higher in Italy and Britain than in Germany, Norway, and Austria. Such a result fits with the fact that, objectively, these benefits and services are probably higher in the latter three than in the former two countries. But to some extent, at least, it also fits the marginal utility argument that as the level of economic development rises, the proportion of people who can take care of their own welfare—and are prepared to do so—increases. And above all, in contradiction to the demand spiral hypothesis, the pattern across the countries suggested that welfare demands are not insatiable.

In a wealthy society with high welfare standards, according to the marginal utility hypothesis, we expect to find declining support for further expansion of the welfare state. This does not imply, however, that cutting central welfare programmes is a popular policy. If governments attempt to curb the public sector during a period of recession, public protest against a deterioration in public health care and in care for the elderly can be strong. Perhaps this explains why support for expanding health services and old age pensions increased between 1985 and 1990 in Italy, Britain, and in Germany. In all three countries there has been vigorous debate about reducing welfare levels, suggesting that the marginal utility principle may not hold in reverse.

In line with the 'new politics' thesis, it might be thought that in the economically most advanced countries, in place of demands for further regulation and redistribution, demands for action to combat environmental pollution and to secure the free transmission of ideas would be particularly strong. However, Chapters 10 and 11 give the impression that other forces are much more decisive, making public opinion unstable and erratic once we move outside the well-trodden fields of economic policy. With regard to communications' policies, for example, the few comparative data available point in different directions. For example, British people are more prone than others to support the censorship of books, but also more prone to allow the publication of material which might damage the government (cf. Tables 10.2 and 10.3). As to environmental policies, attitudes favouring environmental protection are especially positive in Greece and Italy, where the objective need is probably also greatest, but they are especially negative in Britain and Ireland. In brief, on questions of social and economic policy, there is considerable cross-national consistency. But outside those well-established fields, consistent patterns are hard to find.

There are certain structural reasons why the level of economic development cannot be expected to stand out as a major factor in our data. In this volume we are dealing with countries which all belong to the upper fourth, even the upper fifth, of the countries of the world in terms of economic development. The limited variance of the economic factor alone means that we cannot expect to find the kind of systematic differences which one often finds in, say, a Unesco or Unicef report.

None the less, there are some striking differences among our countries in regard to beliefs about the scope of government. We suspect that some of these differences are more subtle north–south or Protestant–Catholic differences—which are difficult to capture in surveys—than outright economic ones. In addition, as we have witnessed, some cross-national differences are likely to be due to the different policies pursued by national governments, or isolated events affecting a single country.

Scope-of-Government Beliefs and Political Participation

Turning to the role of beliefs about government in influencing mass political behaviour, we attempt to draw conclusions with regard to two interrelated hypotheses. One is that, because of the expansion of the public sector, these beliefs have become increasingly important in partisan choice, giving rise to a high level of issue voting among West European publics during the last two decades. The other hypothesis is that such a high level of political strife regarding policy demands has led to a decline in general political support.

Many of the issue or policy areas subsumed under the scope of government have traditionally been subject to intense political conflict. They have largely constituted the backbone of the party system and its projection on the left–right axis since the advent of universal suffrage. We cannot expect other issues, of more recent origin, to have become fully expressed in the party systems as yet. Therefore, our findings on partisan differences and left–right differences have concentrated on the classic issues of economic security and equality, economic interventionism, and the size and power of the state in general.

Beginning with the latter, Table 4.9 showed that, on average, across eight issues voters for parties on the left assigned more responsibility to government than voters for parties of the right. The correlations (*r*) oscillated around 0.40 in Norway and Britain as against only 0.15–0.20 in Germany and Ireland, suggesting that the Anglo-Scandinavians tend to view the function of the state in a clear-cut left–right perspective unmitigated by Catholic Christian Democratic ideology. Corroboration of this interpretation comes from Table 7.5, which shows that reducing income difference is a particularly 'hot' issue in Finland, Britain, and the Netherlands, but much less so in Germany, Italy, Switzerland, and Austria. The correlations with party preference ranged between 0.25–0.35 in the former group of countries as against 0.04–0.16 in the latter group. The demand that the government provide a job for everybody yielded correlations with party choice which went in the same direction: the 1973–6 question elicited the highest correlation in Finland, and the 1987 question displayed particularly high correlations in Britain (0.42) and the Netherlands (0.35).

The security dimension of welfare—the provision of benefits, pensions, and health care services—also displayed clear partisan differences, as discussed in Chapter 8. Support for expanding old age pensions correlated with party choice particularly in Denmark, Sweden, and Britain (Table 8.11). With regard to expanding two other policy areas on the security dimension, namely health care and unemployment benefits, again Britain presents fairly high correlations between attitudes and partisan choice, whereas Germany shows lower correlations and Austria still lower ones again. Attitudes toward tax progressiveness are a third type of beliefs which are subject to intense partisan conflict, at least in the northern countries of Western Europe. Table 6.1 showed correlations with partisanship to be above 0.20 in Britain, Norway, and the Netherlands, around 0.20 in Germany, but much lower in Switzerland and Ireland.

When it comes to government intervention in the economy, we

noticed significant variation by party preference, although generally not of the same magnitude as on welfare issues. In the 1990 data, we found that in Britain 50 per cent of Labour voters but also 31 per cent of Conservative voters could be classified as interventionists; in Germany, 51 per cent of Social Democratic voters and 35 per cent of Christian Democratic/Christian Social voters were so classified (Table 9.9). When respondents were asked in the Eurobarometer surveys around 1980 whether they wanted more government management of the economy, party differences were much smaller. Indeed, in 1981, the partisan differences almost vanished in Britain under Mrs Thatcher's first government—which makes us suspect that the meaning of the term 'government management' is subject to different ideological interpretations. None the less, it is evident that beliefs about the scope of government in the economic field are of major consequence for partisan choice. Especially in Britain, Scandinavia, and the Netherlands they seem to provide much of the fuel for electoral competition. But we have no direct evidence that, in this respect, issue voting increased during the 1970s and 1980s.

The second hypothesis suggests that these issue conflicts have negative consequences for general political support. In particular, we expect voters who disagree strongly with government policy to exhibit low levels of political support. This was corroborated in Chapter 12 for Britain, Germany, and Italy, the countries for which adequate data could be retrieved. Within three different policy areas—matching the three issue agendas—perceived distance from government policy was shown to be positively related with voting for the opposition, with political distrust, and, in certain cases, related also with sympathy for protest behaviour. Of these policy areas, welfare policies appear to be the most important for the maintenance of political support; that is, voters demanding an expansion of welfare made up the bulk of the politically dissatisfied. As we have just seen, such voters are, logically enough, especially frequent in countries where the standards of welfare are comparatively low—for example, in Italy rather than Germany. Thus, if we consider a high level of trust in government as a 'benefit' from welfare politics, our finding on this point confirms the declining marginal utility of welfare policies. It is where welfare standards are low that the political benefit of expanding welfare is high.

Thus, what we find is that the micro-level relationship between perceived policy distance and relatively low political support does not translate into a similar relationship at the aggregate level. The

Scandinavian party systems display intense political conflict over issues about the scope of government but, at the same time, the citizens of Scandinavian countries are also among the most satisfied. This is probably because the conflict is balanced and the level of social equality relatively high. The danger of political overload and crises of legitimacy is greater in countries where the welfare programmes have been unable to keep pace with rising expectations.

Social Position and Beliefs about Government

In discussing the social origins of beliefs about the scope of government, we may again take our point of departure in the notion of the marginal utility of different types of government activity. The same hypothesis which predicts that the economically advanced nations will lose interest in redistribution and social equality would also predict that it is underprivileged groups, in particular, who need the economy to be protected by the state.

On many points such a prediction is borne out by our data. Table 4.9 showed that people with low education, low income, and working-class identification were much more likely than educated middle-class people to assign responsibility to the government. Again, Table 7.5 showed that workers are more likely than others to support equality policies and job guarantees. Especially in Britain and the Netherlands, these correlations were substantial. In line with this finding, people with relatively little education support redistribution policies in most countries. This is especially the case in Germany and the Benelux countries, but Britain and Ireland are exceptions to the rule (Table 7.7).

The fact that some redistribution already takes place through taxation means that attitudes towards the tax burden vary by income in less predictable ways. Three different hypotheses about this relationship were discussed in Chapter 6. The outcome was the simplest: people with low income support progressive taxation (Fig. 6.2).

That people characterized by low education and low income tend to support redistribution does not mean that they can be relied upon to support all types of social policies. Low income is generally associated with support for expanding old age pensions (Table 8.7), and also with support for more spending on health care and unemployment benefits (Tables 8.8–8.9). However, in the Scandinavian data for the

1970s, it was the better educated who wanted to expand social benefits (Table 8.5).

Compared with status variables, gender and age exert comparatively little impact on the beliefs we have studied. Regarding gender, women might be thought to have a particular interest in the state as a protector of physical safety and economic rights. In line with this expectation, Chapter 4 found that women typically assign more responsibility to government than men, at least in Germany, Britain, Italy, and Norway. However, the correlations are modest. In a few countries, women are significantly more supportive of old age provision than men. This is the case, especially, in Norway and to a lesser extent in Germany and Italy (Table 8.7). The findings are much the same for health care provision (Table 8.8); Italian women are exceptional in their support for unemployment benefits in 1990 (Table 8.9). With regard to state intervention in the economy, a more general finding is that women are more positive than men (Table 9.14), which seems natural considering that economic life is largely dominated by men. Finally, the domain where we expected the largest differences, namely environmental protection, shows few consistent findings. For example, women are more concerned than men about the environment, but men are more likely to demand strong state action to protect the environment (Chapter 11).

With regard to age or generational differences, too, our findings have disappointed us by being minor and erratic. In some countries, especially Italy, older people assign more responsibility to the state than younger people (Table 4.9). But on such an obvious issue as extending old age pensions it is by no means everywhere that we find older people to be more supportive than the young. This is the case in Britain and Italy (Table 8.7), but in Sweden the relationship is reversed (Table 8.5). When it comes to social benefits, the young certainly do not seem to have abandoned the welfare state; and in comparison with the middle-aged, the young also tend to be more supportive of economic management (Table 9.14).

Some of these findings about differences in beliefs about government as between the old, the middle-aged, and the young appear to fall in line with life-cycle explanations rather than generational explanations. In modern societies the young, along with the old, are dependent on the state because economic ties within the family have weakened. This situation pits them against, especially, employed middle-aged men who believe themselves to be less dependent on the state. Other findings fall in line with generational explanations, which pit the young against the old in a simple linear relationship. However, we have to admit that the two types of explanation cannot be separated in our data. This was the case, for example, with the finding that in a number of countries the young were less inclined toward censoring books than were the old (Table 10.8). Still other findings surprised us by the lack of any systematic relationship. For example, we found no relation between age and demands for state action against pollution of the environment (Chapter 11). Here we had expected that, as a 'new politics' theme, environmentalism would be carried by the younger generations.

Studying Scope-of-Government Beliefs

In view of the inadequacy of our data on many important points, one may well wonder whether beliefs about the scope of government is a worthwhile topic of study. It may be argued—and, in fact, was argued many times in the course of our project—that these beliefs, as we find them reflected in survey data, are neither valid nor reliable indicators of the role of citizens in politics. The tendency toward under-budgeting and the resistance to taxes noted in Chapters 4 and 5, question the utility of beliefs about government as instruments of political control.

However, even our fragmentary data sources reveal meaningful relationships between policy demands and several other variables. These relationships suggest two rather contradictory tendencies. Sometimes we can point to a positive correlation across countries between the actual size of the public sector and the expectations of citizens. It is hardly coincidental, for example, that the public share of health care expenditure is low in Switzerland and that the Swiss rank low in assigning responsibility for health care to their government. But sometimes an opposite tendency prevails: people seem to demand what they miss, their wants being affected not so much by the prevailing political arrangements as by objective criteria. The widespread demand for welfare in Italy or the widespread demand for action against pollution in Greece are cases in point.

A positive relationship between public demands and actual policy is in line with a 'political culture' view of national differences. The relationships we observe in the data are often the end result of a long process in which a number of forces have interacted. To illustrate, one can view the weakness of the welfare sector in Switzerland, compared most plausibly with Austria, as the result of the absence of a strong socialist movement in Switzerland compared with the influence of socialism in Austria after the Second World War. The differences between the two countries in regard to ideology and political organization, in turn, have a much longer prehistory. But the fact that, today, both societies exhibit a high level of political stability suggests that a mutual adaptation between demands and actual policy has taken place over time.

A negative relationship between policy demands and actual policy probably has a more complex underlying causality. It signals a distance between policy and public opinion which may be almost habitual, as seems to be the case in Italy. But the distance may also signal growing opposition and a warning to governments who are carrying their line of policy so far that the middle-of-the-road electorate can no longer follow or understand it. Thus, whereas a positive relationship limits a government's freedom of action, a negative relationship offers an opportunity for innovative policies, at least for one or two election periods.

There are many examples of policies being conducted, in the shorter run, against the will of the majority of voters. Many policies of Mrs Thatcher's Conservative governments were carried out without widespread support among the British electorate, although it might be argued that they were in accord with British public opinion during the period of the foregoing Labour government. Another example is offered in Chapter 14, which serves as a kind of epigram to this volume. That chapter pointedly argues that, even though health care is sacrosanct in the eyes of the public, this has not prevented health care expenditure from being tightly checked in advanced societies.

Which comes first, a change in policy or an increase in people's demands for that policy? To what extent are these demands translations of 'real' social problems rather than phantoms arising in the political process? Unfortunately these questions, so critical for our purpose, cannot be answered—neither in a general sense nor in any specific case. In our view, the process by which beliefs about the scope of government are formed depends to a large extent on the success—or the failure—of policies in solving social or national problems. But this view implies that, in a sense, policy demands are provisional in nature and cannot always be taken seriously by a party or a government which has set itself reformist goals. If the policy turns out to be successful, public opinion will often change towards consent.

On the one hand, policy demands are not to be considered autonomous phenomena but malleable by government and opposition parties as well as by the mass media. On the other hand, policy demands are clearly related to objective needs. What is needed is source material which allows us to study more closely the process by which beliefs about the scope of government are formed in different policy fields—both as reactions to social problems and values, and as reactions to actual policy measures. Here, the social choice approach makes assumptions which are overly rational. The public in general is not equipped to formulate policies or to compare political programmes. Rather, the public reacts against policies whose results it does not like, such as cutting health care or old age pensions, thereby creating political tension and instigating a search for alternatives. In such situations, the ensuing political debate seems, to a surprising degree, to become a matter of public concern. To only a minor extent are public reactions in such matters dictated by personal interests. Public choice theory is well aware of the dilemma that nobody has an interest in holding down the level of taxation whereas everybody has an interest in some particular form of state expenditure. None the less, the fact is that, during the 1980s, increasing taxation has become the surest way to political defeat in many countries, and the cost of a new bill has become the first question to be asked by political opponents.

For the most part, during the 1980s, West European governments overcame the crisis of economic growth and distribution which was rooted in the energy crises of the 1970s. However, at the same time, governments in Western Europe stand accused of a lack of solidarity with minorities and social losers (including, to some extent, the unemployed). According to social choice theory, these minorities should form special interest groups and exert pressure on their governments. According to the average taxpayer's logic, government investment in improving the conditions of the minorities is of no use. It is hard to say which argument is the more rational. But a third argument, equally rational, is that if the effects of government policies were transparently successful, support for welfare policies—to alleviate poverty or urban deprivation—would be widespread. In other words it is not rational assumptions but empirical study which clarifies the interplay of policy, popular beliefs, and social problems.

Finally, we need to study more closely the ways in which people express their policy beliefs. In the long run, beliefs about the scope of government must lead to certain kinds of political behaviour in order to have any impact on public policies. If they are the beliefs of spectators rather than participants, governments and parties will soon learn to disregard them. If they are the beliefs of active, democratic citizens, then we need to know more about the role of scope-of-government beliefs in the dynamics of party choice and the mobilization of political movements. In the final analysis, research into mass beliefs about the scope of government is justified by showing that these beliefs are of some consequence for the functioning of a democratic system.

14

Public Attitudes and Changes in Health Care Systems: A Confrontation and a Puzzle

ACHILLE ARDIGÓ

One of the traditional precepts of democracy is the importance of citizens grouped together as a 'public' to legitimate governments. The critical question here, of course, is what criteria define citizenship. With the growth of a bourgeois middle class, a broader—but nevertheless limited—concept of citizenship came to emphasize public opinion as a sphere in which private individuals become publicly important and in which, through political confrontation, such individuals can take part in rational public debate.

It is clear that the concepts of citizenship and public opinion are both subject to historical transformations. For example, Marshall (1964) speaks of a process of enlarging citizenship from civil and political rights to encompass the rights of social citizenship. In this process, public opinion depends on the freedom of speech, opinion, association, assembly, and—above all—of the press. Due to this process, however, public political discourse is no longer a matter of rational deliberation, but now operates—in the words of Habermas (1962: 337–8; my translation):

> through the internal channels of parties and associations . . . The parties and public associations, in their roles as large, bureaucratized organizations, hold an oligopoly of the organization of unions and associations which is effective in terms of publicity and which carries political weight . . . As a form of disintegration of the middle-class public sphere, it gives rise to a demonstra-

tive and manipulative form of publicity, developed by the organizations, over the heads of the public who are influenced by the mass-media.

From the early 1970s until the present time, in advanced Western democracies, there has been stagnation or even decline in the participation of citizens in political parties and trade unions while non-institutionalized involvement in social movements has increased. These developments reflect, not least, increasing individualization along with the fragmentation of communities and cultures, and they are sometimes interpreted as a corollary of a growing crisis of the modern European welfare state. Not only have governments become painfully aware of these trends, but they have also become aware of changes in the public mood, which is now regularly and competently assessed by modern techniques of public opinion research.

The point should be made, however, that although surveys are increasingly used to sound out public opinion, some social scientists have voiced criticism and dissent about the political uses of public opinion research. They argue that because of the complexity and selective self-referencing nature of decision-making, and the increasingly supranational character of economic and political linkages, the power of non-manipulated public opinion declines continually. In large part, this is because democratic control of the mass media, which in many instances have grown into multi-media corporate giants, has become quite difficult.

According to the élite theorists of yesterday and today—from Pareto, Mosca, and Michels to Schumpeter, Aron, Lasswell, and Wright Mills—the functioning of modern democracies is limited, at best, to the alternation of élites. For those contemporary social theorists who dwell on notions of self-sufficiency and the self-referencing nature of social systems, the political opinions of the *quidam de populo* are considered insufficient and incongruous when it comes to influencing effectively the process of government in complex societies. According to one recent interpretation, 'public opinion' in the era of surveys should be restricted to the producers and the influential consumers of information within the bounds of the political system; that is, according to Luhmann (1981), to the 'politically relevant public'.[1] Luhmann states that, in complex societies, societal modernization has replaced a hierarchical political system with a self-referential circulation of information within and between—and somewhat restrained by—certain subsystems. The 'relevant' public is an element within the political system.

Luhmann's thesis that the public (*Publikum*) constitutes part of the political subsystem only in so far as it is politically relevant, suggests that he believes part of the electorate to be mere environment—or background 'noise'—not only with respect to the political system at large, but even with respect to the limited segment of the *Publikum*. This is borne out in a number of passages in *Politische Theorie*, and in later studies. In *Politische Theorie*, Luhmann states that the self-referential *Publikum* lacks the objective and scientifically valid criteria of authentic politics. Consequently, he wonders whether the cues supplied by the *Publikum* are sufficient to manage all the problems of the human environment in a given society. It may be that the political system is in danger of working too selectively and remaining too tied to its own functional necessities.

In a book written together with de Giorgi eleven years later, Luhmann (1992) further expounds his thinking, arguing that public opinion is unable fully to penetrate reality by receiving and decoding messages from its human environment. With regard to the relationship between politics and its environment, the authors maintain that 'public opinion acts like a non-transparent mirror'; it just reflects the information communicated in large quantities by the political system itself. Thus, as Luhmann puts it: 'an immense redundancy is produced, and this makes it quite useless to do research into what individuals really know and think . . . Public opinion [in complex societies] is not, at this juncture, either the medium of a rational form of enlightenment or the invisible power that eighteenth-century thinkers believed would supersede traditional thinking . . . ' (Luhmann and De Giorgi 1992: 389–90). In their view, public opinion is not capable of constituting a systematic and complete link between the political system and the environment.

These ideas, which are part of a refined theoretical approach, reflect conclusions which had been arrived at earlier in some of the sociological literature. As far back as 1959, C. Wright Mills wrote (1959: 52):

> What were called 'publics' in the eighteenth and nineteenth century are being transformed into a society of 'masses'. Moreover, the structural relevance of publics is declining as men at large become 'mass men', each trapped in quite powerless milieux. In this school's (abstract empiricism) study of political life, 'voting behavior' has been the chief subject matter, chosen I suppose because it seems so readily amenable to statistical investigation. The thinness of the

results is matched only by the elaboration of the methods and the care employed.[2]

Three years later, Habermas (1962: 352–3; my translation) stated:

the material in surveys—opinions of any type of any group—does not qualify as public opinion . . . The reflection of group opinions defined by the criteria of an empirical investigation, concerning both the processes of government and administrative activity, and the formation of a political will influenced by publicity put forward in a manipulative or demonstrative fashion, cannot mend the rift between the pretence of public opinion in public law and the socio-psychological dissolution of the concept thereof . . .

Habermas believed that, in order to create effective public opinion for a democratic political system, it was necessary to mediate survey materials and, more generally, the expression of public opinion in the political system, with informal communicative contexts 'through a competent public activated during critical junctures of the parliamentary organizations'.

More recently, Giddens (1992: 681) has summarized similar critical reflections on the potential of surveys and their limits. The material gathered may be superficial; where a questionnaire is highly standardized, important differences between respondents' viewpoints may be glossed over; and responses may be what people profess to believe rather than what they actually believe. In our view, such critical thoughts on public opinion and its media, with its fundamental theoretical ramifications, at least deserve serious consideration.

In this chapter, we reflect on what citizens perceive to be the responsibilities of their governments and the way they assess the activities of government concerning the management of the welfare state, with particular reference to health services. First, we draw some conclusions from a secondary analysis of data from cross-national sample surveys which contain questions on the role of national governments in providing health services. Secondly, these findings will be related to data on recent variations in public health service expenditure. On account of the major revisions currently taking place in health services in all advanced Western nations, health services provide a particularly promising field for examining the problem of objective trends and subjective perceptions as mirrored in survey data.

The Survey Evidence

Reviewing the available comparative evidence on the relationship between government and health services, we pay attention especially to data from two surveys: the Political Action study (1973–6) and the 1985 ISSP study on the role of government. A second Political Action study was carried out in 1979–81, but this covered only three countries (the United States, Germany, and the Netherlands), so comparison over time is not possible for all eight of the original countries.[3] Other major comparative surveys, such as that conducted by Verba, Nie, and Kim (1978) which ran between 1966 and 1971, or the 1981 and 1990 European Values Surveys, do not contain specific items referring to health services. Also, unfortunately, very few items relevant to the topic under consideration can be found in the Eurobarometer surveys.

In the first Political Action study, the attitudes of citizens towards the role of government in dealing with selected issues were assessed along three dimensions: the importance of the issue; the perceived responsibility of the government for that issue; and how the issue has been managed by national governments. Altogether eleven issues were listed. The one item on the list which relates to health services is 'providing good medical care'. We examine how the scope of government in relation to health is assessed, and how government action and management are evaluated.

A first look at the data in Table 14.1 reveals that, according to respondents, 'providing good medical care' is the most important of the issues posed. Pooling the data for all eight countries, it was considered 'very important' by 83 per cent of respondents. Moreover, as Table 14.2 shows, 60 per cent of all respondents across the eight countries regarded 'providing good medical care' as 'an essential responsibility' of the government, thereby ranking medical care not much lower than 'fighting inflation' (72 per cent) and 'guaranteeing neighbourhoods safe from crime' (65 per cent). As to the question 'how well the government is handling these problems', Table 14.3 shows that respondents generally tended to evaluate government performances on 'providing medical care' very highly. Furthermore, looking at things from the other side, the negative answers ('very bad' and 'bad') add up to only 29 per cent—about one-third of those who were dissatisfied with the government's performance on combating inflation (83 per cent). These findings are the more remarkable since, in general, the issues posed in the survey score quite low percentages.

TABLE 14.1. *The importance of eleven issues*

	Very important	Important	Not very important	Absolutely unimportant
Good medical care	83	16	1	0
Fight rising prices	81	16	2	1
Jobs for everyone	80	18	2	1
Neighbourhoods safe	77	20	3	1
Good education	74	23	2	0
Old people	71	27	1	0
Fight pollution	68	27	4	1
Adequate housing	64	31	5	1
Men/women equal	37	41	18	4
Even out wealth	35	36	22	7
Ethnic minorities	26	44	23	8

Notes: Entries are percentages of the pooled sample. The item 'Fight rising prices' was not available in the surveys for Britain, the United States, and Switzerland. For the full text of the item, see Table 3.6.
Source: Political Action (1973–6).

TABLE 14.2. *Government responsibility for eleven issues*

	Essential	Important	Some	None
Fight rising prices	72	22	5	1
Neighbourhoods safe	65	26	8	1
Good medical care	60	31	8	1
Jobs for everyone	56	33	10	1
Good education	55	36	9	1
Fight pollution	54	34	11	1
Old people	50	41	9	1
Adequate housing	43	38	17	2
Even out wealth	29	35	25	12
Men/women equal	24	42	27	7
Ethnic minorities	23	41	29	6

Notes: See Table 14.1.

As a general trend, in the years during which the first Political Action survey was carried out—the period of the first severe economic crisis connected with rising oil prices during and just after the Yom Kippur war—consensus about government health policy seems to have remained quite strong. The results of the survey show no traces of the first anti-welfare and anti-tax reactions which emerged in the 1970s. However, only a few years later, there were strong reactions

TABLE 14.3. *How well government is handling these problems*

	Very good	Good	Bad	Very bad
Good medical care	15	56	23	6
Good education	15	58	22	5
Jobs for everyone	12	47	33	9
Ethnic minorities	9	53	31	8
Old people	9	51	33	7
Neighbourhoods safe	8	40	36	16
Men/women equal	7	55	33	6
Adequate housing	6	43	39	12
Fight pollution	5	38	43	14
Even out wealth	4	34	42	19
Fight rising prices	2	15	45	38

Notes: See Table 14.1.

of this kind in California, where Proposition 13 was approved, and in Denmark, with the electoral surge in favour of Glistrup's anti-tax party which campaigned on issues of welfare cuts.

Despite the consensus, it is possible to observe in Table 14.4 some differences in the responses to the Political Action item when the data are disaggregated by country. The general trend was towards a high degree of responsibility being attributed to government for 'providing good medical care'. But significant differences emerge when comparing countries with a strong public health system and countries with a largely private health system. We should note, in particular, that Italy (at the time ruled by a centre–left government) and Britain (the homeland of a national health service) show the highest levels of consensus in attributing to government 'an essential responsibility' for health matters. Clearly, people in Italy and Britain were largely agreed in expecting their government to assume primary responsibility for providing good medical care. By contrast, the least favourable scores for government involvement in health care were registered in the United States and Switzerland.

However, a very large difference between Italian and British respondents can be detected when government performance in health care is considered. As we can see from Table 14.5, Italy and Britain are, in effect, at opposite poles when the government's handling of medical care is evaluated. Italian respondents were very dissatisfied with their government's performance, while the British accorded their government the highest proportion of 'very good' and 'good' evaluations, followed by respondents from the Netherlands, Germany, and Austria.

The Political Action study combined responses to all three questions—about importance, responsibility, and performance—into an index of 'policy dissatisfaction'. We find that the index scores for dissatisfaction with health policies varies very much from one country to the next (data not shown here). Italy is once again located on the most negative pole, followed at a distance by the Americans. Whereas 49 per cent of Italians said they were highly dissatisfied, this is true for only 20 per cent of the Americans, 17 per cent of the Finnish, and 16 per cent of the Swiss. In Germany, Austria, Britain, and the Netherlands, this proportion ranges around 10 per cent. In all, more than half the

TABLE 14.4. *Assignment of responsibility to government for providing good medical care*

	Essential	Important	Some	No
Italy	79	16	4	1
Britain	74	21	5	0
Germany	63	32	6	0
Austria	62	32	6	0
Netherlands	55	38	6	1
Finland	55	40	5	0
Switzerland	48	38	13	1
United States	42	36	20	3

Notes: Entries are percentages. For the full text of the item, see Table 3.6.

Source: Political Action (1973–6).

TABLE 14.5. *Evaluations of government's handling of medical care*

	Very badly	Well and very well	Other
Italy	23	38	39
United States	10	61	29
Finland	4	71	25
Switzerland	4	72	24
Austria	2	79	19
Germany	3	81	16
Netherlands	2	84	14
Britain	3	85	12

Note: Entries are percentages of national samples.

Source: Political Action (1973–6).

respondents from Britain, Austria, and Germany expressed very little political dissatisfaction in the field of health care.

We turn now to the 1985 ISSP cross-national survey on the role of government. Five countries in this survey were included in the first Political Action survey (Germany, Britain, Austria, Italy, and the United States). The sixth country is Australia. One interesting opportunity for analysis stems from the distinction between ideological orientations and practical—that is, financial—considerations with respect to health care regimes. Here we can bring together a question about the government's responsiblity for care of the sick and a question asking respondents whether they agree or disagree with specific items of public expenditure which include expenditure on health.

In this instance, respondents were asked: 'On the whole, do you think it should be or should not be the government's responsibility to . . .', with seven different items being proposed. As Figure 14.1 reveals, even a decade after the Political Action study, the ISSP data for six countries show the extent to which people still attribute high responsibility to governments for providing health care. Next to 'providing health care for the sick', the item 'providing a decent standard of living for the old' takes the second position among the seven items; both items also have

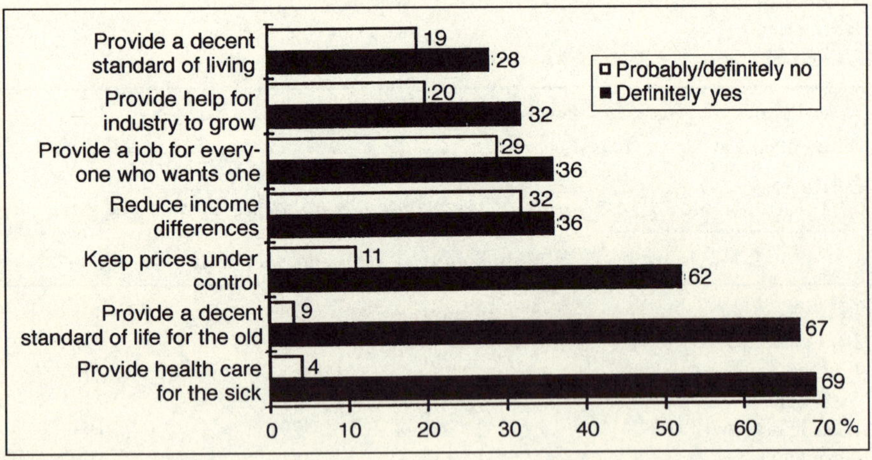

FIGURE 14.1. *Attitudes towards government responsibility for seven policy issues*

Note: Based on the question: 'On the whole, do you think it should or should not be the government's responsibility to . . . ?'

Source: ISSP (1985).

the lowest proportion of negative responses ('probably should not be' and 'definitely should not be').

Those responses which refer only to the health care item are highlighted for six countries in Figure 14.2. These figures reveal the degree of polarization between the supportive and negative answers to this item. They point to the very different position in the United States when it comes to the provision of health care.

A further item for evaluating beliefs about the organization of health care was introduced in the 1985 ISSP survey with a question about whether respondents would like to see more or less government spending in certain policy areas. It is interesting to recall that, by adding the comment 'remember that if you say "much more" it might require a tax increase to pay for it', the question explicitly referred to the link between public expenditure and taxes. Once again, among seven areas of government spending, it was public health care which received by far the most backing for increased spending, notwithstanding the note of caution about tax increases being required to pay for it. In all, 69 per cent of the pooled sample agreed that there should be more or much more spending on health; only 5 per cent said there should be less. By selecting the very positive response category ('spend much more') and summing the 'spend less' and 'spend much less' responses, shown in

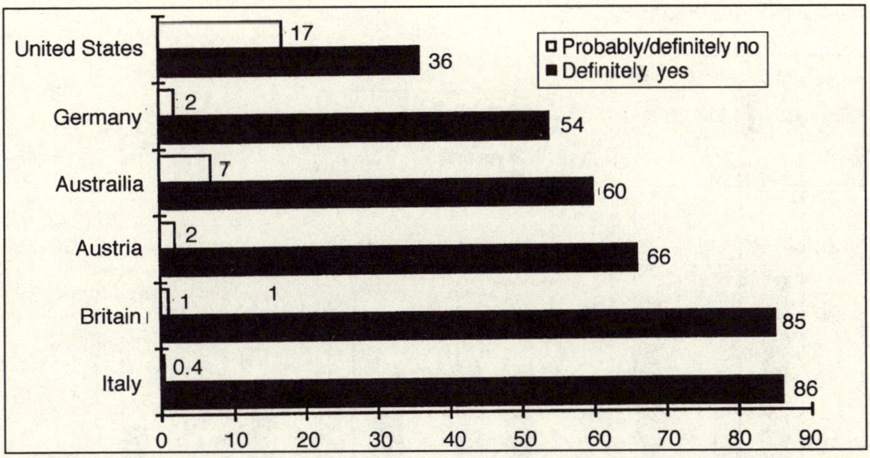

FIGURE 14.2. *Attitudes towards government responsibility for providing health care for the ill*

Note: Based on the question: 'On the whole, do you think it should or should not be the government's responsibility to . . . provide health care for the sick?'

Source: ISSP (1985).

Figure 14.3, we can fully appreciate the prominent role of the demand for more public expenditure on health services—especially when compared with six other fields of welfare spending.

There are national differences in these matters, as would be expected. The general agreement on more public health expenditure—ranging

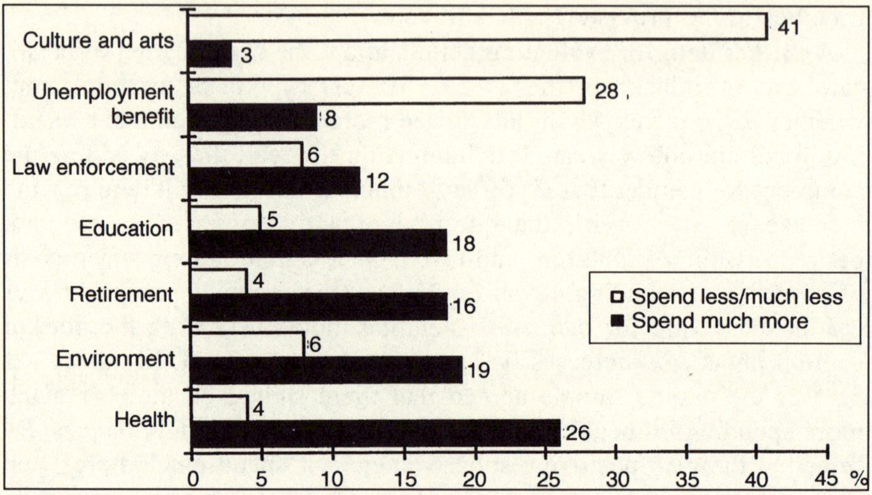

FIGURE 14.3. *Attitudes towards government spending in seven policy areas*
Source: ISSP (1985).

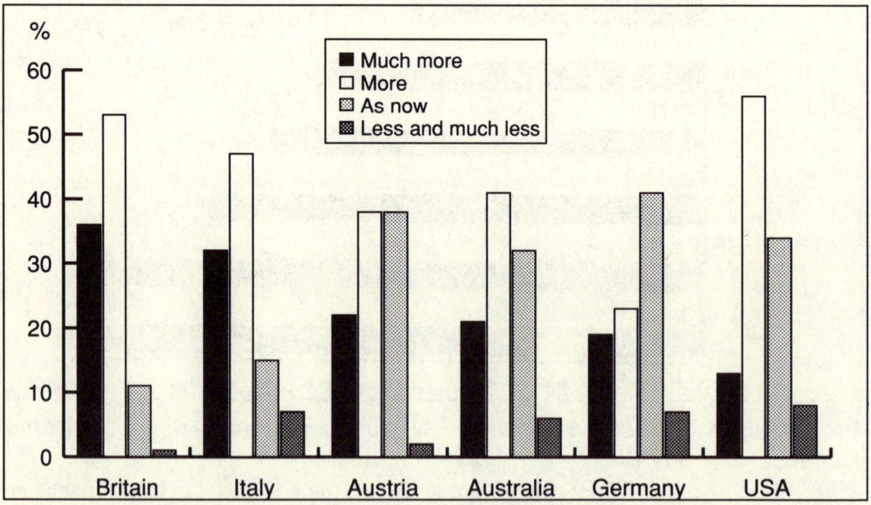

FIGURE 14.4. *Attitudes towards government spending on health*

from 52 per cent in Germany to 88 per cent in Britain—seems to hide a variety of different realities. In Figure 14.4, we show that the United States and Germany are both at the low end of the spectrum; these two countries have completely different traditions in public support for the health system. At the high end of the spectrum, we find Britain and Italy once again, while Austria and Australia occupy middle positions.

It seems plausible to argue that those respondents who favour more health expenditure are also the ones least satisfied with the health system in their country. A sort of polarization can be observed in Germany and the United States between those in favour of further health expenditure and those who want to keep spending levels low or to see them go even lower. It may well be that such a polarization is related more to the high degree of satisfaction with their health services among Germans[4] than to ideological opposition to government responsibility for health care, a point which is probably more relevant to the United States.

Given the nature of the Political Action and the ISSP surveys, a systematic comparison between them is difficult, despite similarities in the choice of items, methods, and countries. In particular, the way in which the health care issue is defined is slightly different.[5] Nevertheless, we can draw some general conclusions.

Both surveys clearly show how important health policies are for people and the extent to which governments are generally expected to take responsibility for health care. Thus the demand for government health services, from the point of view of the public, seems to constitute a strong and permanent feature of the modern democratic welfare state. The proportion of respondents in the 1985 ISSP data who would accept further taxation provided that health expenditure increased can be assumed to indicate that institutionalized policies in this sector rest on an even larger consensus than is generally supposed (cf. Alber 1988: 181–207).

It also appears from both surveys that such consensus has persisted, and even increased, over the period 1973–85. Notwithstanding the possible—even quite likely—effects of a backlash starting with the 1973–4 economic crisis, health matters seem to remain above debate as a responsibility of the government in welfare states. If anything, ten years after the first Political Action survey, an even stronger legitimation of the welfare state in the field of health services may be detected.

Continuity and Change in Health Systems

In this section we confront the survey data with some 'hard' evidence from government spending statistics and reflect on the outcome of this comparison. The picture obtained from the surveys showed such continuity that we have to ask ourselves how this squares with the macroscopic evidence of a significant change in health policy programmes in major developed Western countries over the 1973–85 period. For this reason, it seems appropriate to return to the question asked at the outset: Can socio-political surveys be considered effective instruments for exercising 'a critical role' in the interaction between the state and civil society?

The answer to this question turns out to be inconclusive. We begin with the observation that, at least *ex post*, such data contribute to our understanding of why most existing health provision has been maintained and why public expenditure on health has increased. This is even true for the United States and Britain, despite the fact that, in the period covered by the two surveys, radical changes took place in these countries—as they did elsewhere. This is evidenced in the emergence of new political philosophies and changes in public opinion, which started to oppose the social democratic and social Christian welfare state models. However, before looking at the data on public health expenditure, we should give some thought to the influences underlying cross-national differences.

It also seems plausible to recognize that socio-economic structural variables have some influence on the distribution of political attitudes in the various countries. However, recalling the persistent differences between the Americans, the Swiss and—although on a different measure—the Germans, on the one hand, and the citizens of the other Western countries included in the surveys, on the other, some empirical generalizations can be attempted. In societies which have reached high levels of economic and civil development, any increase in the gross national income is accompanied by a more than proportionate increase in both public and private per capita spending on health. The growth of private expenditure which is taking place within highly developed welfare states is due to the increased interest of individuals in their own health status. In other words, their attitudes towards health care are not governed simply by their interest in the level of taxation.

Data from the two surveys are also useful in understanding why in the United States, notwithstanding some dissatisfaction with belated and very partial health schemes, there were no reforms to the major injustices and paradoxes of the health system even at the end of the 1980s. The American health system, although characterized by a certain medical excellence and with the highest health expenditure in the world, does not provide any health protection—public or private—for some 35–37 million American citizens.[6] There was simply not enough public pressure to change this situation so long as the opposition of the majority of Americans—as evidenced among respondents in the surveys—to public responsibility in health care remained intact. This survey is a clear example of a situation where attitudes reflect the dominant national culture and the interests of policy makers, but not the interests of sizeable disadvantaged minorities.

Still, one has to wonder why the national samples we have looked at do not show any change over time, either regarding people's conception of health welfare or the growing budgetary crisis over its provision. Where are the traces in the public mind of either the anti-tax revolts or the ideological and financial turnarounds which took place in many Western states during the later 1970s and the 1980s? After all, it was these macro-level changes which led towards the privatization of health services and towards a new mix of health management, coupling public and private resources. And there is not even the slightest reflection in the survey data of tendencies towards the improvement of public health care through innovations emphasizing the responsible participation of health clients rather than direct management by a centralized welfare state.

We now come to look at those other data which enable us to appreciate the extent of such changes in the policies and practices in health systems during the period under consideration. Thus, we present some figures on the evolution of public health expenditure and the variation of such expenditures. Particularly interesting are comparisons of health expenditures as a proportion of national wealth (measured by GNP) and total national expenditure (public and private) on health during the years when the two surveys took place. Subsequently, changing trends in the overall health care complex will be addressed in more qualitative terms.

An essential reference in dealing with the health care responsibilities of governments are the statistics on public health expenditure. In Table 14.6 we show the variations in effective public expenditure for health as a percentage of GNP in the countries under consideration, calculated from OECD statistics.

TABLE 14.6. *Public health expenditures as a percentage of GNP, 1973–85*

	1973	1974	1975	1985
Australia	2.92	3.02	3.62	5.05
Austria	3.54	3.71	5.11	6.18
Italy	5.23	5.25	5.24	5.41
Finland	4.45	4.48	4.99	5.65
Netherlands	5.13	5.40	5.90	6.28
Switzerland	3.83	4.11	4.83	5.24
Britain	4.10	4.71	4.97	5.20
United States	2.93	3.23	3.56	4.42
Germany	5.14	5.68	6.28	6.37

Source: OECD (1990: table 6).

Even at a first glance, a comparison of the first and fourth columns shows the extent to which public expenditure on health has continued to grow as a proportion of GNP in each country. But how do these data square with attitudes towards health care as assessed in the two surveys discussed above?

No relevant differences emerged over time among the national samples in the two surveys. By contrast, the public expenditure figures show a trend towards growing public commitment—at least, financial commitment—to health, as a proportion of GNP, precisely in those countries in which, at the beginning of the period, public expenditure on health was lower and respondents were more resistant to attributing responsibility in the field to the government. As we can see in Figure 14.5, this is the case in Austria, Australia, the United States, and Switzerland.

However, no clear trend towards an increase in public expenditure on health, calculated as a percentage of total health expenditure—public and private—can be detected from 1973–5 (when the first survey was conducted) through to 1985. Rather, changes in public expenditure as a proportion of total national expenditures on health, shown in Table 14.7, reveal considerable heterogeneity.

In four countries—Italy, the United States, Britain, and Germany—over the period in question, the public share of total health expenditure declined somewhat. In the other four countries, expenditure increased, markedly so in Austria and Australia. It is especially worth noting that, over the period, health expenditure in the United States—as a proportion of GNP—continued to grow. This implies that this growth disproportionately took place in private health expenditure.

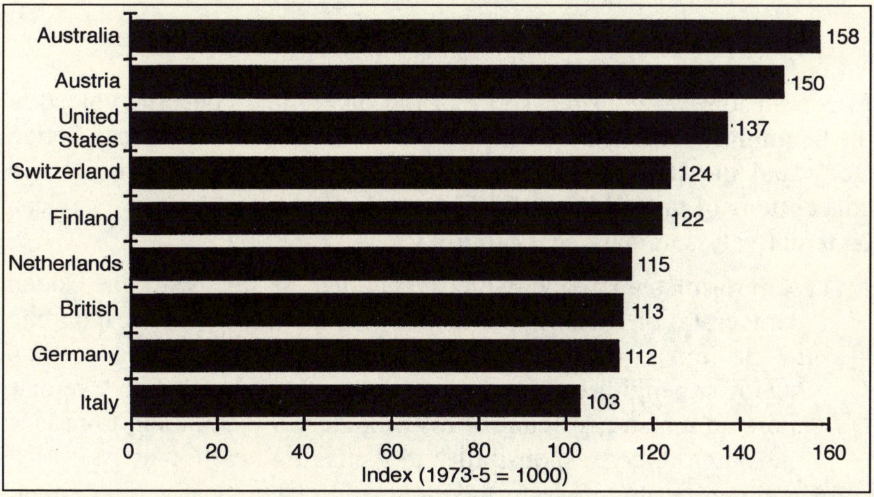

FIGURE 14.5. *Growth of public health expenditure as a percentage of GNP, 1973–5 to 1985*

Source: OECD (1990).

TABLE 14.7. *Public health expenditure as a proportion of total health expenditure, 1973–5 and 1985*

	Average 1973–5	1985
Italy	87	79
United States	41	38
Britain	90	87
Germany	79	78
Netherlands	75	76
Finland	78	79
Switzerland	67	68
Austria	67	76
Australia	61	72

Note: Entries are percentages of GNP.

Source: OECD (1990: table 2).

Conclusions

In conclusion, we consider some of the theoretical concerns voiced at the beginning of the chapter. In the decade between the Political Action study and the ISSP survey, at least three different lines emerged in conceptions of the public and the societal role of health care. They can be tentatively summarized as follows:

(1) A reformist approach which remained in line with the social democratic or social Christian models of welfare, but responding to the impact of increasing public expenditure deficits on total health expenditure. Here, governments have tended to exercise more administrative control over the health system and to reduce their own direct responsibility in managing health matters.

(2) A line opposing the reformist approach, centred on the privatization and deregulation of health care, and aiming to achieve an overall reduction in public—or government—responsibility for managing health systems. According to this approach, a new role for the public is proposed as a way of controlling public expenditure on health care.

(3) A third, and still doubtlessly a minority line, questions both the prevailing bureaucratic model and the market model. Instead, this approach looks to new forms of public health centred on the customers' involvement. This approach stresses the subjective and intersubjective change in people's life-styles, especially consumption styles, in the context of collective living conditions which reflect environmental pollution and artificial health risks.

Another influence on this last line of thought is a growing awareness of the changes taking place in the current study of diseases. This is particularly true with respect to rolling back beliefs in the general responsibility of governments for health care. For example, it is suggested that governments should be responsible only for urgent care, and promoting greater individual interest in, and collective responsibility for, prevention. Such an approach can already be seen in tackling AIDS, coronary diseases, brain and breast cancer, drug and alcohol dependency, diseases deriving from smoking, domestic and road accidents, the consequences of inadequate nutrition, and the health problems arising from poverty and pollution (Baggot 1991: 191–213; Ardigó 1994).

Thus, what we have to ask is: why did the two surveys not reflect those discontinuities in the interaction between governments and public opinion which already, at least tentatively, existed in the years when the surveys were carried out? One plausible hypothesis is that the deficiency reflects the rationale of the survey questions: in both surveys, the questions were thought of, primarily, within the context of the reformist line of reasoning. In all fairness, it must be added that neither study was designed to examine the complexities of the health-care field. In this sense, the purpose of the original questions does not entirely fit with our analytic interest. This situation is typical in secondary analysis and has impinged on quite a few of the topics covered by the Beliefs in Government project.

In the two studies referred to in this chapter, questions about health emphasized 'providing good health care' and 'providing health care for the sick'. People had no opportunity of expressing their views about different forms of public health, especially health-care arrangements which are more sensitive to personal and interpersonal responsibility, to preventive care, or to ecological risks. We can speculate that the building of beliefs in the new systems of health care did, indeed, move along the lines we have indicated, both in questioning the classic welfare and market models, and in addressing the different mix of the two—and also in confronting the hegemony of the medical professions. Since the data do not contradict these propositions we may continue to put them forward even though the surveys carried out in 1985 did not positively detect such trends.

Given the shortcomings in the data we have reviewed, the basic question raised at the outset remains unanswered: is survey research by its very nature incapable of discovering such trends? Thus, is survey research really a useful tool in building an educated public opinion? In other words, would surveys have detected the early signs of these trends if an adequate conceptual underpinning and good operationalization of this issue had been been available? On the current evidence, this has to remain an open question.

NOTES

1. In *Politische Theorie im Wohlfahrtstaat*, Luhmann (1981: ch. 6), states that a transformation of the political system has taken place in complex societies from stratification to a three-dimensional circularity (*selbst Reflexivität*). Politics (political parties) and the 'politically relevant public' are said to be continuously interacting in

a circular way. This sub-system is said to enter 'all political operations, acquiring a co-determinant importance'.

2. C. Wright Mills was criticizing the well-known study by Lazarsfeld, Berelson, and Gaudet (1948), *The People's Choice*.
3. A further problem is that the completion rate is markedly lower than in the earlier survey.
4. See Confalonieri (1989: 102 ff.). Confalonieri shows that, when the 1985 ISSP survey was carried out, 82 per cent of German respondents were highly satisfied with their health services.
5. In the Political Action study, the issue is 'providing good medical care', whereas in ISSP (1985) the wording is 'providing health care for the sick'. Thus there is a different emphasis on the quality of health care provided, and limiting health care to the sick implies—at least logically—excluding public health care for everybody; for instance, individual and collective prevention or health education.
6. A recent OECD publication observes that the United States 'devotes to health care almost 12 per cent, soon 15 per cent, of their GDP, but still the 17.5 per cent of the population under the age of 65 has no public or private health care coverage . . . ' (Enthoven 1990: 63).

REFERENCES

Abramson, P. R. (1983). *Political Attitudes in America: Formation and Change*. San Francisco: W. H. Freeman.

Alber, J. (1982). 'Some Causes and Consequences of Social Security Expenditure Development in Western Europe'. EUI, Working Paper No. 15, Florence.

——— (1984). 'Versorgungsklassen im Wohlfahrtsstaat: Überlegungen und Daten zur Situation in der Bundesrepublik'. *Kölner Zeitschrift für Soziologie und Sozialpsychologie* 36: 225–51.

——— (1988). 'Is There a Crisis of the Welfare State? Cross-National Evidence from Europe, North America and Japan'. *European Sociological Review* 4: 181–207.

Almond, G. A. (1980). 'The Intellectual History of the Civic Culture Concept'. In *The Civic Culture Revisited*, ed. G. A. Almond and S. Verba. Boston: Little, Brown.

——— and Powell, G. B. Jr (1980). *Comparative Politics Today: A World View*. Boston: Little, Brown.

——— and Verba, S. (1963). *The Civic Culture: Political Attitudes and Democracy in Five Nations*. Princeton, NJ: Princeton University Press.

———, Powell, G. B. Jr, *et al.* (1978 2nd edn.) (1960 1st edn.). *Comparative Politics: System, Process, and Policy*. Boston: Little, Brown.

Alt, J. E. (1983). 'The Evolution of Tax Structures'. *Public Choice* 41: 181–222.

Alwin, D. F. *et al.* (1990). *Attitudes to Inequality and the Role of Government*. International Social Survey Programme. Rijswijk: Sociaal en Cultureel Planbureau.

Andersen, J. G. (1982). 'Den folkelige tilslutning til velfœrdsstaten'. In *Partier, ideologier, väljare*, ed. D. Anckar, E. Damgaard, and H. Valen. Åbo: Åbo Akademi.

——— (1990). 'Environmentalism, New Politics, and Industrialism: Some Theoretical Perspectives'. *Scandinavian Political Studies* 13: 101–18.

Ardant, G. (1975). 'Financial Policy and Economic Infrastructure of Modern States and Nations'. In *The Formation of National States in Western Europe*, ed. C. Tilly. Princeton, NJ: Princeton University Press.

Ardigó, A. (1994). 'Per una sociologia della salute'. In *L'arco di Giano*, iv, *Salute e diritto alla salute nella società in trasformazione* 4: 111–25.

Ashford, S., and Timms, N. (1992). *What Europe Thinks: A Study of Western European Values*. Aldershot: Dartmouth.

Baggot, R. (1991). 'Looking Forward to the Past? The Politics of Public Health'. *Journal of Social Policy* 20: 191–213.

Baker, K. L., Dalton, R. J., and Hildebrandt, K. (1981). *Germany Transformed: Political Culture and the New Politics*. Cambridge, Mass.: Harvard University Press.

Barnes, S. H., Kaase, M., *et al.* (1979). *Political Action: Mass Participation in Five Western Democracies*. Beverly Hills, Calif.: Sage.

Bartolini, S., and Mair, P. (1990). *Identity, Competition, and Electoral Availability: The Stabilization of European Electorates 1885–1985*. Cambridge: Cambridge University Press.

Beck, U. (1992). *Risk Society: Towards a New Modernity*. London: Sage.

Bell, D. (1973). *The Coming of Postindustrial Society: A Venture in Social Forecasting*. New York: Basic Books.

——— (1976) (1979 2nd edn.). *The Cultural Contradictions of Capitalism*. New York: Basic Books.

Bennulf, M., and Holmberg, S. (1990). 'The Green Breakthrough in Sweden'. *Scandinavian Political Studies* 13: 165–84.

Bernard, J. (1981). *The Female World*. New York: Free Press.

Birch, A. H. (1984). 'Overload, Ungovernability and Delegitimation: The Theories and the British Case'. *British Journal of Political Science* 14: 135–60.

Bosanquet, N. (1983). *After the New Right*. London: Heinemann.

Bourdieu, P. (1977). 'Question de politique'. *Actes de la recherches en science sociales* 16: 55–89.

——— (1980). *Le sens pratique*. Paris: Les Editions du Minuit.

Bowles, S., and Gintis, H. (1982). 'The Crisis of Liberal Democratic Capitalism: The Case of the US'. *Politics and Society* 11: 51–93.

Brittan, S. (1975). 'The Economic Contradictions of Democracy'. *British Journal of Political Science* 5: 129–59.

Brown, L. R. (1992). 'Launching the Environmental Revolution'. In *State of the World*, ed. L. R. Brown. London: Earthscan.

Budge, I., and Hofferbert, R. (1990). 'Mandates and Policy Outputs: US Party Platforms and Federal Expenditures'. *American Political Science Review* 84: 111–31.

Bulpitt, J. (1986). 'The Discipline of the New Democracy: Mrs Thatcher's Domestic Statecraft'. *Political Studies* 34: 19–39.

Butler, D., and Stokes, D. (1969) (1974 2nd edn.). *Political Change in Britain: The Evolution of Electoral Choice*. London: Macmillan.

Cameron, D. (1978). 'The Expansion of the Public Economy: A Comparative Analysis'. *American Political Science Review* 72: 1243–61.

Campbell, A., Converse, P. E., Miller, W. E., and Stokes, D. E. (1960). *The American Voter*. New York: John Wiley.

Campbell, A., Converse, P. E., Miller, W. E., and Stokes, D. E. (1966). *Elections and the Political Order*. New York: John Wiley.

——— ——— and Rodgers, W. L. (1976). *The Quality of American Life: Perceptions, Evaluations, and Satisfactions*. New York: Russell Sage Foundation.

Castles, F. G. (1978). *The Social Democratic Image of Society*. London: Routledge and Kegan Paul.

——— (ed.) (1982). *The Impact of Parties: Politics and Policies in Democratic Capitalist States*. London: Sage.

Centro de Investigaciones Sociologicas (CIS) (1988). *Politica Fiscal, Gasto Publico e Impuestos*. Madrid: Centro de Investigaciones Sociologicas.

Citrin, J. (1974). 'Comment: The Political Relevance of Trust in Government'. *American Political Science Review* 68: 973–88.

——— (1979). 'Do People Want Something for Nothing? Public Opinion on Taxes and Government Spending'. *National Tax Journal*, 32, Supplement: 113–19.

Clark, T. N., and Ferguson, L. (1983). *City Money*. New York: Columbia University Press.

Commission of the European Communities (1984). *Television without Frontiers*. COM (84) 300, 14/6/1984, Brussels.

Confalonieri, M. A. (1989). 'La giustizia distributiva e il Welfare State'. In *Governo e cittadini*. Milan: Angeli.

Converse, P. E. (1964). 'The Nature of Belief Systems in Mass Publics'. In *Ideology and Discontent*, ed. D. Apter. New York: Free Press.

Coughlin, R. M. (1980). *Ideology, Public Opinion and Welfare Policy*. Berkeley, Calif.: Institute of International Studies, University of California.

Crewe, I. M. (1988). 'Has the Electorate become Thatcherite?' In *Thatcherism*, ed. R. Skidelsky. Oxford: Basil Blackwell.

Crozier, M. J., Huntington, S. P., and Watanuki, J. (1975). *The Crisis of Democracy: Report on the Governability of Democracies to the Trilateral Commission*. New York: New York University Press.

Dalton, R. J. (1986). 'Wertewandel oder Wertewende. Die neue Politik und Parteienpolarisierung'. In *Wahlen und politischer Prozeß: Analysen aus Anlaß der Bundestagswahl 1983*, ed. H.-D. Klingemann and M. Kaase. Opladen: Westdeutscher Verlag.

Davis, J. A. (1986). 'British and American Attitudes: Similarities and Contrasts'. In *British Social Attitudes: The 1986 Report*, ed. R. Jowell, S. Witherspoon, and L. Brook. Aldershot: Gower.

Debbasch, C. (1989). *Les Privatisations en Europe*. Paris: Editions du CNRS.

Deitch, C. (1988). 'Sex Differences in Support for Government Spending'. In *The Politics of the Gender Gap*, ed. C. M. Mueller. London: Sage.

Dennis, J. (1973). *Socialization to Politics: A Reader*. New York: John Wiley.

Douglas, J. (1976). 'Review Article: The Overloaded Crown'. *British Journal of Political Science* 6: 483–505.

Douglas, M., and Wildavsky, A. (1982). *Risk and Culture: An Essay on the Selection of Technological and Environmental Dangers*. Berkeley, Calif.: University of California Press.

Downs, A. (1959). 'Why the Government Budget is Too Small in a Democracy'. *World Politics* 12: 541–63.

——— (1972). 'Up and Down with Ecology: The Issue-Attention Cycle'. *Public Interest* 28: 38–50.

Dunlap, R. E. (1989). 'Public Opinion and Environmental Policy'. In *Environmental Politics and Policy*, ed. J. P. Lester. Durham, NC: Duke University Press.

Dunleavy, P. (1980). 'The Political Implications of Sectoral Cleavages and the Growth of State Employment'. *Political Studies* 38: 364–83 and 527–49.

——— (1989). 'The End of Class Politics?' In *Politics in Transition*, ed. A. Cochrane and J. Anderson. London: Sage.

——— and Husbands, C. (1985). *British Democracy at the Crossroad*. London: Allen and Unwin.

Easton, D. (1965*a*) (1979 2nd edn.). *A Framework for Political Analysis*. Chicago: Chicago University Press.

——— (1965*b*). *A Systems Analysis of Political Life*. New York: John Wiley.

——— (1975). 'A Re-Assessment of the Concept of Political Support'. *British Journal of Political Science* 5: 435–57.

——— and Dennis, J. (1967). 'The Child's Aquisition of Regime Norms: Political Efficacy'. *American Political Science Review* 56: 25–38.

Eckerberg, K. (1990). *Environmental Protection in Swedish Forestry*. Aldershot: Gower.

Edgell, S., and Duke, V. (1982). 'Reactions to Public Expenditure Cuts: Occupational Class and Party Realignment'. *Sociology* 16: 431–9.

——— ——— (1984). 'Public Expenditure Cuts in Britain and Consumption Sectoral Cleavages'. *International Journal of Urban and Regional Research* 8: 177–201.

——— ——— (1991). *A Measure of Thatcherism*. London: Harper Collins.

Eduards, M. L., Gustafsson, G., and Jónasdóttir, A. (1989). 'Könsmakt och maktlöshet i nationalstaten'. In *Kvinnors makt och inflytande*. Report No. 15. Stockholm: JÄMFO.

Eichenberg, R. C., and Stoll, R. (1990). 'Straightjacket: Public Support for Defense Spending in Four Western Democracies, 1960–1988'. FIB Papers. Wissenschaftszentrum Berlin für Sozialforschung. Mimeo.

Eichenberger, K. (1977). 'Der geforderte Staat: Zur Problematik der Staatsaufgaben'. In *Regierbarkeit. Studien zu ihrer Problematisierung*, i, ed. I. Band, W. Hennis, P. G. Kielmansegg, and U. Matz. Stuttgart: Ernst Klett.

Elazar, D. (1970). *Cities of the Prairie*. New York: Basic Books.

Elklit, J., and Tonsgaard, O. (eds.) (1984). *Valg og välgeradfærd*. Aarhus: Forlaget Politica.

——— ——— (eds.) (1989). *To folketingsvalg*. Aarhus: Forlaget Politica.

Enthoven, A. C. (1990). 'Que peuvent apprendre les Européens des Americains?' In *Les systemes de santé: A la recherche de l'efficacité*. Paris: OECD.

Esping-Andersen, G. (1980). *Social Class, Social Democracy and State Policy*. Copenhagen: New Social Science Monographs.

——— (1985). *Politics Against Markets*. Princeton, NJ: Princeton University Press.

——— (1990). *The Three Worlds of Welfare Capitalism*. Cambridge: Polity Press.

Euromedia Research Group (1992). *The Media in Western Europe*. London: Sage.

Farah, B. G., Barnes, S. H., and Heunks, F. (1979). 'Political Dissatisfaction'. In *Political Action: Mass Participation in Five Western Democracies*, ed. S. H. Barnes, M. Kaase, *et al*. Beverly Hills, Calif.: Sage.

Feinberg, J. (1973). *Social Philosophy*. Englewood Cliffs, NJ: Prentice-Hall.

Ferrera, M. (1986). *Cittadini e Fisco in Italia: Le Indicazioni di un Sondaggio*. Milan: Universita L. Bocconi.

Fietkau, H. J., Kessel, H., and Tischler, W. (1982). *Umwelt im Spiegel der öffentlichen Meinung*. Frankfurt: Campus.

Flanagan, S. C. (1987). 'Value Change in Industrial Societies'. *American Political Science Review* 81: 1303–19.

Flora, P. (ed.) (1986*a*). *Growth to Limits: The Western European Welfare States since World War II*, i. Berlin: de Gruyter.

——— (ed.) (1986*b*). *Growth to Limits: The Western European Welfare States Since World War II*, ii. Berlin: de Gruyter.

——— and Heidenheimer, A. (eds.) (1981). *The Development of Welfare States in Europe and America*. London: Transaction Books.

——— Alber, J., and Kohl, J. (1977). 'Zur Entwicklung der westeuropäischen Wohlfahrtsstaaten'. *Politische Vierteljahresschrift* 18: 705–72.

Franklin, M., and Mughan, A. (1978). 'The Decline of Class Voting in Britain'. *American Political Science Review* 72: 523–34.

——— Mackie, T. T., Valen, H., *et al*. (1992). *Electoral Change: Responses to Evolving Social and Attitudinal Structures in Western Countries*. Cambridge: Cambridge University Press.

Fraser, D. (1979). *Power and Authority in the Victorian City*. Oxford: Basil Blackwell.

Free, L., and Cantril, H. (1967). *The Political Beliefs of Americans: A Study of Public Opinion*. New Brunswick, NJ: Rutgers University Press.

Frey, B. S., and Weck, H. (1983). 'Estimating the Shadow Economy: A ''Naïve'' Approach'. *Oxford Economic Papers* 35: 23–44.

Fuchs, D. (1989). *Die Unterstützung des politischen Systems der Bundesrepublik Deutschland*. Opladen: Westdeutscher Verlag.

Funkhouser, G. R. (1973). 'The Issues of the 1960s: An Exploratory Study in the Dynamics of Public Opinion'. *Public Opinion Quarterly* 37: 62–75.

Gamble, A. (1988). *The Free Economy and the Strong State: The Politics of Thatcherism*. London: Macmillan.

Gamson, W. A. (1968). *Power and Discontent*. Homewood, Ill.: Dorsey Press.

Gans, H. A. (1988). *Middle American Individualism*. New York: Free Press.

Garrard, J. (1983). *Leadership and Power in Victorian Industrial Towns*. Manchester: Manchester University Press.

Gerlach, L. P. (1986). 'Protest Movements and the Construction of Risk'. IIUG Discussion Paper, Berlin, pp. 86–110.

Giddens, A. (1992). *Sociology*. Cambridge: Polity Press.

Gilljam, M., and Holmberg, S. (1993). *Väljarna inför 90-talet*. Stockholm: Norstedts Juridik.

——— ——— and Bennulf, M. (1991). *Swedish Election Study 1988: Technical Report*. Göteborg: Depårtment of Political Science.

Goodin, R. E. (1976). *The Politics of Rational Man*. London: John Wiley.

——— (1992). *Green Political Theory*. Cambridge: Polity Press.

Gould, F. (1983). 'The Development of Public Expenditures in Western Industrialised Countries: A Comparative Analysis'. *Public Finance* 39: 38–69.

——— and Roweth, B. (1978). 'Politics and Public Spending'. *Political Quarterly* 49: 222–7.

——— ——— (1980). 'Public Spending and Social Policy: The United Kingdom 1950–1977'. *Journal of Social Policy* 9: 337–57.

Graubard, S. R. (ed.) (1986). *Norden: The Passion for Equality*. Oslo: Norwegian University Press.

Gunter, B., and McLaughlin C. (1992). *Television: The Public's View*. London: John Libbey.

Gustafsson, G. (1972). 'Strukturomvandling och politisk socialisation'. Umeå universitet, Statsvetenskapliga institutionen.

——— (1987). *Decentralisering av politisk makt*. Stockholm: Carlsson Bokförlag.

Habermas, J. (1962). *Strukturwandel der Oeffentlichkeit*. Neuwied: H. Luchterhand Verlag.

——— (1973). *Legitimationsprobleme im Spätkapitalismus*. Frankfurt: Suhrkamp.

——— (1975). *Legitimation Crisis*. Boston: Beacon Press.

——— (1989). *The Structural Transformation of the Public Sphere: An Inquiry into a Category of Bourgeois Society*. Cambridge: Polity Press.

Hadenius, A. (1985). 'Citizens Strike a Balance: Discontent with Taxes, Content with Spending'. *Journal of Public Policy* 5: 349–63.

Haller, M., Höllinger, F., and Raubal, O. (1990). 'Leviathan or Welfare State? Attitudes Toward the Role of Government in Six Advanced Western Nations'. In *Attitudes to Inequality and the Role of Government.* International Social Survey Programme, ed. D. F. Alwin *et al.* Rijswijk: Sociaal en Cultureel Planbureau.

Heidenheimer, A. J. (1981). 'Education and Social Security Entitlements in Europe and America'. In *The Development of Welfare States in Europe and America*, ed. P. Flora and A. Heidenheimer. London: Transaction Books.

Hernes, H. (1987). *Welfare, State and Women Power: Essays in State Feminism.* Oslo: Oslo University Press.

Hibbs, D. A., and Madsen, H. J. (1981). 'Public Reactions to the Growth of Taxation and Government Expenditure'. *World Politics* 33: 413–35.

Hildebrandt, K., and Dalton, R. J. (1978). 'The New Politics: Political Change or Sunshine Politics?' In *Elections and Parties: Socio-Political Change in the West German Federal Election of 1976*, ed. M. Kaase and K. von Beyme. Beverley Hills, Calif.: Sage.

Hintze, O. (1975). 'Military Organisation and the Organisation of the State'. In *The Historical Essays of Otto Hintze*, ed. F. Gilbert. New York: Oxford University Press.

Hirschmann, A. O. (1970). *Exit, Voice, and Loyalty.* Cambridge, Mass.: Harvard University Press.

Hofferbert, R. I., and Klingemann, H.-D. (1990). 'The Policy Impact of Party Programmes and Government Declarations in the Federal Republic of Germany'. *European Journal of Political Research* 18: 277–304.

Hofrichter, J., and Reif, K. (1990). 'Evolution of Environmental Attitudes in the European Community'. *Scandinavian Political Studies* 13: 119–46.

Holmberg, S. (1981). *Svenska väljare.* Stockholm: Liber.

——— and Asp, K. (1984). *Kampen om kärnkraften: En bok om väljare, massmedier och folkomröstningen 1980.* Stockholm: Liber.

——— and Gilljam, M. (1985). *Swedish Election Study 1982: Technical Report.* Göteborg: Department of Political Science.

——— ——— and Oskarson, M. (1988). *Swedish Election Study 1985: Technical Report.* Göteborg: Department of Political Science.

Inglehart, R. (1977). *The Silent Revolution: Changing Values and Political Styles Among Western Publics.* Princeton, NJ: Princeton University Press.

——— (1979). 'Value Priorities and Social-Economic Change'. In S. H. Barnes, M. Kaase, *et al.*, *Political Action: Mass Participation in Five Western Democracies.* Beverly Hills, Calif.: Sage.

——— (1984). 'The Changing Structure of Political Cleavages in Western Society'. In *Electoral Change in Advanced Industrial Democracies*, ed. R. J. Dalton., S. C. Flanagan, and P. A. Beck. Princeton, NJ: Princeton University Press.

Inglehart, R. (1990). *Culture Shift in Advanced Industrial Society*. Princeton, NJ.: Princeton University Press.

International Social Survey Programme (ISSP) (1985, 1990). *Role of Government: Codebook ZA. Nos. 1490 and 1950*. Cologne: Zentralarchiv für Empirische Sozialforschung, University of Cologne.

Janowitz, M. (1976). *Social Control of the Welfare State*. Chicago: University of Chicago Press.

Jennings, M. K., Van Deth, J. W., *et al.* (1989). *Continuities in Political Action: A Longitudinal Study of Political Orientations in Three Western Democracies*. Berlin: de Gruyter.

Johansson, O. (1993). 'Swedes' Reactions to the Assassination of the Swedish Prime Minister Olof Palme'. Forskningsrapport: Umeå Universitet.

Johnston, M., and Wood, D. (1985). 'Right and Wrong in Public and Private Life'. In *British Social Attitudes: The 1986 Report*, ed. R. Jowell, S. Witherspoon, and L. Brook. Aldershot: Gower.

Karran, T. (1985). 'The Determinants of Taxation in Britain: An Empirical Test'. *Journal of Public Policy* 5: 365–86.

Kay, J. A. (1990). 'Tax Policy: A Survey'. *Economic Journal* 100: 18–75.

Kenski, H. C. (1988). 'The Gender Factor in a Changing Electorate'. In *The Politics of the Gender Gap*, ed. C. M. Mueller. London: Sage.

King, A. (1975). 'Overload: Problems of Governing in the 1970s'. *Political Studies* 23: 284–96.

King, D. (1987). *The New Right*. London: Macmillan.

Klages, H. (1984). *Wertorientierungen im Wandel*. Frankfurt: Campus.

Klingemann, H.-D. (1982). 'Conflicting Modes of Political Orientation, or What Happens to the German Left? The Case of West Berlin'. Presented at the Conference on 'Representation and the State: Problems of Governability and Legitimacy in Western European Democracies', Stanford University, October.

Kolberg, J. E. (1992). *The Study of Welfare State Regimes*. New York: M. E. Sharp.

——— and Pettersen, P. A. (1981). 'Om velferdsstatenes politiske basis'. *Tidskrift for samfunnsforskning* 22: 193–222.

Korpi, W. (1981). *The Democratic Class Struggle*. Stockholm: Tiden.

Kosonen, P. (1987). 'From Collectivity to Individualism in the Welfare State?' *Acta Sociologica* 30: 281–93.

Kristensen, O. (1982). 'Tax Structure and Public Spending, or How the Electorate is Deceived into Paying for Bigger Public Spending than It Really Wants'. *Scandinavian Political Studies* 9: 317–36.

Kyle, G. (1989). 'Kvinnorna och historien'. In *Kvinnors makt och inflytande*. Report No. 15. Stockholm: JÄMFO.

Lane, J.-E., and Ersson, S. (1987) (1991 2nd edn.). *Politics and Society in Western Europe*. London: Sage.

Lane, J.-E., McKay, D. and Newton, K. (1991). *Political Data Handbook: OECD Countries*. Oxford: Oxford University Press.

Lane, R. E. (1986). 'Market Justice, Political Justice'. *American Political Science Review* 80: 383–402.

Lazarsfeld, P. F., Berelson, B., and Gaudet, H. (1948). *The People's Choice*. New York: Columbia University Press.

Lewis, A. (1980). 'Attitudes to Public Expenditure and the Relationship to Voting Preferences'. *Political Studies* 28: 284–92.

——— and Jackson, D. (1985). 'Voting Preferences and Attitudes to Public Expenditure'. *Political Studies* 33: 457–66.

Lijphart, A. (1971). 'Comparative Politics and Comparative Method'. *American Political Science Review* 65: 682–93.

Lipset, S. M., and Horowitz, I. L. (1978). *Dialogues on American Politics*. New York: Oxford University Press.

——— and Rokkan, S. (1967). 'Cleavage Structures, Party Systems, and Voter Alignments: An Introduction'. In *Party Systems and Voter Alignments: Cross National Perspectives*, ed. S. M. Lipset and S. Rokkan. London: Macmillan.

Listhaug, O. (1990). 'Explanations of Political Support'. Paper presented at ESF conference on the Beliefs in Government Project, Group 1. Rome.

——— and Miller, A. H. (1985). 'Public Support for Tax Evasion: Self-Interest or Symbolic Politics?' *European Journal of Political Research* 13: 265–82.

——— ——— and Valen, H. (1985). 'The Gender Gap in Norwegian Voting Behaviour'. *Scandinavian Political Studies* 8: 187–206.

Löfstedt, R., and White, A. L. (1990). 'Chernobyl: Four Years Later the Repercussions Continue'. *Environment* 32: 2–4.

Lowery, D., and Sigelman, L. (1981). 'Understanding the Tax Revolt: Eight Explanations'. *American Political Science Review* 75 : 963–74.

Luhmann, N. (1981). *Politische Theorie im Wohlfahrtstaat*. Munich: G. Olwog Verlag.

——— (1990). *Political Theory in the Welfare State*. Berlin: de Gruyter.

——— and de Giorgi, R. (1992). *Teoria della società*. Milan: Angeli.

Marshall, T. H. (1950). *Citizenship and Social Class and Other Essays*. Cambridge: Cambridge University Press.

——— (1964). *Class, Citizenship, and Social Developments: Essays by T. H. Marshall*. New York: Doubleday.

Martinussen, W. (1993). *Velferdsfellesskap. Medvirkning og solidaritet i nærmiljø, yrkesliv og politikk*. Allforsk AVH: Senter for Samfunnsforskning.

McDonough, P., *et al.* (1986). 'Economic Policy and Public Opinion in Spain'. *American Journal of Political Science* 30: 446–74.

McQuail, D., and Windahl, S. (1981). *Communication Models for the Study of Mass Communications*. London: Longman.

Messere, K. (1993). *Tax Policy in OECD Countries*. Amsterdam: IBDF Publications.

Michelat, G., and Simon, M. (1985). 'Determinations socio-économiques, organisations symboliques et comportement électoral'. *Revue Française de Sociologie* 36: 32–69.

Miliband, R. (1969). *The State in Capitalist Society*. London: Weidenfeld and Nicolson.

Miller, A. H. (1974). 'Political Issues and Trust in Government 1964–1970'. *American Political Science Review* 68: 951–72.

——— and Listhaug, O. (1990). 'Political Parties and Confidence in Government: A Comparison of Norway, Sweden and the United States'. *British Journal of Political Science* 20: 357–86.

Mills, C. W. (1959). *The Sociological Imagination*. New York: Oxford University Press.

Morrison, D. (1986). *Invisible Citizens: British Public Opinion and the Future of Broadcasting*. London: John Libbey.

Morrissey, O., and Steinmo, S. (1987). 'The Influence of Party Competition on Post-War UK Tax Rates'. *Policy and Politics* 15: 195–206.

Nie, N. H., Hull, C. H., Jenkins, J. G., Steinbrenner, K., and Bent, D H. (1975). *Statistical Package for the Social Sciences*. New York: McGraw-Hill.

Nielsen, H. J. (1976). 'The Uncivic Culture: Attitudes towards the Political System in Denmark and the Vote for the Progress Party'. *Scandinavian Political Studies* 11: 147–56.

Niskanen, W. A. (1973). *Bureaucracy: Servant or Master? Lessons From America*. London: Institute of Economic Affairs.

O'Connor, J. (1973). *The Fiscal Crisis of the State*. New York: St Martin's Press.

——— and Brym, R. J. (1987). 'Public Welfare Expenditure in OECD Countries: Towards a Reconciliation of Inconsistent Findings'. *British Journal of Sociology* 34: 47–68.

OECD (1968). *National Accounts, 1950–68*. Paris: OECD.

——— (1981). *The Welfare State in Crisis: An Account of the Conference on Social Policies in the 1980s*. Paris: OECD.

——— (1983). *National Accounts, 1964–81*. Paris: OECD.

——— (1985*a*). *Social Expenditure 1960–90*. Paris: OECD.

——— (1985*b*). *Measuring Health Care 1960–83*. Paris: OECD.

——— (1987*a*). *Taxation in Developed Countries*. Paris: OECD.

——— (1987*b*). *National Accounts 1973–85*. Paris: OECD.

——— (1990). *Les systèmes de santé: A la recherche de l'efficacité*. Paris: OECD.

——— (1992). *National Accounts, 1985–90*. Paris: OECD.

OECD (1993). *Health Systems*. Paris: OECD.

Offe, C. (1976). 'Überlegungen und Hypothesen zum Problem politischer Legitimation'. In *Bürgerlicher Staat und politische Legitimation*, ed. R. Ebbighausen. Frankfurt: Suhrkamp.

——— (1980). 'The Separation of Form and Content in Liberal Democratic Politics'. *Studies in Political Economy* 3: 5–16.

——— (1984). *Contradictions of the Welfare State*, ed. J. Keane. London: Hutchinson.

——— (1985). 'New Social Movements: Challenging the Boundaries of Institutional Politics'. *Social Research* 52: 817–68.

——— (1987). 'Democracy Against the Welfare State? Structural Foundations of Neo-Conservative Political Opportunities'. *Political Theory* 15: 501–37.

O'Higgins, M., Schmaus, G., and Stephenson, G. (1989). 'Income Distribution and Redistribution: A Microdata Analysis for Seven Countries'. In *Poverty, Inequality and Income Distribution in Comparative Research: The Luxembourg Income Study (LIS)*, ed. T. M. Smeeding, M. O'Higgins, and L. Rainwater. New York: Harvester Wheatsheaf.

Olson, M. (1965). *The Logic of Collective Action*. Cambridge, Mass.: Harvard University Press.

——— (1990). *How Bright Are the Northern Lights? Some Questions about Sweden*. Lund: Institute of Economic Research, University of Lund.

Page, E. (1983). *Laws and Orders in Central-Government Relations*. Glasgow: CSSP Studies in Public Policy, No. 106.

Pappi, F. U. (1977). 'Einstellungen zum Wohlfahrtsstaat'. In *Probleme der Modernisierungspolitik*. Mannheimer Sozialwissenschaftliche Studien, xiv, ed. W. Zapf. Meisenheim am Glan: Anton Hain.

Peacock, A., and Wiseman, J. (1967). *The Growth of Public Expenditure in the UK*. London: Allen and Unwin.

——— ——— (1979). 'Approaches to the Analysis of Government Expenditure Growth'. *Public Finance Quarterly* 7: 3–23.

Pechman, J. A. (1988). *World Tax Reform: A Progress Report*. Washington, DC: Brookings Institution.

Peltzman, S. (1980). 'The Growth of Government'. *Journal of Law and Economics* 23: 209–87.

Pennock, J. R. (1966). 'Political Development, Political System and Political Goods'. *World Politics* 18: 415–34.

Percheron, A. (1971). 'La Conception de l'autorité chez les enfants français'. *Revue Française de Science Politique* 21: 103–28.

Peters, B. G. (1991). *The Politics of Taxation*. Oxford: Basil Blackwell.

Peterson, A. (1984). 'The Gender-Sex Dimension in Swedish Politics'. *Acta Sociologica* 27: 3–18.

Petterson, O., Westholm, A., and Blomberg, G. (1989). *Medborgarnas Makt*. Stockholm: Carlssons Bokforlag.

Pierson, C. (1991). *Beyond the Welfare State?* Cambridge: Polity Press.

Pliatsky, L. (1982). *Getting and Spending*. Oxford: Basil Blackwell.

Pommerehne, W. P., and Schneider, F. (1978). 'Fiscal Illusion, Political Institutions, and Local Public Spending'. *Kyklos* 31: 381–408.

Pöntinen, S., and Uusitalo, M. (1986). *The Legitimacy of the Welfare State: Social Security Opinions in Finland 1975–1985*. Report No. 15. Helsinki: Suomen Gallup,

Poulantzas, N. (1978). *State, Power, Socialism*. London: New Left Books.

Rasler, K. A., and Thompson, W. R. (1985). 'War Making and State Making: Governmental Expenditures, Tax Revenues and Global Wars'. *American Political Science Review* 79: 491–507.

RePass, D. E. (1971). 'Issue Salience and Party Choice'. *American Political Science Review* 65: 389–400.

Ringen, S. (1987). *The Possibility of Politics: A Study in the Political Economy of the Welfare State*. Oxford: Clarendon Press.

Robinson, R. V., and Bell, W. (1978). 'Equality, Success, and Social Justice in England and the US'. *American Sociological Review* 43: 125–43.

Rogers, E. M., and Dearing, J. W. (1988). 'Agenda-Setting Research: Where Has It Been, Where Is It Going?' In *Communication Yearbook*, xi, ed. J. A. Anderson. Newbury Park, Calif.: Sage.

Rokeach, M. (1973). *The Nature of Human Values*. New York: Free Press.

Roller, E. (1991). 'Goals of the Welfare State: Analytical and Empirical Bases'. Presented at the meeting of the ESF Project 'Beliefs in Government', Group 3, Umeå.

——— (1992). *Einstellungen der Bürger zum Wohlfahrtsstaat der Bundesrepublik Deutschland*. Opladen: Westdeutscher Verlag.

Rose, C. (1990). *The Dirty Man of Europe: The Great British Pollution Scandal*. London: Simon and Schuster.

Rose, R. (ed.) (1980). *Challenge to Governance*. Beverly Hills, Calif.: Sage.

——— (1983*a*). *Getting By in Three Economies: The Resources of the Official, Unofficial, and Domestic Economies*. Glasgow: University of Strathclyde.

——— (1983*b*). *The Role of Laws in Comparative Perspective*. CSSP Studies in Public Policy, No. 103.

——— (1984). *Understanding Big Government: The Programme Approach*. London: Sage.

——— (1985). 'Maximising Tax Revenues While Minimizing Political Costs'. *Journal of Public Policy* 5: 289–320.

——— and Karran, T. (1987). *Taxation by Political Inertia*. London: Macmillan.

——— and Peters, B. G. (1978). *Can Government Go Bankrupt?* New York: Basic Books.

Saunders, P. (1985). 'Public Expenditure and Economic Performance in OECD Countries'. *Journal of Public Policy* 5: 1–21.

Schemeil, Y. (1985). 'Les Cultures politiques'. In *Traité de Science Politique*, iii, ed. M. Gratwitz and J. Leca. Paris: Presse Universitaire de France.

Sears, D. O. (1974). 'Political Socialization'. In *Handbook of Political Science*, ed. F. L. Greenstein and N. Polsby. Reading, Mass.: Addison-Wesley.

——— and Citrin, J. (1982). *Tax Revolt: Something for Nothing in California*. London and Cambridge, Mass.: Harvard University Press.

———, Hensler, C., and Speer, L. (1979). 'Whites' Opposition to Bussing: Self-Interest or Symbolic Politics?' *American Political Science Review* 73: 369–84.

———, Lau, R. R., Tyler, T. R., and Allen, H. M. Jr (1980). 'Self-Interest vs. Symbolic Politics in Policy Attitudes and Presidential Voting'. *American Political Science Review* 74: 670–84.

Shapiro, R. Y., and Young, J. T. (1990). 'Public Opinion toward Social Welfare Policies: The United States in Comparative Perspective'. In *Research on Micropolitics*, iii, ed. S. Long. Greenwich, Conn.: JAI Press.

Sharpe, L. J. (1981). 'Is There a Fiscal Crisis in Western European Local Government? A First Appraisal'. In *The Local Fiscal Crisis in Western Europe: Myths and Realities*, ed. L. J. Sharpe. London: Sage.

——— and Newton, K. (1983). *Does Politics Matter?* Oxford: Oxford University Press.

Sorensen, R. (1992). 'Fiscal Illusion; Nothing but Illusion?' *European Journal of Political Research* 22: 279–305.

Stedman-Jones, G. (1971). *Outcast London*. Oxford: Clarendon Press.

Stephens, J. D. (1979). *The Transition from Capitalism to Socialism*. London: Macmillan.

Stockholm International Peace Research Institute (1990). *SIPRI World Armaments and Disarmament*. Oxford: Oxford University Press.

Svallfors, S. (1989). *Vem älsker Välfärdsstaten*. Lund: Arkiv avhandlingsserie.

Tajfel, H. (1981). *Human Groups and Social Categories: Studies in Social Psychology*. Cambridge: Cambridge University Press.

Tarschys, D. (1975). 'The Growth of Public Expenditures: Nine Modes of Explanation'. *Scandinavian Political Studies* 10: 9–31.

Taylor-Gooby, P. (1983*a*). 'Ambivalence and Altruism: Public Opinion about Taxation and Welfare'. *Policy and Politics* 11: 15–39.

——— (1983*b*). 'Legitimation Deficit, Public Opinion, and the Welfare State'. *Sociology* 17: 165–84.

——— (1985). *Public Opinion, Ideology and Social Welfare*. London: Routledge and Kegan Paul.

——— (1993). 'What Citizens Want from the State'. In *International Social*

Attitudes: The 10th BSA Report, ed. R. Jowell., L. Brook, and L. Dowds. Aldershot: Gower.

Thomassen, J. (1989). 'Economic Crisis, Dissatisfaction, and Protest'. In *Continuities in Political Action*, ed. M. K. Jennings, J. W. Van Deth, *et al.* Berlin: de Gruyter.

Thorndike, E. L. (1911). *Animal Intelligence*. New York: Macmillan.

Tilly, C. (ed.) (1975). *The Formation of Nation States in Western Europe*. Princeton, NJ: Princeton University Press.

Trappel, J. (1991). 'Born Losers or Flexible Adjustment? The Media Policy Dilemma of Small States'. *European Journal of Communication* 6: 355–71.

Trettner, B. (1974). *Die Steuermentalitat: Ein Internationaler Vergleich*. Berlin: Duncker and Humblot.

United Nations (1972). *Conference on the Human Environment*. Stockholm: UN.

Uusitalo, M. (1984). 'Comparative Research of the Determinants of the Welfare State: The State of the Art'. *European Journal of Political Research* 12: 403–22.

Valen, H. (1981). *Valg og politikk—et samfunn i endring*. Oslo: Forbruker og administrasjonsdepartementet. NKS-forlaget.

Van Dijk, T. (1987). *Communicating Racism*. Newbury Park, Calif.: Sage.

——— (1991). *Racism and the Press*. London: Routledge.

Van Snippenburg, L. B., and Vettehen, P. G. (1992). 'Dutch Youth in Transition to Adulthood: Differential Changes in their Political and Sociocultural Values since the Seventies'. *Journal of Youth and Adolescence*, 21: 573–91.

Vedung, E. (1991). 'Miljöpartiet, Nedfrysningen och den Järnhårda Oligarkilagen'. In *Människa, Miljö, Samhälle, Samhällsvetenskapliga fakulteten*, ed. B. Gustaffson. Uppsala: Uppsala University.

Verba, S., Nie, N. H., and Kim, J.-O. (1978). *Participation and Political Equality: A Seven-Nation Comparison*. Cambridge: Cambridge University Press.

——— *et al.* (1987). *Elites and the Idea of Equality: A Comparison of Japan, Sweden, and the United States*. Cambridge, Mass.: Harvard University Press.

Vig, N. J., and Kraft, M. E. (1990). *Environmental Policy in the 1990s*. Washington, DC: Congressional Quarterly Press.

Waernes, K. (1987). 'On the Rationality of Caring'. In *Women and the State*, ed. A. Showstack-Sassoon. London: Hutchinson.

Wagner, A. (1890 3rd edn.). *Finanzwissenschaft*. Leipzig.

Weale, A. (1992). *The New Politics of Pollution*. Manchester: Manchester University Press.

Welch, S. (1985). 'The ''More for Less'' Paradox: Public Attitudes on Taxing and Spending'. *Public Opinion Quarterly* 49: 310–16.

Whiteley, P. (1981). 'Public Opinion and the Demand for Social Welfare in Britain'. *Journal of Social Policy* 10: 453–70.

Wilensky, H. L. (1975). *The Welfare State and Equality: Structural and Ideological Roots of Public Expenditures*. Berkeley, Calif.: University of California Press.

——— (1976). *The 'New Corporatism', Centralization, and the Welfare State*. Beverly Hills, Calif.: Sage.

——— (1981). 'Leftism, Catholicism and Democratic Corporatism: The Role of Political Parties in Recent Welfare State Development'. In *The Development of Welfare States in Europe and America*, ed. P. Flora and A. J. Heidenheimer. Princeton, NJ: Transaction Books.

Wilson, H. H. (1961). *Pressure Group*. London: Secker and Warburg.

Wolman, H., and Goldsmith, M. (1987). 'Local Government Fiscal Behaviour and Intergovernmental Finance in a Period of Slow National Growth: A Comparative Analysis'. *Environment and Planning, C: Government and Policy* 5: 171–82.

——— ——— (1992). *Urban Politics and Policy: A Comparative Approach*. Oxford: Basil Blackwell.

Worre, T. (1980). 'Class Parties and Class Voting'. *Scandinavian Political Studies* 3: 299–330.

Young, O. (1989). *International Cooperation: Building Regimes for Natural Resources and the Environment*. Ithaca, NY: Cornell University Press.

Zapf, W. (1986). 'Die deutsche Version des Wohlfahrtsstaates'. In *Wirtschafts und Sozialstatistik: Empirische Grundlagen und politische Entscheidungen*, ed. K. Hanau, R. Hujer, and W. G. Nebauer. Göttingen: Vandenhoeck and Ruprecht.

AUTHOR INDEX

Subject Index